THE LIMITS OF EXPERTISE

Ashgate Studies in Human Factors for Flight Operations

Ashgate Studies in Human Factors for Flight Operations is a series dedicated to publishing high-quality monographs and edited volumes which contribute to the objective of improving the safe and efficient operation of aircraft.

The series will achieve this by disseminating new theoretical and empirical research from specialists in all relevant fields of aviation human factors. Its foundation is in applied psychology, presenting new developments and applications in such established fields as CRM, SA and decision-making. Its range also encompasses many other crucial areas such as fatigue and stress, the social environment, design, technology, communication and training.

Submitted work relevant to the objective of the series will be considered for publication by the board of editors. The series is intended for an international readership and so books with a broad geographical appeal are especially encouraged.

Series editorial board

The Limits of Expertise
Rethinking Pilot Error and the Causes of Airline Accidents

R. Key Dismukes
NASA Ames Research Center, California

Benjamin A. Berman
NASA Ames Research Center/
San Jose State University Foundation, California

Loukia D. Loukopoulos
NASA Ames Research Center/
San Jose State University Foundation, California

ASHGATE

Published by
Ashgate Publishing Limited
Gower House
Croft Road
Aldershot
Hampshire GU11 3HR
England

Ashgate Publishing Company
Suite 420
101 Cherry Street
Burlington, VT 05401-4405
USA

Ashgate website: http://www.ashgate.com

British Library Cataloguing in Publication Data
Dismukes, Key
    The limits of expertise : rethinking pilot error and the
    causes of airline accidents. - (Ashgate studies in human
    factors for flight operations)
    1.Aircraft accidents - Human factors - Case studies
    2.Aircraft accidents - Investigation - Case studies
    I.Title II.Berman, Benjamin A. III.Loukopoulos, Loukia D.
    363.1'2414

Library of Congress Control Number: 2006938316

ISBN: 978-0-7546-4964-9 (HBK)
ISBN: 978-0-7546-4965-6 (PBK)

Printed and bound in Great Britain by MPG Books Ltd, Bodmin, Cornwall.

Contents

List of Figures

List of Tables

Foreword

Investigators for the US National Transportation Safety Board and its sister agencies worldwide do an extraordinary job of piecing together the evidence in major airline accidents and determining the causes of these tragedies under the most difficult circumstances. Every time I participated in an investigation or reviewed a staff report, I was struck by the extent of destruction of the wreckage, the mystery of what happened, and the difficulty of obtaining evidence. I was uniformly proud of the work of our staff in overcoming these difficulties to unveil the causes of the accident and to identify ways to prevent recurrence.

Crew error plays a central role in many airline accidents. Uncovering the causes of such error is one of investigators' greatest challenges because human performance, including that of expert pilots, is driven by the confluence of many factors, not all of which are observable in the aftermath of an accident. Although it is often impossible to determine with certainty why accident crewmembers did what they did, it is possible to understand the types of error to which pilots are vulnerable and to identify the cognitive, task, and organizational factors that shape that vulnerability. And it is possible to identify recurrent themes of vulnerability across a large set of accidents.

That is why this book is of essential importance. The authors go beyond accident investigation, asking not why the accident crews acted as they did but why any highly experienced crew in such circumstances might have been vulnerable to error. This is not a mode of inquiry appropriate to the investigation of the causes of a specific accident. It is, however, extremely pertinent to the development of strategies for reducing vulnerability to error in human endeavors involving complicated undertakings, dynamically changing circumstance, and underlying risk.

I expect that this book will profoundly influence the perspectives of accident investigators, designers of equipment and procedures, and trainers in occupations where professional skills are paramount. Experts are subject to the human limitations that we all share. Improving safety requires understanding the interaction of those limitations with task demands, operating procedures, and organizational pressures. This understanding can provide a basis for improving equipment, training, procedures, and organizational policy across a broad array of complex human operations.

The Honorable Carl W. Vogt
Former Chairman, US National Transportation Safety Board
Trustee Emeritus and Former Chairman, Flight Safety Foundation
Former Member, White House Commission on Aviation Safety and Security

Preface

We had difficulty deciding whether Berman or Dismukes should be the first author of this book. Although our contributions differed in nature, they were equally important. Failing to persuade our publisher to run half of the printing with Berman first and half with Dismukes first, we decided somewhat arbitrarily to make the order: Dismukes, Berman, and Loukopoulos.

Acknowledgments

We wish to express our gratitude to several individuals who critically reviewed portions of this book. Tom Chidester reviewed successive drafts of all chapters and provided many invaluable suggestions. Patty Jones also reviewed the entire manuscript in its final stages and made helpful comments. Sean Belcher, Barbara Durian, Evan Byrne, Rahul Dodhia, Jon Holbrook, David Keeling, Dick McKinney, Jessica Nowinski, Robert Sumwalt, and Frank Tullo also read specific chapters and made helpful suggestions based on their particular areas of scientific or operational expertise. Kim Jobe provided expert assistance in searching the literature and preparing the manuscript. North Georgia College & State University graciously provided the first author with an office in which to retreat from other duties while working on this book. This work was supported by NASA's Aviation Safety Program.

To Barbara.

To Suzanne and Rose.

To Louisa and Dimitris, with admiration and appreciation.

Introduction

Most airline accidents are attributed to errors made by the flight crew (Boeing, 2004). But what does this mean? Why do highly skilled professional pilots make errors, with consequences sometimes fatal to themselves as well as to their passengers? How should we think of the role of these errors in accidents when we seek to prevent future accidents? This book seeks to address these questions in the light of what scientists are learning about the nature of skilled performance of humans performing complex tasks.

The level of safety achieved by major airlines in the United States and in most other developed countries is one of the great success stories of modern industry. The probability of becoming a fatality on a US airline flight is roughly eight in a hundred million flight segments (Sivak and Flannagan, 2003). In comparison, if one were to drive the distance of an average airline segment in a passenger car, the risk of death would be about 65 times greater (*ibid*.). This is a dramatic improvement over the early days of airline operations, when accidents were common and every airline pilot could list colleagues killed on the job (Gann, 1961; Hopkins, 1982). This improvement came about through steady advances in the design and reliability of equipment systems, operating procedures, and training over the second half of the twentieth century.

In spite of these advances the industry must constantly strive to maintain and improve safety. Every accident is a profound tragedy for the victims and their families. The horrible nature of a crash of a passenger-carrying airplane is large in the minds of the public, who rightfully demand the highest level of safety achievable. Further, the level of safety that has been achieved requires unremitting effort to maintain, in part because it is so high. The inherent nature of complex sociotechnical systems is to devolve if not constantly attended (Reason, 1997, p. 6). Economic forces contribute to this tendency. Since de-regulation in 1978 the airline industry has operated on razor-thin profit margins, and since the 11 September 2001 terrorist attacks most US companies have had to institute substantial cost-reduction programs to survive. Although no airline we are familiar with would knowingly compromise safety to cut costs, it is extremely difficult to know *a priori* whether changes designed to improve efficiency of operations and training will affect safety. Thus it is now more crucial than ever before to understand what makes the aviation system vulnerable to failure. Because most aviation accidents have been attributed historically to deficiencies in the performance of the flight crew, it is especially important to understand what makes pilots vulnerable to error.

In this book we review the 19 major[1] accidents in US air carrier operations from 1991 through 2000 in which crew errors played a central role, according to the National Transportation Safety Board (NTSB), the US government agency responsible for investigating and determining the causes of all US civil aviation accidents. It is noteworthy that these 19 accidents comprise slightly more than half of the 37 major accident investigations that the NTSB conducted during this period.

Our sources of information about what happened in these accidents are the NTSB reports and associated documents that are publicly available. The NTSB conducts extensive investigations of major accidents. Analyzing wreckage, aircraft design and performance characteristics, and data from flight data recorders (FDRs) and cockpit voice recorders (CVRs), investigators are in most cases able to reconstruct the events of the accident flight to a remarkable degree.[2] The NTSB's investigative approach is to assign a multi-disciplinary team (the "go-team") to a major accident; the team is assisted by technically competent specialists from the aircraft manufacturer, airline, unions, and the Federal Aviation Administration (FAA), as appropriate to the circumstances of the accident. The NTSB also routinely evaluates how the crewmembers were trained, how they performed in training and in flight check rides, and how they were regarded by their fellow pilots. And of course, if the crewmembers survive, the investigators interview them extensively. Major NTSB investigations carefully scrutinize human performance issues and any crew errors and analyze how these issues and errors may have contributed to the accident. The final report[3] on each accident analyzes the crew's performance from both an operational and human factors perspective.

Modern airline operations are highly scripted. Airlines write flight operations manuals (FOMs)[4] that provide crews with instructions for all aspects of operation, both normal and non-normal (for example, emergencies). Hundreds of procedural steps are required to set up and check the correct operation of a large airplane's equipment systems before flight. These procedural steps, as well as the procedures for navigating and controlling the airplane in the air, are performed according to written scripts detailed in the FOM. These written scripts establish the correct way to perform procedures and provide standardization across pilots. Standardization is crucial because airline captains and first officers are frequently re-paired (most commonly after each three- or four-day trip), and it is common for pilots starting a trip together to be meeting for the first time if they fly for a large airline that employs thousands of pilots. Standardization also helps individual pilots to learn procedures and, with practice, remember how to execute those procedures without excessive mental demand.

Accident investigators identify crew errors in part by comparing the actions of the accident crews to the FOM written scripts and to the training provided by the airline.[5] Investigators also analyze the adequacy and appropriateness of the guidance contained in the FOM. The NTSB (1994a) has cited crew procedural errors as the largest category of primary errors in airline accidents (see also Karwal, Verkaik, and Jansen, 2000; Helmreich, Klinect, and Merritt, 2004); however, to interpret this observation meaningfully one must determine why deviations from procedures occur. Our analysis in this book suggests that many factors are at play. It is important to recognize that the scripts provided by FOMs represent an ideal. Actual line operations present complex situations not fully provided for by FOMs

(Loukopoulos, Dismukes, and Barshi, 2003, 2006), and the norms of actual line operations sometimes diverge from the ideal because of sociocultural, professional, and organizational factors (Reason, 1997; Helmreich and Merritt, 1998).

We use the NTSB's operational and human performance analysis of the accident as the starting point for our own analysis. We do not second-guess the NTSB as to what errors were made or how those errors contributed to the accident. However, our analysis differs in a subtle but crucial way from that of NTSB investigators because we are asking a different kind of question from the ones the Board is charged to address. The NTSB's charter requires it to determine the probable cause of each specific accident. As far as possible, the human performance group of the investigation team attempts to identify factors that may have contributed to the crew's errors; however, to cite such factors the NTSB must be reasonably certain that these factors did in fact contribute significantly to the errors and, by extension, to the particular accident under consideration.

Unfortunately, in many cases this is not possible. For example, consider the case of a crew preparing for takeoff who inadvertently fail to set the flaps to the takeoff position. (Setting the flaps is a highly practised procedural step that the crew would have performed thousands of time before without failure.) Although the NTSB might be able to determine with confidence that the crew failed to set the flaps, it is usually not possible to determine with any certainty why the crew overlooked a step. Indeed, if the crew survives and are interviewed, they themselves typically cannot explain the oversight. The investigators may be able to identify various factors, such as distraction or a poorly designed checklist that might contribute to an error such as this, but rarely can the degree of influence of such factors be determined. The most common result in a situation like this is that the NTSB will identify the error made by the crew (failure to set the flaps), discuss the human performance issues that could have affected the crew's performance, but stop short of drawing conclusions that link the error to the underlying causes.[6]

We face the same limitation as NTSB investigators and do not attempt to go beyond their reports in analyzing what actually caused the accident crews to make the errors they did. What we do is ask a subtly different question, one that is profoundly important to aviation safety: if a population of pilots with experience and skills comparable to those of the accident crew faced a situation similar, though not necessarily identical, to that which confronted the accident crew, would this population of pilots be vulnerable to making the kinds of errors made by the accident crew and, if so, why? Thus our purpose is different from that of the NTSB, which must attempt to determine what actually happened to the specific crew in a specific accident, to the extent it is possible to do so. In contrast, we attempt to understand the nature of vulnerability of all skilled pilots to error in situations similar to those faced by the accident pilots.

It would be impossibly cumbersome for us and tedious to the reader if, in discussing the many errors identified in the accident reports, we were to use over and over the formulation "A population of pilots similar to the accident crew might have had some degree of vulnerability to making this particular error made by one of the accident pilots because ..." Thus for simplicity we typically say "The captain (or first officer) might have been vulnerable to this error because ..." but periodically remind the reader that we are really talking about a population. Behavioral scientists often use the percentage of a population of individuals making an error in a situation as equivalent to the probability that an individual from that population would make that error.

Drawing upon rich literatures in experimental psychology and human factors, especially research on cognitive mechanisms underlying the skilled performance of experts, we are able to identify factors that make all pilots vulnerable to specific kinds of errors in various situations. A central perspective emerging from the scientific literature is that the occasional errors made by pilots and other skilled experts occur in a somewhat random fashion; thus scientists speak of factors *influencing the probability of errors* rather than *causing errors*. Multiple factors, not all of which can be determined and measured, interact to produce an error in a given instance.

Many people assume that if an expert in some domain (aviation, medicine, or any other) makes an error, this is evidence of lack of skill, vigilance, or conscientiousness. This assumption is both simplistic and wrong (see "bad apple theory" in Dekker, 2002). Skill, vigilance, and conscientiousness are of course essential for safe, effective performance but are not sufficient. A particularly problematic misconception about the nature of skilled human performance is that, if experts can normally perform some task without difficulty, then they should always be able to perform that task correctly. But in fact experts in all domains from time to time make inadvertent errors at tasks they normally perform without difficulty. This is the consequence of the interaction of subtle variations in task demands, incomplete information available to the expert performing the task, and the inherent nature of the cognitive processes that enable skilled performance.

In this book we discuss at length the vulnerabilities of human cognitive processes such as attention, memory, and decision-making. Those vulnerabilities must be considered in the appropriate context. Computer technology has advanced to the point that it is in principle possible to operate an aircraft from takeoff to landing without human intervention. However, for compelling reasons, this is not done. Computers have extremely limited capability for dealing with unexpected and novel situations, for interpreting ambiguous and sometimes conflicting information, and for making appropriate value judgments in the face of competing goals. These functions are appropriately reserved for human experts. Humans are able to perform some tasks far beyond the capabilities of computers because of the way our brains have evolved, but part and parcel of our unique abilities is inherent vulnerability to characteristic forms of error in certain situations. As will become apparent in our analysis of airline accidents, human skill and vulnerability to error are closely linked through underlying cognitive processes.

Human operators are expected to make up for the deficiencies in the design of systems, and this is manifest in aviation operations. Airline crews routinely deal with equipment displays imperfectly matched to human information-processing characteristics, respond to system failures, and decide how to deal with threats ranging from unexpected weather conditions to passenger medical emergencies. Crews are able to manage the vast majority of these occasions so skillfully that what could have become a disaster is no more than a minor perturbation in the smooth flow of high-volume operations. But on the rare occasions when crews fail to manage these situations, it is detrimental to the cause of aviation safety to assume that the failure stems from deficiency of the crews. Rather, these failures occur because crews are expected to perform tasks at which perfect reliability is not possible for either humans or machines. If we insist on thinking of accidents in terms of deficiency, that deficiency must be attributed to the overall system in which crews operate.

Contributing to the misunderstanding of the vulnerability of experts to error is that the presence and interaction of factors contributing to error is probabilistic rather than deterministic. Accidents are rarely, if ever, caused by a single factor but rather by a complex interplay of multiple factors, combining in ways driven in large degree by chance, each factor influencing the effects of the others (Reason, 1997). After analyzing many accident reports – not just those described in this book – we strongly suspect that small random variations in the presence and timing of these factors substantially affect the probability of pilots making errors leading to an accident. In addition to variations in the interaction of external factors, we must recognize that individuals themselves vary moment to moment in the fine-grained detail of their responses to external factors. Thus if it were somehow possible to identically replicate in large numbers the crew of an accident and put each replica crew in exactly the same initial situation, they would not all perform identically, and the differences would grow as the situation unfolded and their reactions altered the interplay of external factors.

To protect and improve aviation safety we must understand what makes pilots vulnerable to error and must understand the interplay of factors contributing to that vulnerability. This book is an attempt to shed light on the nature of the vulnerability of pilots and other experts to error when performing tasks at which they are highly skilled. Fortunately scientists have now learned a fair amount about the cognitive processes and the conditions that shape the form and probabilities of errors. To a large degree the errors made by experts are driven by four factors:

1) specific characteristics of the tasks performed;
2) events in the environment in which tasks are performed;
3) demands placed on human cognitive processes by task characteristics and environmental events; and
4) social and organizational factors that influence how a representative sample of experts would typically operate in particular situations (including both the ideals expressed in training and formal guidance and the 'norms' for actual operations).

Our analysis of pilots' vulnerability to error systematically considers the interaction of these four types of factors in the kinds of situation faced by the pilots in the 19 accidents examined in this book. We also adhere to the assumption of local rationality (Woods and Cook, 1999): experts typically do what seems reasonable to them at the time, given their understanding of the circumstances. This does not mean that experts never fail to be conscientious, but we suggest that errors are not *de facto* evidence of lack of conscientiousness and that the burden of proof falls on anyone claiming an expert was not conscientious.

In seeking to understand the errors made by expert pilots, it is crucial to avoid hindsight bias (Fischhoff, 2003; Dekker, 2002, pp. 16–20), a term cognitive scientists use to describe distortion of evaluators' judgments by knowledge of the outcome of the situation that is being evaluated. Knowing the disastrous outcome of a flight makes it easy to identify things the crew could have done differently to prevent the accident. But of course accident crews cannot foresee the outcome of their flights; as far as they can tell, up until the moment when things start to go wrong, they are conducting flights as routine as thousands they have flown before.

We believe our approach can contribute to aviation safety by helping the understanding of the nature of vulnerability of skilled experts to error, which in turn will lay a foundation for developing countermeasures to reduce that vulnerability. However, there are limitations to our approach: it is inherently speculative. Accident reports do not provide sufficient fine-grain detail of the many factors involved to determine the probability of a particular kind of error, and scientific understanding of the cognitive processes underlying skilled human performance is far from complete. Thus we cannot say what percentage of a large population of airline pilots would have made errors similar to those made by the accident crew if placed in their exact situation, but we are reasonably certain that some of this large population would make similar errors – however, this is not an indication of deficiency on the part of those pilots who did make errors. The probability of any pilots – including the accident pilots – making a particular error in a given situation is quite low, and the probability of that error combining with other circumstances to create an accident is extraordinarily low. But because exposure to opportunity to error is very high – almost 17 million flights are conducted worldwide every year (2003 data, commercial jet airplanes, >60,000 pounds maximum gross weight) (Boeing, 2004) and each flight has numerous opportunities for error – errors do occur regularly. We can say with reasonable confidence from our analysis of cognitive vulnerabilities in the 19 accidents discussed in this book, and from the fact that the kinds of error in these accidents also occur regularly in non-accident flights (Loukopoulos et al., 2003, 2006), that few if any pilots are immune from making the kinds of error that occurred in these accidents. Thus it is essential to understand the true nature of vulnerability to error in order to reduce that vulnerability, to devise ways to help pilots catch errors before they become consequential, and to making the aviation system resilient to errors that are not caught.

To provide a good sample of the range of situations and the range of errors leading to accidents, we chose to treat all 19 major US accidents attributed at least partly to crew error in the period 1991 through 2000. This allowed us to identify common themes underlying the accidents; these common themes and their implications are discussed in the final chapter (Chapter 21). This approach also allows our book to serve as a companion piece to a previous study by the NTSB, for which the second author served as the principal investigator while on the NTSB staff: *A Review of Flightcrew-involved Major Accidents of US Air Carriers, 1978 through 1990* (NTSB, 1994a). Accidents in the NTSB study were selected using criteria similar to our own. The NTSB study provided a statistical analysis of characteristics of the operating environments, characteristics of crewmembers, errors committed, and the contexts in which the errors occurred in the 37 accidents during that 12-year period. Among the interesting findings of this study were that the captain was flying in more than 80 per cent of the accidents, and that the crew were flying together for the first time on the day of the accident in 73 per cent of accidents for which data were available. Chapter 20 of our book provides a comparable statistical analysis that updates and extends the NTSB study.

The 19 accident chapters of this book follow a common format. We first provide a brief description of the accident and the NTSB conclusions about the causes of the accident and contributing factors. We then discuss the significant events leading to the accident in chronological order, first briefly describing the event and then discussing crew actions, errors identified by the NTSB, and our thoughts on why pilots may be vulnerable to these kinds of errors. Each accident chapter concludes with a short summary and discussion of implications of our analysis. The accident chapters can be read independently of each other, so readers who are especially interested in a particular accident or particular type of situation can go directly to the chapter of interest. The statistical summary chapter comes after these accident chapters, and in the final chapter we attempt to draw together what we have learned in this study and suggest specific ways to improve aviation safety.

This book is written for a diverse audience. It will of course be of particular interest to the aviation operational community and to scientists studying aircrew performance. Beyond that it should be useful for anyone interested in aviation safety and those interested in understanding why skilled experts in any domain make errors, sometimes with disastrous consequences. To make the book as widely accessible as possible we explain technical terms and concepts in endnotes to the extent practical. For further information the reader without experience in aviation might consult books such as *The Turbine Pilot's Flight Manual* (Brown and Holt, 2001). Also, Walters and Sumwalt (2000) provide a very readable summary of a wide cross section of aviation accidents.

Notes

1   The NTSB defines an accident as major when a 14 CFR 121 aircraft was destroyed or multiple fatalities occurred or one fatality occurred and a 14 CFR 121 aircraft was substantially damaged. However, the NTSB adopted this definition recently and thus did not use these criteria in selecting the cases for its 1994 safety study on flight crew performance in major US air carrier accidents (NTSB, 1994a). To facilitate comparison with the earlier study, we selected these 19 accidents using two criteria that closely matched the ones used by the NTSB in 1994: (1) the NTSB conducted a major investigation (signified by an

NTSB accident ID in the "MA" series) or produced a major accident report in the NTSB AAR report series, and (2) the NTSB cited deficient performance of the flight crew as a causal or contributing factor.

2   CVRs and FDRs (see glossary) are essential tools for accident investigation. In this book we make extensive use of the NTSB transcripts of CVR recordings (the actual recordings are not publicly available) and of FDR data in NTSB reports. The CVR data are our primary factual source for what the crewmembers were doing through the sequence of events in an accident; however, this source of information is inherently incomplete. The recording captures only utterances and other audible sounds and provides no information about non-verbal communications or about movements of the crew such as pointing and touching. Further, transcribing the recording inherently requires varying degrees of interpretation. The FDR data, used in conjunction with the CVR transcript, help flesh out the picture of crew actions, but it is not possible to know everything the crew was thinking and doing.

3   Most major aviation accident investigations performed by the NTSB result in a detailed final report known as a "Bluecover" report (the name is derived from an earlier – but not current – color scheme) that follows the ICAO Appendix 13 format for an accident report, first summarizing relevant factual information about the accident, then analyzing the facts, and finally reporting the agency's findings, causal determinations, and recommendations for safety improvement. Such a report was available for 17 of the 19 accident cases that we review in this book. Sometimes the NTSB publishes the results of a major investigation in a less extensive, "summary" or "brief format" report. In most of these summary reports the discussion of the facts and analysis of the accident is much less extensive than in a Bluecover report. For the two major accident cases we analyze for which the NTSB did not produce a major accident report, we also reviewed publicly available background reports by NTSB investigators ("group chairman factual reports") in the areas of flight operations, human performance, and data recorders.

4   The FOM is based on but more detailed than operating manuals provided by the aircraft manufacturer.

5   And from the standpoint of scientists studying skilled performance of experts, airline operations provide an excellent domain for investigation because it is easier to distinguish correct from incorrect performance than in many other domains of skilled performance.

6   The NTSB's ultimate goal is to identify safety improvements that can prevent recurrence of accidents from the same causes. Recognizing the need to identify factors that contribute to the errors of aviation personnel, the NTSB increasingly discusses factors that might have contributed to errors and makes related safety recommendations, even if it is not sufficiently certain of the degree of influence of those factors to cite them as probable causes or contributing factors in a particular accident.

Chapter 1

USAir 1016 – Windshear Encounter

Introduction

On July 2, 1994 at 1843 eastern daylight time, USAir flight 1016, a Douglas DC-9-31, crashed into a residential neighborhood shortly after executing a missed approach from the instrument landing system (ILS) approach to runway 18R at Charlotte/Douglas International Airport in Charlotte, North Carolina. There were 37 passenger fatalities, and the remaining 20 passengers and crewmembers were injured. The airplane was destroyed in the accident.

Flight 1016 departed from Columbia, South Carolina, and after a brief en route segment it proceeded normally through the initial descent into the Charlotte area, only 20 minutes after takeoff. The first officer was the flying pilot; the captain was the monitoring pilot. Flight 1016 was the fourth leg that the crew had operated on the day of the accident, which was the first day of a planned three-day trip together.[1] The two pilots were highly experienced in their respective crew positions and in flying the DC-9: the captain had logged 1,970 hours as a DC-9 pilot-in-command, and the first officer had 3,180 hours as a DC-9 second-in-command.

According to the NTSB's analysis of aircraft performance and weather data, after abandoning the attempted ILS approach, flight 1016 encountered a microburst (a localized, severe downdraft condition associated with thunderstorms) as it began its missed approach maneuver. The NTSB determined that the probable causes of the accident were:

1) the flight crew's decision to continue an approach into severe convective activity that was conducive to a microburst;
2) the flight crew's failure to recognize a windshear situation in a timely manner;
3) the flight crew's failure to establish and maintain the proper airplane attitude and thrust setting necessary to escape the windshear; and
4) the lack of real-time adverse weather and windshear hazard information dissemination from air traffic control.

all of which led to an encounter with and failure to escape from a microburst-induced windshear that was produced by a rapidly developing thunderstorm located at the approach end of runway 18R (NTSB, 1995a, p. vi).

The NTSB also cited several factors as contributing to the accident:

1) the lack of air traffic control procedures that would have required the controller to display and issue airport surveillance radar ... weather information to the pilots of flight 1016;
2) the Charlotte tower supervisor's failure to properly advise and ensure that all controllers were aware of and reporting the reduction in visibility and the runway visual range value information and the low-level windshear alerts that had occurred in multiple quadrants;
3) the inadequate remedial actions by USAir to ensure adherence to standard operating procedures; and
4) the inadequate software logic in the airplane's windshear warning system that did not provide an alert upon entry into the windshear (NTSB, 1995a, p. 120).

Significant events and issues

1. The crew avoided precipitation cells in the terminal area and prepared for an anticipated visual approach

At 1822:59, while the airplane was entering the Charlotte area, the captain obtained the latest weather observation for the destination airport by listening to the automated terminal information system broadcast. He then accurately summarized the weather conditions for the first officer as "[sky condition] five thousand scattered, [visibility] six in haze, [surface temperature] 88 degrees, wind's 150 [degrees] at eight [knots] ..."

Despite this report of benign conditions at the Charlotte airport, within the next several minutes the crew detected convective weather ahead conducive to thunderstorms and began to consider how it might affect their flight. The captain was concerned that the airplane's onboard weather radar equipment was showing heavy precipitation ahead. Beginning about 14 minutes before the accident, the CVR recorded conversations between the captain and first officer about changing the flight's heading to avoid this weather. The crew coordinated several heading changes with air traffic control (ATC) to avoid buildups and obtain a smooth ride for the passengers. At 1833:17, about 10 minutes before the accident, the captain again discussed deviating for weather with the approach controller. The controller acknowledged that he was aware of the weather area and told the captain that flight 1016 would be turning before it reached the radar-indicated precipitation.

Any crew operating in this situation might develop an expectation from these observations and communications that their flight would probably reach better weather at the destination airport after flying around or through the precipitation areas ahead of them. During this portion of flight 1016, the crew appropriately sought out weather information and responded appropriately to the cues they received from onboard weather radar. The recorded information suggests that the captain was actively managing the situation to avoid severe weather while he communicated with ATC and while the first officer concentrated on flying the airplane. The information that the crew had received about weather along the route and at the destination airport was consistent with continuing the approach.

At 1835 the captain, conducting the checklist used to begin the descent to their destination, called: "Approach briefing" and the first officer responded: "Visual backup ILS". Shortly after this conversation the approach controller transmitted to the flight: "… vectors to the visual approach to 18 right". Crew comments captured on the CVR indicate that the first officer set up the navigation instruments for the ILS approach as a backup to the planned visual approach; however, the crew did not explicitly brief the ILS approach. We suggest that the highly abbreviated approach briefing by the first officer, which is common in air carrier operations when a crew expects to conduct a visual approach, meant that the crew of flight 1016 was still anticipating an improvement in weather conditions before the end of the flight. The controller's vectors for the visual approach supported the crew's expectation.

2. Lacking significant information, the flight crew continued the approach into an area of heavy precipitation and windshear

In the minutes that followed, the approach controller noticed a radar return consistent with a heavy precipitation storm cell that "popped up" on his radar display at the south end of the airport. He told the crew of flight 1016, at 1836:59: "May get some rain just south of the field … just expect the ILS now". However, the controller did not mention the details of the weather. The NTSB's investigation found that the intensity of the precipitation displayed to the controller at this time was Level 3, indicating heavy precipitation; the agency noted that air traffic procedures required the controller to provide specific information about the intensity of this precipitation to the crew As a result of the controller's omission of this information, the crew of flight 1016 continued their approach unaware of the magnitude or severity of the weather threat.

At 1838:38, as the flight continued toward the runway with the airport apparently remaining in sight, the captain commented: "Looks like it's sittin' right on the …" The remainder of his comment was unintelligible on the CVR, but he was most likely referring to a weather area in close proximity to the airport with which he had visual contact or was observing as precipitation echoes on his weather radar display. The captain continued: "If we have to bail out it looks like we bail out to the right". This apparently referred to a turn that the captain was planning for the flight to execute in the event of a missed approach to avoid what he considered to be the worst of the weather. The first officer replied: "Amen". The captain added: "Chance of shear". With the plan thus set, the crew continued to descend the airplane toward a landing in or near the heavy precipitation area.

These recorded discussions between the captain and first officer about the location of the weather and the possibility of windshear necessitating a missed approach, as well as their communication of an explicit plan to turn right to avoid the weather, suggest that the crew quickly and effectively put aside their earlier mind-set of good weather for landing. Their conversations further suggest that they were planning effectively for the contingencies associated with a weather cell in the vicinity of the airport. The crew demonstrated good awareness of the threat situation and responded with a contingency plan. Their conversation also may have helped to prepare for a missed approach or a windshear recovery maneuver, should either become necessary.

Given the information that the crew of flight 1016 had received by this time, their decision at this point to continue the approach is understandable. Summer thunderstorms are common in the vicinity of many airports, and airline operations typically continue in a routine fashion, deviating around the storm cells as necessary. If continuing to the destination looks questionable, crews often defer decisions about diverting to holding or to an alternate airport until the situation becomes clear, because in most cases it is possible to continue the approach and land. Although the crew of flight 1016 received and acknowledged the cues that the situation had worsened, the situation confronting them at this stage still did not clearly dictate an immediate missed approach.

However, as the approach continued and the actual weather ahead of flight 1016 worsened to a truly hazardous condition, the crew was not provided with all of the available information in a timely manner. As a result, their concept of the situation was at best incomplete. The flight crew was not told by air traffic controllers that the intensity of the precipitation near the airport was rapidly increasing to Level 6 (extreme intensity). Also, controllers did not provide the crew with updates on deteriorating visibility as the rain intensified at the airport. Because of inadequate communication inside the control tower cab, the crew was not informed of a report by a departing aircraft that "there's a storm right on top of us". However, controllers did relay a pilot report from the aircraft landing on runway 18R directly ahead of flight 1016, informing the crew that the preceding aircraft's ride was smooth on final approach and inadvertently misleading the crew of flight 1016 still further.

Reports of weather conditions by pilots who are operating ahead on the approach are highly salient to air carrier pilots; this report of smooth conditions may have been strong encouragement for the crew of flight 1016 to continue their approach, especially in the absence of the other available information that would have suggested a rapidly worsening situation. At this time, the crew of flight 1016 could see rain, which they later characterized as a "thin veil," between their aircraft and the runway; thus, the crew's own weather observations did not clarify the situation for them.

At 1840:27, when the flight was about 4.5 miles from the runway (less than two minutes' flying time), the low-level windshear alert system (LLWAS) alerted controllers to windshear activity inside the airport boundary. The controller handling flight 1016 did not immediately provide this windshear alert to the flight, initially transmitting the wind report only as a single, steady value (100 degrees at 19 knots – well within the aircraft's landing capability). At 1841:06, the controller transmitted a windshear alert, but again the controller provided only the wind information from a single sensor at the center of the airport and omitted additional wind reports from sensors in multiple quadrants of the field that would have given a more complete picture of the changing weather conditions on the ground.

We note that pilots do not necessarily associate an LLWAS alert accompanied by windspeeds below 20 knots with flight conditions that make air carrier operations unsafe. Airlines typically do not direct a missed approach based solely on an alert from the LLWAS, because flight operations can be safely continued with many of these alerts. This ambiguity about the significance of an LLWAS alert reduces the usefulness of this system as a decision tool for pilots. Improvements to the system in recent years have made the information more useful, but there will have to be a period of adjustment, accompanied by education about the reduced false-alarm rate of the newer LLWAS installations, before air carrier crews have the confidence to rely upon the improved LLWAS. At the time of the accident, an LLWAS alert should have primed a crew to be ready for a missed approach, as this crew was. We suggest, though, that the flight crew's continuation of the approach at this point was still reasonable, given the information they had received from the controller and typical experience with LLWAS performance.

Citing the controllers' failure to provide the crew of flight 1016 with the detailed information about the intensity of the precipitation, updated reports of deteriorating visibility, and detailed windshear advisories, the NTSB concluded that:

> [the] flight crew initiated the approach into an area of convective activity that, based on information from other sources, was not considered to be threatening ... [T]he crew's decision to continue the approach, even though the weather conditions were rapidly deteriorating, might have been influenced by the lack of significant weather information, or reported information, that led the crew to believe that the weather conditions still did not pose a threat to the safe completion of the flight (NTSB, 1995a, pp. 98–9).

What the crew most critically lacked at this time was the specific information that the windshear within the thunderstorm cell ahead of them was rapidly becoming severe. A microburst with downdrafts of up to 30 feet per second was developing within the storm cell, apparently just as the flight reached the weather area. Explicit information about this threat would have strongly suggested the desirability of a different course of action to the crew; in particular, earlier execution of a missed approach. Flight 1016 did not have predictive windshear detection equipment on board, which was coming into use around the time of this accident and might have provided valid real-time information about the weather threat that lay ahead of the flight. Further, even the most advanced ground-based windshear detection equipment available at the time of the accident (terminal Doppler radar, which was not installed at the Charlotte airport when the accident occurred) probably would not have provided information about the rapidly developing microburst quickly enough to be useful because this system requires up to several minutes to integrate its radar data. The hints of this microburst threat that were implicit in the visibility and wind reports that controllers did not pass along to the crew also might have prompted executing a missed approach earlier; however, we suggest that this indirect information about the nature of the storm was probably not sufficient to completely disambiguate the situation. Crews often persist with a planned approach when cues about the feasibility of the approach are ambiguous. (This "plan continuation bias" is discussed in more detail in later chapters and in Nagel, 1988, and Orasanu et al., 2001).

The truly hazardous nature of the weather – which was not apparent to the crew of flight 1016 – made it highly desirable to execute a missed approach before entering the area of changing and gusting winds (this area is known as the wind field) associated with the thunderstorm cell. Microbursts challenge flight operations because they can cause drastic changes in airplane performance that require rapid and large control inputs from the crew. An airplane often first encounters the flow of air exiting the downdraft and spreading out along the ground as a headwind component that initially enhances the performance of the airplane, causing it to climb or gain airspeed (performance-enhancing shear). Then, just as the pilot reduces power to compensate for this headwind shear, the airplane may penetrate the core of the microburst in which the air is sinking rapidly in a severe downdraft, and the airplane may then encounter a tailwind that further saps its performance as it adjusts to the changing wind within which it is immersed (performance-decreasing shear). These effects may exceed the capability of the aircraft to climb or even to maintain altitude. As the NTSB described the microburst encountered by flight 1016:

> ... the airplane encountered a windshear 6 to 8 seconds after the missed approach was initiated ... the wind shifted from a headwind of about 35 knots to a tailwind of about 26 knots in 15 seconds. The vertical velocity component of the wind field was also examined and it was determined that the vertical wind velocity increased from about 10 feet per second (fps) down to about 25 fps down, and increased further to 30 fps down as the airplane attained its maximum altitude and transitioned into a descent (NTSB, 1995a, p. 91).

Given only the information that was actually available to the crew of flight 1016 – initial visual contact with the airport, windshear report with winds less than 25 knots, small diameter of the storm cell on their radar, and pilots ahead reporting smooth conditions – and operating practices common in the airline industry, it seems likely that many or even most crews in this situation would have continued the approach for at least as long as the accident crew before deciding on a missed approach. Air carriers routinely operate flights in conditions such as these, as is revealed by the succession of other air carrier flights that were arriving and departing Charlotte at the time of the accident: two flights landed less than four minutes prior to the accident airplane and two flights also departed during the same period, with the last of these taking off just at the time of the accident and reporting a smooth ride in heavy rain during its takeoff roll.

Two other USAir flights (806 and 797) decided to delay takeoff because of the weather situation. The radio transmissions between these flights and the control tower were recorded in the cockpit of flight 1016. We cannot ascertain whether the crew of flight 1016 heard, or used, the information about these other company flights postponing takeoff, but we note that flight 1016 began a missed approach approximately 30 seconds after these radio transmissions.

Penetration of storm cells by airliners in the vicinity of airports may not be as uncommon as one might expect. We are aware of only one study providing data on this issue, but that study is revealing. MIT Lincoln Laboratory scientists evaluating new weather radar equipment correlated weather radar returns with flight radar tracks of aircraft inbound to the Dallas/Fort Worth airport during periods of heavy thunderstorm activity (Rhoda and Pawlak, 1999). They discovered that most flight crews confronted by thunderstorms on approach penetrated the storm cells at some point. The likelihood of cell penetration increased for aircraft within 10–15 miles of the airport and for aircraft following other aircraft on the approach.

Airline crews may be biased to continue approaches to airports in the vicinity of airports by several factors. On-time arrival at the planned destination is highly valued by passengers and by the companies competing for their business. Frequent and successful operations in the vicinity of thunderstorms may lead pilots to develop a false sense of security: having no information about how close to the margins of safety these "successful" approaches may have actually been, pilots may unwittingly build up an inaccurate mental model of the degree of risk involved. Lacking unambiguous information about the level of risk during the approach, pilots may give too much weight to the ride reports of the flights arriving before them. Unfortunately, little hard evidence exists to reveal at what point a large population of airline pilots might break off an approach in the situation confronting the crew of flight 1016, but the limited data available do not suggest that this crew fell outside the range of typical decision-making in the airline industry – the "norms" of everyday flight operations.

3. Captain commanded, and first officer initiated, a missed approach

At 1841:59, the first officer stated: "There's, ooh, ten knots right there". The captain replied: "Okay, you're plus twenty". These comments referred to the airspeed margin above the flight's target airspeed and suggested that the airplane was entering the increasing headwind (performance-increasing) portion of a microburst. The pilots recognized the significance of the 20-knot airspeed increase: at 1842:14, the captain stated: "Take it around, go to the right". At this time the airplane was about 200 feet above ground level. The first officer initiated a missed approach and turned the airplane to the right, as pre-briefed by the captain, in an attempt to avoid flying through the heart of the precipitation cell during the missed approach. But, as it turned out, the cell had shifted position to the right of the runway threshold. The turn ordered by the captain resulted in the airplane penetrating the downdraft portion of the microburst.

We suggest that the crew's response to the gain of airspeed by abandoning the approach was prompt. The crew's actions were possibly facilitated by their earlier briefing about the possibility of windshear. In retrospect, with our full knowledge of the actual location and severity of the microburst, it is clear that the crew's decision to turn to the right worsened their situation; however, their actions were consistent with the only information available to them at the time. Further, during the missed approach maneuver there was insufficient time for the crew to manipulate the airborne weather radar or use any other method to update their information about the weather threat.

As the missed approach began, the captain stated: "Max[imum] power". The first officer repeated: "Yeah, max power". According to FDR information, the crew increased the power enough to provide for climb performance, but the thrust remained approximately nine per cent less than maximum (go-around) thrust. It is not clear why the crew did not set the power to maximum as they had discussed; most likely, it was an inadvertent slip caused by workload and stress. The first officer then called for the flaps to be retracted to 15 degrees. The captain retracted the flaps in response to the first officer's request. The crew did not retract the landing gear.

In its *Pilot's Handbook* for the DC-9, the air carrier had established two procedures that the crew could have considered using in the circumstances existing at this time in the flight. One procedure, the normal missed approach, called for the crew to set the engine power levers to command go-around thrust (the maximum thrust value approved for continuous use; the relevant callout was "Maximum power"), retract the flaps to 15 degrees to reduce drag, rotate the nose upward to begin a climb, adjust the airplane's pitch attitude to maintain an optimum airspeed for climb performance, and retract the landing gear after the aircraft began a positive rate of climb (NTSB, 1995a, pp. 58–60). The other procedure, the windshear/microburst recovery maneuver, called for the crew to push the engine power levers full forward (exceeding normal thrust limits; the relevant callout was "Firewall power"), maintain the existing flap and landing gear configuration, rotate the nose to 15 degrees above the horizon (a very high pitch angle), and then maintain the 15-degree pitch attitude regardless of airspeed loss unless the stall warning stickshaker indicated that the airplane was nearing the absolute minimum speed at which the wings could produce lift.

The difference in pitch guidance between the two procedures was critically important. Performance studies had indicated that a flight would have the best chance of surviving a windshear encounter if the crew maintained the high nose-up pitch attitude of the windshear recovery procedure and used the energy available from excess airspeed to avoid ground contact. In contrast, crews following the normal missed approach procedure of maintaining a fixed target airspeed might pitch the airplane down into the ground when it experienced a loss of airspeed from the downdraft/tailwind components of the windshear.

The preponderance of the crew's actions during this period (callouts, adding partial climb thrust, retracting the wing flaps) suggests that they initially attempted to execute the normal missed approach procedure after abandoning the ILS approach at approximately 200 feet above the ground in response to the increasing airspeed.[2] Reviewing the information available to the crew of flight 1016, the NTSB concluded that they "should have recognized that a windshear condition existed, and they should have executed a windshear [recovery] maneuver" (NTSB, 1995a, p. 107). We note that the windshear recovery procedure would have been an optimal response for the crew when the increase in airspeed was initially encountered and suggest that it became critical later, when conditions deteriorated. However, in the specific situation confronting the crew of flight 1016, several factors might have mitigated against any crew's execution of this response, either as an initial action when abandoning the ILS approach or, later, while already executing a missed approach procedure.

We think that many crews confronted with a similar airspeed gain in this kind of situation might also respond with the normal missed approach procedure. As the NTSB suggested in its analysis of the accident, prior to entering the performance-decreasing downdraft and tailwind portions of the wind field, crewmembers might think that they were avoiding the windshear rather than recovering from it. In this regard, the actions of the crew of flight 1016 were supported by company procedures as stated in the carrier's DC-9 *Pilot Handbook*: "If on approach and an increasing performance shear is encountered, a normal go-around, rather than recovery, maneuver may be accomplished" (NTSB, 1995a, p. 59).

In the seconds that followed initiation of the missed approach, flight 1016 entered the downdraft and tailwind (performance-decreasing) portion of the microburst wind field, and the airplane began to sink toward the ground despite its nose-up attitude and climb thrust setting. The best way for the crew to respond to this deterioration in airplane performance would have been to change plans and execute the windshear recovery maneuver. Even though the windshear was reducing the flight's airspeed alarmingly, the crew's best hope for escape was to hold the airplane's pitch attitude high and sacrifice airspeed. (However, NTSB performance calculations indicated that flight 1016 could have escaped the windshear successfully if the crew had completely performed either the normal missed approach or the windshear recovery procedure.)

In order for the crew to recognize that they needed to switch from a normal missed approach to the windshear recovery procedure, they would have had to note and interpret additional cues resulting as the aircraft's performance began to deteriorate – decreasing airspeed and poor climb performance – but this would have required the pilots to integrate and interpret information from multiple sources while under workload, time pressure, and stress. Because integration of multiple cues is challenging, especially under severe workload and stress, when human attention tends to narrow (Baddeley, 1972; Stokes and Kite, 1994, Chapter 3), the FAA mandates that air carrier airplanes provide direct warning of windshear with an onboard windshear detection system. Flight 1016 was equipped with a windshear detection system that was "reactive"; that is, it was designed to activate once the airplane had entered a windshear condition. (This contrasts with the "predictive" type system that is designed to provide advance warning of windshear; predictive windshear equipment was coming into use at the time of the accident but was not yet widely installed in the US air carrier fleet.) Although it could not have provided any advance warning of windshear, the reactive system installed on the airplane should have provided the crew with both visual and aural windshear warnings once entering the shear.

But flight 1016's windshear detection system never activated. Although the NTSB was unable to determine with certainty why the system did not activate, the agency found that it included "a design feature in the software that desensitizes the warning system whenever the flaps are in transition, thus reducing nuisance warnings" (NTSB, 1995a, p. 15). Flight 1016 encountered the performance-decreasing effects of the windshear during the 12-second period while the flaps were retracting. Thus the crew's retraction of the flaps (part of the normal missed approach procedure but not the windshear escape procedure) may have inadvertently caused the onboard system to fail to warn them. The absence of this warning may have been critical. If the crew had received the warning they would have been more likely to shift to the windshear recovery procedure, and if they had shifted they would have been more likely to apply maximum continuous (or greater) thrust and would have been more likely to hold a high pitch attitude rather than lower the nose to maintain a constant airspeed.

The crew's failure to execute the windshear recovery procedure in the presence of several windshear cues demonstrates that crews can be strongly misled by the absence of an expected cue – in this case, the onboard windshear warning. In simulator training for windshear encounters, the windshear warning reliably alerts pilots to the encounter, and through repeated association during training this warning cue may be stored in memory as a central aspect of windshear encounter. Consequently the absence of this expected warning cue may make pilots slower to interpret their situation as a windshear encounter, even though other cues occur. Also, in this regard, the NTSB noted that in the company's training scenarios turbulence always signaled the onset of windshear. But flight 1016 entered the performance-decreasing portion of the windshear without encountering turbulence. Consequently, another expected windshear cue was missing.[3]

Other cues, such as deteriorating airspeed and poor climb performance, occurred to alert the crew that they were encountering performance-decreasing windshear. However, the absence of some of the expected, clearly defined cues about windshear encounter can be problematic because it is inherently difficult for humans under the stress and workload of a windshear encounter to rapidly and reliably assess multiple, complex, and ambiguous cues that require effortful, analytical thought. Pilots are specifically trained to expect that a microburst encounter beginning with a performance-increasing shear will likely transition to a performance-decreasing shear, and the crew of flight 1016 very probably understood this, at least intellectually. However, as the crew proceeded deeper into the windshear, the stress and workload would have made it increasingly difficult to quickly recognize, assess, and respond to the cues that they were now entering the performance-decreasing domain.

Company-approved procedures authorizing a normal missed approach in response to a performance-increasing windshear have the undesirable by-product of exposing crews to the difficult task of switching to the windshear recovery maneuver at a critical and pressured time.[4] In general it is best to avoid placing crews in situations in which they must make a rapid change in plan under high workload. Consequently, the aviation industry might want to consider writing procedures that call for crews to initiate only a windshear escape maneuver, rather than a normal missed approach, in the case of a performance-increasing windshear. This procedural change would eliminate the need to reassess the situation and switch to a different procedure, and this would reduce workload and might improve reliable execution of windshear recovery.

4. Captain ordered, and first officer executed, a pitch-down during the windshear encounter

At 1842:22, just after the first officer had pitched the airplane to the missed approach attitude of 15 degrees nose-up and as the airplane was transitioning into the downdraft and increasing-tailwind portion of the microburst, the captain ordered: "Down, push it down". The first officer responded by reducing the airplane's pitch attitude over a period of seven seconds, eventually reaching a minimum of five degrees nose-down. As a result of both the nose-down control inputs and the performance-decreasing effects of the windshear, the airplane entered a steep descent. Investigators determined that this pitch-down input was the key factor in the airplane's inability to fly through the windshear encounter.

Although the reasons for the captain's "down" command and the first officer's nose-down pitch inputs cannot be determined with certainty, several possibilities are suggested by evaluation of the cues that the crew would have been receiving at the time. It is conceivable that the captain's "down" command might have been his response to the airplane's initial pitch-up from increasing headwind at the onset of the windshear; in this case, he may have been urging the first officer to modulate the pitch-up rate so as not to exceed 15 degrees. Alternatively, the captain may have based his comments on the airspeed decrease that occurred as the airplane transitioned into the performance-decreasing portion of the shear; in that case, his command may have been meant to urge the first officer to decrease the airplane's pitch attitude so as not to allow the airspeed to decay.

The NTSB evaluated the airplane's longitudinal trim[5] status at the time of the pitch-down and found that the airplane was operating approximately 29 knots below its in-trim speed; to maintain the existing nose-up attitude the first officer would have been maintaining approximately 24 pounds of back pressure on the control column. As a result, he would not have been required to push forward on the control column to obtain the pitch reduction that occurred after the captain's "Down, push it down" statement; instead, he needed only to relax some of the back pressure that he had been exerting. The NTSB commented: "While it is possible that the first officer intentionally released the pressure to comply with the [captain's] directive, this action might also have been instinctive because pilots are unlikely to ignore an out-of-trim condition" (NTSB, 1995a, p. 98). We would further add that if the first officer did deliberately pitch down to maintain airspeed, the out-of-trim condition may have produced a greater nose-down reaction than he desired. Afterwards there was little time for the crew to correct for this reaction.

Whether prompted by the captain or by his own view of the airspeed indicator, the first officer may have pitched the nose down because of the significant loss of airspeed that was occurring at the time and because the onboard windshear warning system did not alert him to do otherwise. As we have noted, had the crew made the mental transition to the windshear recovery procedure, they would have been more likely to maintain the airplane's pitch attitude at the expense of airspeed, the most effective strategy in windshear. However, even making this transition does not guarantee correct performance. Pilots develop a deep and powerful habit to maintain a "safe" target airspeed, and this habit is reinforced in all flight situations except for windshear. The difficulty of overcoming this habit is recognized in current air carrier pilot training requirements, which provide more frequent simulator training for the windshear recovery procedure than for most other emergency procedures.

This point is illustrated by a recent study of newly hired airline pilots' performance in recovering from various aircraft upset attitude situations (Gawron, 2002, pp. 115–26). In this study, recovery performance was evaluated in an actual aircraft – a Lear Jet with computer-driven control responses that mimic the performance and handling of a large jet aircraft and provide the sensations and cues available only from actual flight – rather than in the type of ground simulator in which airline pilots are typically trained. Thirty-five of 36 subject pilots recovered from a windshear scenario based on the flight 1016 accident; however, the performance of a substantial fraction of these pilots was far from optimal. Five of the 36 subjects, like the accident crew, reduced pitch attitude in an attempt to maintain airspeed. These results suggest that airline pilots may have difficulty with the procedure of sacrificing airspeed to hold a high pitch attitude in actual flight, even though they have received ground simulation training in the windshear recovery procedure.

5. The crew did not challenge the high sink rate and were unable to recover before impact

At 1842:28, approximately seven seconds after the captain's "down" command, the "whoop, whoop, terrain" ground proximity warning (GPWS) activated and continued until impact. The airplane was descending through 330 feet above ground level when the GPWS alert began. Concurrently, the CVR recorded a crewmember stating "[unintelligible] power". After the accident, the captain testified that in response to the GPWS activation he had stated "Firewall power", the command for thrust consistent with windshear recovery and the terrain escape maneuver. FDR information shows that the thrust increased above the normal go-around value, and one second later the crew moved the control column sharply aft; however, they began these recovery inputs too late. One second later the FDR recorded the nose still below the horizon and the rate of descent continuing to exceed 2,000 feet per minute. The stickshaker activated at 1842:33, indicating that further nose-up control inputs would be ineffective. Ground impact occurred shortly thereafter.

A total of about 13 seconds elapsed from the captain's "down" command to the first sounds of impact. The foregoing analysis suggests that the crew was taking action to recover during the second half of this period, thus roughly six seconds was potentially available for a quicker and possibly more effective recovery. We find it understandable, though, that the crew had difficulty taking advantage of all 13 seconds that were available, because of cognitive limitations to which all humans are subject. During this period, the crew had to integrate the messages of the flight instruments concerning the rapidly developing sink rate. This task may have been particularly difficult for the captain. The NTSB noted that while the first officer would have been actively scanning the flight instruments as the flying pilot, the captain may not have been scanning the instruments as actively.

We also note that, having just commanded a pitch-down (not recognizing that recovery actually required maintaining a nose-up pitch attitude), the captain would have required some time to re-organize his understanding of the situation. It is difficult to change mind-set quickly under time pressure and stress; further, because people tend to interpret cues in a way that confirms their mind-set and often fail to process conflicting cues (confirmation bias, as discussed in: Einhorn and Hogarth, 1978; Mynatt and Doherty, 1999, Chapter 21; Wickens and Hollands, 2000, pp. 312–13), the captain's pitch-down mind-set could have delayed his comprehension of and reaction to the cues that the sink rate was getting worse. Although six seconds is generally more than adequate for reacting to an unambiguous signal, the situation in which the crew of flight 1016 found themselves at this time was saturated with a confusing array of cues. No data exist on how long it would take a large sample of airline pilots to sort out this situation and respond appropriately, but we suspect the range of response times would be considerable and that many might not respond more quickly than this crew. Further, we suspect that the variability would occur not only across pilots but within pilots – individuals' response times to complex situations often vary considerably as functions of happenstance details of the situation and the individual's cognitive state at the moment.

Concluding discussion

In its statement of probable cause for this accident, the NTSB concluded that the crew of flight 1016 made a poor decision to continue their approach until entering the windshear, failed to recognize the windshear in a timely manner, and failed to make the proper control inputs to recover from the windshear. While all of these conclusions are valid in hindsight and with the benefit of full information (the NTSB explicitly recognized in its other causal and contributing factor determinations that the crew received inadequate information), we have suggested in this chapter that the crew's actions in all of these aspects of performance are understandable in terms of the limited information available to the crew, typical airline operating practices, and human cognitive processes.

Lacking adequate information about the weather threat ahead of them, the crew of flight 1016 continued their approach until actually penetrating a severe microburst. The history of thunderstorm-related air carrier accidents and recent research on penetration of thunderstorms by airline flights suggest that the series of decisions and reactions that led the crew of flight 1016 to the microburst penetration was consistent with norms for airline flight operations, given incomplete information about the specific nature of the threat. At the beginning of the sequence of events, the crew's decisions to continue with the approach were arguably correct, as the NTSB recognized. Later in the sequence, the crew's decisions remained "locally rational"; (see Introduction) that is, they were correct based on the information possessed at the time. The limited normative information available on this subject suggests that many, or even most, airline crews would have taken the same initial course as the accident pilots under the same circumstances – to steer clear of the defined confines of the cell, continue inbound to the airport, remain watchful for windshear, and be prepared for a missed approach or windshear escape maneuver. In most line operations conducted in these weather conditions, the cells can be avoided or, if inadvertently encountered, they do not overwhelm aircraft control; as a result, airline crews receive repeated reinforcement to expect that approaches conducted in these conditions are safe. Occasionally, however, a small cell harbors a powerful microburst, and in these rare instances a crew following the normal strategy may unwittingly encounter such a hazard. The fact that crews frequently continue approaches under seemingly identical conditions and the ambiguity of available cues in these conditions may desensitize crews to the grave danger that the situation sometimes poses.

This accident illustrates the tendency for flight crews to persist with an existing plan despite receiving new information suggesting the plan should be changed. It seems likely that this kind of mind-set is more powerful and more likely to influence flight crews when, as in the case of this accident, the cues suggesting the situation has changed are ambiguous, and when time pressure, competing workload, and stress increase the difficulty of interpreting the cues.

Once the crew of flight 1016 entered the microburst while attempting to execute a missed approach, they were unable to change plans to execute the windshear recovery procedure in time to escape from the microburst. The airline's standard operating procedures allowed a normal missed approach in response to performance-increasing windshear, which was the first cue about the microburst that the crew received. By exposing the crew to the need to reassess their situation during the missed approach and change their plans under a heavy cognitive load, this procedure increased the probability of crew error. (However, airlines also have to consider the cost of executing a windshear recovery that might not be required.) Further, the failure of the airplane's onboard warning system to alert the crew and the absence of turbulence, which are cues that pilots associate with the presence of windshear, may have slowed the crew's identification of the performance-decreasing effects of the microburst.

In the final seconds of the flight, the crew's nose-down control input undermined the recovery. We can never know why the crew responded this way, but their response may have been triggered by the highly trained and constantly practised habit of all pilots to adjust pitch to maintain airspeed. The crew's performance was shaped by characteristic human cognitive tendencies under high workload, time pressure, and stress: attention narrows, integration and interpretation of multiple and ambiguous cues are delayed, and retrieval of declarative knowledge that might override established habits is impaired. Thus, in complex, dynamic situations such as that of flight 1016 that do not map perfectly against training scenarios, we expect considerable variability in pilots' performance.

We suggest that the aviation system, as currently operated, puts airline crews in the position of being expected to operate in proximity to hazardous weather without the information that they need to judge the situation accurately. This accident can be viewed as the probabilistic outcome of repeatedly operating flights without adequate information in the vicinity of thunderstorms. The performance of the crew of flight 1016 in many ways demonstrated high levels of professional competence. The aspects of their performance that were less than perfect illustrate that highly skilled professionals are inherently vulnerable, probabilistically, to making characteristic forms of errors some percentage of the time as a function of the particular circumstances of the situation and chance. Recognizing that error rates can be reduced but not completely eliminated, leaders in the airline industry have begun developing training to help crews detect errors and manage the consequences of errors (Gunther, 2004a). In addition to this training, we suggest that to reduce the probability of accidents such as that of flight 1016 the aviation system must provide accurate, unambiguous, and timely information to enable crews to identify and avoid truly hazardous weather,[6] or it must adopt substantially more conservative policies for operating in the vicinity of thunderstorms, which of course would increase operating costs and flight delays.

Notes

1 Paired with another captain, the first officer had also flown a company flight that arrived in Pittsburgh at 0930 on the morning of the accident.

2 The crew did not retract the landing gear after beginning the missed approach, as specified by the missed approach procedure (but not the windshear recovery procedure, which specified leaving the gear extended). Perhaps the crew did not retract the landing gear because they were intentionally waiting to achieve a solid, continued climb and safe altitude. Alternately, they may have inadvertently omitted the landing gear retraction step of the missed approach procedure in the stress and workload of the combined missed approach, turn for weather avoidance, and the ensuing windshear encounter.

2 This discussion illustrates how even well-intentioned training that is largely well-designed may not adequately prepare flight crews to deal with situations that occur somewhat differently in actual flight operations. While it is not feasible to give simulator training in all possible variants of every situation that crews may encounter, we suggest that training scenario designers should explicitly consider what cues to provide and in what manner to present the cues to avoid engendering inappropriate habits and expectations among the pilots trained.

4 We are not aware of any current air carrier windshear training scenarios that would allow crews to practise this kind of transition from a normal missed approach to a windshear recovery.

5 This trim control is normally set for a given airspeed so that the pilot does not have to exert forward or backward force on the yoke to maintain that airspeed.

6 Onboard predictive windshear warning systems and ground-based terminal Doppler weather radar systems with microburst detection are now mature technologies (installed on many, but not all, aircraft employed in airline service and at a select number of high-

volume runways at major airports) and could greatly improve crews' ability to assess windshear threats accurately and make decisions early enough to reduce or avoid desperate maneuvers. These information sources could be combined with improved display systems that provide the information in real time and provide the proper flight guidance.

Chapter 2

TWA 843 – The Power of Suggestion

Introduction

On July 30, 1992 at 1741 eastern daylight time, TWA flight 843, a Lockheed 1011, rejected takeoff shortly after liftoff on runway 13R at John F. Kennedy International Airport in New York. Six seconds after liftoff the airplane landed hard, damaging the right wing spar and starting a fire. As the airplane approached the end of the runway, the captain realized that he would not be able to stop on the paved surface and steered the airplane onto the grass at the left edge of the runway. The airplane came to rest about 300 feet to the left of the runway departure end. One serious injury (a broken leg suffered during emergency evacuation) and 9 minor injuries were reported among the 280 passengers and 12 crewmembers. Visual meteorological conditions prevailed at the airport at the time of the accident, which occurred during daylight.

The crew of flight 843 were highly experienced in their respective positions and in flying the L-1011. The captain had accumulated more than 15,000 hours in over 27 years with the airline, and he had 2,397 hours of experience in the L-1011, 1,574 of which were as a captain. The first officer had accumulated nearly 14,000 hours of flight time in 25 years with the company, and he had 2,953 hours as an L-1011 first officer. The flight engineer was in his third year with the company and had 2,266 hours of experience as an L-1011 flight engineer. Also, two other captains who were qualified on the L-1011 occupied jumpseats at the rear of the cockpit.

The flight was normal through pushback, engine start, taxi-out, and the takeoff ground roll. The flight was loaded to within 1,000 pounds of the airplane's 430,000-pound maximum allowable takeoff weight. The first officer was the flying pilot for the takeoff. Consistent with the company's procedures, the captain (who was the monitoring pilot) retained sole responsibility for the decision to reject a takeoff and thus maintained control over the throttles during takeoff. As specified in these procedures, the captain advanced the throttles to takeoff thrust and then kept his right hand on the throttles to be prepared to reject the takeoff if necessary. When the captain called out "V1" (takeoff decision speed) at 1740:58, he removed his right hand from the throttles and guarded them from behind,[1] prepared at that point to continue the takeoff in the event of an engine failure. (V1 speeds are set for the specific conditions under which an aircraft is operating and are provided to the crew in performance charts. At V1 the pilot can reject the takeoff and still be able to stop the aircraft on the remaining runway. Beyond V1 crews are trained to continue the takeoff in most situations, including failure of one of the engines.)

The captain called "Vr" (the "rotation" speed at which the pilot pulls the nose up to begin the climb) at 1741:03, and the first officer began to pull back on the control column to rotate the nose upward at about 2 degrees per second. Liftoff occurred six seconds later, at approximately 11 degrees of pitch. Shortly after liftoff, according to the crew's recollections, the stall warning stickshaker activated. This is a motor-driven, highly salient vibration of both pilots' control yokes designed to alert crews to a critically high wing angle of attack as the aircraft approaches stall speed.

During the moments following activation of the stickshaker, the first officer announced that the airplane would not fly and turned over the flight controls to the captain, who then made what he later described as a "split-second decision" to return the airplane to the runway. The airplane sustained damage during the ensuing hard landing and excursion off the runway surface. The NTSB determined that:

The probable causes of this accident were design deficiencies in the stall warning system that permitted a defect to go undetected, the failure of [the airline's] maintenance program to correct a repetitive malfunction of the stall warning system, and inadequate crew coordination between the captain and first officer that resulted in their inappropriate response to a false stall warning (NTSB, 1993a, p. 46).

Significant events and issues

1. False stall warning at liftoff

Post-accident inspection and testing revealed that the stall warning system malfunctioned, causing it to signal the crew that the airplane was stalling after liftoff, when in fact it was not stalling. During the checks that the crew performed in preparation for flight, nothing in the cockpit would have indicated that this system was malfunctioning. The L-1011 stall warning system was designed to suppress stall warning indications until after liftoff. Consequently, the stickshaker activated just after liftoff. Immediately the first officer stated: "Getting a stall".

The L-1011 flight deck overhead panel includes a "Stall Warning System Fail" light that was supposed to alert the crew to malfunctions of the stall warning system; however, the monitoring circuit was not designed to detect the particular fault that occurred in the accident. As a result, this warning light did not illuminate, and there was no direct annunciation to the crew that the stickshaker activation after takeoff was a false stall warning. Presumably, two annunciations did occur as a result of the system failure that caused the false stall warning: (1) an "Autothrottle System Fail" light also located on the overhead panel above the pilots' heads, and (2) an amber "Flight Control Panels" annunciation on the lower part of the center instrument panel. However, neither indication would have illuminated until two seconds after the stickshaker had activated because of a time delay that was included in the warning system design All other instrument indications, aircraft configuration, and aircraft performance were normal, as the aircraft was not, in fact, stalling.

Interviewed after the accident, the crew of flight 843 did not recall seeing any of the warning lights, and we find it unsurprising that the crew did not notice these lights. The overhead panel is outside the normal instrument scan patterns during aircraft rotation and initial climb, and the lower center instrument panel is also not the crew's primary focus area at these times. Further, even if the crewmembers had noticed the illuminated lights, neither the "Autothrottle System Fail" nor the "Flight Control Panels" light had a direct and unambiguous connection to a stall warning system failure. Perhaps most significantly, by the time the built-in two-second delay had elapsed and the warnings had begun, the crew was already reacting to the stickshaker activated by the false stall warning, and the critical decisions were in process or already made. Therefore, we suggest that the L-1011 warning system design did not provide timely and clear annunciation of a false stall warning to flight crews.

The L-1011 stall warning system suppresses stall warnings on the ground to avoid nuisance warnings, but the same design feature has the unintended consequence of allowing a false stall warning indication to remain latent during taxi-out and takeoff and first be annunciated to the crew just after the airplane lifts off the ground. This design forces pilots to evaluate and attempt to deal with a stall warning under extreme time pressure, when workload is high and they have little time to ascertain whether the warning is false.

The NTSB noted the difficulty of this situation in a discussion of the false stall warning in its accident investigation report. However, during its investigation the NTSB learned that the airplane involved in the accident had also presented a false stall warning just after takeoff to a different flight crew on an earlier flight. The NTSB cited this excerpt from the report about the incident submitted by the captain of that other flight:

> The preflight, taxi, and takeoff up through the liftoff were normal; however, after the liftoff the stickshaker activated on a continuous basis. The airspeed showed V2 [takeoff safety speed] plus 2 or 3 knots, the takeoff/climb attitude was normal, and all center panel engine indications were normal. The aircraft flew normally, and responded to control inputs normally. I instructed the … first officer and … flight engineer to deactivate the stickshaker while I flew the aircraft. In all, the stickshaker was activated for approximately 15 seconds (NTSB, 1993a, p. 35).

Based in part on this evidence of a crew that was able to successfully identify and handle a false stall warning under similar circumstances, the NTSB concluded that the crew of flight 843 should have been able to cope with the situation:

> … The Safety Board does not consider the onset of the stickshaker stall warning as an emergency condition that justifies actions that can place the airplane in jeopardy. The stickshaker activation is a warning indication that the wing is at an [angle of attack] approaching a stall condition, but a significant margin of safety is provided before the actual aerodynamic stall angle occurs. Moreover, the captain had called out V1 and Vr, presumably by reference to the airspeed indicator, and the airplane was accelerating through V2 and beginning to climb. Based on their awareness of air speed and flap configuration, the pilots should have concluded that the stickshaker was a false stall warning (NTSB, 1993a, p. 52).

Several cues to the airplane's normal performance status coexisted with the false stall warning cues. According to the captain of the flight involved in the previous incident, he was able to rapidly cross-check other indications and immediately deduce that the stall warning was false. Still, it is important to recognize that making this assessment rapidly and accurately is quite challenging. The period immediately after an airplane leaves the ground is critical because anything that goes wrong may pose a large threat, and the crew must be prepared to react quickly and correctly to diverse situations. Under normal conditions the flying pilot[2] concentrates on controlling the airplane, watching out the cockpit windscreen, and being prepared for any non-normal events. The other pilot monitors the instrument panel, aircraft performance and trajectory, and the actions of the flying pilot. Mental workload is relatively high during this period.

False stall warnings at takeoff are so rare that few pilots have experienced them; airlines do not train for them, and it is likely that few pilots have mentally prepared for this extraordinary event. A stall warning at this moment causes surprise and a sense of urgency for immediate response because it signals threat at a time when the aircraft is especially vulnerable. Stress may also come into play and combine with high workload and time pressure to impede deliberate, thorough cognitive, analysis of the situation and identification of alternative interpretations of conflicting cues. Individuals forced to make high-stakes decisions under time pressure tend to favor simpler interpretations and strategies that make fewer demands on limited working memory resources than does deliberate, analytical thought (Stokes and Kite, 1994, Chapter 3; Wickens and Hollands, 2000, p. 489; Staal, 2004, p. 76). Under these circumstances pilots are likely to be heavily influenced by automatic retrieval from memory of the strong association of stickshaker activation with approach to a stall.

Given sufficient time all experienced airline pilots would probably sort through the conflicting cues and reach the correct interpretation. If a false stall warning occurred at cruise altitude, when threat and time pressure are much lower, we suspect most crews would probably work through the situation slowly enough to decide that the stall warning is false. The successful performance of the crew in the previous incident reveals that at least some of the time it is possible for a crew to reach the correct interpretation quickly enough to disregard the stall warning during takeoff; however, no data exist to reveal what proportion of a large population of pilots would be so successful. From a cognitive perspective, we suspect that many would make errors under these conditions. The variability in performance is not just a function of differences among pilots; under challenging conditions such as these each individual's performance would vary as a function of minute aspects of the situation too subtle to be revealed by what is known about the accident flight and the incident flight that preceded it (see discussion of "replica" pilots in the Introduction).

2. First officer stopped takeoff rotation and decreased pitch attitude

According to flight data recorder information, after reaching 12.6 degrees of pitch immediately following takeoff, the airplane's nose-up attitude began to decrease. The first officer explained in post-accident interviews that he felt the stickshaker, then felt the aircraft sinking, which reinforced his impression that the airplane was stalling. The captain recalled after the accident that he had heard the stickshaker, sensed the airplane beginning to sink, and heard the first officer say that the airplane was not flying.

Results of post-accident simulation studies indicated that the "sinking feeling" both pilots perceived (shown in FDR data as a slight reduction in vertical G loading) was the product of nose-down control inputs made by the first officer. The reduction in G loading was consistent with the airplane's pitch attitude reduction produced by a forward motion of the control column. The NTSB concluded that the first officer must have pushed the control column forward, or at least relaxed some of the back pressure that he had been applying to the column.

When the stickshaker activated, the first officer probably relaxed back pressure on the control column as a highly practised, automatic response to the indications of stalling. It seems likely that most pilots would have initially responded in this automatic fashion, though some might have quickly checked this response and pulled the nose back up to takeoff attitude. The investigation found that the airline did not provide formal training for recovering from stall warning activations immediately after takeoff. As is common at most airlines, the company's stall training stressed applying maximum power and slightly reducing pitch, the correct response in most situations (NTSB, 1993a, p. 47).[3] In contrast, if any special procedures and training for coping with a stall warning immediately after takeoff were developed, they would probably have to differ from standard airline stall recovery, and would be more akin to the windshear avoidance maneuver that stresses maintaining or increasing to a high pitch attitude – close to stickshaker activation – to avoid ground contact. But providing this special training, besides being an expensive remedy for a rare situation, would put pilots in the situation of having two different stall recovery maneuvers and having to choose the correct one under time pressure. This discussion illustrates the dilemmas and trade-offs confronting airlines attempting to provide effective procedures and training for a wide range of non-normal situations, not all of which can be anticipated.

The first officer's pitch reduction in response to the stall warning indication (understandable, at least as an initial, immediate response) caused the airplane to remain in critical proximity to the runway surface; the airplane never achieved an altitude greater than 15 feet. Further, the sinking feeling caused by the pitch attitude reduction would have strongly reinforced the message of the stickshaker that the airplane was stalling. In combination, the stickshaker and the sinking sensation very likely drove the impression of both the captain and first officer that the airplane was not performing normally.

3. First officer transferred aircraft control to the captain

At 0741:13, about two seconds after liftoff and while the airplane's pitch attitude was beginning to decrease in response to the first officer's pitch control inputs, the first officer stated: "You got it". The captain heard the first officer and took control of the airplane, replying "OK" at 0741:14.

The NTSB concluded that the first officer's transfer of control to the captain did not conform with procedures established by most air carriers for a positive transfer of control (NTSB, 1993a, p. 53), ones that ensure someone is flying the airplane at all times and that the pilot assuming control is aware of the flight's status and prepared to fly. Ordinarily, a flying pilot wanting to transfer airplane control to the monitoring pilot would first direct an order or inquiry to the monitoring pilot (such as "You have the aircraft" or "Can you take it?"), next, the monitoring pilot would response positively ("I have the aircraft") and the other pilot would acknowledge ("You have the aircraft").

Under the circumstances of flight 843, there was not time for a complete discussion of this sort, although a brief inquiry to the captain may have been possible and could have better prepared the captain to assume control. The first officer's sudden turnover of control to the captain without verbal exchange clearly hampered coordination of the two pilots' efforts. Thrust into the flying pilot role without warning, the captain had little time to analyze the (false) warning of the stickshaker and the sinking sensation normally associated with reduction of aircraft climb performance. Although the first officer did not recognize that his own pitch control inputs were causing the sinking sensation during the very brief period before he gave control to the captain, we suggest that, in general, a pilot making a nose-down input is more likely to link the control input to the sinking sensation than would a pilot not on the controls. The close correlation of aircraft response to the direction, magnitude, and timing of control inputs provides strong feedback to the pilot making the inputs, though if distracted by some other event, as was the first officer, pilots may not be aware of their control inputs. Thus there are strong advantages to having the flying pilot remain in control of the aircraft in dynamic, time-pressured situations, at least until an orderly transfer of control is possible. If the first officer of flight 843 had not given control to the captain, he would have had several additional seconds to recognize that his pitch inputs were causing the airplane to sink, and the captain would have been able to focus on analyzing the situation.

We note that any training the crew of flight 843 received about change in control was probably generic and certainly was not emphasized or practised in this specific context. In any case, with little time to react to the situation and coordinate a response, the first officer was forced to make an instantaneous decision. It seems likely that the first officer recognized that the aircraft was not climbing (without realizing it was due to his own control input), felt unable to make sense of the situation, and was confused about what to do. Interviewed after the accident, the first officer did not articulate an explicit reason for suddenly turning over control to the captain. In this confused and stressful situation, with a strong sense of time pressure and threat from an airplane that did not seem able to fly and with the remaining runway that was available to land rapidly growing shorter, it is not surprising that the first officer focused on the fact that the more experienced captain might handle the situation better, rather than on how best to transfer control. Impulsive, disorganized responses to unfamiliar situations are not uncommon when individuals are under time pressure and stress (Stokes and Kite, 1994, Chapter 3).

The NTSB analyzed company procedures and training for rejected takeoffs to see what light these might shed on the first officer's thought processes. The NTSB suggested that the first officer may have turned over control to the captain because the first officer considered the airplane to be in a rejected takeoff situation, despite already being airborne, and also recalled that company procedures authorized only the captain to initiate and perform the rejected takeoff maneuver. Alternatively, the NTSB suggested that the first officer may have actually initiated a rejected takeoff with his nose-down pitch input, and that he might have been influenced to take this unauthorized action by simulation training in which first officers were allowed to perform the rejected takeoff maneuver (at its normal time, prior to V1 speed). If these two factors suggested by the NTSB did play a role in the first officer's thought processes, we suggest it did not occur as deliberate, thoughtful analysis but as confused reaction that may not have been entirely conscious.

Unfortunately, no data exist to reveal how many of a large population of first officers would make similar errors or other problematic responses in this situation. However, the general literature on stress and cognition suggests that some would make mistakes (Stokes and Kite, 1994, Chapter 3; Driskell and Salas, 1996; Staal, 2004).

4. Captain returned the aircraft to the runway

Interviewed after the accident, the captain recalled that immediately after accepting control of the airplane he reduced engine thrust to idle and continued the reduction of pitch attitude begun by the first officer to five degrees (approximately the normal landing attitude). FDR data indicated that the airplane leveled off over the next two seconds, then descended rapidly to the surface. It was airborne for only six seconds. The maximum airspeed of 181 knots was achieved one second before ground contact.

When he was suddenly given control of the airplane, the captain was faced with what he described as a "split-second decision" either to continue the takeoff, or to reject the takeoff despite already being airborne and return to the runway. The captain stated that he based the decision to return to the runway on his sense that the airplane would not fly normally and his observation that sufficient runway existed to land and stop. Airline pilots are trained to continue a takeoff once past V1 speed in most situations, even including an engine fire. The logic for this guidance is that in most situations, it is safer to deal with an emergency in the air (using the onboard fire extinguishers, in the example of an engine fire) than to reject the takeoff after V1 and run off the end of the runway as a result. The V1 decision is formally based on considerations of an engine failure at this critical speed; V1 is established such that aircraft performance capabilities allow for a safe rejected takeoff prior to V1 and a safe continued takeoff at and beyond V1 despite the failed engine.

Conceivably, though, there are some situations in which it would be better to reject the takeoff after reaching V1 speed, even if the consequence is running off the end of the runway. Among these are icing- or windshear-induced loss of climb performance, both of which, we note, could manifest themselves as a stickshaker warning just after rotation Therefore, the idea of rejecting a takeoff after V1 is one that most airline captains would probably consider if under the impression that their aircraft was not capable of climbing.

While in hindsight the captain's decision to effectively reject the takeoff well past the formally specified decision speed (V1) was incorrect based on actual flight conditions and dynamics (nothing was wrong with the airplane), we suggest that his decision is readily understandable given the cues he was receiving that the airplane was stalling (stickshaker, sinking feeling). Further, the first officer's statements reinforced the cues that the airplane was not flying normally. Also, the first officer's pitch control inputs, which were reducing the airplane's climb and changing the pitch from the takeoff attitude toward landing attitude, may have biased the captain to continue in the direction already established, to reject the takeoff. The captain correctly recognized that he did not have much time to decide – the available runway was quickly being consumed with engine power set at takeoff thrust and the airplane accelerating through 180 knots. During the last two seconds prior to touchdown, the first officer and the flight engineer voiced conflicting suggestions to the captain. The first officer said: "Abort, get it on [the ground]". The flight engineer said: "Get it off". Each crewmember then stated, once again, the action that he was advocating. But by the time the captain would have heard these statements, he was already landing the airplane.

The captain was put in a very difficult position by the first officer's sudden and unexpected transfer of control. At that moment the captain was trying to make sense of a highly unusual situation; the stickshaker is a very salient, attention-grabbing stimulus and was perceived as a serious threat rather than a nuisance alarm. With this mind-set, the captain indeed had to make a split-second decision on whether to continue or abandon the takeoff. Very probably the captain had never experienced or been trained to expect a false stickshaker at this moment. He perceived that the aircraft was not climbing normally and apparently did not notice the slight forward motion that the first officer had applied to the control column (which otherwise might have cued him as to the source of the downward trend). Without that information, the available cues may have triggered memory of a number of scenarios that can lead to failure to climb, including undeployed flaps or leading edge devices, icing, or incorrect thrust indications. Indeed, accidents caused by just these conditions had been widely publicized at the time of flight 843.[4] Rapid decisions by experts are often driven by automatic retrieval from memory of scenarios from past experiences and other knowledge that seems to match the current situation (described as "recognition-primed decision-making" by Klein, 1997). The situation as perceived by the crew of flight 843 may have triggered a match for memory of circumstances in which aircraft in fact are not able to climb from takeoff. If this was the case, the match of perceived situation to memory was misleading and may have biased the captain to reject the takeoff.

In situations combining threat, urgency, and ambiguous, conflicting cues, we cannot expect pilots to quickly review all available indications, analyze the situation, and reach the correct interpretation with a high degree of reliability. In general, humans, no matter how expert, are fallible when making decisions about unfamiliar situations especially under time pressure and stress. For this reason the industry in recent years has emphasized training crews to continue takeoff after V1. However, typically the simulation training is based on engine failure shortly after V1, as mandated by the FAA, and does not include other anomalies or ambiguous cues, especially those that suggest the aircraft may not be able to fly.

5. The airplane landed hard and the right wing spar failed

Witnesses observed the airplane land hard, with the wings flexing down and the landing gear struts compressing. The witnesses reported that the airplane immediately began to shed parts, and a fire broke out. The NTSB determined that the right wing spar failed at touchdown because the load on the structure (from the airplane landing overweight and at a descent rate of approximately 14 feet per second) exceeded its design strength and certification requirements. As far as can be determined, the captain had no previous experience to apply to this immediate transition from takeoff to landing in the L-1011, a maneuver inherently difficult to accomplish smoothly.

Concluding discussion

This accident involved a problematic aircraft design feature (vulnerability to false stall warnings without alerting for failure until after takeoff) closely coupled with a time-critical situation that made thorough analysis quite difficult. In this situation, the crew was forced to make two "split-second" decisions in close sequence: whether the airplane was stalling or flying normally and, immediately after that, whether the takeoff should be continued or abandoned.

In hindsight, the crew of flight 843 made both of these decisions incorrectly, which accounts for the NTSB's citation of inadequate crew coordination and actions as one of the probable causes of the accident. However, given the information available to the crew at the time, and the characteristics and limitations of human information-processing, both the first officer's actions and the captain's decisions are not surprising. Generally, crews are likely to treat stall warnings as valid when the warnings are salient and there is insufficient time for analytical thought. Even when other cues are present that might reveal the stickshaker warning to be false, it is quite difficult for pilots to sort through and analyze conflicting non-salient cues with a high degree of reliability when under time pressure, high workload, and threat. Further, subtle cues such as seat-of-the-pants sensations and statements by other crewmembers can powerfully influence the reactions of a pilot who is under time pressure.

All of these factors came together in the extremely brief period available for decision and reaction by the crew of flight 843. We do not know what percentage of pilots in identical situations would have taken the same actions; we can only guess that some would. The NTSB, noting that another crew had correctly diagnosed a stickshaker warning as false and had continued their takeoff, inferred that it should have been possible for the crew of flight 843 to do the same. But the detailed circumstances of the previous incident were not investigated by the NTSB and probably were not identical – for example, the first officer may not have relaxed back pressure on the yoke, reducing climb performance, and presumably the first officer did not transfer aircraft control unexpectedly to the captain.

It is crucial to understand that in these types of situations, retrieval of information from memory, assessment of diverse cues, and rapid choice of action are probabilistic and variable, even among highly competent professionals. We do not have sufficient data to know what proportion of airline pilots might make errors similar to those of the crew of flight 843, but we are certain that all pilots would be vulnerable to some degree to error in this challenging situation. We argue that it is not appropriate or useful to assume that crews who do make errors in these difficult situations are in some way different from their peers.

As a result of this accident, the NTSB recommended that air carriers be required to establish training and procedures "for crew coordination briefings on actions to take in the event of abnormal situations during the takeoff and initial climb phase of flight, and the proper techniques for the transfer of control of the airplane, especially during time-critical phases of flight" (NTSB, 1993a, p. 68). While the training and procedural improvements called for in this recommendation are valuable, we must also realize that it is simply not possible to train extensively for all situations, and that no amount of training and procedural development and discipline can equip humans to perform with the flawless reliability demanded of commercial aviation under highly dynamic conditions involving ambiguity, high cognitive load, and stress.

Because training and procedures are unlikely to achieve the required levels of safety and reliability in situations like these, we suggest that if the consequences of a false indication or warning are likely to be severe, substantial attention should be devoted to preventing these false warnings. Generally, under FAA aircraft certification requirements, much effort has been devoted to minimizing the occurrence of false *negative* warnings – failure of warning systems to alert pilots. For example, airliners have dual redundant stall warning systems, either of which shakes both pilots' control columns. But activation of the stickshaker when an aircraft is flying normally without danger of stalling is an example of a false *positive* warning. We suggest that the dangers of false positive warnings should be carefully explored, and in situations in which the consequences of a false positive warning could be severe designers should develop appropriate safeguards.

Generally, to significantly improve flight crew performance in these "split-second" decision situations, crews must be provided with all relevant information in a way that they can assimilate much more easily and quickly. Training can also help by emphasizing the need to strongly bias decisions in ambiguous situations shortly after V1 toward continuing the takeoff. In recent years the airline industry and its regulators have put more emphasis on this "go orientation" (FAA, 1994), but more could be done. For example, crews could be given opportunities in simulation to practise go/no-go decision-making in ambiguous situations, rather than only in the traditional V1 engine-cut scenario. Buttressed with classroom training, this simulation practice would enable crews to more reliably choose to continue a takeoff after reaching V1 when their senses are telling them to stop.

Notes

1   Possible reasons for the company's procedure to guard the throttles from behind after V1 include preventing inadvertent power reduction from throttle slippage, facilitating the addition of full (firewall) power if required during initial climb, and facilitation of fine power adjustments during the initial climb.

2   On each flight either the captain or the first officer is designated as the pilot to fly the airplane (often termed the flying pilot) and the other is responsible for a range of other duties (and is sometimes called the monitoring pilot).

3   The crew did not increase power from the takeoff thrust setting to the absolute maximum thrust that the engines were capable of producing (disregarding normal operating limitations). This absolute maximum power value, commonly referred to as "firewall thrust", is optimal for a stall recovery. Similarly, crews involved in several other accidents, including USAir flight 1016 discussed in the preceding chapter (NTSB, 1995a), Air Florida flight 90 (B737-222, Washington DC, January 1982 – NTSB, 1982), and Delta flight 1141 (Dallas/Fort Worth, August 1988 – NTSB, 1989) did not set firewall thrust when it may have been desirable. These accidents suggest that crews may not think to add power when already commanding takeoff thrust, which is at or near normal operating limits.

4   This accident occurred within several years of major accidents in which air carrier aircraft were unable to take off and climb successfully because of incorrect flap configuration, icing, windshear, and other external factors; see, for example, the Pan Am windshear accident (flight 759, B727, New Orleans, July 1982 – NTSB, 1983), the Northwest Airlines flap configuration accident (flight 255, MD-80 Detroit, August 1987 – NTSB, 1988a), the Delta Airlines flap configuration accident (flight 1141, B-727, Dallas/Fort Worth, August 1988 – NTSB, 1989), the Ryan Air icing accident (flight 590, DC-9 ,Cleveland, February 1991 – NTSB, 1991 and Chapter 7 of this book), and the USAir icing accident (flight 405, Fokker 28, New York, March 1992 – NTSB, 1993b and Chapter 12 of this book). Airline crews were generally aware of these accidents at the time of flight 843, and this may have predisposed the crew to consider that airplanes sometimes do not climb normally after takeoff despite operating at normal pitch attitudes and airspeeds. In response to the accidents involving attempted takeoffs with improper flap/slat configuration, some air carriers instructed pilots to respond to a stall indication at takeoff by checking the configuration. However, it is not clear how likely crews are to remember and have time to perform this configuration check under stress and high workload.

Chapter 3

American 1572 – Accumulation of Small Errors

Introduction

On November 12, 1995 at 0055 eastern standard time, American Airlines flight 1572, a McDonnell Douglas MD-83, struck trees on a ridge of terrain about 2½ miles from the threshold of runway 15 while executing a VOR approach at Bradley International Airport, Hartford/Windsor Locks, Connecticut. Heavily damaged, with one engine failed and the other producing only reduced thrust, the flight continued toward the airport and landed just short of the runway surface. The airplane was substantially damaged in the accident, and one passenger received minor injuries during the emergency evacuation. There were five crewmembers and 73 passengers aboard the scheduled flight from Chicago, Illinois.

The accident occurred on the second day of a two-day crew pairing for the captain and first officer, during which they had operated several flights in the afternoon, evening, and late night periods. These flights had been running late on both days. Flight 1572 departed Chicago about 1½ hours late, at 2305, and the operation was routine through descent in the Hartford terminal area. The captain was the flying pilot and the first officer was the monitoring pilot.

The captain and first officer were both highly experienced in their respective crew positions and in flying the MD-80 aircraft type. The captain had logged 1,514 hours as an MD-80 captain, and he had also accumulated 2,716 second-in-command hours in type. The first officer had logged 2,281 hours of second-in-command time in the MD-80.

The NTSB investigation found that the airplane's three altimeters were not set to the latest surface barometric pressure in an environment of rapidly falling pressure. As a result, the airplane was operating at a lower altitude than was indicated on its altimeters. Further, the NTSB determined that the captain did not level the airplane at the specified minimum descent altitude (MDA) and the first officer challenged that error too late to prevent impact with the trees. However, the NTSB also recognized the crew's excellent flight skills and crew resource management in bringing the airplane safely to the runway after striking the trees.

The NTSB determined that the probable cause of the accident was "the flight crew's failure to maintain the required MDA until the required visual references identifiable with the runway were in sight". Contributing factors were "the failure of the ... approach controller to furnish the flight crew with a current altimeter setting, and the flight crew's failure to ask for a more current setting" (NTSB, 1996a, p. vi).

Altimetry

The altitude indicated by altimeters varies with barometric pressure, which is a function of atmospheric conditions at a given time over a given location. To ensure consistency among aircraft and adequate terrain separation, altimetry procedures require air traffic controllers to provide the appropriate pressure value at certain points in flight, and pilots adjust their altimeters to reflect this value to ensure that their altimeters indicate the correct altitude. Fast-moving aircraft traveling at altitudes higher than 18,000 feet are generally not concerned with proximity to the ground, but rather with proximity to each other. Rather than continuously updating the barometric pressure to reflect the conditions on the ground over which they are flying, US air traffic procedures require all aircraft to use a standard pressure value (29.92 inches of mercury) when operating above 18,000 feet; this establishes a common reference altitude to avoid collisions. Operating below 18,000 feet, especially during climb-out or during descent to land, proximity to the ground is critical, so pilots set their altimeters to the local atmospheric value provided by air traffic control (and also by the air carrier's dispatcher/operations department in some cases). Depending on local weather conditions, pilots may need to reset altimeters more than once as they reach the vicinity of the airport. This ensures that altimeters are correctly adjusted for local variations in atmospheric pressure.

Altimeters may be set to read either height above sea level, a setting called QNH, or height above the airport, a setting called QFE. After landing, an altimeter set to QNH will indicate the elevation of the airport above sea level, while an altimeter set to QFE will indicate 0. QNH is the standard in the US for flight operations below 18,000, and controllers provide pressure settings for QNH, but not QFE. Using QNH settings, pilots must maintain awareness that their altimeters indicate height above sea level, and that terrain and airports are typically above sea level. Controller instructions are given in terms of height above sea level, and most instrument approach plates indicate required altitudes above sea level, with height above the airport in parentheses. At the time of the accident American Airlines used a combination of QNH and QFE. QFE, used successfully by several airlines for many years, has the advantage of indicating altitude above the airport directly to the pilots, which can help maintain awareness of proximity to the ground, especially under instrument conditions in which the point at which the crew must decide to land or go-around (decision height or MDA, depending on the type of approach) can be as little as 200 feet above the ground. However QFE also has disadvantages, as will become apparent in the discussion below. (For various reasons American Airlines stopped using QFE after this accident.)

Significant events and issues

1. The crew set an incorrect barometric pressure into their altimeters, the approach controller failed to furnish an altimeter update on initial contact, and the crew did not request an update

At 0030, the airline's operations department provided the crew of flight 1572 with the altimeter setting for Bradley (the destination airport) via datalink. The datalink message included a QNH setting of 29.42 and a QFE setting of 29.23. The airline's procedures required crews to set all three of their altimeters (primary instruments on the captain's and first officer's panels and a standby instrument on the center panel between them) to QNH when descending through 18,000 feet and then to re-set the two primary altimeters to QFE when passing through 10,000 feet. The standby altimeter, which provides reference altitude for the autopilot, was to remain set on QNH, and crews were to fly by reference to this standby altimeter in order to comply with ATC (air traffic control) altitude assignments, until descending below the final approach fix. (This fix is usually several miles from the airport and is crossed 2,000 feet height or less above airport elevation, depending on local terrain.) Descending from the final approach fix, crews were to monitor the primary altimeters, set on QFE, to determine when to level off at MDA.

At 0033, ATC provided a Bradley altimeter setting of 29.40 (QNH) to flight 1572 – this was the setting they would need after descending below 18,000 feet. The crew could not enter this setting into any altimeter immediately after receipt because the altimeters had to remain set to the standard 29.92 pressure setting as long as the flight was above 18,000 to comply with ATC altitude assignments. Subsequent crew conversation recorded by the CVR suggests that the pilots did not write down the 29.40 setting as a way to remember it later. We do not know how many pilots write down altimeter settings in this situation, but suspect that pilots may underestimate vulnerability to forgetting or remembering these numbers incorrectly, because the task seems so easy.[1] Also, the crew of flight 1572 could not use a technique many pilots at other airlines use to remember the altimeter setting to be used below 18,000 feet: putting the destination airport pressure setting in the standby altimeter. Because of QFE procedures at this airline, the standby altimeter, which provided altitude information to the autopilot, had to remain on 29.92.

At 0038:45 the crew of flight 1572 set their altimeters for the descent below 18,000 feet. This involved adjusting all three altimeters to the QNH setting. At this time the captain recalled a setting of 29.50 (which was the setting received earlier in an automated terminal information service (ATIS) broadcast). The first officer suggested, incorrectly, "They called 29.47 when we started down ... whatever you want." The captain replied: "Okay". Post-accident wreckage inspection revealed that the standby altimeter was set to 29.47 at impact, suggesting that the actual altimeter setting provided by air traffic control (29.40) was never entered into the altimeters. As a result, the aircraft operated about 70 feet lower than assigned altitudes during the approach; however, this error did not contribute to the accident, as will be discussed later.

The ATIS weather broadcast received by the crew included remarks that atmospheric pressure was falling rapidly. This should have been a cue for flight crews and controllers to attend carefully to changes in altimeter settings, because the changes could affect altitude readings substantially. Company procedures outlined in the company's *Flight Manual* (Part 1, Approach and Landing section) required crews to cross-check primary and secondary altimeter settings after the changeover to QFE at 10,000 feet[2] and instructed crews: "Throughout the approach, monitor barometric changes and update the altimeters accordingly" (NTSB, 1996a, p. 128). On most flights the altimeter setting provided by the company prior to descent would not change significantly prior to arrival, so there would be little need to update the QFE. However, barometric pressure changes were significant on the night of flight 1572.

The NTSB investigation did not reveal to what extent the airline's training emphasized frequent updating of altimeter setting during uncommon occasions of rapid pressure change, nor did it reveal to what extent crews actually followed this practice. Under conditions of rapid pressure change, the airline's use of QFE altimetry would add to flight crew workload. Crews are notified of pressure changes by air traffic controllers, and this information is provided as a QNH setting. Upon receiving an updated QNH altimeter setting from ATC, flight crews would have to convert QNH to QFE. This would require additional communications with company operations or a calculation or a table lookup by the pilots every time a new pressure setting was received. This additional workload, during the approach when crews are already busy, increases opportunities for error.

The flight established contact with Bradley approach control at 0043:41. In his response to this initial contact the controller failed to provide an updated altimeter setting, as required by air traffic control procedures,[3] and the crew of flight 1572 did not ask for an update. Because controllers normally provide updated settings at this point, we suspect that many pilots unwittingly become dependent on receiving this update and do not develop personal techniques to prompt themselves to think about pressure changes. The altimeter setting that the controller would have provided at this time was 29.38 (QNH), a pressure reduction that equates to an additional 20-foot discrepancy between the indicated altitude and the flight's actual altitude. Comparing the 29.38 setting with the previously issued 29.42 setting on which the QFE setting of 29.23 had been based, the NTSB estimated that by this time in the flight, the crew's failure to obtain and enter the current altimeter setting resulted in the airplane operating as much as 40 feet lower than it should and would have been if the most current altimeter setting had been used. Of course, to take advantage of the new altimeter setting the pilots would have had to obtain or calculate the corresponding QFE value.

Barometric pressure continued to decrease rapidly as the flight continued. Post-accident investigation revealed that the QNH altimeter setting had decreased to approximately 29.24 at the time of the accident. Without any updates from air traffic control or by the crew, we estimate that this caused the airplane to be flying approximately 170 feet lower than the altitude indicated on the altimeters.[4] However, air carrier and air traffic control standard procedures did not provide for continued altimeter updates following initial contact with the approach controller. Further, by this time the control tower had closed because of a broken window in the tower cab. The broken window was a rare event, but even without that event the circumstances of this accident suggest that the air carrier operations system is vulnerable to rapid changes in barometric pressure during approaches to landing.

2. Autopilot would not hold the VOR course centerline and the captain changed the lateral automation mode to heading select

The airplane intercepted the final approach course about 15 miles from the runway at 3,500 feet. The captain recalled, in post-accident interviews, that at this time the autopilot was unable to track the VOR course automatically[5] so he changed the lateral mode to heading select. Using the heading select mode required the captain to closely monitor the flight's lateral alignment and make manual adjustments with the autopilot heading selector knob to bracket and track the VOR course. This required additional attention from the captain, especially given the strong crosswinds existing at initial approach altitude. Radar and FDR (flight data recorder) data show that the airplane repeatedly deviated on both sides of the approach course as the captain attempted to track the course. These repeated deviations suggest the captain may have been overloaded, and correcting the deviations conceivably may have reduced attention to other cockpit tasks. It is also possible that lack of practice in executing an approach with the autopilot in heading select mode contributed to the captain's difficulty in tracking the course. The accident report did not provide information about the captain's recent experience and level of proficiency in this specific task, or about how often airline pilots in general practise it.[6] Clearly, though, the captain was forced to use a less desirable mode of lateral control when the crosswinds prevented him from using his accustomed mode.

3. First officer did not provide the required callout on reaching MDA and the captain did not level the airplane quickly enough at MDA

While he was correcting the flight's lateral course tracking in heading select mode, the captain was also managing its vertical path on the non-precision approach. Without an electronic glideslope or other vertical guidance along the final approach path, the captain's goal would have been to descend the airplane to 2,000 feet above sea level (QNH) until after crossing the final approach fix, then descend and level the airplane at the MDA of 908 feet above the airport (QFE). The captain used the autopilot's vertical speed mode to descend to the final approach fix crossing altitude. The captain also used the altitude preselect feature to cause the autopilot to level the airplane automatically at 2,000 feet, with the autopilot using QNH data from the standby altimeter. The first officer announced passing the final approach fix at

0052:45, stating: "That's it". The captain stated: "Coming back [on thrust]" and ordered the flaps to be configured for landing. The first officer confirmed descending to the height above airport (QFE) value published for the MDA, stating: "Okay, going down to nine oh eight, huh?" which the captain confirmed. The first officer continued: "Set and armed", to which the captain replied: "Naw you don't have to do [unintelligible] … three thousand".s The first officer then stated: "Three thousand missed".

This exchange suggests that as the descent to MDA began, the first officer started to set up the automation to again use the altitude preselect function, in which case the autopilot would automatically level the airplane at MDA. However, the captain apparently did not intend to use this function. He instructed the first officer to set the altitude selector for the missed approach altitude rather than the MDA. The captain chose to use the autopilot to maintain a constant vertical speed in descent (1,000 feet per minute), while he monitored his altimeter, evidently intending to manually capture the MDA by pressing the autopilot altitude hold button when the airplane reached that altitude.

The captain's method was consistent with the company's QFE procedures and training, and with both pilots' reference to MDA as a QFE value. In contrast, it would have been awkward to use the altitude preselect function while also using the QFE procedures because the autopilot depended on QNH information from the standby altimeter. If the pilots had chosen to use altitude preselect they would have needed to confirm the MDA in height above sea level, which was 1,080 feet, and set that value in the altitude selector. Perhaps this is what the first officer had done when he stated: "Set and checked", but there is no way to ascertain the meaning of his statement from the accident report. In any case, given the airline's altimetry procedures, to use altitude preselect for capturing the MDA would have imposed greater workload at a critical phase of the final descent. But the method chosen by the captain for leveling the airplane (pressing the altitude hold button when reaching the MDA) would require close monitoring of the altimeter and would generate greater workload as the airplane reached MDA, an even more critical phase of the flight.

The accident investigation revealed that for smoothness the MD-80 altitude hold function was designed to allow the airplane to sink below the altitude at which it had been engaged, then smoothly recover back to that altitude with a gentle climb. Post-accident simulations showed that if the altitude hold button were pressed when the airplane was descending at 1,100 feet per minute, which was flight 1572's descent rate when it passed MDA, it would sink an additional 80 to 130 feet before leveling off. The tests showed that the greater altitude loss would occur in turbulent conditions; flight 1572 was operating in moderate turbulence, so we would expect the autopilot to have allowed the airplane to sink below the MDA by as much as 130 feet even if the captain had pressed the button at the instant that the airplane reached MDA.

The information available from the accident investigation did not allow us to ascertain whether the captain was aware that the airplane was designed to initially overshoot the selected altitude when using the altitude hold button to level off from a descent; however, we assume this was common knowledge among the airline's pilots. Normally the flying pilot would anticipate the overshoot and press the altitude hold button shortly before reaching MDA (and then press the button again to fine-tune the altitude at which the aircraft leveled). The investigation did not reveal to what extent the airline had established explicit procedures or had taught specific techniques for level-off at MDA.

Combining the effects of the uncorrected altimeter settings with the overshoot behavior of the altitude hold function, we estimate that the airplane could have descended as much as about 300 feet below the MDA. These effects were compounded by the captain's delayed action to level the airplane at the MDA. At 0053:43 the first officer stated, "Showing you going through the course" (apparently referring to an increasing deflection of the course deviation needle of the horizontal situation indicator that was on each pilot's instrument panel). This statement and FDR data show that the captain was still working on the course alignment task as he performed the final descent and monitored the altimeters for MDA. At 0055:06 the first officer stated, "There's a thousand feet [above airport elevation]", which was a required callout for the non-precision approach. Five seconds later he stated: "Now nine hundred feet is your ah … your bug", which was a prompt that the airplane was approaching MDA. The captain replied: "Okay". The NTSB's correlation of FDR, CVR, and radar data confirm that the airplane was approaching the MDA at this time. However, FDR data indicated that the autopilot remained in the vertical speed mode, and the airplane continued to descend through the MDA at approximately 1,100 feet per minute. At 0055:26, the first officer challenged, "You're going below your …".

The first officer's prompt to the captain approaching MDA at 0055:26 did not conform precisely with American Airlines' procedures for standard callouts, according to which he should have stated, "100 feet above MDA" (NTSB, 1996a, p. 41). However, the first officer issued his MDA prompt when the airplane was approximately 100 feet above MDA, and the captain appeared to have understood (or at least acknowledged) the first officer's message that the airplane was approaching MDA. The first officer apparently did not provide the next required callout, which should have been made upon reaching MDA. In post-accident interviews the first officer told investigators that after he made the callout approaching MDA, he looked away from his flight instruments and out the windshield to see if the flight was in visual contact with the runway environment. He had ground contact straight down but did not see the runway environment. When the first officer looked back to his instruments the airplane had descended through MDA, and he made the "You're going below …" statement to the captain.

We suggest that if the first officer had continued monitoring his flight instruments rather than looking outside as the flight approached MDA, he might not have missed the MDA callout, and he would have been able to provide a more timely warning that the flight was descending through MDA. However, in looking outside to establish visual contact with the ground, the first officer was following a natural desire of pilots to check for the airport position as they break out of clouds. The accident investigation report does not indicate whether the company's procedures provided specific guidance for the monitoring pilot (the first officer in this case) to maintain attention to instrument references and ignore the view out the windshield during an instrument approach. With specific guidance for the monitoring pilot to concentrate on the instruments while the flying pilot (the captain in this case) looked outside, the first officer might have kept his attention directed to the instruments and might have alerted the captain sooner.

However, even if the airline had provided this guidance (which some other airlines do), ensuring that monitoring pilots consistently resist the temptation to look outside at this critical phase would require training, standardization, and checking. Because no adverse consequences, other than an occasional missed callout, normally follow from looking away from the instruments momentarily, monitoring pilots may not even realize that their monitoring is inadequate and may not maintain the required discipline. Consequently, relaxed monitoring may become the norm among pilots, undercutting a major defense against error so insidiously that neither pilots nor airline managers may notice until an accident occurs (Sumwalt, Thomas, and Dismukes, 2003).

It is not possible to ascertain with certainty why the captain did not start to level flight 1572 until below the MDA,[7] despite the first officer prompting him about approaching MDA only a few seconds earlier. We may speculate, though, on several possibilities consistent with the situation existing at the time and common human reactions.

Concentrating on controlling the aircraft and looking outside to see the airport when the aircraft would break out of the clouds, the captain may have inadvertently stopped scanning the altimeter momentarily. Also, he may have been unwittingly depending on the first officer's callouts as his cue to take each action on the approach. If this was the case, when the first officer did not call out MDA the captain missed his cue to level the airplane and did not take that action. Although it seems strange that the commander of the flight, handling the controls, may have been so dependent on cues from the first officer, it is fairly common when executing non-precision approaches for the flying pilot to concentrate on aircraft control and for the monitoring pilot to prompt each step of the procedure. This is not meant to result in overdependence on the monitoring pilot's prompts, but habit patterns such as this build up without individuals being aware that they rely on external prompts to trigger a highly practised response. Wiener and Curry (1980) describe examples of this phenomenon in aviation operations, referring to it as "primary-backup inversion," in which a backup cue such as an altitude alert becomes the primary signal to which pilots respond. If this happens, most of the crew-based bulwarks against error and the possibilities for error-trapping are lost. There would be little overt evidence if this monitoring and error management function were to degenerate into one pilot unwittingly becoming dependent on the prompts of the other pilot, and this inadvertent degeneration of procedures would be difficult to identify either in accident investigations or during air carrier training and checking.

Alternatively, or additionally, the captain may have been waiting unconsciously for the autopilot to level the airplane at MDA, even though it was not set to do so. Although he explicitly declined to use altitude preselect on this approach, the captain would have been far more accustomed to using altitude preselect for level-offs in general. He would have used this feature for nearly all climbs and descents on line flights, and he would have had relatively few occasions to use the altitude hold button in line operations. It is common for habits to capture behavior, especially under high workload, when the non-habitual behavior is rarely practised, and the habitual behavior is normally triggered by cues similar to those supposed to trigger the non-habitual behavior (Reason, 1990, p. 68; Betsch, Haberstroh, Molter, and Glöckner, 2003; Loukopoulos et al., 2006). If this were the case on this accident approach, when starting the descent the captain may have intended to press the altitude hold button at the MDA, but then, while attending to other demands, he may have unwittingly reverted to the habit of relying on the autopilot to capture the altitude automatically.

Although instrument flying inevitably involves dividing one's attention and coping with distractions, this approach may have presented an unusually heavy workload for the captain. As we have mentioned, he was required to switch to and use the heading select mode to track the final approach course. Using this lateral automation mode during an instrument approach was probably unusual for the captain, although the accident report is silent on this issue. As he neared the MDA, the captain remained off course and apparently was still paralleling or gradually closing on the centerline. Any pilot could become preoccupied with correcting an off-course deviation such as this one. Further, heavy rain and moderate turbulence during the final approach segment may also have distracted the crew. Although certainly well within airline crews' capability, non-precision approaches are inherently more challenging and thus more vulnerable to crew error. Recognizing this, airlines have limited use of non-precision approaches in US operations as much as possible. (A movement is under way to eliminate non-precision approaches in airline operations altogether by providing electronic slope guidance for all approaches, as discussed in the last section of this chapter.) But a consequence of limited use of non-precision approaches is that airline pilots may not maintain as high a level of proficiency as they would if they flew these approaches frequently.

4. Captain responded to the first officer's challenge by using automation to level the airplane

FDR and CVR data indicate that the captain pressed the altitude hold button after the first officer's below-MDA challenge. However, the airplane continued to descend, as indicated by three "sink rate" annunciations from the GPWS that were recorded on the CVR. At 0055:30, the airplane hit trees at about 770 feet above sea level, and about 310 feet below the published MDA.

As we have suggested, the captain's use of automation to level the airplane when he realized the flight had descended below MDA may have been a factor in the accident because the altitude hold function has a built-in altitude loss that consumed the remaining margin above the trees. The accident investigation report did not specifically analyze the outcome that would have ensued if the captain had switched to manual control to level the airplane once he realized he had descended below MDA. Conceivably, a maximum-effort, manually controlled, level-off or go-around might have prevented the tree strike if the captain had been able to initiate it very quickly after receiving the first officer's prompt.

We do not know why the captain used the automation to level the airplane even after being challenged for descending below MDA, but it is consistent with several factors. Because the captain had already planned to use this mode, he would have automatically responded to the first officer's challenge by pressing the altitude hold button unless he quickly recognized that continuing his original plan would further increase danger to the flight. But the captain had little reason to suspect life-threatening danger at this point; he was unaware that the altimeter was incorrectly set, the approach chart did not depict the ridge on the approach course as an obstacle, the overshoot aspect of using altitude hold may not have come quickly to mind, and he may have been unaware of how little margin for altitude error some non-precision approaches provide. It is not certain that most airline pilots are aware that US instrument approach design standards provide as little as 250 feet of clearance above obstacles at a non-precision MDA, and even if they know this it is not clear that they would quickly remember it in situations such as this. Further, both research and anecdotal evidence reveal that it is fairly common for pilots to use automation modes even when manual control is a better way to get out of a critical situation (Curry, 1985; Wiener, 1989). Although the cause of this tendency is not well understood, the fact that it continues to occur despite admonitions in training suggest that the cause is deeply rooted in the interaction between human cognitive processes and the nature of cockpit automation.

Concluding discussion

Controlled flight into terrain is one of the most common types of fatal airline accidents. A frequent scenario in controlled flight into terrain is crashing short of the runway while executing a non-precision approach requiring stepdown fixes based on DME (distance measuring equipment). The risk for many non-precision approaches is substantially higher – around five-fold – than for precision approaches.[8] The higher risk is probably a function of several factors working together: flight path guidance is less precise, terrain clearance in some cases allows little margin for error (probably less than crews realize), and crew workload is higher. The combination of these factors increases the variability of crew performance, vulnerability to errors, and the consequences of error.

In addition to the typical challenges of a non-precision approach in night instrument conditions, the crew of flight 1572 faced several other challenges. These included unusually rapid changes in atmospheric pressure, moderate turbulence and strong crosswinds forcing use of heading select for lateral control and increasing workload, and the airline's use of an altimeter-setting procedure that contributed to workload demands. The crew made several errors that contributed directly to the accident; however, we suggest that the types of error this crew made are not uncommon among experienced airline pilots and are best understood as inherent vulnerability resulting from the interaction of human cognitive processes, the nature of the specific tasks, and incomplete availability of relevant information.

Flight 1572 descended below MDA in part because rapidly falling barometric pressure caused the aircraft altimeters to read incorrectly during final approach to the airport. The crew did not update altimeter settings during the latter part of the approach, even though company procedures called for them to do so. Multiple factors probably contributed to this failure; central among those factors was the inability of aviation meteorology, air traffic control, and the company to provide frequent updates of rapidly falling barometric pressure to the crew. This illustrates a vulnerability of the overall aviation system's procedures for dealing with rapidly changing weather conditions. Also, we do not know how many crews in the situation of flight 1572 would have initiated requests for updated barometric pressure during a busy descent, and unfortunately the investigation did not reveal the extent to which company training and standardization emphasized frequent updating of pressure settings in this situation.

The final approach segment of flight 1572 was characterized by lateral and vertical tracking tasks that required greater monitoring and manual intervention by the crew compared with their tasks on most other flights. These tasks increased the workload on the accident crew and may have contributed to the crew's failure to level out at MDA. In particular, habit-capture and primary-backup inversion, to which humans are especially vulnerable under high workload, may have played a role.

We argue that airline crews should be trained to recognize the accumulation of workload and consequent snowballing of vulnerability to error. Ideally, crews confronting the circumstances of this accident would recognize that the combined effects of the strong crosswinds, failure of the autopilot to hold the VOR course, rapid pressures changes, late night operations, the non-precision approach, and a closed control tower were approaching the limits imposed by human attention and working memory constraints. But without explicit training in this issue, crews immersed in challenging high workload situations frequently have difficulty recognizing that they are getting overloaded and changing their strategy do deal with the overload. A variant of crew resource management training, "threat and error management", teaches pilots to recognize that these situations pose considerable threat and helps pilots develop strategies to deal with these types of threat (Helmreich, Klinect, and Wilhelm, 1999; Gunther, 2004a). This issue is also addressed in the Flight Safety Foundation's controlled flight into terrain (CFIT) checklist, which provides crews with a specific tool they can use in real time to identify complex, high workload, high risk situations and which encourages crews to respond conservatively to these sorts of threats (FSF, 2003).

We argue that flight 1572 is a classic example of a "systems accident". Several hazards pre-existed in the system. Normally pilots manage these hazards with a high degree of reliability; however, when by chance several hazards combine in the same flight, the margin of safety is reduced substantially. It is unrealistic to expect crews to fly without making errors. Errors occur in most normal line flights under benign conditions; fortunately, most of these errors are either inconsequential or are caught before escalating into a bad outcome (Klinect, Wilhelm, and Helmreich, 1999; FSF, 2005). However, in challenging and high workload situations the frequency of errors and the difficulty of catching errors go up. Thus it is crucial to design aviation operations, systems, and training to deal with the reality that multiple hazards and random errors will sometimes combine to threaten safety.

Airlines design their procedures and systems to provide multiple safeguards against human error. In principle these safeguards are supposed to work independently of each other, so that if one safeguard fails another will catch the problem. But in practice, safeguards that were designed to be independent can devolve in a way that removes independence and reduces the level of protection. For example, approach controllers are required to provide barometric pressure information when flights are handed off to them, and flight crews are also held responsible for obtaining the current altimeter setting. But when controllers routinely provide this information without being requested, pilots may unwittingly become dependent on being provided this information to trigger them to think about updating altimeter settings. (This is another example of ways in which experts become dependent on normally present cues in the environment to automatically trigger habitual responses – see Chapter 9.) But in this habitual form of responding, the crew has become dependent on the controller's action and no longer provides an independent safeguard. Because the process normally works quite reliably, no one in the system may recognize that the safeguard has been compromised.

This chapter illustrates several ways in which error-trapping procedural safeguards can become subtly compromised, reducing the level of safety. To prevent this degradation pilots must be constantly on guard and companies must provide effective training, buttressed by periodic checking. Line operations safety audits (LOSAs) provide a specific method by which companies can systematically examine fleet operations for latent threats and evaluate the effectiveness of procedural safeguards (ICAO, 2002a; Klinect, Murray, Merritt, and Helmreich, 2003). In a LOSA a large number of normal line flights are observed from the cockpit jumpseat by trained observers using a template form to note threats encountered, errors made, and detection and resolution of errors. This provides a statistical sample large enough to analyze systemic vulnerabilities.

Given that airline accident rates are significantly higher for non-precision approaches in instrument conditions, it would be helpful to tilt the odds in favor of safety by reducing the risks of non-precision approach operation. This strategy is being pursued worldwide by the aviation community in the wake of this and several other recent accidents involving controlled flight into terrain. One strategy involves creating a constant angle glidepath for the non-precision approach (similar to a precision approach glideslope) that provides continuous guidance during descent until the missed approach point is reached (FSF, 2002) This strategy, which would combine current and future flight management system technologies, would reduce the need for automation programming and would eliminate intermediate level-offs during final approach, thereby reducing workload and potential sources of error.

Another strategy attempts to reduce the risk of non-precision approaches by providing pilots with better information about hazardous proximity to terrain. This is being implemented by installing enhanced ground proximity warning (EGPWS) or terrain avoidance warning (TAWS) systems and by providing better depiction of terrain hazards on approach charts. These programs, which reduce workload, remove procedural elements highly vulnerable to error, and improve the quality of information presented to pilots, probably would have prevented this accident and certainly will reduce the risk of similar accidents in the future.

Notes

1   When busy with other tasks, individuals are vulnerable to forgetting or to incorrectly remembering any information that has been recently acquired and not processed elaborately (Brown and Craik, 2000). This vulnerability is especially high when the new information resembles other information processed frequently or recently (described as "proactive interference" by Keppel and Underwood, 1962). Altimeter settings usually do not vary greatly; thus pilots may confuse in memory the most recently received setting, say 29.87, with one of many previous settings, say 29.97 (see Johnson, Hashtroudi, and Lindsay, 1993 for a review of this concept of "source memory confusion"). Note that in this example three of the four numbers are the same. Although the difference in these two settings represents only 100 feet, that difference can be crucial at decision height (DH) or minimum descent altitude (MDA).

2   The CVR reveals that the crew began a cross-check and apparently the first officer started to notice inconsistency in the QNH setting of the standby altimeter with the QFE setting of the primary altimeters. However the crew did not follow up to determine the source of the inconsistency, which was that they had not updated QFE to reflect the (incorrect) QNH setting of 29.47 they had entered earlier. Even if they had completed this cross-check it would not have caught the initial error of entering an incorrect value for QNH, nor could it catch any other errors that might have been made updating altimeter settings later in the approach. Although the QNH error caused the flight to be 70 feet lower than indicated during the descent, it did not contribute to the accident because at level-off at MDA the crew was now using QFE on the primary altimeters.

3   The FAA's handbook for air traffic controllers (FAA, 2004a) requires terminal approach controllers to provide a current altimeter setting to pilots of inbound aircraft "on initial contact or as soon as possible thereafter", and also to "issue changes in altimeter setting to aircraft executing a non-precision instrument approach as frequently as practical when the official weather report includes the remarks 'pressure falling rapidly'" (as was the case for flight 1572).

4   In its accident investigation report, the NTSB estimated the altimeter error at this time to have been 76 feet, apparently based on the difference between the barometric pressure provided to the crew by the approach controller but not converted to QFE and entered

by the crew into the altimeters (29.42) and the pressure that was recorded in a weather observation that was taken four minutes prior to the accident (29.35).

5   This may have been a function of the intercept angle and crosswind. The captain recalled that the autopilot was applying a 30-degree crosswind correction but was unable to track the course.

6   Airline training records typically do not contain this level of detail.

7   The accident report does not mention the captain's recollections of this part of the accident sequence. Presumably he was asked but perhaps he did not recall this part clearly

8   A joint NLR/Flight Safety Foundation study estimates that the risk of CFIT during a non-precision approach is approximately five times that of a precision approach operation (Enders, Dodd, Tarrel, Khatwa, Roelen, and Karwal, 1999).

Chapter 4

American International 808 – The Strobe Light that Wasn't There

Introduction

On August 18, 1993 at 1656 eastern daylight time, American International Airways flight 808, a Douglas DC-8-61 freighter, crashed ¼ mile from the approach end of runway 10 at Leeward Point Airfield, Guantanamo Bay, Cuba, after the captain became concerned about the position of his airplane relative to the Cuban border (a strobe light normally marking the border was inoperative) and then lost control of the airplane while maneuvering for landing. Flight 808 was an international, non-scheduled, military cargo contract flight from Norfolk, Virginia to Guantanamo Bay. The three flight crewmembers aboard (captain, first officer, and flight engineer) were seriously injured, and the airplane was destroyed in the accident.

The flight crewmembers were highly experienced as air carrier pilots and in their respective crew positions on the DC-8. According to the findings of the NTSB's investigation, the crewmembers were well regarded for their skills. However, they had limited experience in the operation that was being attempted when the accident occurred: prior to the accident flight, the captain had never flown to Guantanamo Bay, which poses special communication, navigation, and aircraft handling challenges; the first officer had only flown there decades earlier in a smaller military aircraft.

The accident occurred during the fifth flight leg of the crew's duty period, which had begun in Dallas/Fort Worth at 2300 on the day prior to the accident. The crew had originally been scheduled off duty in Atlanta after flying through the night and arriving there at 0752 on the day of the accident. The captain, who lived in Atlanta, had left the airport and was driving home when he learned that the air carrier wanted him to fly an unexpected trip. Departing from Atlanta, the crew flew the aircraft to Norfolk to be loaded with cargo for Guantanamo Bay. Flight 808 arrived in Norfolk at 1140 and departed for Guantanamo Bay at 1413. The flight then operated normally until arriving in the vicinity of the destination. The captain was acting as the flying pilot and the first officer as the monitoring pilot. As the crew approached Guantanamo Bay they had been on duty nearly 18 hours and awake for periods ranging from 19 hours to more than 23 hours (the captain had been awake the longest).[1]

The NTSB determined that the probable causes of this accident were:

> … the impaired judgment, decision-making, and flying abilities of the captain and flight crew due to the effects of fatigue; the captain's failure to properly assess the conditions for landing and maintaining vigilant situational awareness of the airplane while maneuvering onto final approach; his failure to prevent the loss of airspeed and avoid a stall while in the steep bank turn; and his failure to execute immediate action to recover from a stall.

The Safety Board cited the following as factors contributing to the cause of the accident:

> The inadequacy of the flight and duty time regulations applied to 14 CFR Part 121, Supplemental Air Carrier, international operations and the circumstances that resulted in the extended flight/duty hours and fatigue of the flight crew members ... the inadequate crew resource management training and the inadequate training and guidance by American International Airways, Inc., to the flight crew for operations at special airports such as Guantanamo Bay, and the Navy's failure to provide a system that would assure that the local tower controller was aware of the inoperative strobe light so as to provide the flight crew with that information (NTSB, 1994b, p. v).

Significant events and issues

1. Captain and first officer were unfamiliar with arrival procedures for Guantanamo Bay

At 1632:17 the CVR recorded the captain saying: "Wonder if we talk to Cuba uh approach at all?" The first officer replied: "Should be". The captain continued: "We're going to be in their airspace here in a little bit". The first officer transmitted the query to the US air traffic controller who was working the flight. The controller informed the first officer that there was no need to contact Cuban air traffic control. The crewmembers then continued to converse about Cuban air traffic control and evinced some confusion about the flight's clearance limit. In a radio transmission at 1634:33, the first officer mistakenly addressed the Guantanamo radar facility (a US Naval facility) as "Havana Center".

Later, the recorded conversations and radio transmissions of the flight crew continued to suggest a lack of familiarity with the special procedures for the destination. At 1636:03 the controller advised flight 808 to report the East Point arrival fix and provided a definition of the fix according to a radial and distance from Guantanamo Bay. The captain did not understand the controller's radial/distance references and the first officer read back the definition of the fix incorrectly. The crew's efforts to understand their clearance to East Point only after receiving it suggests that they were not well prepared to fly the arrival routing into Guantanamo Bay. The recorded conversations of the crewmembers about the "number" assigned to East Point does imply, though, that the crew had programmed the arrival fixes into the airplane's inertial navigation system. At 1642:40 the first officer requested a clarification from air traffic control about the location of another of the arrival fixes, Point Alpha. The crew spent portions of the next 5 minutes discussing the fix definition among themselves and with controllers, and setting up navigation radios to identify Point Alpha.

The accident investigation revealed that the flight crew possessed current navigational publications that described the procedures to use for arrival at Guantanamo Bay. The crew's confusion about flight 808's position as they entered the area, their lack of knowledge about procedures to use for transiting Cuban airspace under visual flight rules, and the difficulties that they experienced identifying, flying to, and reporting passage of the intermediate approach fixes (East Point and Point Alpha) suggest that the crewmembers were not fully conversant, however, with the special procedures for Guantanamo Bay. This is consistent with their lack of recent experience operating in the area.

The US Air Force Air Mobility Command contract administrator at Norfolk informed NTSB investigators that he normally provided flight crews inbound to Guantanamo Bay with a briefing form about the special procedures for operating there. However, recognizing the captain during flight 808's ground time at Norfolk on the day of the accident, the contract administrator mistakenly thought that the captain had been to Guantanamo Bay many times and therefore would not require the briefing. Further, the crewmembers did not request a detailed briefing even though the captain and first officer were aware from company training that special approach procedures were in effect at Guantanamo Bay.

We do not know whether the crew's apparent lack of preparedness for navigating to the destination would have been mitigated by information that the company or Air Force failed to provide them, whether it was derived from incomplete arrival preparations and briefings by the crewmembers during the flight, or if other factors such as fatigue contributed to this problem. Further, it is not clear whether the workload that the crew experienced coping with their unprepared state affected their subsequent preparation for and execution of the approach when they arrived at the airport several minutes later.

2. Captain changed his plan to land on runway 28 for the more challenging approach to runway 10

The winds were southerly, making operations possible on either runway 28 or 10. Originally advised by the controller that runway 10 was the active arrival runway, the flight crew during initial descent requested to use runway 28, which had an unobstructed final approach path and an uncomplicated approach. However, at 1641:53 the captain stated: "Ought to make that [runway] 10 approach just for the heck of it to see how it is. Why don't we do that, let's tell them we'll take 10. If we miss we'll just come around and land on 28". The first officer replied: "Okay", and he transmitted the captain's request to ATC. The flight engineer made no comment about the runway change.

Because of the proximity of Cuban airspace and high terrain to the west of the airport, the approach to runway 10 required a low-altitude turn from base leg to final and a short final approach segment. Flights inbound to Guantanamo Bay were prohibited from entering Cuban airspace, which began less than 1 mile from the threshold of runway 10. However, the large turning radius of big transport aircraft also required these aircraft to fly the base leg of the approach as close as possible to the Cuban border, in order to have enough space to align on the runway without having to bank at a dangerously steep angle. If the spacing from the runway and initiation of the turn were not performed and timed perfectly, the angle of bank required to avoid overshooting the final approach course could become very steep. All of these factors made the turns from downwind to base and then to final approach very critical maneuvers in a large aircraft such as the DC-8. After the accident, investigators determined that for flight 808 there was only a 2-second time period within which to start the turn from base leg to final approach to be able to line up with the runway using a normal bank angle (30 degrees).

• The first officer had viewed the air carrier's qualification video for Guantanamo Bay only five days prior to the accident. The captain had viewed the video about five months prior to the accident. FAA regulations for special airport qualifications did not require the flight engineer to be trained or qualified for a special airport. For the approach to runway 10, the video showed a view from the cockpit and described the tight geographic confines for conducting the approach, the foreshortened final approach segment, and the southerly prevailing winds. However, as the NTSB noted, the video did not discuss "the factors that make the approach particularly challenging to the pilots of airplanes with high approach speeds" (NTSB, 1994b, p. 71), including the criticality of timing the initiation of the turns and the need to maintain adequate speed margins because of increased load factors in the steeper-than-normal turns.

The captain's spur-of the moment decision to change flight 808's arrival runway from 28 to 10 substantially increased the difficulty of the approach, as will be apparent later in this chapter. He did not appear to have explicitly weighed the risks of undertaking this approach; nor did the first officer or flight engineer verbalize any special concerns about the captain's decision. The failure of company and Air Force contractor briefings about Guantanamo Bay to inform the crew about the criticality of the base leg and final approach spacing and turns may have made the captain of flight 808 less likely to recognize the dangers of a quick change to runway 10.

We suggest that last-minute changes such as these are inherently vulnerable to error because they do not allow time to identify special demands of the approach, assess potential threats, and plan accordingly. Last-minute changes often increase time pressure and workload, making it difficult to fully brief the revised plan, even though a thorough briefing is especially important when the original plan is changed. The lack of an approach briefing may have distanced the first officer and flight engineer from full participation in flight management, making them less likely to challenge the decision to land on runway 10, and undercutting the crew's performance during the approach. However, we note that last-minute runway changes under time pressure have become commonplace in US air carrier operations (Helmreich et al., 2004), although these are usually initiated by air traffic control, rather than by crews. Conceivably crews have become inured to last-minute runway changes and underestimate the risks involved.

Although the crew of flight 808 did not brief the details of the approach to runway 10, the captain did brief the possibility of a missed approach and his contingency plan to land on the opposing runway, which implicitly invited the other crewmembers to call for a missed approach if they felt it was needed later in the flight. The captain's quick, one-sentence briefing about the plan in the event of a missed approach demonstrated good leadership and crew communication, and – all other factors aside – should have primed the crew to be prepared to abort the approach if it did not work out. (However, other factors can counteract the benefits of such a briefing – for example, plan continuation bias, discussed later in this chapter.) Apparently the first officer understood that the captain's intention to land on runway 10 would be subject to change, because at 1642:18 the first officer mentioned this plan to air traffic control, transmitting almost incoherently: "... requesting uh, land uh, east and if we uh, need to we'll uh, make another approach uh, but we'd like to make the first uh, approach anyway uh, to uh, the east th – this afternoon".

3. During the maneuver to final approach the flight crewmembers attempted to sight a strobe light marking the US/Cuban border, and the captain allowed airspeed to deteriorate

Closing on Guantanamo Bay, the crew spotted the runway and maneuvered the airplane onto a downwind leg south of the airport. At 1651:37, the first officer prompted the captain to configure the airplane for the approach, querying: "You want to get all dirty [configure landing gear and flaps for landing] and slowed down and everything?" The first officer had a clear view of the runway on the right-hand side of the aircraft, while the captain's view of the runway would have been obstructed for some of the downwind leg. The first officer cautioned the captain to avoid flying an excessively tight pattern, advising: "I'd give myself plenty of time to get straight ... maintain a little water off [the wingtip] because you're gonna have to turn ... I think you're getting' in close before you start your turn". After that, the flight engineer also began to caution the captain about the airplane's position on the approach, stating: "Yeah, the runway's right over here, man ... you're tight on it". The captain responded to these challenges, but apparently did not correct the flight's position on downwind. He responded: "Yeah I got it, yeah I got it ... going to have to really honk it [turn steeply to avoid overshooting final]".

Beginning at 1652:03, the air traffic controller cautioned the flight not to extend its downwind leg, transmitting: "Cuban airspace begins three quarters of a mile west of the runway you are required to maintain within this, within the airspace designated by a strobe light". The first officer replied: "Roger, we'll look for the strobe light". The investigation revealed, though, that the strobe light was inoperative on the day of the accident and that the controller's reference to it was made in error.

At 1653:22 the flight engineer challenged: "Slow airspeed". The first officer challenged: "Check the turn". The captain responded: "Where's the strobe?" The captain made six additional inquiries about the strobe light over the next 33 seconds. At the same time, the airplane was turning more steeply, descending, and continuing to lose airspeed. As the captain continued to focus on the strobe light, the first officer was also engaged in the search for the strobe light (based on references to the light that were recorded by the CVR). Meanwhile, the flight engineer was calling out to the pilots: "You know we're not getting our airspeed back there ... we're never going to make this … watch the … keep your airspeed up". The only response the captain made to these challenges was when the first officer asked him, at 1653:58: "Do you think you're gonna make this?" The captain replied: "Yeah". Then he added: "If I can catch the strobe light".

The captain's continued references to the strobe light suggest that his inability to see the light led to his becoming preoccupied with that task and distracted from managing the approach and from basic airmanship. As a result he lost awareness of the runway's position and the airplane's airspeed. The degree to which the captain was preoccupied by the search for the strobe light is indicated by his repeated statements about it while he was not responding to the critically slow airspeed that had developed and multiple challenges from his flight crew. Further, in his preoccupation with the search for the strobe light the captain did not use other cues that were available to help him align the airplane on its approach, such as the roadway along the Cuban border and other visual checkpoints.

The captain's preoccupation with the strobe light was cited by the NTSB as evidence of his impairment by fatigue. The NTSB cited testimony from a NASA human fatigue researcher who indicated that when fatigued: "People get tunnel vision … they can literally focus on one piece of information to the exclusion of other kinds of information …" (NTSB, 1994b, p.51). Later in this chapter we will have more to say about the role of fatigue in this accident, but, recognizing the documented effect of fatigue on the narrowing of attention and performance in general, we suggest that other factors may also have been at play in the crew's fixation on finding the strobe light.

The captain's concerns about remaining extremely close to, but clear of, Cuban airspace were valid. There were severe penalties for violating Cuban airspace and, as we have indicated, the airplane's positioning along the Cuban border was critical to obtaining an adequate turn radius for maneuvering to the runway. Of all the possible means of positioning his aircraft with respect to the Cuban border, we believe that it was natural for the captain to focus so heavily on seeking the strobe light for guidance because the air traffic controller specifically mentioned the importance of the strobe. The captain could not find the strobe because it was inoperative, yet the controller's assertion of its operation probably made the captain's inability to find the light even more frustrating and reduced the likelihood he might deduce that it was inoperative. Unsure of the Cuban border, the captain may have compensated by aligning the airplane too close to the runway, unwittingly reducing the available maneuvering radius by one third of the already restricted area. The captain's preoccupation with the strobe light and his consequent narrowing of attention and distraction exemplify the powerful effects that incomplete or, especially, false information can have on pilots' allocation of attention, decisions, and control actions (Stokes and Kite, 1994, Chapter 3).

As will be discussed later, fatigue probably contributed greatly to the captain's preoccupation with finding the strobe and distraction from controlling the airplane. However, even in the absence of fatigue, pilots are vulnerable to this sort of distraction. Cockpit tasks often require pilots to shift attention back and forth among multiple tasks. The cognitive mechanisms for shifting attention leave pilots vulnerable to preoccupation with one demanding task to the neglect of others, as evidenced by many incident reports (Dismukes, Young, and Sumwalt, 1998).

4. Captain overshot the runway centerline, forced the approach, and stalled the airplane

At 1654:07 the first officer called out: "140 [knots]", indirectly indicating that airspeed had decreased to 7 knots below the calculated approach speed for the flaps 50 configuration. At that time the airplane was in the turn from base leg to final, and its bank angle was increasing to greater than 50 degrees.

Because of the limited radius of airspace that was available for the base leg and final approach, even if the approach had been executed perfectly the airplane would have been established on final approach only 1,300 feet prior to the runway threshold at an altitude of 120 feet above ground. In comparison, on a normal visual approach a heavy transport aircraft typically would be established on final approach at least 2 miles prior to the runway threshold at about 600 feet above the ground. Moreover, the captain's positioning of the airplane ¼ mile inside the Cuban border on base leg rather than just inside the border and his late initiation of the turn from base to final meant that the approach could not be flown with normal bank angles, airspeeds, and stall margins. NTSB calculations indicated that the flight could not have avoided overshooting the runway centerline without exceeding a bank angle of 55 degrees, compared to a normal maximum bank angle of 30 degrees. At the 55-degree bank angle, the airplane was operating at the onset of a stall.

One second after the first officer's airspeed challenge, the CVR recorded the sound of increasing engine thrust. This suggests that the captain was beginning to respond to the loss of airspeed. However, as a result of the decreasing airspeed (to 136 knots) and the increasing load factor from the steep bank angle, the stall warning system activated at 1654:09. During the next 4 seconds the CVR recorded "stall warning" statements from the first officer and flight engineer. The captain's response was: "I got it ... back off", uttered simultaneously with another crewmember's call for "max power". In the following 5-second period that was available for stall recovery, the captain did not apply maximum thrust; nor did he use roll controls (which remained effective in the stalled condition) to restore a wings-level condition. The airplane continued to slow down, bank angle increased to 60 degrees, and ground impact occurred at 1654:20.

Much of the crew's performance during this last portion of the flight was clearly problematic; however, the first officer and flight engineer took several highly appropriate actions attempting to return the flight to safe operation. They encouraged the captain not to crowd the runway on downwind, prompted him to configure the airplane, and tried to alert him that airspeed was decaying below safe margins. Unfortunately the captain, in his fatigued and preoccupied condition, did not respond adequately to the crew's challenges. In retrospect, the first officer would have done better to have explicitly called for the captain to go around, which he might have done at any point from the moment it became apparent they were unable to identify the Cuban border with certainty through the time when the stickshaker activated. However, in many other accidents the first officer did not challenge the captain forcefully or explicitly enough to turn the situation around (NTSB, 1994a). Also, recent NASA research conducted in flight simulators reveals that first officers tend to couch challenges to the captain more indirectly and less emphatically than captains' challenges to first officers (Fisher and Orasanu, 2000).

Factors affecting crew performance across events

Many aspects of the crew's performance, especially during the last moments of the flight, strongly suggest that the crew were impaired by fatigue, and the NTSB analysis concentrated on crew fatigue as the critical factor in these events. The NTSB also recognized other factors, such as the inherent difficulty of flying this approach and the captain's inability to view the runway through the windshield during the turn to final from his position on the left-hand side of the airplane, but in citing fatigue as the probable cause of the accident, the NTSB implied that the accident would not have occurred if the crewmembers had been better rested.

No one could reasonably argue that a flight crew's performance would be unimpaired by having been awake for 19–23 hours. Further, the captain's public hearing testimony about his mental state was consistent with the effects of fatigue:

> ... I felt very lethargic or indifferent. I remember making the turn from the base to the final, but I don't remember trying to look for the airport or adding power or decreasing power ... On the final, I had mentioned that I had heard [the first officer] say something about he didn't like the looks of the approach. And looking at the voice recorder, it was along the lines of, are we going to make this? ... I remember looking over at him, and there again, I remember being very lethargic about it or indifferent. I don't recall asking him or questioning anybody. I don't recall the engineer talking about the airspeeds at all. So it's very frustrating and disconcerting at night to try to lay there and think of how this – you know – how you could be so lethargic when so many things were going on, but that's just the way it was (NTSB, 1994b, p. 60).

In testimony, the first officer reported that he was not fatigued during the accident approach. In contrast, he described himself as feeling "alert and exhilarated" as they approached the airport (NTSB, 1994b, p. 60). However, scientific evidence indicates that self-evaluation of fatigue is often inaccurate (Rosekind, Gander, Connell, and Co, 2001). Further, the repetitiveness of some of the first officer's statements and his inability to recall and use information that had only recently been provided suggests that the first officer was in fact affected by fatigue, which he acknowledged to investigators during his post-accident review of the air traffic control voice recordings. (An example was the radio transmission mistakenly addressed to Havana Center made shortly after ATC told the crew they would not need to contact Havana.)

Review of the evidence by NASA fatigue researchers established that cumulative sleep loss and the long period since the crewmembers of flight 808 awoke must have impaired their performance. One of the researchers testified during the NTSB public hearing that sleepiness during waking hours can affect every aspect of human capability and performance, including decision-making. The researcher stated that when fatigued, people have difficulty processing critical information and choosing among alternatives (NTSB, 1994b, p. 51; see also Durmer and Dinges, 2005).

Fatigue may have affected many aspects of the crew's performance. For example, it probably made it more difficult for the crew to process the navigation and communications challenges of flying in the Guantanamo Bay terminal area, compounding any inadequacies in the crew's preparation and knowledge. Fatigue probably contributed to the captain's last-minute decision to change runways, difficulty in maneuvering the airplane, preoccupation with the missing strobe light, loss of control, and failure to recover. Fatigue may also have undercut the effectiveness of the efforts of the first officer and flight engineer to challenge the captain.

We suggest that the insidious effects of fatigue go beyond undermining performance of normal cockpit tasks – fatigue also impairs individuals' ability to judge their own performance and the performance of other crewmembers and impairs their ability to recognize that a situation is getting out of hand. Thus fatigued individuals have difficulty recognizing that they are impaired and in danger. Also, though no specific research exists on this point, fatigue may exacerbate crews' vulnerability to plan continuation error. Recent research shows that pilots, like all individuals, are vulnerable to plan continuation bias, which makes them slow to recognize that an original or habitual plan of action is no longer appropriate to the situation and must be revised.

The cognitive mechanisms of plan continuation bias are not well understood, but we suspect several factors are involved. Plan continuation errors in aviation have most often been reported during the approach-to-landing phase of operation. During approach, crews normally must make small adjustments to control flightpath and airspeed, sometimes deviate around weather, and often alter the approach in response to ATC instructions. The crew's goal is normally framed as landing the aircraft (safely, of course), and their focus is on progress toward that goal and making adjustments as necessary to complete it. This way of framing goals may make crews less sensitive to cues that conditions have changed and that the goal should be abandoned. (Consider an alternate way the goal might be framed: "After each stage in the approach we will determine whether to continue the approach or to abort it". This particular formulation may not be practical for everyday flying, but it illustrates that goals can be framed in ways to keep alternatives in mind.) Workload is often high during approach – the workload of the crew of flight 808 was quite high – and high workload makes it more difficult for crews to proactively assess changing conditions and re-evaluate goals. Under high workload, individuals tend to rely on highly practised procedural routines, whose demands on limited cognitive resources are less than the demands of effortful analysis and deliberation. The most highly practised procedural routines during approach involve adapting and adjusting to continue the approach, which pilots can do in a relatively automatic fashion even under heavy workload.

Thus, fatigue was not the only challenge confronting the crew of flight 808. The complexity and unfamiliarity of the approach, inadequate information about the specific challenges of the approach, and misleading information about the missing strobe light came into play. These other factors combined in a way that put the crew in a high workload situation that in itself made the crew vulnerable to error. Adding fatigue to the mix greatly amplified this vulnerability, producing a snowballing effect that made recovery increasingly difficult. Fatigue may prevent a crew from noticing or correctly interpreting a latent threat, leading them into a high-workload situation that is inherently difficult to manage, and fatigue may then interfere with the crew's ability to recognize that the situation is deteriorating and requires a change of plan.

Our discussion so far has focused on fatigue, the challenges of the flight, and the errors made by the crew of flight 808. However, it is crucial to understand that this crew did not choose to fly fatigued and that the aviation system in which they operated placed them in a situation in which any crew would have been in danger of having an accident. Regulations for flight, duty and rest times are hotly debated within the aviation industry; however, most knowledgeable parties recognize that regulations that essentially allowed unlimited continuous duty for supplemental air carrier crews invited accidents (some aspects of the regulations have changed since this accident). The president of this crew's airline acknowledged that they "work everything right to the edge of what was allowed by the Federal regulations" (NTSB, 1994b, pp. 30–32). Further, the training and flight reference materials provided the crew were inadequate to prepare them for the challenges of the flight, even if they had not been fatigued. Thus the snowballing situation that ended in the crash of flight 808 began before the crew got in the airplane with inadequacies in the aviation system.

Concluding discussion

In our view this accident resulted from the interplay of many factors: fatigue, lack of adequate information, misleading information, an ill-chosen decision by the captain to make an extremely difficult approach with which he was unfamiliar, inadequate briefing for this approach, the failure of the other crew members to challenge the captain's decision or to argue for aborting the approach when it became no longer viable, the all-too-human vulnerability to persist in plans that require revision, the captain's inadequate response to crew warnings, and his inadequate response to decaying airspeed, overbanking, and stall. The crew was highly experienced and their skills were well regarded; thus, we must regard the errors that they made as ones to which all pilots are vulnerable in similar situations. This vulnerability is a function of the situation, task demands, and the inherent nature of human cognitive processes. In fact, the NTSB cited an October 10, 1993 incident in which a Northwest Airlines DC-10 flight landed at Guantanamo Bay with one main landing gear off of the runway surface. This DC-10 flight shared most of the factors at play in the accident of flight 808.

AIA 808 was a landmark accident because it was the first time that the NTSB felt it had sufficient objective evidence to name fatigue as the primary cause. Fatigue was clearly central to the errors made by the crew, yet it is important to recognize that experienced pilots sometimes make these types of errors even in the absence of fatigue, as illustrated by numerous reports pilots have made to the Aviation Safety Reporting System (ASRS) database.

AIA 808 illustrates how the operating environment, specific circumstances, and human vulnerability interact to produce accidents in ways that can only partly be predicted. Had some of the circumstances of this accident been different – for example, if the strobe light had been operating – the accident might not have occurred. This accident also illustrates the way in which factors interact in an escalating fashion that makes the situation increasingly difficult to manage. Fatigue and inadequacy of briefing materials about special aspects of the approach probably contributed to the captain's last-minute decision to use runway 10 and the captain's failure to brief the new approach adequately, which in turn made it more difficult for the other crew members to challenge the decision. The inoperative strobe light, the controller's guidance to use the strobe light for orientation, and fatigue interacted and greatly amplified the captain's vulnerability to preoccupation with finding the strobe and distraction from controlling the airplane. Fatigue almost certainly made it difficult for the captain to respond adequately to the airplane's performance deterioration and the warnings of the first officer and flight engineer, and the inherent vulnerability of all crew members to plan continuation bias made them less likely to abort the approach as the situation deteriorated.

This accident also reveals hidden vulnerability in the defenses against threats and errors that the airline industry has carefully constructed in recent decades – defenses that have proven their value countless times over the years. These diverse defenses are intended to provide multiple, independent barriers to threats and to errors, so that if one defense fails, others will prevent escalation of the threat or the consequences of an error. Unfortunately, the defenses are not in fact entirely independent, and all of them can be eroded by a common factor such as fatigue. Also, some of the defenses are not as strong as intended. For example, the NTSB (1994a) reported that inadequate monitoring and challenging were prevalent factors in airline accidents between 1978–1990, and we find the same problem in our sample of 1991–2001 accidents.

This accident is an organizational accident in that the crew was placed in a situation with substantially heightened risk because of fatigue generated by job requirements and because the crew was not provided critical information. In airline operations, as in many industries, crews are implicitly expected to make up for the deficiencies of the system in which they operate by using skill and judgment, which they do successfully the vast majority of the time. But when they fail on rare occasion to make up for deficiencies in the system, blaming the crew for an accident is detrimental to the cause of aviation safety. A far more constructive approach is for the industry to focus on making operations resilient to diverse threats to safety.

We suggest several ways operational resilience can be increased. The most obvious is to not send crews out fatigued. The specific provisions of federal regulations of flight, duty, and rest times are debated within the airline industry. Without entering that debate, we suggest that, although the content of these regulations is crucial, it is not sufficient. Operating safely requires that companies commit themselves to not putting crews in the position of having to fly fatigued, and requires pilots to commit themselves to not undertaking flights when fatigued, whether induced by work requirements or personal activities. Doing this in practice is not simple. Fatigue is not an all-or-nothing state; we all experience some degree of fatigue at work, the question is: how much is too much? Unfortunately, subjective impressions of fatigue often underestimate the degree of performance impairment. Training programs exist that can help both crews and company managers understand and combat fatigue (Rosekind et al., 2001).[2]

Monitoring and challenging are essential defenses against a wide range of threats and errors (Sumwalt, Thomas, and Dismukes, 2002), yet this and other accidents reveal that procedures and training for monitoring and challenging need more work. Training should also be expanded to inform pilots about subtle vulnerabilities such as plan continuation bias and disruption of attention by concurrent task demands, and to give them realistic practice in coping with these factors. Further, operating procedures should be analyzed periodically to identify hidden vulnerabilities and to restore independence of multiple barriers to threats and errors.

Notes

1   If the accident had not occurred, the flight crew would have ferried the airplane back to Atlanta, empty. This flight would have been permitted under the air carrier regulations pertaining to flight, duty, and rest time because ferry flights were not subject to these regulations.

2   Fatigue management in aviation is the research area of NASA's Fatigue Countermeasures Group – for more information and links to relevant publications, see http://humanfactors. arc.nasa.gov/zteam/fcp/FCP.pubs.html.

Chapter 5

Southwest 1455 –
Unstabilized Approach at Burbank

Introduction

On March 5, 2000 at 1811 Pacific standard time, Southwest Airlines flight 1455, a Boeing 737-300, crashed through a 14-foot-high metal blast fence at the departure end of runway 8 while landing at Burbank, California. The airplane continued past the airport boundary and across a street, coming to a stop near a gas station. Of the 142 persons aboard, two passengers were seriously injured, and the captain and 41 passengers incurred minor injuries. The airplane was substantially damaged.

Flight 1455 departed from Las Vegas, Nevada approximately two hours behind schedule. This was the first flight that the captain and first officer had operated together, and it was the beginning of a planned three-day trip for the crew. The crew were highly experienced in their respective positions and in the 737: the captain had 5,302 hours of experience as a 737 pilot-in-command, and the first officer had 2,522 hours of experience as a 737 second-in-command. Both crewmembers had several days free from duty immediately prior to the day of the accident.

The accident investigation revealed that the airplane was high and fast as it joined the final approach course to runway 8. The captain, who was the flying pilot, landed the airplane at 182 knots, more than 40 knots faster than the computed target speed, after descending on a steep gradient during final approach. The pilots were unable to stop the airplane within the confines of the runway surface after realizing that the airplane was traveling so fast.

The NTSB determined that the probable cause of this accident was "the flight crew's excessive airspeed and flightpath angle during the approach and landing and [their] failure to abort the approach when stabilized approach criteria were not met". The NTSB further determined that "contributing to the accident was the [air traffic] controller's positioning of the airplane in such a manner as to leave no safe options for the flight crew other than a go-around maneuver" (NTSB, 2002, p. 22).

Significant events and issues

1. Changing surface wind conditions at the destination required the crew to change their arrival plan

The flight entered the Burbank area on a standard terminal arrival routing from the northeast. During the descent the first officer obtained ATIS information for the destination indicating that there were strong westerly winds at the surface and that aircraft were landing on runways 26 and 33. At 1754:21, the captain gave an approach briefing to the first officer, including his plan to land the flight on runway 33. Because of high terrain located to the north, east, and south of the airport, the most common approach path to runway 33 was via the ILS approach to runway 8 (overflying lower terrain to the west of Burbank) with a circle-to-land maneuver southwest of the airport for the landing on runway 33. However, at 1802:52, air traffic control advised the crew that the ATIS had been updated and they should expect an ILS approach straight in to runway 8. (The strength of the westerly surface winds had decreased substantially, allowing aircraft to land to the east.) This was the most commonly used runway at Burbank, and the crewmembers had flown ILS and visual approaches to it many times in the past. The crew prepared for the new landing runway by confirming their previously planned final flap setting of 40 degrees and calculating a final approach target airspeed of 138 knots. After checking the new ATIS broadcast, the first officer informed the captain at 1804:49 that the westerly surface winds had decreased from the previously reported 18–26 knots to 6 knots.

The runway change occasioned by the reduction in surface winds required the pilots of flight 1455 to change their arrival and approach plans. Although the CVR data indicate that they articulated the change clearly and verified it with each other, any runway change during descent also carries implied or explicit pressure to accept the air traffic control instruction without consuming much time to consider the new runway assignment. As a result, pilots may not recognize implications of the change that may not be readily apparent. Also, they may accept and implement the runway change without adequately briefing themselves for the circumstances of using the new landing runway. Crews can always "buy time" for decisions, preparations, and briefings by requesting delay vectors from air traffic control. However, in practice they often eschew this option, perhaps reflecting industry concerns with on-time performance and fuel efficiency, and perhaps not recognizing the risks of rushing decisions and setting up an approach to a new runway hurriedly. Also, crews may come to accept runway changes automatically because they happen fairly frequently in airline operations, usually with benign outcome, and these successful outcomes over time may lead crews to underestimate the possibility and consequences of not having enough time to prepare adequately for a runway change.

However, for the crew of flight 1455, the change from runway 33 to runway 8 had critical implications that may not have been immediately evident to them. The change resulted in a significant decrease in the flying time and distance that would be available for reducing the airplane's speed, configuring it for landing, and descending to touchdown. Compounding the reduced time and distance, this change also meant that the final approach would be flown with a tailwind aloft, in contrast to the headwind component that the flight would have encountered landing on runway 33. Although the tailwind was light on the ground, the pilots were to discover that it was significantly stronger aloft.

The crew of flight 1455 did not appear to be bothered by the change to runway 8, however. The captain's reaction to learning about the change was to tell the first officer: "Okay, good". Given his familiarity with landing on runway 8, the captain may have even felt relieved to perform the straight-in precision approach that he would have been most comfortable with instead of the more challenging and less common circling approach near terrain. The crew's subsequent discussion about surface winds, final flap setting, and target approach speed indicates that they were properly considering the direct implications of the runway change for adequacy of the runway length and the best airplane configuration for landing on it.

The crew had slightly more than 5 minutes to prepare for landing on the new runway, from their first notification to expect runway 8 to the time that they were cleared for the approach. The airplane was flying assigned headings and descending steadily with the autopilot engaged during this period, so the flight control workload was relatively low. However, we note from the CVR transcript that there was nearly constant conversation during this period between the two crewmembers and air traffic control, all related to the approach preparations, obtaining the new ATIS broadcast, and spotting traffic to follow. The time that was potentially available for thinking about and briefing the new descent and landing plan was nearly all consumed by routine communications and searching for traffic.

Runway 8 at Burbank is relatively short for a Boeing 737, with 6,032 feet of paved surface. The runway length is adequate for landing but provides little margin for error. According to his post-accident statements, the first officer did not consult the onboard performance computer (OPC) in preparation for the landing on runway 8. The OPC contained detailed information about landing distance requirements, target speeds, and target power settings. Company procedures found in the "Landing Performance" chapter of the *Flight Reference Manual* did not require consulting the OPC but stated that the system "should be used anytime landing performance capabilities ... are in question and include (but are not limited to) the following conditions: tailwind, high gross weight, short runway" (NTSB, 2002, p.18). These were in fact the conditions facing flight 1455 after the runway reassignment; however, if the first officer had consulted the OPC, he would have learned that the operation was permissible and would not have necessarily received any additional information that was operationally relevant. On the other hand, if the first officer had explicitly considered whether conditions required consulting the OPC, he might have been sensitized to challenging aspects of the approach that would demand careful attention. Still, the crew's plan to use flaps 40 for landing suggests that they recognized the short runway situation in which they were operating. We can therefore assume that they were generally aware that this would be a relatively critical approach and landing.

During this period the first officer appeared to be monitoring the flight appropriately, and the two pilots were communicating effectively, as revealed by a conversation recorded on the CVR at 1755:59. While the flight was being vectored in the terminal area the first officer told the captain: "Check your orange bug, Howard. If you're happy, I'm happy". The captain replied: "Nooo, I'm not [then apparently reset the bug] ... okay, now I am, thank you".

2. Air traffic control caused the flight to be both fast and high when beginning the approach

While the first officer was obtaining the new ATIS, the captain received and acknowledged an air traffic control instruction to maintain 230 knots or greater "till advised". At 1805:13 the captain informed the first officer about the airspeed restriction. The flight received vectors to a base leg intercepting the final approach course approximately 7–8 miles from the runway. Air traffic control then offered the crew a visual approach and pointed out another company flight that was several miles ahead on the same approach to runway 8. The first officer asked the captain whether he wanted the visual approach. The captain acknowledged to the first officer, at 1806:11: "Yeah I think so, we'll just wait a second, I want to get through these clouds but I think the visual will be fine ...". The crew then sighted the company traffic, and at 1808:19 the controller transmitted: "Southwest 1455, cross Van Nuys at or above 3,000 [feet], cleared visual approach runway 8".

According to radar data, the flight was approximately 3 miles north of the extended runway centerline and 9 miles west of the runway threshold at 4,200 feet MSL (approximately 3,400 feet above airport elevation), traveling at about 230 knots indicated airspeed when it was cleared for the visual approach. This clearance signified that the crew could maneuver at their discretion toward the airport, align with the final approach course, and begin their descent. Without explicitly stating so, clearance for the visual approach also lifted the 230-knot minimum airspeed restriction that the controller had earlier imposed. (Pilots are provided with this guidance by the FAA in Chapter 4 of its *Aeronautical Information Manual* (FAA, 2004b).) We note that from the moment that flight 1455 was cleared for the approach (and the airplane's flightpath and speed thus became subject to the captain's management), the flight had to slow 95 knots and descend 3,400 feet to reach a runway that was approximately 10 miles away by the planned ground track. Based on these parameters and the flight characteristics of the 737, it would have been difficult and perhaps impossible for the crew to have established the airplane on a stabilized approach prior to touchdown even if the captain had taken the most aggressive action possible to slow and descend the airplane once cleared for the approach. The NTSB concluded that the controller had "positioned the airplane too fast, too high, and too close to the runway threshold to leave any safe options other than a go-around maneuver" (NTSB, 2002, p.22).

During this period leading up to approach clearance the crew was receiving information that, to a pilot experienced in flying the 737, would suggest an impending high/fast situation. The controller's assignments of a 190-degree heading setting up a base leg to the final approach course and 230 knots airspeed reduced the length of the final approach segment and placed the airplane at the extremes of its capability to both descend and slow in the limited distance remaining to the runway. The crew of flight 1455 presumably recognized they were being put in a "slam-dunk", a not uncommon clearance that puts flights in a high/fast situation and challenges crews to get the aircraft stabilized on target airspeed, descent rate, and glideslope before landing.

Most pilots operating in a terminal area iteratively evaluate how far they are from the runway and how much speed and altitude they must dissipate over that distance to obtain a stabilized approach to the runway. We do not know from the accident records whether, or in what way, the captain was thinking about these issues at this time. He did not evince any special concern when he told the first officer about the speed assignment, but he may well have been engaging in the routine descent-planning thought processes. The first officer also did not express concern, but we cannot ascertain his thoughts about the situation at that time either. Although pilots use rules of thumb to iteratively evaluate their descent profile, no precise algorithms exist by which crews can calculate whether they can establish a stabilized approach from a given position on base leg. Their judgments depend on experience in similar situations. Almost certainly, both pilots of flight 1455 had often dealt with slam-dunk clearances and thus did not regard their situation as extraordinary.

The crew continued to be very busy during this portion of the flight. Both pilots were coping with the new runway assignment at the time that the captain received and acknowledged the new heading and speed assignments. The first officer was not monitoring the air traffic control frequency at that time because he was obtaining new weather and runway information on a different frequency. The workload from the change of runways and the change from an ILS to a visual approach may have interfered with the crew's perception of the significance that the heading and speed assignments had for their flight situation. We speculate that one of the dangers of high workload is that crews may fall into a reactive mode, responding to events as they occur, rather than strategically assessing the evolution of their situation. This reactive mode reduces cognitive demands, but leaves the crew slow to recognize latent risks.

3. The captain attempted to descend to the runway without using maximum efforts to slow

Slightly more than one minute elapsed from flight 1455's clearance for the visual approach until the captain commanded the first aircraft configuration change: "Flaps 5". Review of FDR data suggests that during this period the captain was slowing the airplane to get below 225 knots, the maximum speed for extending the flaps to 5 degrees (he was operating the airplane with the autopilot engaged and manually commanded idle thrust, as per the company's operating procedures). In quick succession, the captain then commanded extension of the landing gear and the flaps, in stages, to 40 degrees. During this period, he also noted on the flight management system display that there was a 20-knot tailwind at the flight's current altitude.

FDR and radar data indicate that the airplane crossed abeam of the Van Nuys navigation aid while still descending to 3,000 feet (2,225 feet above airport elevation) and slowing through 225 knots. The airplane slightly overshot the final approach course with the course intercept commanded by the autopilot. It rejoined the course as the captain disconnected the autopilot. Then, while the captain ordered the flap and gear configuration changes, the airplane maintained 3,000 feet until approximately 3 miles from the runway threshold. At this time the airspeed had decreased to approximately 180 knots, and the captain then began descending at more than twice the normal 3-degree gradient path in order to aim for his desired touchdown point just beyond the runway threshold.

The captain's actions from the time that he first commanded flap extension indicate that he was aware the airplane was higher and faster than the normal profile. The quick configuration of the airplane for landing suggests the captain's desire to slow the airplane rapidly.[1] The captain commanded extension of the flaps to 40 degrees ("Put it to 40") while the airspeed was above 180 knots, which further suggests his awareness of the need to dissipate airspeed. The first officer recalled responding by pointing to the airspeed indicator to alert the captain that the airspeed exceeded 156 knots, the maximum speed allowed for extending flaps to 40), and the captain continued: "It won't go, I know that, it's all right ...". The captain would have been aware that the 737 flap system uses load protection devices that prevent extension of the flaps to the 40-degree position until airspeed reduces to the limit speed. Presumably, he called for the flap handle to be set to the 40-degree position in advance so that the flaps would extend to the maximum position as soon as he was able to slow the airplane sufficiently. (In fact, the flaps did not extend to 40 degrees until after touchdown because airspeed remained above the limit speed of 156 knots throughout the approach.)

Although the captain was clearly attempting to cope with the flight's high and fast situation, his actions suggest that he did not immediately recognize the extreme criticality of the need to slow and configure, that an all-out effort, including maximum slowing in the air, would be required to stop the airplane on the runway. If the crew had recognized the need to slow down more rapidly, they could have extended the landing gear immediately after receiving the visual approach clearance, before the airplane slowed to the flaps 5 limit speed. Highly experienced in the 737, the pilots would have known that this is the quickest and most efficient way to slow down. Instead, by using the normal procedure of waiting to slow to flaps 5 speed and then extending the flaps before the landing gear, the crew forsook a great deal of potential drag and speed reduction. Thus, the crew reconfigured the airplane at a rapid pace but not in the most efficient manner for slowing down. Also, while constrained to maintaining at least 230 knots by the air traffic controller's earlier instruction prior to receiving clearance for the visual approach, the crew could have asked the controller to permit them to slow down sooner.

All this is consistent with the post-accident recollections of both pilots that they thought the situation was under control until after the airplane touched down. They may have thought the situation was under control because they were using the same techniques to control their descent profile that they had used on previous slam-dunk approaches, which all worked out successfully (that is to say, no accident occurred – we do not know whether this crew previously exceeded stabilized approach criteria or how common it was for other company crews to exceed these criteria). Further, the crew's failure to request a speed reduction or greater spacing on the base leg is also consistent with the normal behavior of many air carrier pilots. Unless the situation is critical most pilots are reluctant to make such a request, perhaps because of their desire to help controllers maintain the flow of traffic or because of professional pride in being able to manage the situation without outside assistance.

To summarize the captain's apparent concept of the situation at this point in the flight, as revealed by his actions, he most likely knew that the airplane was not in a position to make a normal approach. However, he did not appear to be aware that the actual situation was extreme or that after he missed the opportunity to slow the airplane rapidly with the landing gear and began to descend before the airplane had slowed to normal approach speed, an accident was now inevitable unless the crew abandoned the approach attempt.

The captain's decision to descend from 3,000 feet before slowing the airplane to below flaps 40 speed conflicted with the advice provided by the airline in a section entitled "Pilot Techniques, FO Operating Technique, Close-in Descent Calculations" in its *Flight Reference Manual*: "If you are really behind – the best choice: level off, configure all the way to flaps 40 – then start down. Remember that the flaps blow up to 30 just above 150 knots. Flaps 40, gear down and 140 knots will give about 1,000 feet per nautical mile (almost 1 for 1)" (NTSB, 2002, p.16). This last reference indicated that a 737 configured at flaps 40 with landing gear extended could achieve three times the normal descent gradient while still maintaining the proper final approach speed – as long as it was slowed down to approach speed before beginning to descend.

Presumably the captain was aware, at least in principle, that the best way to accomplish an approach from a high/fast starting position in the 737 is to fully configure and slow the airplane before descending, so it is not clear why he started to descend before configuring and slowing. When asked after the accident why he descended before slowing, the captain replied that he had wanted to descend out of the 20-knot tailwind prevailing at 3,000 feet. It is true that getting lower would improve the airplane's position somewhat[2] but whatever advantage this offered would be more than offset by the excessive airspeed.

Other factors may also have contributed to the captain's decision to descend before slowing. The captain recalled being surprised that the flight had progressed beyond the Van Nuys navigational aid when he noticed the displayed distance to that fix increasing. He looked back over his left shoulder to visually confirm passing Van Nuys. Thus, while busy attempting to slow down the captain had imperfect awareness of his proximity to the Burbank Airport, and then he had to contend with the surprise of being closer than he had thought. At some point he would have observed the perspective of the runway at Burbank growing increasingly steep, well beyond normal. There is a strong tendency for pilots to begin descending when the sight picture of the runway indicates that the airplane is high on the final approach descent path, because beginning a steep descent makes the sight picture start coming back to normal immediately. Consequently, when pilots find themselves high on approach, discipline and a good grasp of the concept of total energy is required to slow the airplane before descending because this technique initially makes the sight picture of the angle to the runway get even worse (steeper) while the airplane is slowing. (The airplane's total energy state is a combination of its altitude and airspeed. An airplane high on approach has excess total energy that can be dissipated only by increasing drag or flying a longer lateral distance to the runway. Increasing airspeed to descend more rapidly does not reduce total energy substantially.) Further, pilots in this situation must apply these somewhat counterintuitive flight control inputs while under the workload and stress inherent in a high and fast situation. Their attention may become increasingly consumed with the threateningly steep sight picture and the accelerating pace of developments as the runway nears rapidly. Conceivably in the case of flight 1455 the surprise, time pressure, and stress from the worsening situation may have impaired the captain's judgment of the best way to manage being high and fast. One of the dangers of excessive workload is that it preoccupies mental resources necessary to assess evolving situations and likely outcomes (Staal, 2004, pp. 76–7).

4. Despite excessive airspeed, the pilots continued with their plan to land and did not execute a go-around

FDR data indicate that the airplane continued descending at a steep gradient of 7 degrees (compared to a normal descent gradient of 3.0 to 3.5 degrees) until the captain began the flare for landing at approximately 150 feet above ground level. Although the captain managed to land the airplane within the touchdown zone (normal part of the runway for landing) by using the greater-than-normal descent gradient, the airplane could not slow down while descending at that angle. Throughout the final approach and landing, flight 1455 continued to operate at least 45 knots faster than its 138-knot target speed, despite engine thrust remaining at idle.

According to FDR data and an NTSB study of radar data (NTSB, 2001a) for the accident flight, when the airplane descended through 1,000 feet above airport elevation (at 1810:27) its airspeed was 197 knots (groundspeed was 211 knots, reflecting a 14-knot tailwind), and it was descending at 2,624 feet per minute. When the airplane descended through 500 feet above airport elevation (at 1810:43, only 16 seconds from touchdown) its airspeed was still 197 knots (groundspeed was 204 knots, reflecting a 7-knot tailwind), and it was descending at 1,974 feet per minute. In comparison, on the normal descent gradient from 1,000 feet to the ground (tracking the centerline of the electronic glideslope when stabilized at the 138-knot target airspeed) the airplane would have been descending at approximately 800 feet per minute. Further, if flight 1455 had been operating on the normal descent gradient but at moderately excessive airspeed when descending through 1,000 feet, the airplane would have had the drag capability to attain the 138-knot airspeed target.

From the beginning of the flight's Final Descent from 3,000 feet, 3 miles from the runway, there were several additional cues that the aircraft was quite high, fast, and descending at a high sink rate. The steeper-than-normal descent gradient made the runway appear foreshortened, cockpit instruments indicated that airspeed and sink rate were substantially above normal target values and that the aircraft was well above the glideslope, the throttles were at idle instead of the setting (nominally 55–65 per cent N1) that normally maintains a 737 in a stable descent at target airspeed; and beginning at 1810:24, when the airplane was descending through approximately 1,200 feet above ground and its descent rate was increasing through 2,900 feet per minute, the GPWS announced its "sink rate" warning continuously which then devolved to the more significant "pull up" warning. However, none of these cues suggested immediate danger until just before touchdown. Through most of the approach, while the cues clearly indicated that the airplane was in an unusual and unstabilized profile, the crew could safely continue the descent and defer a decision about whether to continue or go around. Cockpit instrumentation does not provide crews information about an airplane's projected touchdown and stopping location as a function of current flight and runway parameters[3] (it would in principle be possible to compute and display this information). Without this specific information, pilots who continue an unstabilized approach at low altitude must attempt to judge from experience whether it will work out.

Several factors may have further impaired the captain's ability to judge whether it would be possible to salvage the unstabilized approach of flight 1455. An analysis by the Southwest Airline Pilots' Association (SWAPA) suggests that the captain would have focused his attention primarily on the sight picture of the angle down to the runway, which was the most salient and compelling cue available (SWAPA, 2002). The captain worked to adjust the flightpath to make this sight picture match that of a normal profile, which he accomplished – by descending at high speed – albeit at the very end of the descent. Consistent with this explanation, the captain reported after the accident he was aware that the speed was high but not aware of the exact value or that it was quite excessive, and he stated that he became fixated on the sight picture. Apparently the captain did not give adequate weight, among the cues available, to airspeed indications. Trying to get the airplane back on a normal descent path under these conditions would have been quite demanding of the captain's attention and probably was stressful. One of the well-demonstrated effects of stress is to narrow the field of visual attention and to disrupt mental processes underlying reasoning and decision-making. To the extent that the crew of flight 1455 was affected by the attention-demanding effects of their immersion in a high/fast situation, they would have been less likely to notice and react to the cues that were available to them suggesting that the approach could not be safely continued to landing.

The captain and first officer also reported being distracted by concerns about whether the airplane that had just landed in front of them would clear the runway in time for flight 1455 to land. The airplane ahead of them did not clear the runway until flight 1455 was only 300–500 feet above ground, so the crew's concerns were valid and would have attracted their attention until moments before the landing flare began. Another possible distraction may have been the auditory warnings from the GPWS that sounded continuously throughout the final moments of the descent. The warning (20 seconds of "sink rate" followed by about 11 seconds of "whoop, whoop, pull up") was certainly a salient cue that should have caused the crew to consider abandoning the approach. Warning alarms are designed to intrude forcefully on pilots' attention; however, they also often have the unintended effect of distracting pilots and interfering with their processing of other information (Stanton, Booth, and Stammers, 1992).

To reduce the cognitive challenges of assessing whether approaches can be continued safely to landing, especially under conditions of time pressure, workload, and stress, most airlines now provide their crews with guidelines that specify criteria for stabilized approaches, including the point on the approach at which flight parameters must meet those criteria. This airline's *Flight Reference Manual* procedures for visual approaches specified that by 1,000 feet above airport elevation pilots should plan to be configured with the landing gear down, at the landing flap setting (40 degrees in this case), with the Final Descent checklist completed. Additionally, by 500 feet above ground the airplane should be "stabilized on final approach with engines 'spooled up'". The manual further stated: "High idle thrust is considered 'spooled up'" (NTSB, 2001b). Another part of the manual, entitled "Normal Operations, Approach – Approach Envelope for All VMC Landing Approaches", discussed the "approach envelope" and defined the portion of the approach between 500 feet above airport elevation and touchdown as "the slot". The manual stated the "final slot conditions" as: "proper sink rate and on glidepath; proper speed (for existing conditions); proper runway alignment – no further turning required; trimmed for zero stick forces; steady-state thrust setting in final landing configuration". The manual cautioned: "IF NOT IN THE 'SLOT' YOU ARE NOT PREPARED FOR A NORMAL LANDING [emphasis in original]" (NTSB, 2002, p. 15).

In a section of the manual entitled "Close-in Descent Calculations" that provided descent gradients for various gear, flap, and airspeed combinations, including those useful for recovering from a high/fast condition, the following information appeared:

> In any case, have the engines spooled up by 500 feet [above ground level]. You must lead with the power – a good technique is to begin advancing the power as the glideslope comes off the bottom of the case or the upper [row of lights of the visual approach slope indicator] turns pink (NTSB, 2002, p.16).

The airline also provided criteria for the monitoring pilot to call out flightpath and airspeed deviations to the pilot flying. The "Normal Operations, Approach, Deviation Callouts for All Approaches" section of the company's manual stated: "If any of the following parameters are exceeded, the pilot not flying will make the corresponding callout and verify that the pilot flying takes appropriate corrective action. The pilot flying will acknowledge the callout verbally with immediate corrective action". The manual provided these parameter limits for callouts that were relevant to the accident flight: "Airspeed – Target speed plus 10 knots (callout: 'Airspeed'); Glideslope – +/- 1 dot displacement (callout: 'Glideslope'); Sink Rate – 2,000 feet per minute when below 2,000 feet above ground, 1,000 feet per minute when below 1,000 feet above ground (callout: 'Sink rate')" (NTSB, 2001c). In another section of the manual, the company provided criteria for a go-around and missed approach. Three of the stated criteria for which "a missed approach must be executed" were: "full scale deflection of the [localizer course deviation indicator] occurs inside the outer marker or [final approach fix] in [instrument meteorological conditions] ...; the pilot determines that a landing cannot be accomplished in the touchdown zone ...; the captain directs the first officer to go around" (NTSB, 2001d).

In a post-accident interview, the airline's vice president of flight operations discussed the procedures for monitoring, challenging, and responding to deviations from the ideal stabilized approach. The NTSB reported:

> [He] said that if a first officer called out an airspeed and/or sink rate deviation, the captain should acknowledge and say: "Correcting". He thought that executing a go-around would depend on the extent of the deviation. If the airspeed were within 6 knots, then probably not. He said that was where judgment came in (NTSB, 2001e).

We suggest that although the company had appropriately established "bottom lines" for a stabilized approach (with airplane configuration criteria at 1,000 feet and additional sink rate, airspeed, and thrust criteria at and below 500 feet), these criteria allowed crews considerable latitude for deciding how to manage deviations rather than mandating specific responses. For example, the manual's statement that the crew should "plan" to configure the airplane by 1,000 feet provided leeway for deviating from this plan and did not mandate a go-around for failing to configure on time. The criteria for "the slot" were comprehensive, but the manual merely suggested that a flight outside the slot was "not prepared" for landing, rather than mandating a missed approach. Further, the criteria for 500 feet mandated that the engines be "spooled up" but also specifically allowed "high idle" thrust to fulfill this requirement, which is puzzling because high idle thrust will not maintain constant airspeed on a normal 3-degree descent path. Finally, the criteria that the airline had established for a mandatory missed approach did not include deviation from glidepath and did not provide specific airspeed, sink rate or path deviation values (other than full-scale localizer deviation). Rather than specifying glidepath deviation limits that would mandate a go-around, the company expected crews to use their own judgment.

Most approaches involve some degree of deviation from the standard of a perfectly stabilized condition. We think that it is highly desirable for air carriers to establish specific definitions for stabilized approach and realistic deviation limits for continuing the approach or changing to a go-around. This helps crews identify how much deviation can be managed safely, which is especially important under situations of high workload and time pressure, when it is difficult for even the most experienced of crews to correctly judge dynamic situations with absolute reliability. Providing explicit deviation limits and mandating a go-around when exceeding them simplifies the mental task for crews and facilitates making timely decisions to go around when appropriate. Explicit mandatory limits also reduce the danger of divergence of perception between the two pilots on whether to go around, and they allow crews to justify their actions to others. Mandatory limits may also be especially effective in encouraging first officers to challenge apparent errors by captains by providing agreed-upon numerical values that trigger a challenge, using standard terminology. This can help first officers overcome the social "power distance" that may otherwise inhibit them from challenging captains (Hofstede, 1980).

According to the company's procedures, the flight crew should have exchanged callouts when the flight descended through 1,000 feet above airport elevation. The manual specified that the first officer called out: "1,000 feet", and the captain repeated: "1,000 feet" and also stated the current airspeed and sink rate (NTSB, 2001f). The CVR data reveal that the crew of flight 1455 did not perform these callouts. The callouts that the manual required at 1,000 feet were different from those we have already discussed, in that crews were required to make them routinely at the specified altitude on every flight instead of making them only when prompted by deviations from the ideal flightpath. We suggest that if the first officer had cued the captain with the regular "1,000 feet" call, the captain's attention might have been drawn to the excessive airspeed and sink rate as he, in turn, prepared for his required response. The captain told investigators after the accident that "everything was stabilized at 500 feet except airspeed", which suggests that the lack of callouts by the first officer did not prevent the captain from recognizing that airspeed was higher than normal. However, callouts from both pilots might have helped the captain recognize just how excessive the airspeed was. The lack of the 1,000 foot callout, furthermore, deprived the captain of the opportunity to recognize the excessive speed at an earlier point when he presumably would have had the opportunity to react better. As the airplane descended through 1,000 and 500 feet, the captain may have subconsciously relied on the first officer's callouts to make habitual checks regarding speed and altitude. The absence of an expected cue is hard to notice (Wickens and Hollands, 2000, p. 217), as further evidenced by the captain's admission that he "did not remember passing through 1,000 feet".

The absence of other verbal challenges from the first officer, including the callouts for excessive airspeed, off-scale glideslope deviation, excessive sink rate, and improper flap configuration for landing (all of which were required by the company manual in the existing situation) is of great concern. The captain had briefed the first officer prior to the flight in a way that invited challenges, telling the first officer that he liked company procedures and did not "do things dumb, dangerous, and different, and if you see anything, speak up". In his post-accident interviews, the first officer showed substantial awareness of the flight's specific airspeed values at several key points in the approach. He recalled that the airspeed was 200 knots when the flight began its descent from 3,000 feet after passing Van Nuys. He also recalled that the airspeed was approximately 180 knots when the captain called for flaps 40. The first officer told investigators that he did not challenge the excessive airspeed because the captain always seemed to be correcting (NTSB, 2001g). This suggests that the first officer, noting the captain's actions to slow the airplane (rapid flap and gear extension, idle power setting), felt that his challenge was not needed because the captain was already aware of the problem.

Taken at face value, the first officer's explanation suggests that the only value of challenging by monitoring pilots is to recognize hazards that flying pilots have missed and bring the information to their attention. However, this ignores the value of independent thought and assessment by the monitoring pilot, and the potential ability of a monitoring pilot to influence the flying pilot's decision-making through the power of suggestion (Besco, 1994; Fischer and Orasanu, 2000). A direct challenge, such as "We should go around", can have a powerful influence on the course of events. Even a milder challenge, such as "Sink rate" or, even better: "Sinking 1,900" can have a strong influence on a flying pilot who may not fully apprehend all aspects or implications of the situation. The first officer of flight 1455 may not have directly suggested a go-around because he, too, may have thought the situation was manageable; however, explicit callouts would have brought attention to flight parameter values that might conceivably have prompted both pilots to reassess the situation.

The situation in this cockpit raises another important but subtle point about crew communication and effective crew resource management. Some crews may think that the only purpose of callouts is to identify deviations and to alert the flying pilot to things going wrong. However, callouts also provide another, more subtle kind of information, especially during approach. Required callouts help keep the flying pilot abreast of events; for example, even the rate and cadence of altitude callouts by the monitoring pilot can help the flying pilot maintain a sense of the flight's descent rate and of how the approach is working out (Kanki and Palmer, 1993). Therefore, monitoring pilots should call out relevant and important pieces of information, even if they think that the flying pilot is aware of the situation. The first officer's omission of the standard altitude callouts deprived both himself and the captain of these accustomed information cues.

Airlines' standard callouts and deviation limits explicitly include the monitoring pilot in the process of recognizing, assessing, and challenging unstabilized approaches because the flying pilot may become so engrossed in conducting the approach that he or she may not be able to assess how well it is working out. However, both flying and monitoring pilots may become desensitized to unstabilized approach parameters from their previous experiences with unstabilized approaches that ended with successful landings. The first officer told investigators that he had previously seen captains successfully perform landings when the airplane had not been completely configured at 1,000 feet, when it had been "out of the slot" at 500 feet, and when idle thrust was required on final approach. Further, we suggest that the company's inclusion of a technique for recovering from a steep, idle-power descent (adding power when the glideslope needle leaves full deflection, with recovery as low as 500 feet) in its flight manual may have been interpreted by some pilots as tacit approval to attempt to salvage highly unstabilized approaches at low altitude. The previous experiences reported by the first officer and the company's procedure for a low-altitude recovery from a steep approach could have led the first officer to accept the way that the captain was conducting flight 1455's approach rather than to challenge the captain.

It would be highly desirable to evaluate the approach phase of flight 1455 in the context of the crewmembers' perceptions, expectations, and habits developed from their own past experiences and the operating norms of the air carrier to which they had been exposed over the course of many years of flying. This perspective is difficult to obtain, unfortunately. Burbank air traffic controllers interviewed by investigators after the accident reported that they had seen airliners "make it" down to a landing on runway 8 from as high as 7,000 feet or as fast as 260 knots ground speed over Van Nuys. This suggests that the steep and fast approach attempted by flight 1455 was not unique among air carrier operations at Burbank, although it may not have been common. Unfortunately, these anecdotal observations fall far short of the kind of data needed, and a full perspective on air carrier and industry norms was not available from the information obtained during the accident investigation. We suggest that evaluation of an individual flight crew's performance is drastically incomplete without understanding how the company's operating procedures are typically enacted in daily line operations; however, we recognize the difficulty of identifying these norms in the aftermath of an accident.

Workload and distractions may also have interfered with the first officer's callouts, analysis of the situation, and performance of checklists. Both pilots were concerned with the airplane that landed ahead of flight 1455 and then did not clear the runway until shortly after the time at which the first officer should have made the 500-foot callout. The abnormally high airspeed and descent rate of flight 1455 reduced the spacing between it and the preceding flight, added to the uncertainty of whether the airplane on the runway would clear in time, and severely reduced time available to accomplish remaining duties and respond to events. During the last 60 seconds before touchdown, the first officer called the Burbank tower controller to reconfirm flight 1455's clearance to land, executed several commands by the captain for flap extensions, and executed items of the Final Descent checklist in response to the captain's call for the checklist. During this period the GPWS auditory warnings were sounding continuously, which may have interfered with the first officer's thinking and communication.

The first officer's radio call to reconfirm landing clearance came only 40 seconds after acknowledging clearance to land on runway 8, and he did not verbalize most of the challenge-response items on the Final Descent checklist as required by company procedures. He stated in a post-accident interview that he was too busy to verbalize the checklist and had to perform and verify the items silently. In addition to the high workload imposed by the very rapid approach and by concern for the preceding aircraft, the unusual and threatening sight picture of the steep descent angle may have absorbed much of the first officer's attention as it did the captain's. Under high workload, individuals typically shed tasks that seem less crucial (Raby and Wickens, 1994; Stokes and Kite, 1994, Chapter 3; Staal, 2004, p. 76). Thus the safety features provided by the normal and flightpath deviation callouts by the monitoring pilot and by the 1,000-foot and 500-foot stabilized approach gates were undermined by the very situation they are intended to guard against. (The hidden vulnerabilities of procedural defenses against threats and errors are discussed further in Chapter 21.)

In time-compressed high workload situations one problem may trigger other problems and one error can create the environment for other errors, resulting in a snowball effect of increasing challenge and decreasing crew performance. Obviously, it is highly undesirable for crews to experience high workload during the crucial last moments of approach and landing, as flight 1455 illustrates. Ironically, high workload, time compression, and stress undermine pilots' ability to assess whether they can adequately assess their situation and make appropriate judgments. We suggest that pilots should be taught to recognize signs of their own overload and to respond conservatively. For example, if the monitoring pilot is too busy to perform the Landing checklist, this is a sign of compromised performance and in itself is reason to consider going around.

With its ample margins of airspeed, flight 1455 could have made a successful go-around at any point in the approach and until just after touchdown (go-arounds are permitted in the 737 until the thrust reversers have been deployed several seconds after landing). The captain told investigators that he had performed pilot-initiated go-arounds (as distinct from those ordered by air traffic controllers) in "lots of places", and so presumably he would not have hesitated to do so on flight 1455 had he seen the need for one. Further, a go-around shortly after the flight began its descent from 3,000 feet with an immediate circle-to-land diversion to runway 33 would have approximated the maneuver that the captain had previously planned and briefed. Recall of the previous plan should have primed the captain to consider a go-around, and it apparently did. The captain told investigators that during final approach he had considered circling from the runway 8 final approach course to a landing on runway 33, but stayed with his original plan because he still thought that he could make the landing on runway 8.

Airline operations are typically conducted with substantial margins of safety, and airline pilots rarely continue an operation if they think the outcome is in doubt, so we must ask why the crew of flight 1455 did not even discuss breaking off their approach. This accident dramatically illustrates the power of plan continuation bias, a phenomenon that may be strongest when a goal (such as landing) is near completion. Although this phenomenon is not fully understood, it probably results from the interaction of aspects of the operational situation with several cognitive factors.

On the operational side, most hand-flown approaches (not using the autopilot) involve making continuous small corrections to flightpath and airspeed, and in challenging conditions, such as strong turbulence or crosswind, larger corrections may be required. Pilots develop strong habits for skillfully correcting for deviations to achieve a safe landing. Unstabilized approaches require correcting for large deviations before touching down on the runway. The cockpit provides no specific information on projected touchdown and stopping location, thus pilots must judge the potential outcome of their corrections on the basis of appearances and experience. There is no absolute or clearly apparent dividing line between deviations that can be corrected to produce a safe landing and deviations that cannot be corrected with high reliability. The vast preponderance of pilots' experience is that their corrections for deviations result in a successful landing, creating an expectation that almost all deviations can be safely corrected, and this may even be true of pilots who have continued to land from unstabilized approaches. Workload and time pressure may impair pilots' ability to assess whether the current situation differs significantly from past experience.

Beyond the specific aspects of high workload approaches, several additional cognitive factors probably make all individuals vulnerable to some degree to plan continuation errors. Among those factors are overconfidence bias, a tendency to overestimate one's own knowledge; confirmation bias, a tendency to seek and notice only those cues that confirm a currently held belief or plan, even though conflicting cues may be more diagnostic of the situation; and the anchoring heuristic, which weighs cues supporting the current plan more heavily than conflicting cues when plans are revised (for a review of biases, see Wickens and Hollands, 2000, pp. 310–313; but also see Klein, 1998, for a contrary view of the role of biases in real-world situations). In general, humans are overly reluctant to abandon a plan in which they have invested time and effort (described as the "sunk costs" phenomenon by Arkes and Blumer, 1985) and seek to avoid outcomes perceived as a loss (the "loss aversion" characteristic described by Kahneman and Tversky, 1984).

More recently, Muthard and Wickens (2003) have also linked plan continuation errors in flight operations to poor monitoring, often the result of cockpit automation that does not guide pilots' attention adequately. Undoubtedly, several external pressures also contribute to this bias in aviation operations. For example, on-time arrival at the planned airport is quite important in the aviation industry, and it may be that the costs of abandoning an approach weigh too heavily in the minds of pilots, consciously or subconsciously. Finally, pilots may respond in a particular way to a type of situation many times over the years without problems and thus build up an erroneous mental model of the margin of safety involved, not recognizing how close they may have come to the margin in times past. In these situations pilots may be unduly influenced by the availability from memory of past experiences with successful outcomes and may fail to analyze the current situation adequately (see Chapter 19 for discussion of availability heuristics). In support of this last point, we note that if the runway at Burbank had not been one of the shortest at which the airline operates, flight 1455 might well have been stopped successfully; this would have then reinforced the pilots' perception that they could make an unstabilized approach work.

Unfortunately, high workload, time constraints, and stress make it difficult for pilots to engage in the slow, deliberative mental activity needed to challenge the faulty perceptions caused by these inherent cognitive biases. Given these limits on the reliability of pilots' judgments about correcting approach deviations, it is crucial to set conservative limits on deviations. Formal procedures that set explicit stabilized approach criteria can provide these limits, but the conservatism of the criteria can tempt crews to "bend" the limits, and consequently the "bottom lines" are no longer bottom-line. Stabilized approach criteria are effective only if airlines clearly enunciate the purpose and importance of the criteria and rigorously train, check, and reinforce the criteria. Also, many companies now recognize that no-fault go-around policies are essential to counterbalance the externally generated and self-generated pressures on crews to continue an approach.

5. Captain delayed application of maximum braking

Performance calculations by the NTSB indicate that the airplane touched down at 182 knots indicated airspeed (188 knots groundspeed with the 6-knot tailwind), 2,150 feet beyond the runway threshold, with approximately 3,900 of runway surface and a total distance of 4,150 feet remaining to the blast fence at the far end of the runway. According to the agency's performance calculations, a 737 landed with the parameters of the accident airplane could have stopped in 3,500 feet with immediate application of maximum manual braking by the pilot flying.

The captain recalled, in his post-accident interview, that deceleration was normal on the landing rollout but shortly thereafter the runway end seemed closer than it should have been. At that time he thought the airplane might hit the blast fence at the end of the runway. He applied braking "pretty good" and used reverse thrust. Near the end of the runway he steered to the right, following which the airplane hit the blast fence. The first officer recalled first perceiving that they were having difficulty stopping when the airplane was about halfway down the runway.

Failure of the airplane to slow in accordance with performance calculations for maximum braking suggests that the captain did not immediately apply and hold maximum brake pressure. This suggests, in turn, that even after touchdown it was still not immediately apparent to the crew from the available cues that the airplane was in a critical situation. The crew's delayed awareness of their situation is corroborated by the post-accident statements by both crewmembers about their developing realization of a critical state partially down the runway – but by then it was too late to stop the airplane. Recognition may have been delayed by lack of specific information about the projected stopping performance of the airplane – if the pilots had been presented with unambiguous information that maximum braking was required, they very probably would have started applying it sooner. Few airline pilots have ever had to exert maximum braking effort to avoid going off the end of a runway, thus it is hard to judge when it is required. Further, the crew undoubtedly would not have landed if they had not expected that they would be able to stop, and this expectation may have delayed processing of visual cues that the airplane was not stopping quickly enough. (See Adams, Tenney, and Pew, 1995, for discussion of how pilots' mental models can bias processing of incoming information.)

The airline's normal procedures for the landing rollout suggested that crews apply reverse thrust immediately after touchdown. The company procedures added: "Normally, the pilot flying will begin braking at 80 knots …. On short runways or with adverse landing conditions, do not hesitate to initiate braking prior to 80 knots if required" (NTSB, 2001h; NTSB, 2002, p. 17).

We suggest that these company procedures and the preponderance of line operations on long runways may have strongly entrenched a habit of not starting to brake until the airplane had slowed to 80 knots. Although the crew of flight

1455 would have known that it was appropriate to start braking at a higher speed if conditions dictated, the habit may have slightly delayed execution of this knowledge that was declarative but not established as procedural habit.

The 737 is delivered from Boeing equipped with an autobrake system, which applies brakes immediately after touchdown to achieve a preselected deceleration rate. However, this airline's policy was to use manual braking rather than autobraking during the landing rollout. Although autobraking may result in slightly longer stopping distances than optimally performed manual braking, in practice, for the reasons indicated above, use of autobrakes may stop the airplane quicker. (Autobrakes may also give better performance when directional control requires large and rapid rudder inputs.) Performance calculations by the NTSB indicated that flight 1455 would not have stopped before hitting the blast fence if maximum autobraking had been used, but the airplane's stopping performance would have been better than that obtained by the accident crew with the manual braking that they applied. One advantage of autobraking during the accident flight would have been its faster application of heavy braking, following which the crew could have taken over with maximum manual braking as soon as they recognized the need for even faster deceleration.

Concluding discussion

Like many others, this accident involved an initiating event – a runway change in this case – that occurs frequently in line operations but rarely escalates to breach all of the defenses the airline industry has established to avoid accidents. Pilots may become accustomed to accepting runway changes without thinking about the associated risk factors, and indeed it is often hard to evaluate at the time air traffic control issues the runway change whether it can be made to work safely. The "slam-dunk" approach assigned by ATC put flight 1455 in the position of operating high and fast early in the approach, but not until much later could it be determined to be unworkable. Unfortunately, in the last moments of the approach the crew had become so busy trying to manage the extreme demands of salvaging the approach that their ability to assess whether they would succeed was severely impaired.

The captain pressed the approach on to landing, perhaps unaware of the extent to which the flight's airspeed was excessive; the first officer, though aware that the flight was exceeding stabilized approach parameters, did not challenge the captain's actions. This accident illustrates the way decisions and errors early in a flight sequence often increase the likelihood of subsequent errors, causing a snowballing escalation of problems. The crew's operation of the airplane at high airspeed and descent rates substantially reduced the time available for completing tasks; this in turn increased workload, which probably contributed to dropping of procedural safeguards and which certainly made it far more difficult for the crew to assess their situation.

Monitoring, including procedural callouts, and challenging are crucial procedural safeguards that dropped out in the final stages of this accident. Pilots may tend to neglect monitoring in these highly pressured situations for several reasons. They may regard monitoring as a secondary task, less important than tasks such as operating controls and communicating on the radio. More insidiously, they may not realize that their monitoring habits are weak or have eroded, because everyday lapses in monitoring only occasionally have severe consequences. The first officer of flight 1455 seemed to be uncertain of the role of monitoring and challenging in a situation in which the captain seemed aware of the situation and was attempting to correct extreme deviations. Hesitancy in monitoring and challenging may also stem from the power gradient between captains and first officers and from stabilized approach criteria that are couched as guidelines rather than as absolute bottom lines that must never be violated.

The NTSB safety study of 1994 identified failures of monitoring and challenging as one of the most common problems in airline accidents. The events of flight 1455 suggest that this continues to be a problem. If monitoring is to be effective in catching errors and preventing their escalation, the industry must develop training and procedures to make monitoring more reliable in the face of the operational pressures.

In some respects the performance of this crew, in pressing a landing at such an excessive airspeed on a relatively short runway, might be viewed as so deviant as to be beyond the realm of expected flight crew performance. That is the view implicitly suggested by the NTSB by citing the flight crew's performance as the probable cause of the accident. The company's vice president of flight operations expressed reliance on pilot judgment when he discussed the company's go-around criteria. Indeed, no matter how well an air carrier defines its procedures and limits and how well it inculcates conformance to procedures in its training and line norms, good pilot judgment is always required. However, we suggest it is counterproductive to consider this accident as merely an instance of pilot judgment that was beyond the pale. To help crews counter the pressures that can lead them into conducting approaches whose outcome is uncertain the industry must understand the task factors, cognitive factors, and social/cultural factors contributing to those pressures. In particular, we must ask: what are the norms for crew actions in situations comparable to that of flight 1455? How often do crews within this airline and within the industry attempt to salvage unstabilized approaches rather than going around? This will be discussed further at the end of this chapter and in Chapter 21.

In this chapter we have discussed the lack of a sharp dividing line with salient, unambiguous indicators to discriminate between normal adjustments and risky salvaging maneuvers during approach and landing. Experienced pilots (like other experts) assess risk in specific situations largely by automatic, non-conscious cognitive processes in which the current situation is compared to previous encounters that seem similar (described as "representativeness bias" by Tversky and Kahneman, 1974). In the absence of unambiguous information, pilots may progressively extend their personal tolerance for approach deviations toward less conservative judgments bit-by-bit through repeated exposure to similar-seeming situations in which the outcome (landing) was successful. Most unstabilized approaches can be salvaged without accident (though the margin of safety is compromised unacceptably); indeed if flight 1455 had not been landing on a short runway we probably would not be writing this chapter. The lack of negative outcome, coupled with the intrinsic rewards of not executing a missed approach (on-time performance, cost savings, etc.) may reinforce this insidious move toward less conservative judgment – and pilots may not even be consciously aware that they have become less conservative.

Especially dangerous are situations that in many ways resemble previous encounters but which differ subtly in critical aspects. For example, a pilot accustomed to being able to manage unstabilized approaches might not recognize that the current approach differs from previous unstabilized approaches because of an unusual combination of a tailwind and a short runway. Furthermore, that pilot's previous experience may not have prepared him or her for the rapid deterioration that can occur as changing conditions combine with human cognitive limitations. In contrast, other pilots may on some occasion have had an uncomfortable result from continuing an unstabilized approach, a landing that felt too close to the edge although no accident occurred. These pilots are likely to develop more conservative judgment and behavior. Thus, even though airline pilot training and operating procedures are highly standardized, individual experiences may produce greater diversity of judgment of risk than is desirable.

More uniform judgment of risk in continuing approaches unstabilized at various points along the flightpath might be facilitated if instrumentation were developed to provide cockpit display of aircraft energy state and projected points for touchdown and stopping. However, since this is not currently available, the main line of defense against variability of pilot judgment in the face of ambiguity must be formal procedures that establish explicit conservative limits within which crews can exercise their skill and judgment without entering regions in which judgment cannot be reliable. Stabilized approach criteria are an especially important case of this principle because of the small tolerances for deviation as the airplane approaches the ground and because workload and time constraints are substantial during this period. It is not clear why the crew of flight 1455 did not adhere to the company's stabilized approach criteria, but in this chapter we have suggested several possible factors: lack of hard bottom lines mandating going around, norms (perhaps industry-wide) in which all crews routinely adjust for minor and moderate approach deviations and at least some crews salvage unstabilized approaches, inherent cognitive biases that distort perception of risk, and the time constraints, high workload, and fixation that were largely the result of the unstabilized approach itself. These factors may combine in other flights; thus it is crucial for the industry to insist that stabilized approach criteria be treated as inviolable bottom lines and to provide training and checking to counter the forces that undermine these bottom lines.

Individuals' attitudes towards their organizations are strongly affected by their perception of their organization's culture and its attitude towards safety and error management (Helmreich and Merritt, 1998, Chapter 4). Pilots' stance towards standard operating procedures greatly depends on whether they perceive management and flight operations to truly demand compliance with operating procedures or merely require lip service. Airlines can therefore encourage compliance with stabilized approach criteria by ensuring that operating pressures and practices do not subtly encourage pushing the margins and by providing crews with training on the issues and factors examined in this chapter. For example, pilots' habits and skills are largely organized around continuing an operation rather than asking: "Should we continue?" Pilots have plenty of practice and much success in adjusting for variable demands in their approaches and landings, in coping with small and sometimes rather large deviations, and in occasionally salvaging a bad situation. Questioning whether to continue is less highly practised, and it also requires more effortful and deliberate critical thought. Unfortunately, humans are less able to carry out these effortful thought processes when workload is high. Just when pilots may most need to evaluate their situation critically, they may be the least capable. Most airline training focuses on developing and maintaining pilots' technical skills (for example, performing maneuvers). Line oriented flight training (LOFT), a full-mission simulation in which crews encounter realistic line scenarios, provides one of the few opportunities for crews to practise judgment in realistic situations and receive feedback in an environment that encourages learning. The analysis in this and other chapters points to the benefits of providing LOFT on a recurring basis rather than only during initial and upgrade training.

   This chapter tells the story of one highly unstabilized approach, but it leaves open the question of how often and how far other flights deviate from the ideal approach, at this airport and at other airports, at this airline and at other airlines. As we have mentioned, several similar accidents have occurred previously, but until recently no data have existed to reveal the extent of approach deviations among the thousands of flights that take place daily around the world. Did these accidents occur because of extreme outliers among crews in unstabilized approach situations, or because of random combinations of circumstances in flights that were operating within the actual normal distribution of flight parameters? How many of the thousands of apparently routine flights conducted every day exceed established safety criteria?

   Emerging data collection programs such as flight operations quality assurance (FOQA) and line operations safety audits (LOSAs) reveal that unstabilized approaches do occur with some frequency. A recent NASA study, discussed in Chapter 21, revealed that a far-from-trivial fraction of unstabilized approaches was continued to landing, albeit without accident. FOQA and LOSA programs, along with well-designed research studies, are essential for uncovering the exposure to risk in airline operations and for determining the nature of risks. Other data sources can also help the aviation industry learn about threats arising in routine flight operations, but the following sources have not been fully exploited for this purpose: air traffic control radar data and controllers' reports, pilots' submissions to confidential incident reporting systems, and training performance data.

   When analyzing data about the frequency and distribution of risky events in line operations, it is important to determine why the crews involved deviated from established procedures. The decisions and actions of airline crews reflect pressures (which may be internalized and not fully conscious) of industry operating practices and cultural norms. For example, crews may be reluctant to decline air traffic control instructions, and they are clearly influenced by industry concerns with fuel costs, on-time performance, and passenger satisfaction. The performance of individual crews should be evaluated in the context of company and industry norms and culture. Unfortunately, little hard data on this context is currently available to NTSB investigators, although we hope emerging data collection and analysis programs will change this picture. Given the lack of normative data on unstabilized approaches and given the issues discussed in this chapter, we are hesitant to assume that flight 1455 was a "fluke" accident caused simply by two pilots not representative of their peers.

Notes

1   The actions of lowering the landing gear and extending the flaps increase aerodynamic drag, slow the airplane, and steepen the descent.
2   The actual effect on flight profile of descending in a tailwind is complicated because decreasing tailwind gradients actually increase airspeed during descent.
3   The heads-up display (HUD) installed in all Southwest Airlines B-737s provides enhanced information about airspeed trends, thrust requirements, and the flightpath. However, this equipment was not capable of displaying the runway required to flare for landing (3,000 feet in the case of flight 1455), the touchdown location, or the runway requirements for braking the airplane to a stop into its displays; thus, the HUD would not have provided definitive information about the impending outcome of the approach to the crew of flight 1455. Use of the HUD was optional, according to the airline's standard operating procedures. Although the HUD would have provided additional, salient cues about the flight's airspeed and flightpath deviations during approach, we are unable to ascertain whether these additional cues would have changed the captain's assessment of the situation or his performance. HUD information is not available to the right seat, where first officers sit.

Chapter 6

FedEx 14 – Pilot-Induced Oscillations in the Landing Flare

Introduction

On July 31, 1997, about 0132 eastern daylight time, Federal Express Inc. (FedEx) flight 14, a McDonnell Douglas MD-11, crashed while landing on runway 22R at Newark International Airport in Newark, New Jersey. The scheduled cargo flight originated in Singapore on July 30 with intermediate stops in Penang (Malaysia), Taipei (Taiwan) and Anchorage (Alaska). On board were the captain and first officer, who had taken over the flight in Anchorage for the final leg to Newark, one jumpseat passenger (a pilot for another airline), and two cabin passengers who were non-pilot company employees. All five occupants received minor injuries in the accident. The airplane was destroyed by the impact and a post-crash fire.

The flight from Anchorage was planned to take 5 hours 51 minutes. The airplane was dispatched with the No. 1 (left) engine thrust reverser inoperative, as approved by the FAA for safe operation in the air carrier's minimum equipment list. The captain served as the flying pilot, and the first officer performed the monitoring pilot duties. Flight 14 was routine through the descent into the Newark area.

The captain had 11,000 hours of total flight time and 1,253 hours of experience in the MD-11, of which 318 were as the pilot-in-command. The first officer, though also highly experienced as a pilot, had accumulated only 95 hours of experience in the MD-11, all as the second-in-command and within the 90-day period preceding the accident. The accident occurred approximately 14 hours after the captain awoke and 8 hours after the first officer awoke. The captain reported that, typical of flights of similar duration, he felt tired at the end of flight 14 but that his performance was not affected. The first officer told investigators that he did not feel tired.

The NTSB's investigation of the accident revealed that the captain became concerned about the relatively short length of the runway that he was attempting to land on, and then during the landing flare (level-off) maneuver he applied a series of nose-down, nose-up, and nose-down pitch control inputs combined with roll control inputs that destabilized the flare and caused the airplane to land hard on its right main landing gear. Absorbing the loads transmitted by the landing gear, the right wing failed in overload and the airplane rolled on its back. A fuel-fed fire ignited before the airplane came to a stop beside the runway. The NTSB determined that the probable cause of this accident was "the captain's overcontrol of the airplane during the landing and his failure to execute a go-around from a destabilized flare". The agency also determined that "the captain's concern with touching down early to ensure adequate stopping distance" contributed to the cause of the accident (NTSB, 2000a, p. ix).

Significant events and issues

1. The captain assessed the situation and became concerned about the length of the landing runway

The CVR recorded a conversation between the crew about runway length and stopping performance beginning at about 0103 as the airplane made its initial descent from cruise. The pilots were discussing how to interpret the data about runway 22R at Newark from the onboard airport performance laptop computer (APLC). In fact, both pilots misinterpreted the data provided by the APLC about the runway length required for landing and stopping the airplane. Apparently they compared the APLC-displayed total required landing distance from the threshold with the runway distance that was available beyond the touchdown target instead of the actual length of the entire runway. This led the crew to overestimate by 1,000 to 1,500 feet the runway length required for stopping the airplane. Based on this misinterpretation, the captain predicted that the airplane would use most of the available runway if he followed the most common procedure of selecting the medium autobrake setting. The pilots had already discussed that one of the thrust reversers was inoperative, and also that maintenance records showed the autobrake system might be unreliable. At 0103:59 the captain stated: "We got a lot of stuff going against us here so we'll go … we'll go with max [autobraking]".

It is apparent from these crew conversations during descent and from similar post-accident statements by the captain that the crew's misinterpretation of the APLC data, combined with knowledge of the inoperative thrust reverser and lack of confidence in the autobrake system, caused the captain to be concerned that the planned landing on runway 22R at Newark would require maximum performance from the airplane and crew. As he related to investigators after the accident, in addition to using maximum autobrakes the captain planned to land the airplane near the beginning of the runway (to gain additional stopping distance) and he wanted to ensure that the airplane would not float during the landing flare.

In reality, the runway length was adequate for normal landing and braking procedures, including the effects of the inoperative thrust reverser. We note that overestimating the runway length requirement would naturally bias a crew to be conservative. There was nothing inherently hazardous about the way that the captain of flight 14 planned to handle the landing, and no one would argue that he did not do precisely the right thing in anticipating, briefing, and taking steps to deal with the perceived need to minimize landing distance. By thinking ahead about potential interactions among runway length, thrust reversers, and autobrakes, the captain demonstrated a highly desirable proactive approach, evidence of strong leadership and resource management skills. In this case, though, the captain's concerns established a mind-set about the importance of landing short that, as we will discuss later in this chapter, would affect his subsequent decisions and actions adversely.

The crew's strong leadership and resource management qualities were also demonstrated during this portion of the flight in the extended conversation they carried out as the descent continued. Research has shown that higher-performing crews communicate more frequently and more effectively with each other than do lower-performing crews (Foushee and Manos, 1981). The captain patiently answered questions posed by the first officer about programming the flight automation systems. The first officer commented: "Yeah, I'm just starting to learn ...", which is consistent with his recent assignment to the MD-11 and limited experience in the airplane. The first officer appeared to have appreciated the information that he was receiving. Then at 0112:27 he pointed out the need to change an altitude entry in the flight management system; this indicates that, despite the instructional nature of the remarks by the captain, the first officer was comfortable enough to continue to monitor and challenge. Overall, with the exception of their joint misinterpretation of the landing performance data, the interaction between the captain and first officer during this portion of the flight suggests a high-performing crew.

2. The captain destabilized the landing flare with a nose-down control input

The flight proceeded uneventfully through the final approach and the beginning of the landing flare. At 0132:16, the captain began to flare the airplane as it descended through 38 feet above the runway surface. The airplane's attitude and airspeed were normal at this time, and the flight was in a position to land within the runway touchdown zone. However, as the airplane descended through 17 feet, about 2 seconds before touchdown, the captain made a nose-down input by moving the control column forward. This destabilized the landing flare. The accident investigation report did not specify how much control force the captain used to lower the nose. However, he had already applied column back pressure to begin the flare at 30 feet, so the control input applied at 17 feet may have been no more than the captain relaxing the back pressure he was holding.

In *Know Your MD-11*, a 1993 all-operator letter (NTSB, 2000a, p.39), the aircraft manufacturer recommended the following procedure for flaring the airplane under normal conditions: "Autothrottles will begin to retard after passing 50 feet, and a slight flare should be initiated between 30 and 40 feet (approximately 2 degrees). The aircraft should touch down in the touchdown zone ... Do not hold the aircraft off".[1] The company's MD-11 flight manual provided an amplified discussion of landing technique, stating: "Holding [the] aircraft off to achieve a smooth landing may result in a long touchdown, unusually heavy braking, a higher pitch attitude and reduced tail clearance." The manual also noted:

> Below 10 feet with the aircraft fully flared (sink rate approximately 2–4 [feet per second]), the basic technique is to maintain attitude by applying the required control wheel pressures. A more advanced technique is to relax the back pressure to lower the nose (approximately 1 degree) prior to main gear touchdown (NTSB, 2000a, p. 39).

The NTSB questioned whether the captain may have been using this "advanced technique" when he applied the nose-down input during the flare maneuver. However, based on the greater magnitude of his input and the higher altitude at which he applied it (17 feet instead of 10 feet), the agency concluded that the captain's actions were not consistent with the technique. We suggest, however, that the captain's nose-down control input was consistent with his desire to land the airplane near the beginning of the runway surface, which was motivated by his expressed concerns about runway length and inoperative equipment. This may have been a deliberate attempt to get the airplane on the ground quickly or it may have been a quite unconscious response to his sense of urgency.

The captain's attempt to touch down early may have run foul of a phenomenon experienced by experts in many fields (such as pilots, surgeons, concert pianists, and golfers) when they try to push a highly practised sensory-motor skill to even greater precision. Well-established sensory-motor skills operate in a largely automatic fashion, rather than under direct conscious control. Attempting to refine the sensory-motor skill, the expert may inadvertently revert to direct conscious control, which instead may produce clumsy over-control. (For example: "thinking too hard" about golf putting may spoil the shot, and the same might be true of an experienced pilot's landing – see discussion in Beilock, Carr, MacMahon, and Starkes, 2002).

3. The captain applied large nose-up and nose-down control inputs in a pilot-induced oscillation, and as a result the airplane bounced after its first landing, then hit hard on the second touchdown

By 0132:17, only 1 second after the initial destabilization of the flare and now approximately 1 second prior to touchdown, the airplane had begun to accelerate toward the ground in response to the captain's nose-down control input. The captain and first officer both recalled sensing that the airplane began a high rate of sink at this time. Within this final second before touchdown, the captain responded with a large-magnitude nose-up column input. Simultaneously he applied a large thrust increase. The captain's pitch and power inputs had just begun to have their effects when the airplane touched down. Also, as a byproduct of his power increase, the thrust lever position prevented the airplane's ground spoilers from deploying on landing (this was a safety feature designed to prevent spoiler extension during a go-around attempt). As a result of the captain's control inputs and the failure of the spoilers to deploy, the airplane had more than enough thrust and lift to support continued flight, and it bounced back into the air.

At 0132:18, just as the airplane was touching down, the captain applied nearly full forward (nose-down) control column input. As the airplane (now airborne) reacted to the large nose-down input, it developed a high sink rate and was accelerating rapidly downward when it struck the runway for the second time. The captain made a final, large nose-up input that was too late to soften the impact. The flight was airborne for only 2 seconds between touchdowns.

The NTSB report described the captain's reversals of control input with increasing magnitude in each reversal as a "classic pilot-induced oscillation (PIO)" in which "the captain made each increasingly larger elevator input in an attempt to compensate for the input he had made in the opposite direction about 1 second earlier". The NTSB continued:

> PIO in the pitch axis can occur when pilots make large, rapid control inputs in an attempt to quickly achieve desired pitch attitude changes. The airplane reacts to each large pitch control input, but by the time the pilot recognizes this and removes the input, it is too late to avoid an overshoot of the pilot's pitch target. This, in turn, signals the pilot to reverse and enlarge the control input, and a PIO with increasing divergence may result (NTSB, 2000a, p. 54).

The NTSB recognized the role of an initiating event in the occurrence of a PIO. The agency cited the following from a 1997 National Research Council study of the phenomenon:

> ... many of the reported [PIO] events have taken place during air-to-air refueling operations or approaches and landings, especially if the pilot is concerned about low fuel, adverse weather, emergencies, or other circumstances. Under these conditions, the pilot's involvement in closed-loop control is intense, and rapid response and precise performance ... are necessary. Even so, these operations usually occur routinely without [PIO] problems. [PIO] events do not occur unless there is a transient triggering event that interrupts the already highly demanding ... operations or requires an even higher level of precision. Typical triggers include shifts in the dynamics of the effective aircraft (the combination of the aircraft and the [flight control system]) caused by increases in the amplitude of pilot commands, [flight control system] changes, minor mechanical malfunctions, or severe atmospheric disturbances. Other triggers can stem from mismatches between pilot's expectations and reality (NTSB, 2000a, p. 54; see also NRC, 1997, pp. 3–4).

In the situation of flight 14, the captain's concerns about landing short and his first destabilization of the flare initiated the PIO. The insidious nature of PIO is that pilots' highly learned habits of adjusting pitch to compensate for normal deviations are precisely the wrong thing to do, because these pitch inputs are inherently out of phase in a PIO. Just as the pilot is correcting for deviation in one direction, the deviation reverses direction too quickly for human response. Because the pilot's inputs are out of phase they cause the magnitude of the oscillation to grow, and the pilot automatically responds with larger inputs, which makes the oscillation grow still worse (Hess, 1997). This closed-loop situation gets out of hand because pilots' highly learned sensory-motor responses are automatic – they are not directly controlled consciously. Indeed, as we have suggested, the skills necessary for flaring and landing an airplane have to be automatic because direct conscious control is too slow and too imprecise for this task. (Landing the airplane using a sequence of conscious thoughts would be somewhat analogous to trying to walk by consciously directing your legs to move one at a time.) But this places the pilot experiencing a PIO in a terrible dilemma: neither conscious efforts to rectify the PIO nor the highly learned automatic responses normally used to land the airplane will work.

In the case of flight 14 several factors may have made the oscillations even worse. The captain may have realized that the airplane had bounced back into the air after the first touchdown. If so, then seeing the remaining runway rapidly being consumed may have made him feel an even stronger sense of urgency to get the airplane down and stopped as soon as possible. This feeling may have been further amplified by concern about controlling the pitch-up rate that the airplane experienced just after the first, bounced touchdown. The company had given its pilots formal instruction about avoiding extreme pitch attitudes close to the ground, to prevent striking the airplane's tail on the runway.[2]

It is also possible that the captain did not recognize that the airplane had bounced back into the air after the first touchdown. We note that with the airplane remaining within 5 feet of the runway, the nighttime visual cues that the crew could have seen through the windshield would not have been adequate to determine that the airplane was not still on the ground. If the captain thought that the airplane's main landing gear remained on the ground, his nose-down input might have been meant to hurry the nose gear to the ground so he could begin maximum braking on the perceived short runway. Another factor, if the captain believed that the airplane remained on the ground, may have been a characteristic that the MD-11 has of pitching up after touchdown, caused by ground spoiler deployment.[3] In fact, after the accident, the captain explained that he had applied the nose-down control input in expectation of this characteristic response. However, the captain's nose-down input was much larger than normally used to compensate for spoiler deployment. Thus, although these factors may have contributed, they were probably overshadowed by the inherent nature of PIOs to engender increasingly large control inputs from the flying pilot.

Once a PIO begins, executing a go-around is probably the only safe option. Why did the captain of flight 14 not do this? Several factors make it difficult for pilots in this situation to recognize quickly enough that they should go around. The PIO develops and gets out of hand so quickly – at most a few seconds – that the pilot has little time to recognize and analyze this unexpected and extremely rare situation. The reduced visibility of nighttime operations may further hamper prompt recognition. The pilot automatically responds in the usual manner of making pitch corrections, which only exacerbates the problem, and, as the oscillations grow larger, the pilot becomes fully occupied with attempting to regain control, leaving few mental resources and precious little time to decide to go around.

Even though most airline pilots in a calm discussion on the ground might identify going around as the best response to a landing PIO, quickly retrieving and executing that declarative knowledge in the midst of a PIO is at best difficult. In contrast to highly practised procedural knowledge (such as manual control skills), retrieval of infrequently used declarative knowledge from memory is often slow and effortful. Few pilots have experienced a major PIO when landing an airliner, and recovering from PIOs is not normally part of airline simulation training. If companies' classroom training addresses PIOs at all, it is likely to be a brief discussion. Also, the captain of flight 14 may have been influenced by his airline's standard operating procedures and training at the time of the accident, which left to pilot discretion whether to respond to a bounced landing by continuing the landing or going around. The crew of flight 14 had received the company's special tailstrike awareness training, which included simulator practice in reacting to bounced landings. Pilots receiving this special training were encouraged to practise salvaging the landing attempt and also practised executing a go-around.[4] Although this training may have been valuable, it would not have engendered a fast, automatic response to go around at the first sign of PIO, and it even could have encouraged continued attempts to salvage bounced landings by suggesting that it is realistic to make a split-second decision, after bouncing, on whether to re-land the airplane or to go around.

4. The captain rolled the airplane right-wing-down after the bounced landing, which contributed to overstress of the right main landing gear and structural failure

After the airplane bounced into the air and during its 2-second flight leading up to the final impact, the captain applied right wheel input together with the nose-down column input. This rolled the airplane to the right as it accelerated the airplane toward the ground. As a result, when the airplane touched down it had a sufficiently high roll angle to bottom the right main landing gear strut before the remaining gear could absorb the impact forces. The concentration of impact forces on a single landing gear was great enough to break the right wing.

We cannot ascertain why the captain rolled the airplane to the right. It is normal to land an airplane on only one of the two main gear when correcting for a crosswind. However, the crosswind prevailing at the time of the landing attempt did not require as large a roll correction as the captain applied. The captain's roll inputs may have been inadvertent; in the midst of making excessive pitch and thrust inputs and then correcting for the still worse conditions that resulted, he may have not realized that he rolled the wheel, perhaps as a result of the airplane bouncing or the captain moving his body in making the other control inputs. The captain also may have had an inaccurate perception of the airplane's attitude and relation to the runway while he was performing the landing, especially during the bounce and attempted recovery. We note that during initial approach the captain had noticed that the left landing light (primarily illuminating the runway ahead of his side of the cockpit) was inoperative. Investigators found that other, overlapping aircraft lights would have illuminated the runway surface ahead of the captain. Further, the captain told investigators that the inoperative light did not affect his performance. However, it is possible that the changes to the normal illumination may have subtly degraded the cues that were available to the captain for judging the airplane's attitude during the brief period between the bounced landing and the ultimate impact. It could have been more difficult for the captain to maintain instantaneous and continuous awareness of the airplane's attitude, perhaps leading to the right roll inputs.

Concluding discussion

One of the seeds of this accident was a seemingly minor knowledge deficiency about interpretation of APLC data. This illustrates the way that a small problem may be dormant for some time but can eventually combine with happenstance events to trigger major problems. (After the accident the company revised its APLC training.) Misinterpretation of the APLC data, combined with concern about an inoperative thrust reverser, led the captain to think that he would have to be very careful to touch down early to avoid running out of runway. This concern may have led to over-control that destabilized the flare, which in turn triggered the classic out-of-phase nose up-and-down control movements intrinsic to PIO.

Once a PIO has started, no pilot, no matter how expert, can be expected to salvage the landing reliably; thus, going around is the best option. The NTSB determined that a go-around could have prevented the accident even if it had not been initiated until after the bounce. Unfortunately, many factors make it difficult for pilots to recognize the need to go around and to respond quickly enough while experiencing PIO: the sudden and unexpected way in which the situation falls apart, the failure of normal responses to correct the situation, the mental demands of trying to control the PIO, and the lack of practice in responding to PIO. In addition to these specific factors, pilots may also be influenced by a more general plan continuation bias, which predisposes individuals to continue an original or habitual plan of action even when changes in the situation reduce the viability of the plan.

This accident, the small margin for error inherent in all landings, and the insidious nature of plan continuation bias suggest that a botched flare/touchdown may be more hazardous than previously recognized. The FAA does not require that air carrier pilots receive training in recovery from a botched landing, and most air carriers do not provide simulation practice in recovery. (This air carrier was an exception in including simulator training on the bounced landing recovery as part of its MD-11 tail-strike awareness program). Also, the decision criteria that air carriers provide pilots for choosing between salvaging a landing or executing a go-around are vague; typically, instructions for salvaging a landing are accompanied by a recommendation to go around in the event of an high, hard bounce, but it is not clear at what point a bounce becomes high and hard enough to require going around. We suggest that merely providing pilots with the declarative knowledge to go around "when necessary" will probably not be adequate to produce the desired response quickly and reliably.

However, pilots' ability to respond appropriately to PIO could be improved considerably by training that included substantial classroom analysis and fairly extensive simulator practice in which pilots always executed a go-around at the first sign of PIO. This raises a policy issue about cost–benefit trade-offs, though. It is not clear how many simulator sessions would be required for pilots to learn to recognize PIO quickly and automatically execute go-around procedures; further, PIO is a very non-linear physical phenomenon, and it might be difficult to put the simulator into PIO consistently in a realistic fashion. Landing PIOs are extremely rare because airline procedures and pilots' skills avoid most situations that might set up PIO. Thus the industry would have to consider the relative benefits of PIO training versus other types of training that might be added, the potential effectiveness of PIO training, and the costs of rare PIOs that end in damaged aircraft or injuries.

Another approach to improving training might combine concern with botched landings and PIOs with concern with unstabilized approaches and the broad issue of plan continuation bias, which appeared in at least nine of the 19 accidents in this book. Classroom training could help pilots recognize and understand plan continuation bias in accidents involving problematic decisions to operate in the vicinity of adverse weather, to continue unstabilized approaches, and to attempt to salvage botched landings. Simulation training could give pilots opportunities to practise responding to problematic approach and landing situations by going around. This training would have to be backed up by establishing no-fault go-around policies and by using checking and other procedures to emphasize that going around is the only acceptable option in many situations. Even though this approach cannot completely eliminate vulnerability to PIO accidents, if pursued emphatically it could make pilots more likely to go around when needed in various situations. Although it will probably never be possible to completely eliminate bias toward plan continuation, it should be possible to substantially increase readiness to break off a problematic approach or botched landing, and this would reduce vulnerability to many of the kinds of accidents described in this book.

Notes

1   "Holding off" means to raise the nose slowly and continuously, which cushions touchdown.

2   The company had provided all of its MD-11 pilots with a special tailstrike avoidance training program that included written, classroom, and simulator components. The instructors' guide for the 1996 Tail Strike Awareness Training program (reproduced in NTSB, 2000a, Appendix F) provided the following: "Some tail strikes have occurred as a result of the pilot attempting to arrest a high sink rate or bounce by quickly adding up elevator. This technique immediately increases both the effective weight of the aircraft and the aircraft's vertical velocity. The resulting increased attitude rate will aggravate the pitching tendency after touchdown and drive the main wheels into the ground, thus compressing the main wheel struts. The aft fuselage will contact the runway at approximately 10 degrees pitch attitude with the struts compressed." NTSB noted that the captain's control responses were not consistent with the tailstrike training provided by the airline.

3   The FedEx *MD-11 Flight Manual* (cited in NTSB, 2000a, p. 39) provided the following information to pilots: "Another contributor to tailstrikes during landing is the nose-up pitching force generated by automatic ground spoiler deployment at main gear spin-up." The manual (section 7-118) added: "This is quickly noted and pilots are taught to

compensate for it during initial and transition training. It then becomes part of the MD-11 pilot's reflexes. Spoiler pitch-up is still present during every landing, and must be counteracted. If touchdown does occur with higher than normal pitch attitude, the nose should be lowered promptly to prevent spoiler deployment from further increasing the pitch attitude."

4   The bounced-landing training scenario is described in the FedEx MD-11 Flight Instructor Guide: "Tailstrike Awareness Training, Training Device" (reproduced in NTSB, 2000a, Appendix F).

Chapter 7

Ryan 590 – A Minute Amount of Contamination

Introduction

On Sunday, February 17, 1991 at 0019 eastern standard time, Ryan International Airlines flight 590, a Douglas DC-9-15, crashed while attempting to take off from Cleveland-Hopkins International Airport. The two pilots, who were the only people on board the cargo flight, were fatally injured. The airplane was destroyed in the accident.

Flight 590 had originated in Buffalo, New York just over 2 hours earlier and had traveled through an area of reported moderate turbulence and rime icing before landing in Cleveland at 2344. The flight arrived on time and was scheduled for an on-time departure. Conditions at the Cleveland airport at the time included dry and blowing snow, and the temperature was 23 degrees F (dew point 20 degrees F).

Together, the captain and first officer of flight 590 had flown six successive nights during the week before flight 590, which was to have been the final leg of their pairing. The first officer, who had joined the airline only a month earlier, was the flying pilot for the flight. The two pilots were highly experienced and had flown the -30 series of the DC-9 aircraft prior to their employment at this airline, but neither was very experienced in the -10 series of the DC-9 that was involved in this accident. The captain had accumulated 505 hours of flight time in the -10 series, and the first officer 30 hours.

The NTSB investigation found that the snowy weather conditions on the ground at Cleveland allowed a thin layer of ice to form on the airplane's upper wing surface. During their 35-minute stay on the ground, the flight crew did not request or receive deicing service. The ice contamination remained on the wings as the flight departed and led to a wing stall and loss of control during the attempted takeoff. The stall warning system failed to activate until 1 second after the stall. Once the stall occurred, it was not possible to recover the aircraft before it crashed.

The NTSB determined that the probable cause of this accident was:

> ... the failure of the flight crew to detect and remove ice contamination on the airplane's wings, which was largely a result of a lack of appropriate response by the FAA, Douglas Aircraft Company, and Ryan International Airlines to the known critical effect that a minute amount of contamination has on the stall characteristics of the DC-9 series 10 airplane (NTSB, 1991, p. v).

Significant events and issues

1. Pilots did not leave the cockpit and apparently did not discuss deicing while on the ground in Cleveland

Interviews with ground personnel indicate that neither pilot left the cockpit during the time on the ground in Cleveland. According to the airline's published standard operating procedures that were in effect at the time of the accident, the flight crew were not required to conduct an external inspection of the airplane during a through-stop such as the one preceding the accident flight.[1] After the accident a company manager contended that there was an unwritten "policy" calling for a walkaround inspection between each flight (NTSB, 1991, p. 36). We note, however, that if in fact this did prevail as a company norm, there was no formal method for reliably transmitting it to newly hired pilots.

The CVR recorded 32 minutes of conversation between the captain and first officer, beginning 3 minutes after the inbound flight landed, continuing for the remainder of the period on the ground, and ending with the accident takeoff. Review of the transcript revealed no discussion of the falling snow, ice accumulation, or deicing during this period. We are not able to ascertain whether the crew may have discussed these issues during taxi-in from the preceding flight, a period not captured by the CVR.

An explicit discussion of the prevailing conditions and the reasons that deicing might or might not be needed would have been good practice. If this discussion had occurred, it might conceivably have led the crew to decide to conduct an exterior inspection. However, the weather conditions (cold temperature, dry snow, and strong winds) prevailing at the airport during the flight's time on the ground would not necessarily suggest upper wing ice contamination to a crew observing these conditions, either from inside or outside the aircraft. The crew of flight 590 may have observed that snow was not accumulating on the windshield or nose of the airplane. Although the view from the cockpit would not have been adequate to determine whether the wings were also free of accumulation, the crew may have assumed the lack of accumulation in areas they could see was indicative of the areas out of view.

Unfortunately, what the crew could observe from the cockpit probably did not accurately reflect icing conditions on critical areas of the upper wing surface. The NTSB investigation determined that the wing leading edges may have remained warm from anti-ice bleed air that had been used during the inbound flight's descent in icing conditions. This residual warmth may have melted the snow that fell on the wing while the airplane was on the ground, and this melted snow may have then refrozen as ice when the wing cooled. This information about hazards of melting and refreezing from a wing that is warm from previous anti-ice system usage was developed only during the accident investigation, so it is unlikely that the crew was aware of the phenomenon.

Individuals, including expert pilots, draw heavily on past experience to evaluate current situations. Finding that some indicator, such as accumulation of snow or ice on the nose and windshield, seems to consistently predict the state of some critical variable, such as wing icing, individuals may come to rely on the indicator without realizing the limits of its predictive power. Individual experiences may not cover the full range of possibilities and thus may lead to incomplete and sometimes misleading mental models of prototypical situations. Thus it is crucial that the airline industry provide pilots with complete information and guidance on how to evaluate critical situations such as wing icing.

Even if the crew had conducted an icing inspection, it is not at all clear that they would have detected the ice accumulation on the wings. The airline had provided its crewmembers with a winter operations bulletin on how to conduct an inspection of the airplane for ice contamination but did not mention the wing upper surface as an area to inspect (NTSB, 1991, p. 37). We suggest that the lack of detailed guidance for an upper wing icing inspection was a serious omission on behalf of the airline in implementing Federal regulations mandating a "clean aircraft".[2] Moreover, the NTSB found that it was very difficult to adequately assess the status of ice contamination on the upper wing surface of a DC-9-15 even with a close visual inspection. The amount of contamination that could critically affect the airplane's performance and handling was so slight that the Safety Board concluded: "The only way to ensure that the DC-9 series 10 wing is free from critical contamination is to touch it" (NTSB, 1991, p. 47). Much of the upper wing surface is not visible and cannot be reached from the ground. Neither this nor other air carriers had provided procedures, equipment, or nighttime lighting for tactile examination of the upper wing surface. Thus, even if one of the pilots of flight 590 had inspected the wing from the ramp, he would not have been able to detect a thin but highly hazardous layer of ice or frost.[3]

In addition to the difficulty of accurately assessing ice on its upper wing surfaces, the specific aircraft design (the -10 series of the DC-9) turns out to be particularly vulnerable to icing on these surfaces. The vulnerability is apparently derived from the lack of wing leading edge high-lift devices, slats or flaps that are mounted on the front portion of the wing of many transport aircraft to improve low-speed performance and delay the separation of smooth airflow on an ice-contaminated wing. As the oldest and smallest series of the DC-9, the -10 series aircraft did not have these devices, which were fitted to the -30 and larger DC-9 aircraft when they were designed later. In the period spanning more than 20 years prior to this accident there were at least four other accidents involving loss of control of a DC-9-10 series aircraft with ice contamination on its wings (NTSB, 1991, p. 29). (Other swept-wing jet transports lacking leading edge devices, such as the Fokker 28, are similarly vulnerable; also see Chapter 12.) The industry, particularly the manufacturer of the DC-9, responded to these accidents by issuing a series of information articles, bulletins, and letters to operators of these aircraft, addressed to the training departments. This information made it clear that the DC-9-10 series aircraft was particularly sensitive to ice accumulation thickness of as little as .02 inches with roughness similar to medium grit sandpaper.

The investigation determined that the company operating flight 590 was not necessarily aware of this information. The airline began its DC-9 operations well after the aircraft manufacturer had originally disseminated the information, and the information was not included in the manufacturer's flight and maintenance manuals, which would have been routinely reviewed by a new operator of the aircraft type (NTSB, 1991, p. 45). Consequently, the critical information about DC-9-10 series upper wing icing vulnerability was not included in the airline's flight crew operating manual or in its winter operations bulletin (NTSB, 1991, p. 46). Further, although both pilots had experience with the DC-9 prior to working for this airline, they had flown the -30 series aircraft, which are less susceptible to the effects of upper wing ice contamination because they are equipped with leading edge devices. The pilots' prior experience would not have provided them with the necessary, critical information about the -10 series. In fact, if they had previously operated successfully in ground icing conditions with the -30 series aircraft, this experience may have decreased potential concerns about upper wing icing in the conditions that prevailed on the night of the accident.

Clearly, the crew's failure to deice the airplane's wings can be traced to multiple inadequacies in the information and guidance they were provided. We note that none of the crews of the other air carrier flights preparing for departure during this period requested deicing services, despite the fact that all necessary equipment was available at this airport (NTSB, 1991, p. 46).[4] This suggests that the crew of flight 590 did not behave abnormally, but were operating comparably to other crews in what was apparently the same situation. (The crew of flight 590 did not know that the difference in the design of the wings of their aircraft made their situation substantially different.)

2. The airplane stalled and rolled uncontrollably immediately after takeoff

The preflight and taxi phases of flight proceeded uneventfully. As the designated flying pilot, the first officer applied thrust for takeoff at 0018:25. The captain called out "V1 ... rotate" at 0018:45, followed by "V2" at 0018:48. He continued to call out airspeed as "[V2] plus 10" and then stated "Positive rate [of climb]" at 0018:50. During the next two seconds the captain repeated "Watch out" three times. FDR data and analysis indicated that the first officer allowed the airplane to remain on the ground past the normal takeoff point and then rotated the airplane normally. Climb performance, however, was deficient. Also, immediately after the airplane lifted off, a series of roll oscillations began and continued until the airplane's impact with the ground. The NTSB attributed the deficient climb performance and the uncommanded rolls to an asymmetric wing stall due to ice accretion on the upper wing surface.

The entire sequence of events, from the beginning of rotation to impact with the ground, lasted approximately 10 seconds. The very brief period after liftoff and before the airplane began to roll uncontrollably, some 2–3 seconds, was the only time during which the flight crew might conceivably have been able to save the airplane, and that would have required holding the airplane only a few feet above the surface, in ground effect, to build airspeed. This action would have required split-second recognition that the airplane was stalling and that normal rotation to a nose-high attitude would not allow the airplane to build enough speed to climb adequately and to maintain control. Given the extremity of the situation and such little time to respond, it is unreasonable to expect any pilot to be able to quickly recognize the stall and identify and execute a novel solution to an extremely unusual situation.

Further stacking the decks against the crew's slim chances of identifying and recovering from the stall was the failure of the stall warning system to activate until about a second after the stall began. Aircraft certification standards require that stall warning systems provide warning of an impending stall with an adequate margin of time before the stall begins, but under some circumstances, including wing icing, the airplane may stall at a lower-than-anticipated angle of attack. This may cause the stall warning system not to activate until after the stall has already begun, which was apparently the case for flight 590.[5] The NTSB concluded that the flight's low altitude and degraded aerodynamic performance precluded any chance of recovery once the airplane stalled. The absence of the stall warning, highly associated in training with approaching stalls, reduced the likelihood of the crew quickly recognizing the cause of the roll oscillations, and may even have suggested to the crew some other cause, such as a flight control malfunction. We note that inadequate information from a stall warning system has also been an issue in other icing-related accidents that occurred after this one (see Chapter 12; also NTSB, 1996b; NTSB, 1998a).

Concluding discussion

Certainly, as the NTSB concluded, a proximate cause of this accident was the failure of the crew of flight 590 to find and remove the ice on the upper wing surface of their aircraft. In hindsight this failure was obviously a major error, but this would not have been at all apparent to the crew at the time, given their experience and state of knowledge. They did not know how very critical even a tiny layer of ice would be for their airplane type and series. Although this information existed and was available to many parties in the aviation system, dissemination of this information through the system was inadequate; consequently, it was not in this company's flight operations documents or otherwise made available to the crew. The pilots also did not know that ice conditions on the wing were very difficult to identify, and that commonly used indicators for inferring conditions on the wing could be misleading. Apparently, at the time of this accident, despite the history of previous, related accidents, the aviation system as a whole failed to recognize that the normal methods that airline pilots were trained to use to inspect for wing ice would be inadequate in this situation.

In electing not to deice their aircraft, this accident crew made the same decision apparently made by all the other crews from other airlines facing what seemed to be exactly the same situation that night. Nothing in their past experience in the DC-9-30 or in their company's training and guidance alerted them that differences in the design of the DC-9-10 made their situation, in reality, profoundly different, with fatal consequences.

Notes

1 The company did require Boeing 727 crews to conduct an exterior inspection prior to each flight. The reason for the difference in procedures for the two fleets is not known.
2 Code of Federal Regulations [CFR] (14CFR91), Section 91.209 and CFR (14CFR121), Section 121.629. We note that requirements for pre-takeoff upper wing inspections in icing conditions were strengthened considerably as a result of this, and similar, accidents.
3 Although inspection procedures have been improved since 1991, tactile inspection procedures have not been implemented; therefore, air carrier operations arguably remain susceptible to the hazards of trace accumulations of upper wing icing.
4 The accident investigation report did not provide the number of air carrier operations that were not deiced during this period.
5 Some stall warning system designs provide for a reduction of the threshold for warning activation to a lower angle of attack during icing conditions, reflecting the aerodynamic degradation from the icing, and maintaining the functionality of the warning prior to the actual stall. Designing stall warning systems that are accurate under both normal conditions and a wide range of icing conditions is a substantial technical challenge. Nevertheless, the absence of this crucial warning can have dire consequences.

Chapter 8

Tower 41 – Loss of Control During a Slippery Runway Takeoff

Introduction

On December 20, 1995 at 1136 eastern standard time, Tower Air flight 41, a Boeing 747-100 bound for Miami, departed the side of runway 4L at John F. Kennedy International Airport, New York while taking off in snowy weather and slippery runway conditions. The airplane came to a stop approximately 4,800 feet from the beginning of the runway and 600 feet to the left of the runway centerline in a snow-covered grassy area. It was substantially damaged by contact with rough terrain and concrete structures during the runway excursion, with one engine separating from the wing and the nose landing gear collapsing into the cabin area. Of the 468 persons aboard, 24 passengers sustained minor injuries and one flight attendant sustained serious injuries.

The crewmembers involved in this accident were well experienced in the Boeing 747 and in their respective crew positions of captain and first officer. The captain had accumulated 1,102 hours as a B-747 captain, and the first officer had 4,804 hours as a B-747 second-in-command. Flight 41 was the first that the captain and first officer had operated together. The flight engineer, who was not rated as a commercial pilot, had 2,799 hours of experience as a B-747 engineer. The captain and first officer had both flown with the flight engineer on previous days.

The crew of flight 41 was aware from the weather information provided for them before the flight that airport surface conditions were slippery, with compacted snow on the runways and taxiways and with some runways closed. Weather reports from the time of the accident indicated that surface winds were from the northwest at between 11 and 22 knots. This was a direct crosswind for flights departing on runway 4L, but the runways aligned with the wind were closed at the time of departure. Flight 41 taxied out for takeoff on runway 4L after pushing back from the gate 36 minutes late and then being deiced.

The B-747 can be steered on the ground using the rudder pedals, which are capable of turning the airplane's nosewheel as much as 10 degrees to the left or right of center while also moving the aerodynamic rudder surface on the tail of the airplane, or by using a steering tiller located on both pilots' sidewall panels. The steering tiller, which is designed to deflect the nosewheel as much as 70 degrees to the left or right of center, is required for parking and other maneuvers involving sharp turns conducted at slow speeds. The tiller is routinely used to steer the airplane on taxiways. As is typical for air carrier operations, the captain of flight 41 controlled the airplane during the taxi-out to the departure runway; further, he was the flying pilot for this flight and thus would continue at the flight controls during the takeoff. According to the captain's post-accident statements, he noticed that the nosewheel skidded slightly in taxi turns, and he also recalled that the airplane slipped forward on the taxiway as he applied power to clear any accumulated ice in the engine inlets. At 1132, flight 41 was cleared into position on runway 4L. The captain continued to control the airplane after aligning it with the runway centerline using the nosewheel steering tiller. He centered the tiller as he brought the airplane to a stop on the runway. He noticed that the runway ahead was partially covered with packed snow, with some bare pavement. Snow was blowing horizontally in the crosswind from left to right across the runway as the captain applied thrust for takeoff.

The NTSB accident investigation revealed that a loss of directional control developed rapidly in the early portions of the takeoff roll. The NTSB concluded that that captain was using the nosewheel steering tiller during the period when the loss of control occurred, and that excess steering angles from his tiller inputs caused the nosewheel to lose traction on the slippery runway surface. The agency also concluded that the captain reduced engine thrust, then reapplied thrust during the loss of control. The NTSB determined that the probable cause of the accident was "the captain's failure to reject the takeoff in a timely manner when excessive nosewheel steering tiller inputs resulted in a loss of directional control on a slippery runway". The NTSB found that "inadequate Boeing 747 slippery runway operating procedures developed by Tower Air, Inc., and the Boeing Commercial Airplane Group and the inadequate fidelity of B-747 flight training simulators for slippery runway operations contributed to the cause" of the accident. NTSB further determined that "the captain's reapplication of forward thrust before the airplane departed the left side of the runway contributed to the severity of the runway excursion and damage to the airplane" (NTSB, 1996c, p. vii).

Significant events and issues

1. The airplane veered left during the initial takeoff roll and the captain responded with nosewheel steering tiller inputs

At 1136 the flight was cleared for takeoff. The captain instructed the first officer to hold left wing down and nose-down inputs on the control wheel and column, respectively, to correct for the crosswind and enhance the effectiveness of nosewheel steering. As the airplane began to move forward, prior to the "80 knots call" from the monitoring first officer, the captain felt the airplane moving to the left. He said that he attempted to return the airplane to the centerline but his control inputs had no effect.

The captain's recollection was that his initial attempt to control the leftward veer was with right rudder and nosewheel steering through the rudder pedals. He recalled using the tiller only after finding his rudder pedal inputs to be ineffective. However, engineering simulations of the event led the NTSB to conclude that the captain must have initially applied tiller inputs much earlier than he recalled. The agency concluded that large nosewheel steering angles resulting from the captain's tiller inputs exceeded the critical angle for nosewheel cornering and traction in the existing slippery runway conditions, causing the loss of directional control. After the nosewheel's traction was lost, even greater nosewheel steering inputs would not have had any effect. Further, the NTSB found that rudder pedal inputs would have been effective for controlling the airplane in the existing runway surface and wind conditions because of the aerodynamic yawing moments available from the rudder surface at the speeds achieved by the airplane during the takeoff attempt. Based on these engineering data, the NTSB concluded that the captain relied on the tiller for directional control and did not apply adequate or timely rudder pedal inputs (NTSB, 1996c, p. 42).

The captain's direction for the first officer to apply crosswind corrections to the control wheel was consistent with a company procedure requiring the captain to "guard" the tiller until accelerating through 80 knots. In order to guard the tiller, the captain of flight 41 would have had to remove his left hand from the control wheel; therefore, the captain needed the first officer to apply the required crosswind corrections to the control wheel and column. Also, as a result of this procedure, which had been established for an earlier series of the B-747 that was not equipped with nosewheel steering through the rudder pedals, the captain's left hand was now in a ready position to use the tiller for directional control. We suggest that this airline's procedures may have increased the likelihood that a pilot would attempt to steer with the tiller during takeoff.

The NTSB's investigation found that although the procedures established by both the manufacturer and the airline urged pilots to use rudder pedal inputs for directional control during takeoff, both sets of procedures also allowed use of the tiller at the beginning of the takeoff roll. The company flight manual instructed pilots to "set takeoff thrust slowly and smoothly and correct deviations with immediate steering and/or rudder action and slight differential thrust if required". (Presumably "immediate steering" refers to use of the tiller, as it is the only way to steer the airplane without rudder action.) However, a company flight standards memorandum that was distributed to pilots during the year before the accident instructed pilots to "use rudder pedal steering for takeoff", but continued, "use of the tiller is not recommended unless rudder pedal steering is not sufficient during the early takeoff roll" (NTSB, 1996c, p. 30). Significantly, post-accident simulations showed that it is precisely during the beginning of the takeoff roll that the airplane is most susceptible, in slippery conditions, to overcontrol of nosewheel steering through the tiller (NTSB, 1996c, pp. 43–4). We suggest that procedures permitting use of the tiller during the takeoff roll could increase the likelihood of tiller use and overcontrol.

We note that the company's flight manuals provided information about using small nosewheel angles for optimal cornering and traction on slippery runways, and the B-747's susceptibility to overcontrol through the tiller was discussed in company ground school training programs. However, proper handling could not be demonstrated to pilots during simulator training because the flight simulators did not accurately reproduce the ground handling characteristics of the B-747 in slippery conditions, in particular the loss of traction from increasing nosewheel deflection. Thus pilots did not have an opportunity to practise the proper control inputs and to avoid using the tiller in these situations. The inadequate simulator fidelity may even have provided the accident crew with negative training or instilled false confidence that the airplane would handle better in slippery conditions than it really did. Consequently, even though pilots received relevant classroom training, the combination of classroom and simulation training was not powerful enough to counter the captain's vulnerability to overcontrol.

The captain stated after the accident that he used the tiller on every takeoff, releasing it after the 80-knot callout. The first officer stated that he also routinely used the tiller early in the takeoff roll when he was performing the flying pilot role. Although company flight managers described proper use of the tiller as "guarding" the control until 80 knots (suggesting that the tiller should be monitored but not necessarily used), the chief of flight standards acknowledged that with pilots regularly using the tiller for taxiing there was a "natural tendency" to revert to using the tiller on the runway (NTSB, 1996c, p. 33).

The statements of the captain and first officer of flight 41 and the flight standards manager suggest that a norm may have developed among the company's pilots to use the tiller during the initial takeoff roll. (The investigation did not generate information about the possible extent of such a norm – such data are hard to obtain, especially after an accident.) This was a harmless habit for most takeoffs, because runways are usually bare and dry. In fact this norm probably reinforced itself by providing pilots with better directional control than they could obtain by using only the rudder pedals during almost all of the takeoffs they performed (that is, the numerous takeoffs on non-slippery runways). However, this norm, combined with the airplane's susceptibility to loss of nosewheel cornering and traction at the increased steering angles available by using the tiller, made it highly likely that loss of control would eventually occur when operating in less frequently encountered slippery runway conditions.

We suggest that operating norms such as using the tiller for the initial takeoff roll develop in part because they work well in most conditions, which reinforces continued use (described as "practical drift" by Snook, 2000, Chapter 6). But these norms may have adverse consequences in less frequently encountered conditions (perhaps why they were not approved in formal procedures). These adverse consequences may occur so infrequently that most pilots do not experience them or learn the downside of the norm. Also, although the company operating flight 41 did not intend the tiller to be used routinely for takeoff, the fact that tiller use was not specifically prohibited and indeed was permitted under some circumstances may have made it easier for this norm to develop.

The captain's control reactions to the rapidly occurring events on flight 41 were probably automatic, habitual responses acquired through many successful flights using a combination of tiller and rudder steering. Even if the captain knew in principle that a different technique was required for slippery conditions, it would have been hard to inhibit the habitual response and quickly substitute an unpractised technique. Further, after his first nosewheel control inputs did not stop the airplane's veer to the left, the captain added more tiller and/or pedal steering but when he exceeded the critical nosewheel angle for cornering and traction, additional tiller inputs only made steering performance worse. We suggest that the captain's actions at this time were understandable as a natural human response to add more input when the initial input does not produce an adequate response. This tendency to keep adding to a control input until the vehicle responds can quite easily lead to overcontrol, especially if there is a delayed response by the vehicle to the inputs (Jagacinski, 1977). Steering a B-747 in slippery conditions may be a notable example of this because of the airplane's sluggish response to steering inputs that results from reduced nosewheel traction. Also, gusty crosswinds like those existing at the time of flight 41's takeoff may contribute to overcontrol by producing transient aircraft motions that can temporarily mask or overcome the airplane's response to control inputs. In a situation such as this, when the addition of more control input is not appropriate, it might be possible to help pilots overcome the natural tendency to add more input by providing training in the specific control responses to use in slippery runway operations. To be effective, this training should provide periodic hands-on practice in a flight simulator that can realistically simulate handling characteristics in slippery conditions. The training that this airline provided – a brief reference in the operating manual and limited practice in an unrealistic simulator – fell far short of this ideal.

Company operating procedures specified that takeoff should be rejected if the airplane could not be controlled directionally (NTSB, 1996c, p. 30). However, these directives begged the question of how much time to spend attempting to control the airplane before rejecting the takeoff. The captain apparently allowed no more than several seconds to elapse after the first indications of uncontrolled yaw before reducing thrust for a rejected takeoff, but even this brief delay was too much to prevent a large heading deviation. The information developed during the accident investigation strongly suggests that the critical cue for rejecting the takeoff should be the *first* lack of response by the airplane to a directional control input, rather than loss of control. A more specific criterion for rejecting the takeoff might have helped the captain resist the tendency to increase control inputs and reject the takeoff before the airplane was leaving the runway surface.

The accident investigation revealed that the airport authority had measured the runway friction coefficient approximately 2 hours prior to the accident, just after the runway had been sanded. Contrary to both port authority and air traffic control procedures, this information was not transmitted to the accident flight crew. Runway friction information might have been useful to the crew of flight 41 if it had been transmitted; however, we note that it is very difficult to translate raw runway coefficient friction data into information that is operationally useful. Air crews would be much more able to interpret information couched in terms of specific steering and stopping performance parameters (such as "20 per cent increase in stopping distance") or at least qualitative descriptors that have been validly and reliably associated with friction data (for example, "Slippery with poor steering and braking") rather than as an abstract coefficient (for example, "0.31 in the rollout area"). The failure of the airport authority and air traffic control systems to provide raw friction coefficient data and the inability of the aviation system to translate coefficients into operationally relevant terms deprived the crew of flight 41 of information that might have influenced their decision to attempt to take off and their control actions during the takeoff. If the crew had been explicitly informed that directional control at low speed would be marginal under the existing runway conditions, this accident might not have happened.

2. As the airplane departed the runway surface the captain added engine thrust

From the CVR,[1] the NTSB determined that engine RPM began to decrease shortly after the flight crew started discussing the loss of directional control. These data are consistent with the captain's statement that he rejected the takeoff. However, the CVR also indicates that engine RPM began to increase again approximately two seconds later, about the time that the airplane left the runway surface. Given the inherent lags in turbine engine response, the throttle levers were apparently moved forward just before the airplane veered off of the runway.[2] The NTSB concluded that the captain had re-applied forward thrust, but because the captain did not recall doing this the NTSB was unable to determine why he might have done so. This thrust increase caused the airplane to travel a greater distance across the airport surface after leaving the runway, crossing several taxiways and another runway (all fortunately unoccupied by other aircraft) and approaching a passenger terminal structure. It also increased the severity of damage to the airplane.

At the time that the airplane left the runway surface its rate of heading change was decreasing and the veer to the left was beginning to flatten. This indicated to the NTSB that the airplane was beginning to respond to the captain's rudder inputs. It is possible that the captain thought he could obtain better directional control on the runway with greater airspeed, or perhaps he recognized that the excursion off the pavement was inevitable and was trying to power the airplane back onto the runway surface. Adding thrust may not have been a clearly thought-out decision but rather an impulsive attempt to salvage a rapidly deteriorating situation that the captain had never previously encountered. Although it is obvious in retrospect that adding thrust was not appropriate, we should keep in mind that humans are quite vulnerable to making such impulsive responses under stress and time pressure in situations in which they have not practised the correct actions to the point of automatic response (Stokes and Kite, 1994, Chapter 3).

Concluding discussion

A lack of specific and realistic training, procedures lacking strict definition, and incomplete and misleading information combined to make the captain of flight 41 vulnerable to losing directional control during takeoff. During their classroom training, the crew were given information about the B-747's nosewheel cornering and traction characteristics during early takeoff roll, but they were not provided with realistic simulator experience that might have helped them apply their classroom training about control inputs appropriate to slippery conditions. Written procedural guidance left room for interpretation and was not well phrased to elicit optimal response from crews. This illustrates that writers of written procedures should think very carefully about nuances of wording and should vet the procedures carefully for effectiveness over the full range of operating conditions.

Air traffic control failed to provide the crew with mandatory information about how slippery the runway was, and even if this information had been provided it would have been given in an abstract form difficult for pilots to interpret in terms of implications for steering and braking.

Apparently a norm had developed among this airline's pilots to routinely use the nosewheel steering tiller at the onset of the takeoff roll. Norms such as this develop because they provide some convenience or advantage in typical operations and because their potential danger is not apparent. (In other situations, norms deviating from formal procedures develop as "work-arounds" in response to conditions unanticipated by those procedures or because the procedures are impractical.) This accident illustrates the unanticipated ways in which habits that seem harmless or even advantageous in routine situations pose a latent threat that may cause harm when circumstances combine in just the wrong way. It is important for airlines to monitor systematically for norms developing in line operations that deviate from formal procedures or that otherwise pose hidden risks. LOSA, discussed in Chapter 21, is one tool that can be used to monitor and assess trends in line operations. Periodic audits can reveal undesirable norms and situations in which procedures and training should be modified. Also, pilots will be much more likely to avoid developing habits that deviate from standard procedures if the nature of the threat from specific habits and the rationale for the established procedures are explained explicitly.

On the basis of the preceding analysis we suggest that this accident is best viewed not as a fluke occurrence but as the probabilistic outcome of providing inadequate information and inadequate training to the crew, allowing inappropriate operating norms to develop, and the occurrence of a difficult handling situation.

Notes

1   The FDR installed on flight 41 was malfunctioning at the time of the accident and no useful data were obtained from it. The NTSB's experience with successfully deriving engine RPM values from sound spectrum analysis of CVRs caused investigators to be confident of their findings about the engine RPM changes that occurred at this time in the accident sequence.
2   The captain stated (and wreckage inspection confirmed) that he did not select reverse thrust, so the engine RPM changes detected on the CVR signified increases in forward thrust.

Chapter 9

Continental 1943 – Gear-Up Landing in Houston

Introduction

On February 19, 1996 Continental Airlines flight 1943, a Douglas DC-9 with 82 passengers and 5 crewmembers aboard, landed at Bush Intercontinental Airport in Houston, Texas with the landing gear retracted. The airplane traveled down the runway on its belly and wings, then came to rest in the grass to the left of the paved surface. The lower fuselage was badly damaged, and 15 passengers suffered minor injuries.

The early morning flight from Washington DC was operating on schedule, and it proceeded normally through initial descent into the Houston area. The first officer was the flying pilot and the captain was the monitoring pilot for this operation. While highly experienced, the captain of flight 1943 was relatively new to captaincy at this air carrier and to flying the DC-9. After achieving his initial upgrade to captain on the Boeing 737 and obtaining 119 hours of pilot-in-command experience over a 3-month period, the captain transitioned to the DC-9 in July, 1995 and flew 220 hours as a DC-9 captain during the 7 months prior to the accident. The first officer of flight 1943 was also relatively new to his crew position and aircraft type. Although he had been a flight engineer at the airline for 6 years (4 years of which he was on leave from the airline for service in the US military), at the time of the accident the first officer had only recently completed his first year as a line-qualified first officer, and he had obtained 450 hours of DC-9 second-in-command experience during that year.

The NTSB investigation revealed that during flight 1943's descent the crew did not select the high pressure setting on the airplane's hydraulic control switches, as specified by company procedures. The DC-9 hydraulic system is designed to operate at reduced hydraulic pressure during cruise flight, sufficient to operate the hydraulically powered flight controls and any other en route requirements. However, if the crew does not manually switch back to the high pressure setting before attempting to extend the flaps and landing gear, there will be insufficient hydraulic pressure to extend these devices. At the time of this accident, company procedures required crews to select the high pressure setting as part of the In Range checklist, which was to be performed during initial descent at an altitude of approximately 18,000 feet. With flight 1943's hydraulic system remaining in low pressure status, the flaps and landing gear did not extend when the crew later attempted to extend them (although, consistent with the airplane's design, there was sufficient hydraulic pressure for the leading edge slats to extend). Unaware that the landing gear had not extended, the crew then continued the flight to landing.

The NTSB determined that the probable cause of this accident was "the captain's decision to continue the approach contrary to [company] standard operating procedures that mandate a go-around when an approach is unstabilized below 500 feet or a ground proximity warning system alert continues below 200 feet above field elevation." The NTSB also cited the following factors as contributing to the cause of the accident:

1) the flight crew's failure to properly complete the In Range checklist, which resulted in a lack of hydraulic pressure to lower the landing gear and deploy the flaps;
2) the flight crew's failure to perform the Landing checklist and confirm that the landing gear was extended;
3) the inadequate remedial actions by [the company] to ensure adherence to standard operating procedures; and
4) the [FAA]'s inadequate oversight of [the company] to ensure adherence to standard operating procedures (NTSB, 1997a, p. vi).

Significant events and issues

1. The captain performed the items of the Descent checklist but did not verbalize the checklist

Beginning at 0841:32 (approximately 20 minutes prior to landing), the CVR recorded the captain talking about some of the items on the Descent checklist (see Figure 9.1). The first officer participated in a discussion about the flight's target airspeed for final approach, which was associated with the final item of the checklist, "Landing Data, Bugs". Then, at 0842:00, the first officer asked the captain to perform the Descent checklist. Three seconds later the captain replied, "Fineto", apparently indicating that the checklist was complete.

According to post-accident statements by the company's vice president of training, the standard operating procedure for performing the Descent checklist was a flow-then-check procedure. This called for the monitoring pilot to first accomplish the four items of the checklist from memory. Then, after the flying pilot called for the Descent checklist, the monitoring pilot was supposed to use the corresponding checklist to visually confirm and verbalize the same items. Checklists are printed on a laminated paper card which, according to the vice president of training, was to be consulted when performing the checklist (in other words, the checklists were not to be performed from memory). Checklists are typically performed in a challenge and response format. The US air carrier industry uses the term "challenge" to denote the querying or command statement that, paired with a response, forms one line item of a checklist.[1] The crewmember issuing the challenge and the crewmember making the response are specified in the design of the specific checklist, as part of formal standard operating procedure. In the design of this Descent checklist the company specified that the monitoring pilot (referred to as "PNF", pilot-not-flying, on the printed checklist) – the captain in this case – was required to perform both the challenges and responses.

The crew's statements recorded by the CVR (on flight 1943) suggest that the captain performed the descent items in a flow procedure but that after the first officer called for the Descent checklist the captain did not perform, or at least did not verbalize, the checklist as required. The captain's silent execution (or non-execution) of the Descent checklist was inconsequential in that all of the necessary items were accomplished; however, because the captain did not verbalize the checklist, the first officer was not able to monitor the captain's performance of the checklist. Further, it established a tone of checklist non-compliance that continued, with more consequential results, in subsequent checklists; this tone may have tended to isolate the first officer from participation in later checklists.

DESCENT

PNF Challenge	PNF Respond
Eng Sync	OFF
Ice Protection	ON/OFF
Pressurization	SET
Landing Data, Bugs	CHECKED, SET (C,F)

IN RANGE

PNF Challenge	PNF Respond
Fuel Boost Pumps, Quantity	#_ ON, CHECKED
No Smoke & Seat Belt Signs	ON
Flight Instrument, Altimeters	CHECKED, SET (C,F)
Hydraulics	ON & HI, CHECKED
Shoulder Harness	ON
Approach Briefing	COMPLETE
Sterile Cockpit Light	ON

APPROACH

PNF Challenge	PNF Respond
Altimeters & Bugs	SET (C,F)
VOR/ADF Switches	SET VOR/ADF
Marker Switches	ON/OFF
Radios	TUNED, IDENTIFIED
Course	INBOUND
Mode Selectors	AS REQUIRED
RAT EPR/TRI	GA
Air Conditioning Auto-Shutoff	ARMED
Landing Announcement	COMPLETE

LANDING

PNF Challenge	PNF Respond
Gear	DOWN, 3 GREEN (C,F)
Ignition	OVRD
Spoilers	LIGHT OUT, ARMED
Flaps, Slats	_'_ , EXT
Annunciator Panel	CHECKED

Figure 9.1   Excerpts from DC-9 "Normal Checklist" (NTSB, 1997a, p. 93).

2. The captain omitted the hydraulic system pressure item during the In Range checklist

At 0845:31, as flight 1943 was descending through 19,000 feet, the first officer called for the In Range checklist. According to the company's flight manual for the DC-9, the monitoring pilot was required to perform both the challenges and responses for the seven items comprising this checklist (see Figure 9.1). The third item, "Flight Instruments, Altimeters" was the only item that required a verbal response by both pilots.

There were no sounds (such as verbalizations by the crew or clicks consistent with switch selections) recorded by the CVR during the minutes immediately before and after the first officer's call for the checklist to suggest that the captain performed the items of the In Range checklist as a flow (as specified by company procedures) before he began the actual checklist. Instead, responding to the first officer's initiation of the checklist, the captain called out the first item, specified on the checklist as "Fuel Boost Pumps, Quantity ... # [number of pumps] ON, CHECKED", by saying: "Uh, fuel boost pumps we got. Number 4 is on". He did not state the quantity. The first officer stated: "No", perhaps questioning or correcting the captain's response about the number of pumps that were turned on. The captain continued, "Number, 4 on. Number 1, 1, 2, 3. Whatever that is, they're on and checked." He continued with the second item on the checklist: "No Smoke Seat Belts [signs], On". Next, he questioned: "Flight Instruments and Altimeters?" The captain continued: "Checked set", but the first officer did not reply about his own instruments. We do not know whether the captain was reading from the checklist, as required, or recalling the checklist items from memory, but he did not follow the correct procedure of challenging one item and then responding to just that item before moving to the next item, and he did not appear to wait for the first officer to respond.

The next item on the checklist was setting the hydraulic pumps to high pressure. According to the Continental Airlines DC-9 Flight Manual, this fourth item on the checklist: "Hydraulics – ON and HI, CHECKED", was to be performed by the monitoring pilot as follows:

> Place the Left and Right Engine Hydraulic Pump switches to the HI position and check both HYD Press gauges within 3000 PSI green arc. Check both Hydraulic Fluid Quantity gauges for indication above red line. Place Alternate and Auxiliary Hydraulic Pump switches to ON position. This is to provide an additional source of hydraulic pressure in the event of an engine pump failure. Verify brake pressure gauges are normal (NTSB, 1997a, pp. 35–6).

The captain did not verbalize this item. Based on the subsequent failure of the flaps and landing gear to extend and the position of the hydraulic switches, found set to low pressure after the accident, the NTSB concluded that the captain omitted the hydraulics item of the In Range checklist.

It is not surprising for a pilot occasionally to inadvertently omit an item of a checklist performed thousands of times previously, often several times a day. When individuals perform a simple task in the same way many times the action often becomes automatic, requiring only a minimum of conscious supervision. In the case of tasks consisting of a sequence of several distinct sub-tasks, such as checklist items, completion of each sub-task automatically triggers retrieval of the next sub-task from memory, which is executed in turn, again requiring little conscious thought. This "automaticity" (Shiffrin and Schneider, 1977) has considerable advantages – it is fast and fluid and makes few demands on attention and working memory, which are the bottlenecks of the cognitive processing of information. But automaticity is vulnerable to error under some circumstances. When individuals are interrupted or distracted while performing a task in a largely automatic manner, the interruption disrupts the flow of sub-tasks, preventing one sub-task from cueing execution of the next sub-task. After the interruption or distraction ends, the individual can easily confuse which sub-tasks have been completed and which have not (Cellier and Eyrolle, 1992; Edwards and Gronlund, 1998; Latorella, 1999).

The reasons for this confusion may involve what is termed "source memory" confusion (see Johnson et al., 1993 for a review of this concept). When a task is performed many times in a largely automatic fashion, the individual episodes of execution are typically quite similar, with little to distinguish one from another. Also, without a certain level of conscious processing, little information is encoded in memory about what few details might distinguish episodes. Consequently, after the end of an interruption, individuals often find it difficult to remember exactly at what point they left off and may have to search the environment for evidence of the state of the task (Reason, 1990, pp. 68–73). Further, performing the last sub-task before an interruption may activate memory of the next sub-task to be performed, even though the interruption prevents it from being performed. This activation may create a new memory, and individuals may confuse having thought about performing the next sub-task with actually having performed it. The probability of confusion goes up under time pressure (Adams et al., 1995). These inadvertent omissions can often be avoided if the individual deliberately pauses after an interruption to explicitly examine the physical state of the environment for evidence of the actual state of the task (in situations in which such evidence exists).

The NTSB found no evidence that the captain of flight 1943 was overtly interrupted while executing the In Range checklist; however, interruptions and distractions are common in flight operations (Loukopoulos et al., 2003), and individuals are frequently interrupted by their own chain of thought. Even a momentary diversion of attention by a stray thought could in principle be enough for an individual to confuse whether a procedural step had just been performed if the procedural flow is performed in an automatic rather than in a deliberate manner. NTSB investigators learned from several other DC-9 pilots that they, too, had occasionally omitted restoring the hydraulic system to high pressure at the proper time in the descent. In those instances, fortunately, the crews were able to catch their error later in the flight by noticing that the flaps and landing gear did not extend. (These crews may have noticed that the handling characteristics and sounds of the aircraft were not consistent with extended flaps and landing gear, or they may have noticed the position of the flap indicator or the absence of three green lights indicating landing gear extension.)

Prospective memory is a fairly new area of research in which scientists are investigating the cognitive mechanisms involved in attempting to remember to perform intended actions that must be deferred (Brandimonte, Einstein, and McDaniel, 1996). Dismukes and Nowinski (2006) recently reviewed a wide range of incidents in which pilots forgot to perform intended actions, and these authors speculate on the cognitive processes underlying pilots' vulnerability to prospective memory errors in various situations.

In its analysis of this accident, the NTSB expressed concern that:

> The normal in-flight operating procedure for the DC-9 hydraulic system deactivates ... hydraulic components, including the landing gear and the flaps, without providing an overt signal to the flight crew of the non-functional status of those components ... If the hydraulic system is not configured properly during performance of the In Range checklist, the error can initially only be determined by direct observation of the hydraulic pump switches and pressure gauges (NTSB, 1997a, p. 40).

The reports from other DC-9 crewmembers suggest that forgetting to switch the hydraulics pumps to the high position was not a rare occurrence; thus, these errors were rooted in inadequate design of the cockpit interface. And what distinguished flight 1943 from other DC-9 flights was not this inadvertent omission but the failure of the crew to catch the error before landing gear-up. The NTSB observed that the air carrier's procedures did not require both pilots to check the hydraulic switch position, which would provide an additional opportunity for one crewmember to catch the omission of this important action by another crewmember.

After skipping the hydraulics item of the In Range checklist, the captain continued with the next item: "Shoulder Harness On", and the first officer responded to this challenge with: "On" (although this acknowledgement was not required by the checklist). Apparently the first officer did not notice the omission of the hydraulics item, for he said nothing about it. Air carriers typically specify that, for a 2-person crew, both pilots are supposed to cross-check and verify the correct performance of all checklist items (for example, this airline's DC-9 flight manual "Use of Checklists" section stated: "Both pilots are responsible for visual confirmation that all checklist items are completed") (NTSB, 1997a, p. 35). However, for several reasons it is not surprising the first officer did not notice this omission. When the captain verbalized a checklist item, the first officer, if he was carefully monitoring execution of the checklist, would be prompted to check the status of that item. But because the first officer was not reading the checklist himself, the captain's failure to verbalize the hydraulics challenge removed the prompt that would normally trigger the first officer to think about that item. Retrieval of information (for example, that a particular item occurs on a checklist after another particular item) depends heavily on the individual perceiving some cue in the environment (such as hearing the challenge for a checklist item) that is directly related to the information to be retrieved from memory (Koriat, 2000). Thus humans are vulnerable to not retrieving information when normal cues are absent. This is an inherent weakness in the checklist procedure – although having the flying pilot confirm the monitoring pilot's execution of checklist items is meant to catch errors by the monitoring pilot, and often does catch some types of errors (such as mis-setting altimeters), it is likely to fail if the monitoring pilot inadvertently omits the challenge for an item.

Another weakness in the system of having the flying pilot monitor the monitoring pilot's execution of checklist items is that the flying pilot is often busy with flying duties and thus must switch attention back and forth between those duties and confirming execution of checklist items. In this situation it is easy to miss a checklist item while attending some aspect of flying duties because attention is a narrow bandwidth channel that generally limits processing to one event at a time (Broadbent, 1958). Further, because the flying pilot is not required to make any response to the checklist challenges unless an item is performed incorrectly, it is hard for the flying pilot to develop and maintain a habit of deliberately attending each item and fully processing the status of that item consciously. It is easier to establish this habit if the flying pilot must make an overt response (a verbal utterance, and/or pointing to or touching the item checked[2]) to the challenge for each item, and if the flying pilot does not have to divide attention with flying duties. Some checklists do require both pilots to respond overtly to at least some of the challenges and to confirm execution of these items, but in many in-flight situations these measures are not practical. No easy solution exists for this dilemma, but it is important to recognize the vulnerabilities of checklist procedures and to recognize that the flying pilot cannot be completely reliable in monitoring execution of checklists.

The company's procedural designers had attempted to provide some redundancy for the In Range checklist by requiring that the items be accomplished first by memory (flow) and then re-checked using the written checklist (Degani and Wiener, 1993). ("Redundancy" is used here in the positive sense of providing a backup if a primary system or process fails.) We note that if the captain of flight 1943 performed the In Range checklist without first performing the flow procedure, as the CVR evidence seems to suggest, he removed the protection provided by this type of redundancy.

Although the airline's vice president of training stated that the company used flow-then-check procedures and the captain may have employed this method for the Descent checklist, it is not clear from the NTSB investigation to what degree the airline had incorporated flow-then-check procedures into its training programs or its norms for line operations. From a line pilot's point of view, the flow-then-check method may seem an inefficient use of time and effort because of its repetitiveness. Thus, it is natural for flows and other intended redundant elements to be dropped out of line operations unless they are rigorously trained and checked. Even when pilots practise the flow-then-check procedure regularly in their daily flying, the quality of execution is vulnerable to deterioration. Considerable effort is required for an individual to deliberately and consciously check the status of an item the individual set only seconds before, perhaps in part because the item is expected to be in the status in which it was thought to be set, and this expectation can bias perception of the actual state of the item. Also, when flows and checklists have been executed many times performance becomes quite automatic, the tempo of execution speeds up, and – for reasons not well understood – individuals find it difficult to slow down a process that has become automatic and to deliberately think about each step of the process (Beilock, Carr, MacMahon, and Starkes, 2002). Thus, procedures requiring pilots to check their own work may in practice provide less redundancy and less reliable error detection than intended. This shortcoming is exacerbated in high workload situations.

After the first officer's response to the captain's challenge about shoulder harnesses, the captain continued the In Range checklist with the challenge: "Approach briefing?" This was a prompt for the first officer to brief the captain on any particulars of the approach not already discussed during the cruise phase of flight. If this briefing had been completed earlier in the flight, at a time not captured by the CVR, the proper response by the captain would have been: "Complete". The captain made no audible response to the approach briefing challenge; without providing time for the first officer to respond, the captain interjected comments about the last item on the checklist: "Sterile Cockpit Light". (The captain's subsequent comments, referring to an earlier version of the checklist and mentioning the changed location of this item on the current checklist, suggest that he was looking at the printed checklist card at that time.) Further, the captain did not call: "In Range checklist complete", as required by company procedures (NTSB, 1997a, p. 35). Later, beginning at 0852:35, the first officer conducted an approach briefing.

This crew's non-standard performance of the In Range checklist and the other checklists of the descent and landing sequence was consistent with a norm of non-standard checklist execution that apparently had developed at this airline prior to the accident. Omitting checklist items and entire checklists, and performing other procedures in a non-standard manner had been noted in two other accidents involving company flights in a 28-month period immediately preceding the accident of flight 1943.[3] After these earlier accidents, the FAA found evidence of poor checklist discipline and compliance during a special inspection of the airline in 1994. In response to these findings, the company strengthened its emphasis on checklist compliance, and a later focused surveillance program by the FAA did not reveal any further systemic deficiencies with procedural compliance at the airline.

After the flight 1943 accident, the company undertook its own internal quality assurance review of line operations and identified several checklist-related deficiencies, including performance of checklists from memory rather than using the checklist card, improper initiation of checklists, and failure to complete checklists after interruptions. Further, the NTSB investigation of this accident found evidence of several norms in flight operations that deviated from established procedures. In its analysis of these deviations, the NTSB concluded that prior to this accident the airline was aware of "inconsistencies in flight crew adherence to standard operating procedures" (NTSB, 1997a, p. 51), that the company had attempted to resolve the identified problems, but that these efforts (and FAA oversight of them) were ineffective until after additional measures were taken as a result of this accident. It seems likely that the norms for relaxed checklist compliance and discipline existing at the time of this accident may have contributed to this crew's deviations from standard procedures.

3. Crew did not notice failure of the flaps to extend

At 0859:00 the first officer asked the captain to extend the wing leading edge slats and to extend the wing trailing edge flaps to 5 degrees. The captain moved the flap control handle through the slats-extend position to the 5 degrees of flaps position, which should have extended both the leading edge slats and trailing edge flaps. The flaps did not extend, however, because of insufficient hydraulic pressure. The leading edge slats extended normally, which created cues (an audible rumble and an illumination of a blue indicator light on the forward panel) that the crew would have associated with normal aircraft responses to moving the flap handle to the slats extend/5 degrees of flaps position.

Neither the captain nor the first officer noticed the failure of the trailing edge flaps to extend at this time, although cues were available that could have alerted the crew to this failure: the flap indicator remained at 0 degrees, the pitch and drag changes normally associated with flap extension were absent, and the "Master Caution" and "Hyd Press Low" annunciator lights may have illuminated, though only momentarily.[4]

Several factors mitigated against recognizing the flap extension failure at this time. Most flight crews are not trained to monitor and verify each intermediate flap extension; this company's Landing checklist required crews to verify only the final flap position. Also, the NTSB found that on the DC-9 the difference in flap indicator needle positions for flap settings of 0 through 5 degrees is not highly salient. Further, DC-9 pilots reported that the pitch and drag changes from extending the slats and flaps to 5 degrees are not great. The pitch and drag changes that would have occurred with only the slats extended were not distinctly different from the changes elicited by extension of both the slats and the flaps to 5 degrees, which the crew expected. Thus, it is not surprising that neither pilot of flight 1943 noticed at this time that the flaps did not extend.

The CVR indicates that both before and after moving the flap handle to the 5-degree position, the captain was devoting some of his attention to a non-operational conversation, which may have distracted both pilots to some degree. At 0858:48, immediately before the first officer made his request for slat and flap extension, the captain stated: "Aw shoot. I can't play tennis when it's like this … Well maybe this afternoon it'll clear up … Actually I've still got a lot of time." After moving the flap handle, the captain stated: "Slats are going to 5", and then, after 10 seconds had elapsed, continued to discuss the weather's effects on his afternoon plans. The NTSB suggested that the captain may have been attending to the scene outside the cockpit, looking at the clouds and the ground, rather than at the cockpit flap indicators and warning lights (NTSB, 1997a, p. 42). This is quite possible, and the captain's conversation conceivably may have further reduced the likelihood of the crew detecting the flap extension failure at this time.

The FAA's sterile cockpit rule (CFR (14CFR121), Section 121.542) prohibits non-essential conversation below 10,000 feet (which flight 1943 was at this time); however, when workload is low pilots may find it hard to resist the temptation to fill in gaps between tasks with idle comments. Indeed an argument can be made that conversation helps maintain alertness. We do not know to what extent the captain's non-essential comments were typical or atypical of other pilots in this situation. Norms may in fact vary widely. CVRs from accident flights not infrequently reveal non-essential conversation below 10,000 feet, but CVRs are not available from non-accident flights (by regulation); thus it is hard to assess how much of a role non-essential conversation might play in creating distractions.

The sterile cockpit rule, which is a conservative measure to reduce distraction from cockpit duties, is vulnerable to compromise because conversation during gaps between tasks may seem harmless to pilots if workload is low. However, pilots may not realize that even light conversation makes substantial cognitive demands and that even momentary diversions of attention may reduce chances of noticing important cues, especially if those cues are not salient (Dismukes et al., 1998). Thus, pilots may unwittingly sacrifice a layer of protection. Rigorous adherence to the sterile cockpit rule may require better education about the distracting effects of conversation. Also, it may be useful to examine whether it is practical or efficacious to require strict adherence to this rule under all low workload situations. For example, it would be hard for a crew to remain totally silent after all tasks have been completed during a long delay waiting in line for departure. Yet crews must be aware of the need to bound conversation so that it does not absorb attention excessively, and to maintain monitoring even in low workload situations.

4. The crew became confused about the flaps not extending and did not perform the Landing checklist

Passing the final approach fix, the first officer asked the captain to extend the flaps to 15 degrees. Shortly thereafter (at 0900:33) the captain stated: "I think the flaps [unintelligible]", apparently noting a discrepancy in the flap extension.[5] Then, over the next 27 seconds, the first officer called for the flaps to be extended progressively to 25, 40, and 50 degrees, apparently unaware that the flaps were not extending or perhaps hoping that additional movement of the flap handle would cause the flaps to extend. During this period, at 0900:35, the CVR recorded three intermittent sounds from the landing gear warning horn. The captain later recalled that he produced those sounds by making rapid throttle movements. After causing the gear warning horn to sound he stated to the first officer: "We know that, you want the gear". Finally, at 0901:00, the first officer stated: "I don't have any flaps".

During this period, the captain continued to set increasing amounts of flap deflection in response to the first officer's calls. The captain may have been confused about the situation, recognizing that something was abnormal but neither drawing together the fragments of information he was perceiving, nor effectively seeking additional information to resolve his confusion. The captain's apparent intentional activation of the landing gear warning horn with throttle movements, which the first officer recalled as having been confusing to him at the time, may have been an attempt by the captain to analyze the situation. If so, it was an ineffective analysis because the throttle test pertained only to landing gear position and did not test for proper flap extension. According to the crew's post-accident recollections, the first officer had by this time pointed to the flap indicator at 0 degrees extension, and the captain had responded by confirming the position of the flap handle. The first officer's clear statement at 0901:00 that the flaps had not extended indicates that he now recognized the problem.

At 0900:38, during this period of confusion about the flaps the first officer called for the landing gear to be extended and for the captain to perform the Landing checklist. At this time flight 1943 was slightly more than 1,000 feet above the ground; at its airspeed of greater than 200 knots, the flight was approximately 1 minute from touchdown. According to the company's DC-9 flight manual, the monitoring pilot was to perform the challenge and response for the five items on the checklist; additionally, both pilots were required to respond to the "gear" challenge (the first item) by verifying that three green lights were illuminated on the forward instrument panel, which would signify that the landing gear were locked in the extended position (NTSB, 1997a, p. 36). CVR information and the recollections of the flight 1943 crewmembers indicate that, after the first officer requested landing gear extension and the Landing checklist, the captain placed the landing gear lever in the down position, but he did not perform the checklist. The first officer did not challenge the captain's failure to perform the checklist, and omission of the checklist removed the challenge that would have prompted both pilots to verify the gear position, as required. Around this time, the landing gear warning horn began to sound again and continued (except for a brief interruption) through the time of impact. Apparently neither pilot reacted to the landing gear warning horn with any action or comment.

Several factors may have contributed to the captain's failure to perform the Landing checklist. Both pilots commented during this period about difficulty in slowing the airplane down. Speed remained high because the retracted flaps and landing gear did not produce the drag normally used to decelerate the airplane to approach speeds. The excessive speed and lack of deceleration were cues that might have alerted the crew to the nature of their problem; however, the excessive speed was causing all of the events during the flight's final approach to happen much faster than normal, which increased the crew's workload. During the final 1,000 feet of the descent, the airplane was traveling more than 70 knots faster than the normal approach speed of 135 knots, which reduced the duration of the final approach from 115 seconds to less than 75 seconds. This left less time than usual to perform the normal landing preparation procedures and allowed little time to think about and analyze whatever was causing the abnormality of their situation.

A few seconds after calling for the checklist the first officer called for flaps 40 and then flaps 50, and the NTSB speculated that these calls may have interrupted the captain just as he would have initiated the checklist. Also at this time the landing gear warning horn started sounding, which would have been a major distraction.

Further, by this time the crew was under high workload because of the abnormally rapid approach and were probably preoccupied with concern about the flap situation. The combination of all these factors probably disrupted the captain's habit pattern of performing the Landing checklist immediately after lowering the landing gear. Also, the situation by this time was inherently stressful, and stress is known to narrow the focus of attention and to impair cognitive processing (Stokes and Kite, 1994, Chapter 3).

It is not surprising that under these circumstances the first officer failed to notice the omission of the Landing checklist. In addition to the effects of stress and workload to which he was subject at this time, it is generally difficult for any flying pilot to monitor initiation and execution of checklists, for reasons discussed earlier in this chapter. Regarding the first officer's failure to verify gear position as required by the Landing checklist, we note that the captain's omission of the entire checklist removed the normal trigger (the "gear" challenge) that would normally prompt the flying pilot to perform this verification. Required actions that are anchored to specific triggers are inherently vulnerable to omission when the normal trigger is unexpectedly absent, as previously discussed. Procedural designers should consider this inherent vulnerability when evaluating the reliability of redundant measures such as having one pilot verify the actions of the other.

The DC-9 is equipped with a landing gear warning horn designed to provide pilots with very salient cues if the landing gear is not extended for landing. This horn functioned as designed, sounding loudly and repetitively during the last portions of flight 1943's approach. When interviewed after the accident, the captain of flight 1943 attributed his failure to respond to the landing gear warning horn to the routine activation of the horn on many other flights when the flaps were extended to 25 degrees before the landing gear had completed its extension cycle. (The extension cycle takes about 15 seconds. The pace of line operations often leads crews to select flaps 25 before the gear extends completely.) Given this somewhat routine activation of the warning horn, the true signal of an unsafe gear status following extension was *continuation* of the horn beyond an initial period. Pilots presumably habituate to initiation of the warning and may not develop a criterion and monitor for how long the horn must continue before truly indicating a problem with gear extension. Also, the DC-9 landing gear horn routinely activates whenever the throttles are brought to idle with the gear retracted, a frequent occurrence during descent. For both reasons, the landing gear warning horn may lose some of its effectiveness as a compelling alert (Degani, 2003, Chapter 13).

The crew of flight 1943 may also have failed to react to the continuing horn for the same reasons they did not verify that the landing gear was extended: high workload, time pressure, stress, and preoccupation with trying to analyze what was going wrong. Further, the loud, continuous noise of the horn may itself have added to the crew's stress and distraction. Highly salient auditory and visual warning alerts are a double-edged sword. High saliency is necessary to attract the attention of a busy crew, but this saliency also makes it extremely difficult for a pilot to process any other information (Stanton, Booth, Stammers, 1992; Staal, 2004, pp. 88–92). Designers of equipment and procedures must consider this trade-off carefully. Generally, it is desirable to either provide the crew with a way to shut off a warning (which has attendant risks) or to mandate a conservative response, such as immediately executing a go-around, that can be practised to the point of becoming automatic. Every effort should be made in the design of equipment and procedures to minimize nuisance alarms (Bliss, Freeland, and Millard, 1999; Bliss and Dunn, 2000).

5. Captain overrode the first officer's challenge to go around and decided to continue the approach, taking control of the airplane less than 200 feet above the ground

At 0901:02 the first officer asked the captain whether they should execute a missed approach, stating: "Want to take it around?" The captain replied: "No that's alright, [unintelligible] keep your speed up here about uh". The first officer said: "I can't slow it down here now". The captain stated: "You're alright", but the first officer continued: "… We're just smokin' in here". At 0901:13 the ground proximity warning system (GPWS) activated, with its repetitive "whoop, whoop, pull up" alert, after which the first officer asked the captain: "Want to land it?" With the statement, "Yeah", the captain accepted control of the aircraft. At 0901:20, approximately 12 seconds prior to landing, the first officer stated: "Your airplane, Captain's airplane". The next sounds recorded by the CVR were those of impact, as the airplane touched down with the landing gear retracted.

What was the crew's understanding of their situation during the last minute of the flight? The first officer seemed to understand fairly clearly that the flaps were not extended. After the accident the captain insisted to the NTSB that he thought the flaps were extended, however the NTSB concluded from the captain's comments on the CVR (such as the ones about keeping the speed up) that he did in fact recognize that the flaps were not extended. But just as clearly, neither pilot recognized that the underlying problem was that the hydraulic system was set to low pressure or understood that the landing gear was not extended (no pilot would land gear-up intentionally). The NTSB investigation revealed that many DC-9 pilots were not trained or knowledgeable about the global effects of failing to switch hydraulic pressure to high on flap extension and gear extension. The DC-9 pilots most likely to be aware of the consequences of failing to switch hydraulic pressure to high were those who reported having made this mistake themselves at some point (though fortunately they caught their mistakes).

Assuming the pilots of flight 1943 had not overlooked setting the hydraulic pressure on some previous flight, we suspect they may have interpreted their problem as a flap extension malfunction, which pilots refer to as a "flap abnormal". Initial and recurrent simulator training provides pilots experience in dealing with flap abnormals, which include failures to extend and retract, partial extension, and asymmetric extension of the flaps. These malfunctions can result from various underlying causes, including electrical problems and mechanical faults with linkages, tracks, and rollers in the flap system, so the occurrence of a flap abnormal does not necessarily imply an underlying problem with the hydraulic system. The first indication of the problem with flight 1943 was the failure of the flaps to extend. The training the crew had received about flap abnormals may have biased them to limit their thinking about their situation to issues with flap extension, and with this mind-set they did not pursue other interpretations.

It is not unusual for experts to react quickly to cues and adopt a response without analysis (a "pop-out" solution). Usually these decisions are made efficiently and correctly, and the tendency to rely on these pop-out solutions is powerfully reinforced by success. Unfortunately, experts can err if their prior experience does not include substantial exposure to conditions matching the current situation but does include experience superficially resembling the current situation. (A partial countermeasure to this particular vulnerability of expert decision-makers might be to caution them about the danger of misdiagnosis from superficial resemblance when operating under time pressure.)

In general, when confronted with a problem, individuals are prone to settle on an explanation that seems consistent with their previous experience (described as "recognition primed decision-making" by Klein, 1997), and once this explanation occurs to them they unwittingly become less likely to notice or correctly interpret cues conflicting with the explanation and more likely to seek information consistent with it. This phenomenon, called confirmation bias, has been observed in diverse settings; for example, among pilots, nuclear power plant operators, military intelligence analysts, and naval radar officers (see Wickens and Hollands, 2000, pp. 312–13 for a review).

The GPWS installed on flight 1943 was an older model that emitted a generic "whoop, whoop, pull up" warning in response to several different types of threatening situations, in contrast to later models that emit a more descriptive warning specific to the particular situation, such as "Too low, flaps" or "Too low, gear". The mind-set of the crew may have been so strong that they interpreted the generic GPWS warning as being related to the high descent rate of their fast approach with retracted flaps; in this way, the GPWS warning would have seemed consistent with the crew's concept of the situation. Conceivably this mind-set might even have biased them to misinterpret the gear warning horn, if they remembered that it has an association with flaps but were too overwhelmed to identify the association correctly. (The gear warning sounds if flaps are extended to landing settings while the gear is up.) Regardless, it is apparent that the crew was at this point so overloaded and confused that they could not think through their situation clearly. Time pressure and workload during the last minute of flight would have made any attempt to gain additional information about the status of the airplane, analyze the problem systematically, or discuss alternative explanations extremely difficult, even if the crew had been so inclined. By this time, going around was the only option that would have given the crew an opportunity to correctly diagnose their situation.

The first officer's statements ("I don't have any flaps" ... Want to take it around? ... I can't slow it down here ... We're just smokin' in here ... Want to land it?") reveal that he was highly uncomfortable with the operation during the last stages of the approach. His discomfort may have resulted from the rapid closure with the runway, his limited experience with no-flap landings, the crew's lack of preparation to make a no-flap landing, the warning horns, his confusion over why the flaps had not extended, and general uncertainty surrounding the entire maneuver. The first officer's comments constituted an appropriate challenge to the captain to re-evaluate the plan to land and to consider going around, which would have been the most appropriate response to the situation.

Why did the captain disregard the first officer's challenges and continue the approach? The reasons are far from clear. The captain may have felt that he grasped the situation correctly as a simple failure of flaps to extend, and that with a very long runway ahead of them he could land safely by keeping speed high. Or if he truly thought the flaps were extended, as he later asserted, then the airplane would have seemed configured to land, although in this interpretation it is far from clear what he thought of the warning horns or why he told the first officer to keep the speed up. But in either case it is abundantly clear in hindsight that the decision to continue the approach was inappropriate. If the flaps were not extended the only appropriate course was to execute a missed approach, verify the problem, and execute the appropriate checklists before setting up a new approach. If the flaps were extended, the confusion, high workload, warning horns, and the first officer's concerned statements were also compelling reasons to execute a missed approach. So why would a highly experienced captain, with no record of reckless disregard of safety, have disregarded all these concerns and continued to a landing?

Several factors may have influenced the captain's actions. By the time of the first officer's challenge to go around, both pilots were in a high workload, time-pressured, stressful situation, full of confusing cues and loud, distracting warning horns. (In another context similar situations have been described as the "fog of war" (Ryan, 1959.) In these situations, human ability to think clearly is often badly impaired and quite unreliable. Particularly insidious is that when individuals are overloaded, their ability to evaluate how well they can deal with their workload and to develop coping strategies is greatly diminished (Staal, 2004, pp. 81–4). One common but undesirable way of responding to the overload and confusion of these situations is to abandon effortful deliberate analysis in favor of simply reacting to events with highly learned automatic responses – in this case continuing the process of landing.

The NTSB suggested that fatigue may have played a role in the crew's thought processes, decisions, and actions throughout this approach. The captain did not have a restful sleep on the night before the accident, reporting that he was awakened several times in the night by traffic and hotel noise before awakening at 0500. Interviewed after the accident, the captain stated that he was tired on the day of the accident and that the wake-up call was especially early because of the change in time zones – his body was adjusted to central time, one hour earlier. The captain did not attribute his performance to the effects of fatigue; however, self-evaluations of the effects of fatigue on performance have been shown to be unreliable (Rosekind et al., 2001). The first officer was upset about his overnight bag being lost on the night before the accident and reported obtaining only five to six hours of interrupted sleep that night. In his post-accident interviews, the first officer stated that he was tired on the morning of the accident and fatigue affected his decisions at the end of the flight. During the approach, the CVR recorded the captain making an apparent reference to both crewmembers' fatigue: "You've been up all night too".

Citing previous transportation accidents in which fatigue affected crew performance, the NTSB stated that:

> There is evidence that obtaining two hours less sleep than normally is required by an individual [this was the sleep status of the crew of flight 1943] can degrade alertness and performance … fatigue can interfere with an individual's capability to deal with rapidly changing events and to direct and sustain attention, and can lead to the tendency to fixate (NTSB, 1997a, p. 50).

This crew's misinterpretation of the nature of the system problem, procedural omissions, ineffective diagnostic efforts, and persisting in the approach were all consistent with fatigue's effects. However, lacking specific evidence linking fatigue to this crew's performance, the NTSB concluded that "there is insufficient information to determine the extent to which it contributed to the accident" (NTSB, 1997a, p. 50).

It is difficult to isolate the performance effects of fatigue, in part because fatigue interacts with other factors affecting performance. In the case of flight 1943, fatigue, high workload, stress, and confusion may have combined in the later stages of the approach to increase the crew's vulnerability to several forms of error, including plan continuation bias. This bias makes individuals prone to continue an original or habitual plan of action even when conditions shift to make the plan problematic. This shows up dramatically in the phenomenon pilots call "get-there-itis".

Was the first officer sufficiently assertive in challenging the captain's decision to continue the approach? Challenges of another crewmember's actions or decisions can range from mild (purely informational or tentative suggestions) through strong (advocating a specific change of action, expressing concern for safety), to directly confrontational (Fischer and Orasanu, 2000). The first officer's explicit query about a missed approach at 0901:02 was a fairly effective challenge in that it got the captain's attention and prompted him to make an explicit decision. After the captain voiced his decision to continue the approach, the first officer several times expressed discomfort about the excessive airspeed – these were milder challenges. His final utterance was to ask the captain to if he wanted to take over the flying pilot duties. This may have been a form of challenge to continuing the approach, or it may have indicated the first officer's resignation from challenging.

We know from the investigation record that events in the first officer's work history at the airline had made him very cautious about challenging captains. In 1994, while serving as a flight engineer, the first officer had been the subject of a complaint by a captain about cockpit behavior. The first officer was interviewed by his chief pilot and underwent a "fitness for duty" examination by a clinical psychologist. He was cleared for line duty and returned to flying the line. According to the NTSB's summary of the first officer's statements about his employment history, he found this incident to be "terribly damaging" professionally. The NTSB summarized the first officer's reactions to the events as follows:

> After the incident [the first officer] adopted what he described as a mode of "captain management" to preclude a recurrence of another similar event. In this mode he would constantly interpret what the captains he flew with really meant or really wanted. He indicated that it was necessary for him to play along and "not stir the hornet's nest". Even though he had been cleared of the accusations, and the record of the incident had been removed from his personnel file, the first officer felt like he was being watched (NTSB, 1997a, p. 10)

Although this crewmember's personality, history and reactions to past events may have made him more hesitant to challenge captains or less forceful in challenging than some other pilots, we note research evidence that first officers, in general, are less direct in challenging captains than captains are in challenging first officers (Fischer and Orasanu, 2000). This difference apparently results from the perceived difference in status and power between the two positions described as "power distance" by Hofstede, 1980). Also, in flight 1943, the first officer's initial challenge ("Want to take it around?") was rebuffed, which may have caused him to soften the form of subsequent challenges. Overall, given the difficulty of maintaining the challenge, we think that the first officer performed reasonably well, at least meeting industry norms at the time for challenging by first officers. We note that some airlines have developed explicit guidance for how monitoring pilots should escalate challenges to which the flying pilot does not respond. Although this guidance is valuable, it does not deal with situations in which the captain overrides the first officer's challenge. The failure of the captain of flight 1943 to take the first officer's discomfort and challenges as prima facie evidence of a problem that must be addressed violates the principles of crew resource management (or CRM – a set of principles pilots are taught to guide interactions and use of human and material resources).

We conclude from this accident that industry standards and training for challenging should be beefed up, especially regarding how to continue a challenge if the initial attempt is not successful. Pilots, especially first officers, should be trained and reinforced to believe that their job may not be done with the first challenge. Challenging becomes harder, but even more crucial when an unsafe situation continues to develop.

When the first officer asked the captain if he wanted to take control of the airplane the captain did so, only 7 seconds before touchdown. We suggest that transfer of control at this critical juncture is inherently risky. The flying pilot may possess information derived from control feel and immersion in the situation that cannot be picked up quickly enough by the pilot taking control to respond appropriately. If it were absolutely essential to transfer control at this low altitude (which was not the case in flight 1943), it would probably be best for the pilot taking control to take the conservative action of immediately executing a missed approach. Low-altitude transfer of control occurred in several other accidents discussed in this book. Although the transfer of control did not contribute directly to the accident in all cases, we suspect that transfer at this point in an approach reveals impulsive decision-making under time pressure, high workload, stress, or some combination of these three factors.

We note that in choosing to continue the approach, the captain violated two "bottom lines", procedures that the airline had established in its *DC-9 Flight Manual* to prevent unsafe continuation of an unstabilized approach.[6] First, procedures required that an approach be discontinued if it was not stabilized below 500 feet above ground level (NTSB, 1997a, p. 36). In this case, not only were the airspeed (84 knots faster than target speed), descent rate, and engine parameters well outside of stabilized approach limits at 500 feet, but also the crew's transfer of aircraft below this limit can be considered an unstabilized condition. Second, the airline's procedures required executing a missed approach if the GPWS activated below 200 feet (NTSB, 1997a, p. 37), which occurred during this approach.

It was unclear to investigators whether these stabilized approach criteria were well trained, or routinely adhered to, in the day-to-day line operations of the air carrier. Following the accident, the air carrier re-emphasized these issues in its written procedures, training programs, line safety audits, and line inspections. Many factors conspire to undercut pilots' recognition that they should execute a missed approach. We believe that airlines must aggressively train and check adherence to stabilized approach criteria. However, to establish norms for adherence that will be reliable in demanding situations that overload pilots' mental resources requires more than just training and checking, as discussed in the concluding portion of this chapter.

Concluding discussion

The chain of events of this accident was initiated by the captain's inadvertent failure to set the hydraulic pumps to the high position, resulting in insufficient hydraulic pressure to extend the flaps and landing gear. Many DC-9 pilots reported having made the same mistake, though apparently the error had always been caught at some point before the airplane landed. Unfortunately we do not know how long these other pilots continued their approaches before catching the error, nor do we know what prompted them to notice the omitted step – that information would shed light on the causes of this accident and might suggest ways to improve safeguards. Whenever human error occurs repeatedly with some particular feature of a system one has to question whether that feature is well-designed for its intended use. The DC-9 design feature requiring pilots to switch hydraulic pressure to high before landing is not common among airliners, although some other airplanes do have this feature. Indications of the status of the hydraulic system are available to the crew through the switch position and readings of the hydraulic pressure gauges. However, one can argue that, because the consequences of not setting the system to the high position are severe, it would be better either to have this function accomplished automatically or to annunciate low hydraulic pressure with a very salient warning when the flap handle is moved to the first of the landing positions.

The crew of flight 1943 missed several opportunities to catch their initial error and made additional errors as they continued the approach. Neither pilot caught the initial error when performing the In Range checklist, which was specifically designed to insure that the hydraulic pumps were set to the high position, along with several other crucial actions. Neither pilot initially noticed that the flaps did not extend when the flap handle was initially operated. Later, as it became apparent that the airplane was not decelerating normally, the first officer did infer a problem with the flaps, which he pointed out to the captain, but the crew failed to analyze the situation and its implications adequately, if at all. The captain failed to perform the Landing checklist when called for by the first officer – this checklist would have directed the pilots' attention to the absence of three green lights indicating gear extension. The first officer became quite uncomfortable with continuing the approach and communicated his discomfort, even suggesting going around, but was not sufficiently assertive and was rebuffed by the captain.

To understand this chain of events we must examine latent weaknesses in the safeguards airlines have carefully erected to prevent single-point errors from causing accidents (Reason, 1990). These safeguards consist of specific defenses in the form of procedures or equipment features. In this chapter we have described specific reasons why each of the defenses was less powerful than intended. Some of these weaknesses are inherent in the interaction of concurrent operational task demands with the limitations of human ability to process information in real time. For example, it is difficult for the flying pilot to reliably divide attention between flying and monitoring execution of the In Range checklist, especially if no overt response is required to individual checklist items.

Other weaknesses in defenses are not intrinsic but creep insidiously into line operations if not guarded against vigilantly. For example, the flow-then-check method of performing procedures provides an important safeguard against omitting crucial actions, but goes against the deep-set bias of humans against redundant action. Rule-based requirements to execute a missed approach if the airplane is not stabilized by a certain altitude or if the GPWS sounds are vital "bottom-line" safeguards, but these safeguards must counter plan continuation bias and the "fog of war" when crews are overloaded, stressed, fatigued, and confused. The company had appropriately established flow-then-check procedures and published appropriate stabilized approach criteria specifying when crews must go around, but the NTSB found that adherence among company pilots was inadequate. We suggest that deviation from these sorts of procedures is not usually a matter of willful disobedience, but rather of a kind of psychological entropy. Norms grow up among populations of individuals to do things in the most economical, convenient manner, especially if individuals do not fully understand reasons for doing things in a more difficult manner, and if the company does not rigorously promote correct use of procedures and frequently check that they are done the right way (Snook, 2000, Chapter 6; Johnston, 2003).

Because no defense against threats and errors can be perfect, the airline industry uses multiple defenses in series, so that if one defense fails, one of the later defenses should catch the problem. The major defenses against gear-up landings, erected by the aircraft manufacturer and the company operating flight 1943, were:

1) the flow-then-check procedure design;
2) making the flying pilot responsible for confirming the monitoring pilot's execution of checklists;
3) use of a Landing checklist with an item for gear extension;
4) green annunciator lights to indicate when the gear is down and locked;
5) a loud gear warning horn;
6) a loud GPWS horn;
7) stabilized approach criteria.

Although each of these defenses had weaknesses (some of which could have been remedied), the combination of the entire set was generally effective in the entire scope of the company's operations, which includes hundreds of thousands of flights annually. Even though many DC-9 pilots at diverse airlines have at one time or another forgotten to switch the hydraulic pumps to high, almost all of these errors were caught before a gear-up landing occurred. Flight 1943 slipped through all these defenses for three reasons:

1) Some of the defenses were not maintained as rigorously as they should have been.
2) Probabilistically, the inherent vulnerability of DC-9 pilots to set hydraulic pressure to high was likely, sooner or later in the course of millions of operations, to combine with latent threats and weakness in defenses against errors to result in a gear-up landing. Among those threats and weaknesses were vulnerability to plan continuation bias, fatigue, lax norms for executing checklists, inadequate training in challenging and monitoring, and happenstance individual differences such as the first officer's previous experience with a captain in the company. Weaknesses often combine synergistically; for example, fatigue, high workload, and stress can greatly exacerbate vulnerability to plan continuation bias.
3) The multiple defenses against a gear-up landing were not entirely independent of each other, allowing an error early in the approach to weaken downstream defenses.

The power of having multiple defenses against threats and errors – crucial to aviation safety – requires those defenses to be independent. If each defense has a fairly high probability of catching an error, then a series of several defenses has an extremely high probability of catching the error, but this is only true if the defenses are independent. This accident illustrates that not all defenses assumed to be independent are in fact so. The initial error made by the crew of flight 1943 later put them in a high-workload, stressful, and confusing situation that substantially increased the probability that they would omit the Landing checklist, fail to notice that the three green landing gear lights were not illuminated, and make errors of judgment. Thus a small error or threat early on, if not caught, can snowball into a situation that progressively deteriorates.

To prevent repetition of accidents such as this one, we suggest several ways existing defenses against threats and errors can be strengthened. Airlines should periodically audit line operations, with especial attention to how standard procedures are typically executed (see Chapter 21). LOSA is a good tool for detecting lax norms and for generating a comprehensive picture of the most prevalent threats and errors in routine line flights. Incident reporting systems can alert company managers to manifestations of hidden threats – for example, frequent reports from pilots of having forgotten to set hydraulic pressure to high should alert the company to a problem in a particular fleet. Companies should periodically evaluate all operating procedures and the typical conditions in which they must be used on the line. A procedure that seems well-designed in the ideal environment envisioned in flight operating manuals may be difficult to perform as intended in the real-world of interruptions, distractions, and shifting environmental conditions (Loukopoulos et al., 2006).

"Bottom-line" rules, such as stabilized approach criteria, are vital safeguards, but they are not likely to be highly effective if they are promulgated only in flight operations manuals and in initial training. Factors such as plan continuation bias and concern with on-time performance and saving face conspire to undercut rigorous adherence to these rules. To counter these factors companies must vigorously promote adherence, educating pilots about the reasons the rules exist, making clear that compliance is mandatory, and establishing no-fault policies for actions such as executing a missed approach. To establish and maintain robust norms for adherence to bottom lines requires a safety culture that is supported unfailingly by operational managers and opinion-leaders among flight crews. Rewards and sanctions must be consistent with the desired norms, and information must be gathered through programs like FOQA and LOSA to monitor what actually takes place in line operations.

Training can be improved in various ways. Pilots can deal with latent threats, such as plan continuation bias, stress, and fatigue, much better if they are educated about the nature of the threats and how they affect crew performance. This and other accidents discussed in this book indicate that initiating challenges, responding to the challenges of other crewmembers, monitoring, and checklist procedures should receive greater emphasis. Training should explicitly address errors of omission and should explain that vulnerability to these errors can be reduced by flow-then-check procedures and by slowing down execution of checking so that it can be performed in a deliberate, conscious fashion rather than relying on automatic execution.

An important topic for air carriers to add to their leadership training for captains is how to respond to situations involving ambiguity. The insidious dangers of mind-set could be explained, and pilots could be encouraged to respond to ambiguity by seeking additional information and systematically considering competing interpretations. In situations in which high workload or time limitation prevented this sort of inquiry, pilots should be trained to select the most conservative response, such as going around.

Notes

1   In a different context, the industry also uses the term "challenge" to refer to a statement by a monitoring crewmember that is intended to question or check another crewmember's understanding of a situation, to ensure that the other crewmember is aware of an error, or to correct an error more directly. One crewmember's challenge of another's error can be done in several ways, ranging from questioning, to expressing discomfort, to direct confrontation; the monitoring crewmember's ease and effectiveness in performing these challenges will vary depending on the situation, the power relationship between the crewmembers (for example, captains may find it easier to challenge their first officers than vice versa), and the characteristics of the individuals involved. In neither context, though, does the term connote insubordination or unwelcome/unexpected intervention by the monitoring crewmember.

2   Sumwalt (1991) describes the following steps for when setting new altitude in MCP:

- pilot not flying communicates with ATC
- pilot not flying sets the altitude alerter/mode control panel
- pilot not flying announces new altitude
- flying pilot points at and repeats new altitude
- pilot flying makes "1,000 feet to go" callout.

3   See Chapter 11. Also, in November 1993 a company Boeing 727 received substantial damage when it contacted the runway during a go-around. The crew had forgotten to extend the landing gear (Continental flight 5148, Chicago – NTSB, 1994c).

4   Some other jet transport types might have provided more salient cues. For example, on the Boeing 737 an amber "Leading Edge Slats Transit" light would have illuminated on the forward instrument panel because of the disagreement between the programmed slat and flap positions. Although this light might draw attention to the nearby flap indicator, it might also confuse a crew by falsely implying that there was a problem with the slats. On other aircraft types equipped with more advanced, electronic crew-alerting functions, the hydraulic and flap problems might have been annunciated more unambiguously.

5   In post-accident interviews, the first officer stated that he had already noticed the flap indicator at 0 by 0900:00 and that he made two comments at that time (unintelligible on the CVR tape) about the flaps. He said that after requesting flaps 15 at 0900:13, he had drawn the captain's attention to the flap indicator pointer at 0 degrees. (See NTSB, 1997a, p. 3.)

6   The Continental Airlines *DC-9 Flight Manual* defined a stabilized approach as "flight on the desired glidepath (visual or electronic) at a steady rate of descent, on the 'target' speed in landing configuration, in trim, and with the proper thrust setting" (NTSB, 1997a, p. 36).

Chapter 10

American 102 – Runway Excursion After Landing

Introduction

On April 14, 1993 at 0659 central daylight time, American Airlines flight 102, a McDonnell-Douglas DC-10 arriving in Dallas/Fort Worth, Texas after a nonstop overnight flight from Honolulu, Hawaii, departed the paved surface of runway 17L while decelerating through 95 knots during its landing roll. The airplane crossed a taxiway and came to rest in soft soil, about 250 feet to the right of the runway. The airplane was substantially damaged and later declared a total loss. Of the 203 crewmembers and passengers aboard, two passengers received serious injuries and 38 passengers and crewmembers received minor injuries. The accident occurred in darkness (1 minute before official sunrise).

After a routine flight from Honolulu, the crew (composed of the captain, first officer, and flight engineer) conducted the approach and landing through an area of rain showers and thundershowers. As the CVR recording began, about 30 minutes prior to landing, the crewmembers were discussing rain showers that they were observing with the onboard radar and the deviations with which they planned to avoid the weather. The first officer was acting as the flying pilot and the captain was the monitoring pilot.

The three crewmembers were highly experienced overall. However, both the captain and first officer were relatively new to the DC-10 aircraft type: prior to the accident flight, the captain had 555 hours of flight experience in the DC-10, and the first officer had 376 hours. All three crewmembers had been off duty for at least 6 days prior to beginning a 3-day assignment that consisted of a round trip to Honolulu, the return trip of which was the accident flight. Their flight from Dallas/Fort Worth (DFW) to Honolulu 2 days prior to the accident had operated between 0900 and 1900 (Dallas time), and the crewmembers reported sleeping for various periods between 2200 pm and 0700 (Dallas time) the night before. The crew spent the next day in Honolulu, napping between 1100 and 1500 (1700 and 2100 Dallas time), and reported for duty on flight 102 just prior to 1700 (2300 Dallas time). Flight 102, planned for 7 hours 7 minutes duration, was a "red-eye" flight operating through the middle of the night relative to the time zone to which the crewmembers' bodies were probably best adapted.

Shortly before the airplane landed the first officer announced he was going around; however, the captain took control and continued the landing. Although the airplane touched down properly aligned with the runway and under control, moments later it veered off the runway. The NTSB determined that the probable cause of this accident was "the failure of the captain to use proper directional control techniques to maintain the airplane on the runway" (NTSB, 1994e, p. vii).

Significant events and issues

1. Captain managed air traffic control and crew resources to avoid thunderstorms

At 0634, while air traffic control (ATC) was vectoring the flight for a landing to the south, the captain's evaluation of the weather radar prompted him to ask the controller whether flight 102 might be able to land in the opposite direction to the prevailing flow of traffic. The captain transmitted: "Is there a lot of traffic coming into DFW at this hour?" The controller replied: "… No sir … matter of fact, I'm not indicating anyone on final right now". The captain continued: "Okay, I was just wondering, uh, just looking at it, it looks like there is at least a remote possibility that you might be able to come in from the south and land to the north, but, uh, we'll keep an eye on it, huh?" After the controller indicated that he might check on the possibility of landing to the north, the captain stated: "Let's wait 'till we get in a little closer …"

For the next several minutes the crew discussed weather radar indications of heavy rain showers ahead of the flight and the best route to fly though the area. Anticipating the possibility of turbulence, the captain ensured that the flight attendants were seated early. At 0642, the CVR recorded a loud rumbling sound and the crew discussed a lightning discharge near or on the aircraft. The captain reported the lightning discharge to the controller and inquired once again about the possibility of landing to the north. The controller replied: "Uh, I doubt it but I will forward that request [to the approach controller]". The captain stated: "Yeah, we're going to have to make a decision here in just a few miles". Told to contact the approach controller, the captain then reiterated his request at 0643: "… Uh, did you get our request for … possibility of landing to the north?" The controller was not encouraging and reported to the captain that several airplanes were waiting at the airport to depart to the south. The captain did not pursue the idea any further. In post-accident interviews, the captain indicated that he had requested an opposite-direction approach because the area to the south was clear of weather cells; however, this area filled in as the flight neared Dallas/Fort Worth, so he acquiesced with the controller's plan for the flight to use the runway 17L approach that traversed the area north of the airport.

After this, the captain requested and received clearance to deviate around weather cells as the flight was vectored for the approach to runway 17L. Then, at 0650:18, the controller transmitted: "American 102 heavy, if able, turn right heading 150 [degrees] and join the runway 17L localizer". At 0650:33 the captain responded, "Uh, I don't think we're goin' to be able to do that, that's a pretty big red area on our scope [heavy precipitation area]". The captain told the controller that he wanted to "just go out, I guess, and wait around [hold, in lieu of commencing the approach] until we see what's goin' on here". ATC responded by informing the captain that another air carrier flight, 8 miles ahead on the approach, was experiencing a good ride through the precipitation. The captain replied: "Okay, uh, we'll head down that way then and, uh, worse comes to worse we'll go out [to the holding pattern] from there".

The captain's requests to land in the opposite direction from traffic and his requests for flexibility to deviate from assigned headings suggest that he was actively and appropriately engaged in managing the weather threat. Although his dialogue with the controller about landing to the north was somewhat tentative, throughout this period the captain was seeking real-time weather information from the onboard radar, continually updating his plan for weather avoidance, and evaluating alternatives. The captain's rejection of the controller's vector to the final approach course and his request for holding was excellent performance in the pilot-in-command role.

However, the captain allowed his decision to be changed by the controller's statement that the airplane operating ahead of flight 102 on the approach was continuing without difficulty. We suggest that in addition to providing the captain with potentially useful information about the lack of turbulence experienced by the flight ahead, the approach controller's reply to the captain's request to hold may have also indirectly pressured him to continue the approach. The captain had announced his decision to the controller and an appropriate reply would have been for the controller to issue clearance to a holding pattern. Instead, in some respect, the controller was urging the captain to continue inbound to the airport, a less conservative action. This was the second time in a matter of minutes that ATC had been an obstacle to the captain's implementation of his decisions.

We are concerned that pilots may be susceptible to being influenced by controllers in ways that are not always appropriate, especially when the controller lacks knowledge of all aspects of the flight's situation. Flights may be exposed to risk if controllers encourage or pressure crews as a means of facilitating the flow of traffic and simplifying the controller's aircraft workload (holding patterns and heading deviations increase controller workload). We recognize that time pressure and frequency congestion often limit pilot–controller communications to terse exchanges and may inhibit discussions that would be adequate for one party to evaluate the appropriateness of the other's suggestions. However, even when adequate time exists and the radio frequency is open, pilots still may refrain from extended discussions with controllers that could provide them with valuable information. The sources of this apparent barrier to communications are not clear, but may be related to habit, tradition, and the work cultures of the two professions.

2. First officer decided to execute a missed approach when the airplane was less than 50 feet above the ground

As the approach continued, the crewmembers had productive conversations about weather conditions, including the first officer's statement at 0652:58: "If anyone sees anything that looks like windshear, let me know". At 0653:32 the CVR recorded a click sound and the crew discussed another lightning strike. At 0655:36 the captain reported a 10–15 knot gain in airspeed to controllers. The crew later recalled that the airplane was established on final approach with a 10-degree crab angle to the right, indicative of a substantial crosswind from the west. Wind reports at the time of the accident suggested a shift in wind direction from the south to the west with increasing wind velocity while the airplane was on final approach. Despite these weather-related factors, the final approach segment was conducted within normal parameters until just before the airplane crossed the landing threshold. At that time the airplane trended high on the glidepath. At 0659:17, when the airplane had just descended through 50 feet above ground, the first officer stated: "I'm gonna go around".

The NTSB conducted extensive interviews with the crewmembers after the accident and summarized the crew's recollections of these events as follows:

> When the first officer had the runway in sight, he disconnected the autopilot but not the autothrottles. He swung the nose of the airplane slightly to the left, and the airplane drifted left. He swung the nose of the airplane back to the right and ... was "not comfortable". He felt that they were "high" and that the airplane would need too much nose-down to accomplish the landing. He announced that he was going to make a missed approach.

> The captain said that he believed the aircraft was drifting to the left, and he felt he could make a safe landing. He did not want to make a missed approach and have to deal with the thunderstorm activity again. He said that they were at 200 feet [above ground] and that he took control of the airplane from the first officer. He made an alignment correction, but said it was not necessary to make an altitude/glideslope adjustment. He was confident that the landing would be within "the desired 3,000-foot touchdown zone." He said that there was no need to go around, no windshear, no airspeed, height, or alignment problem (NTSB, 1994e, p. 66).

When the first officer announced his decision to execute the missed approach just prior to landing, he did not provide the captain with any warning or background discussion for his decision. The post-accident interviews suggest that the captain may have misunderstood the reason for the first officer's desire to reject the landing: the first officer was concerned about the high approach and consequent long landing, while at the time the captain did not believe that the airplane was too high and assumed that the first officer was concerned about the airplane's lateral runway alignment in the freshening crosswind that had developed during the last seconds of the approach.

If the first officer had articulated his concerns before announcing his decision to go around or amplified on his decision at the time he announced it, he might have convinced the captain that the airplane was too high (the first officer was correct: the airplane was too high to be landed as required in the touchdown zone, the first 3,000 feet of the runway) or might have at least convinced the captain to permit a go-around. He could have stated his reasons as a lead-in to the decision statement (perhaps: "We're too high, I'm gonna go around") or as a form of stronger assertion when the captain did not agree with the go-around (such as: "I'm uncomfortable because we're going to land too long").

However, in considering how the first officer might have strengthened his argument to obtain the desired go-around, we must recognize that the time available to him was short with the airplane already descending below 50 feet, just seconds from the usual beginning of the landing flare. Further, the high workload that he was experiencing (aligning and flaring the airplane in the dynamic situation of gusting crosswinds) required his full attention. There was not a lot of time to explain, so what the CVR recorded was a shorthand version of assertion/advocacy[1] from the first officer – he leapt directly to stating his conclusion.

In time-critical situations such as this, crews could reduce misunderstandings by voicing concerns earlier in the approach when more time is available for discussion. Comments such as "We are getting too high" or "I am having trouble staying on the glidepath" might have provided more time for the captain to grasp the situation and react. However, talking through every small correction during a routine approach and landing would seem tedious and unnecessary, and conceivably the flying pilot would have to verbalize all of these corrections in a continuous flow of commentary to be able to adequately communicate the situation to the monitoring pilot. Furthermore, airlines typically do not train pilots about the dangers of truncated communication, which is common in routine cockpit discourse. Perhaps air carrier training should emphasize the need to "talk through" procedures when circumstances are less than ideal (Foushee and Manos, 1981).

3. Captain overruled the first officer, took control of the airplane, and landed

Less than 1 second after the first officer announced the go-around, the captain stated: "No, no, no, I've got it". The first officer confirmed the transfer of control, stating: "You got the airplane". Concurrent with the first officer's confirmation, the radar altimeter provided its "30 feet" aural annunciation.

The situation when the captain took control was challenging. Rain and thundershowers were crossing the runway, and gusty, quartering tailwinds were getting stronger. The airplane had tracked the electronic glideslope during most of the approach but crossed the runway threshold about 100 feet above ground level, twice the normal height for that position. Despite this and the difficulties that the first officer had experienced with lateral alignment, the captain continued the approach and landed. Interviewed after the accident, the captain said he took control and continued the approach because of concern with conducting a missed approach with thunderstorms in the vicinity (NTSB, 1994e, p. 66).

Taking control was consistent with the active command role the captain played throughout the approach. "Basic Procedures and Crew Coordination Practices Applicable to All Instrument Approaches", published in the company flight manual (NTSB, 1994e, p. 76), stated that the "captain is in command and must be prepared to take over at any time" during an approach. However, these procedures also cautioned captains against "last-minute changes in planned procedure". Thus captains were allowed considerable discretion in this situation.

We suggest that changing the pilot who is flying the airplane at 50 feet above the ground has inherent risks. The pilot assuming control has very little time to get in the loop, feel the controls, and develop a clear sense of the flight dynamics, especially with a fluctuating crosswind. Furthermore, overriding a flying pilot's decision to go around at 50 feet is problematic, even when the monitoring pilot is the captain, because the flying pilot may be responding to conditions or concerns not apparent to the captain. In general, the most conservative response in this situation would be to accept and support the first officer's decision to go around. Indeed, many captains make a point of telling first officers before starting an approach (that is, during the approach briefing) that they will execute a go-around if either pilot feels uncomfortable with the approach.

The captain of flight 102 may have felt that the risks of executing a missed approach in threatening weather outweighed the risks of taking control and landing. The crew could not have known the exact location and intensity of storm cells around the airport at that moment. (The NTSB investigation did not attempt to assess the degree of threat involved in going around – indeed, it may have been impossible to obtain the weather data needed for this assessment.) The captain did not have time to make a reasoned analysis of the relative risks of the two options, and thus was forced to make a very fast decision. Rushed decisions with inadequate information often fail to hit on the best choice, but rather than blaming this captain we suggest that airlines might explicitly train pilots in the risks of rushed decisions and might provide explicit guidance for the most conservative response when split-second decisions must be made.

As it turned out, the captain's decision to take control and land does not seem to have contributed directly to the loss of control after landing. The NTSB found no clear evidence of fault in the captain's decision. Despite the challenging winds the airplane was aligned with the runway when it touched down on the centerline, and the landing was soft. The airplane did land abnormally long, more than 4,300 feet from the runway threshold, but adequate runway remained to stop the airplane had it not veered off the side of the pavement.

The NTSB noted there was no evidence that the crew conducted an approach briefing (as typically accomplished at the beginning of the descent phase), perhaps because Dallas/Fort Worth was the crew's home base and they were quite familiar with the arrival procedures and approaches there. (Conceivably the crew might have conducted the briefing before the 30-minute period captured by the CVR.) The company required pilots to conduct an approach briefing, although it was not a checklist line item. Arguably, conducting a briefing might have prompted both pilots to discuss criteria for going around, made the first officer more likely to talk about his concerns during the last moments of the approach, and biased the captain in the direction of accepting a go-around. However, this crew seemed to communicate well in other respects, and we doubt that a briefing by itself would have greatly influenced the captain's time-pressured decision.

4. Captain relaxed crosswind control inputs and attempted to steer the airplane with the nosewheel steering tiller during the landing roll

As the captain flared the airplane for landing, the wind was blowing across the runway from right to left at approximately 15 knots with higher gusts, and wind velocities were increasing (1 minute after the accident, northwesterly winds of 22 knots gusting to 33 knots were recorded at the airport).

The airplane remained aligned with the runway centerline for the first 6 seconds of the landing roll. FDR data indicated that the captain was applying control inputs to correct for the crosswind that was coming from the airplane's right side. His left rudder pedal inputs were counteracting the weathervaning effect of the crosswind, which was pushing the airplane to turn to the right, into the wind. (These rudder pedal inputs provided aerodynamic yawing moments through the rudder as well as cornering through the nosewheel steering system.) His forward pressure on the control column was placing greater weight on the nose landing gear, which provided more friction to hold the airplane's nose straight against weathervaning and provided additional cornering capability for the nosewheel steering. However, about 7 seconds after touchdown the rudder, elevator, and aileron control inputs that had been keeping the airplane tracking straight down the runway were all moved toward their neutral position. In response, the airplane began to turn to the right and off the paved surface of the runway.

Interviewed after the accident, the captain recalled that at this time he noticed the airplane yawing to the right, weathervaning into the wind, and that he responded "instinctively" by attempting to steer the airplane using the nosewheel steering tiller located to his left.[2] The tiller is intended for use during low-speed taxi and parking operations; consequently, it is capable of deflecting the nosewheel to a far greater extent than the rudder pedals (68 degrees to the left or right, compared to 10 degrees for the rudder pedals). When a pilot deflects the nosewheel sharply using the tiller, the DC-10 can turn tightly when maneuvering on dry pavement. However, on slippery pavement the nosewheel can lose traction at wheel deflections of only a few degrees, especially at higher speeds. In contrast, the airplane's rudder (controlled through the rudder pedals, and unaffected by the tiller) would have more than adequate control authority to hold the airplane straight down the runway at the speeds at which flight 102 was traveling during the initial seconds of the landing roll, even considering the crosswind and runway surface conditions that existed at this time in the flight. For these reasons, the DC-10 nosewheel steering tiller is not normally used during the high-speed portions of the landing rollout.

The airline provided its flight crews with some information about the negative effects of large nosewheel steering inputs in the "Operating Techniques" section of its flight manual:

> If the nosewheel steering angle becomes excessive, because of inadvertent steering wheel [tiller] inputs or even rudder pedal inputs on a slippery runway, the desired corrective force will be greatly decreased or even reduced to practically zero. In this situation, it may be necessary to reduce the nosewheel steering angle until steering force is regained … (NTSB, 1994e, p. 72).

However this company did not provide specific instruction on when not to use the steering tiller. In contrast, the manufacturer of the DC-10 communicated, in a 1986 *All Operators Letter* and other publications:

> The control input from the hand wheel [tiller] is much more sensitive than from rudder pedal steering at high speeds. Its use may result in overcontrol of nosewheel steering. Because it is difficult to judge and control the amount of hand wheel input at high speeds, it is recommended that use of the hand wheel be restricted to taxiing and never be used for control of the aircraft on the runway at ground speeds in excess of 15 knots (NTSB, 1994e, p. 69).

The information in the airline's flight manual was perhaps minimally adequate for the captain to know that using the steering tiller at high speed when landing on a wet runway in a gusty crosswind was not appropriate. However, under time pressure, surprise, workload, or stress individuals are often unable to retrieve quickly from memory all information relative to the situation, especially if that information is not elaborated or is not used frequently. Among the distinctions cognitive psychologists make about the ways in which information is organized and stored in memory is a distinction between *declarative* knowledge and *procedural* knowledge (Eysenck, 1994, pp. 93–5). Declarative knowledge is that to which individuals have conscious access and can state directly in some form. In contrast, individuals do not have conscious access to procedural knowledge, which is demonstrated through action. Declarative knowledge, by its nature, is flexible, allowing general principles to be applied to diverse situations. Procedural knowledge is much more specific to situations; individuals develop a characteristic response pattern to specific situations to which they respond repeatedly – this is the basis of habit. Retrieval and execution of procedural knowledge is largely automatic, not requiring much conscious effort – indeed, effort is required to inhibit a strongly established habitual pattern of responding. Thus it is not surprising that the captain failed to retrieve on a challenging landing the modest and seldom-used declarative knowledge about nosewheel steering that he presumably gained from having read the DC-10 flight manual. In contrast, the procedural knowledge associated with taxiing – and conceivably from landing other aircraft – would have been retrieved automatically. In a situation like this one, demanding immediate and precise procedural response, crewmembers are more likely to respond correctly if they have received adequate hands-on training and practice; for example, in a flight simulator that can reproduce the ground handling characteristics of the airplane.

The NTSB's analysis of the FDR information indicated that the loss of control during the landing roll was precipitated by the captain relaxing his previously effective rudder pedal and control column inputs. He removed these inputs when he attempted to use the steering tiller to control the airplane's heading down the runway. The geometry of the cockpit control locations forced the captain to remove his left hand from the control column to reach the tiller. (Presumably his right hand remained on the thrust reverser levers.) This caused the elevator to return to the neutral position and removed the nose-down input necessary to maintain nosewheel traction and cornering. As he began using the tiller the captain relaxed his rudder inputs, either inadvertently or because he anticipated the tiller would provide more effective directional control.

FDR data also revealed that when the airplane headed away from the runway centerline and began to leave the runway surface the captain made only a single, brief rudder pedal input in the correct direction, after which the rudder remained neutral. This suggests that he continued to rely on the tiller as the situation continued to worsen. This is not surprising. Only about 6 seconds elapsed from the moment that the captain relaxed his rudder input to the airplane departing the runway, and the captain's mental workload must have been high as he focused on regaining control, reducing still further the likelihood that he would retrieve from declarative memory information that would help him analyze the cause of loss of control. Also, as in Tower Air flight 41 (Chapter 8), the nature of manual control skill is to increase control input if the vehicle does not respond adequately to initial input (Jagacinski, 1977; Wickens and Hollands, 2000, p. 404).

The NTSB raised the possibility that fatigue may have affected the performance of the crew of flight 102 adversely. Fatigue can impair pilots' reactions and decisions, slowing processing of information, narrowing attention, and perhaps biasing pilots against accepting delays, even when needed (Durmer and Dinges, 2005). The entire crew was well rested prior to starting the three-day trip during which the accident occurred, and the investigation did not uncover any evidence of chronic fatigue. Also the pilots reported adequate amounts of sleep the night before the accident flight. However the crew was not in Hawaii long enough to adapt thoroughly to local time. The flight was a "red-eye" and the accident occurred just before dawn and at the crew's normal circadian low. The NTSB concluded that the possibility of fatigue having affected the crew's performance could neither be supported by the evidence nor dismissed.

5. First officer did not assist the captain with aircraft control as the airplane yawed off the runway centerline

The first officer told investigators that he would have assisted the captain on the controls if he had been asked. In hindsight, he could have improved the airplane's response to the captain's tiller steering inputs by adding forward column pressure, and he might even have recovered control of the airplane himself by pressing on the left rudder pedal. The captain did not ask for help, and the first officer did not intervene as the airplane traveled off the runway and into the grass.

At the time of this accident, the airline did not require the first officer to normally assist the captain upon landing by applying forward control column (nose-down elevator) to improve nosewheel friction. The airline's procedures did not reflect guidance published by the manufacturer in the same *All Operators Letter* cited above: "The pilot not flying must apply sufficient forward pressure to maintain the nosewheel firmly on the ground for maximum directional control" (NTSB, 1994e, p. 70). If the airline had established this as a procedure, including training and standardization to make it a norm, the first officer presumably would have applied forward column pressure; however, we do not know whether this control input would have prevented the accident.

The first officer may have not made rudder pedal input because he thought the captain was doing all that he could or because he thought that having two pilots trying to control the airplane without prior coordination might aggravate the situation. He may also have been hesitant to intervene in a captain's flying – especially one who, seconds earlier, had countermanded his own decision to go around and who had taken the airplane away from him. NTSB investigators interviewed several of the company's first officers to obtain their thoughts about assisting captains with aircraft control or intervening with captains' flying during the landing roll. The NTSB report summarized diverse responses from these first officers:

> Some stated that they would not make control input, with the captain at the controls, unless directed. Others stated that they would assist with nosewheel steering by putting forward pressure on the yoke. When asked if the airplane were about to depart the runway, whether they would make undirected control inputs to assist the flying captain, some said they would not; others said that they would do whatever was necessary to keep the airplane safely on the runway (NTSB, 1994e, p. 94).

These diverse responses reveal the dilemma confronting a first officer forced to make a split-second decision in this situation, especially given the lack of explicit company guidance.

Concluding discussion

In this accident, after the crew performed well maneuvering through a weather area as they approached the flight's destination, the first officer of flight 102 experienced difficulty handling the airplane and, seconds before landing, announced that he was executing a missed approach. The captain immediately overruled the first officer, assumed control of the airplane, and made a long but otherwise normal landing. Then, after holding the proper rudder and control column control inputs to correct for the existing crosswind conditions through the first several seconds of the landing roll, the captain lost directional control of the airplane when he over controlled the nosewheel by using the tiller at high speed and simultaneously relaxed the rudder and control column inputs.

This accident probably would not have happened if the captain had not overruled the first officer's decision to go around, but the NTSB found no evidence that taking over at this late stage in the approach contributed to the loss of control. Conceivably the captain performed less adroitly than he would have had he been on the controls throughout the approach, but if so the effect was subtle because the airplane touched down aligned with the runway. Nevertheless, split-second decisions such as this are inherently risky because humans simply cannot evaluate all aspects of the situation and potential outcomes quickly enough to choose the best option reliably. Rather than second-guessing the captain's decision, we recommend that airlines establish and rigorously train the desired conservative response to situations in which there is not sufficient time for deliberate analysis.

The captain's loss of control from using the tiller illustrates how several latent weaknesses in an operation can on occasion combine in unanticipated ways. The slippery runway and gusty crosswind, though well within the limits airline pilots can normally manage, set the stage. The company did not provide its pilots all pertinent information about vulnerability of nosewheel steering in the DC-10, the captain had relatively low experience in landing the DC-10, his experience with other types of aircraft may have carried over inadvertently and inappropriately, and the well-established procedural skill of maintaining directional control with the tiller during taxi may have been retrieved from memory and executed automatically before less well-established declarative memory could be retrieved. Once factors such as these combine to start an incident, severe time constraints, high workload, surprise, and stress conspire against pilots' efforts to understand and correct what is happening.

Unfortunately, it is unrealistic to hope that an airline can detect and remove all latent weaknesses or predict the countless ways weaknesses might on some occasion combine. However, several things can be done to reduce vulnerability. Not providing pilots with all cautionary information available or not following procedural recommendations from aircraft manufacturers should be done, if ever, only after deliberate and thorough analysis. This accident and Tower 41 illustrate a specific vulnerability to misuse of hand wheel steering that can be addressed through explicit procedures and thorough training and checking. More broadly, a large fraction of the accidents discussed in this book reveal the vulnerability of complex situations in which crews must respond very rapidly. Because humans cannot adequately think through such situations quickly enough, we suggest educating pilots about this vulnerability and whenever possible establishing bottom-line conservative procedures to which pilots can default without attempting to analyze the situation. These issues are further discussed in Chapter 21.

Notes

1   One of the tenets of CRM training is that pilots should clearly articulate their concerns and advocate an appropriate course of action. This tenet is usually couched in terms of "assertiveness" and "advocacy". Captains ultimately decide the course of action but are supposed to consider input from subordinates carefully.

2   Nosewheel steering control inputs were not recorded by the FDR, so the NTSB used the captain's recollected control inputs to establish the sequence of these events.

Chapter 11

Continental 795 – High-Speed Takeoff Decision with Poor Information

Introduction

On March 2, 1994 at 1759 eastern standard time, Continental Airlines flight 795, a McDonnell-Douglas MD-82, overran the end of runway 13 at LaGuardia Airport, Flushing, New York after the captain rejected the takeoff at high speed. The airplane stopped on a dike with its nose section on a mudflat in Flushing Bay. The airplane was substantially damaged in the accident, but there were no fatalities or serious injuries among the two pilots, four flight attendants, or 110 passengers aboard. The accident occurred at night.

Flight 795 was the return leg of a planned round trip between Denver and New York. The crew had operated the inbound trip from Denver on time. The captain and first officer, who had been paired together for a trip earlier in the year, were well experienced in their crew positions and in the MD-80 series aircraft. The captain had 24 years of experience in the DC-9/MD-80 and had more than 6,000 hours in this type of airplane. The first officer had four years and 2,400 hours of experience as a DC-9/MD-80 second-in-command pilot.

It was snowing in New York on the evening of the accident, and the taxiways and runways at LaGuardia were covered with a thin layer of slushy accumulation as the flight prepared for departure. Prior to pushback the crew ordered deicing procedures, which the ground personnel completed at the gate at 1724. The first officer called air traffic control for taxi clearance at 1731. The crew elected to taxi out with one engine operating to save fuel (in anticipation of departure delays) and with the flaps retracted to avoid contamination from the slushy taxiways.

Between 1753:35 and 1754:42 the first officer was in the passenger cabin, conducting a pre-takeoff inspection of the upper wing surface by shining a flashlight through cabin windows. At 1756:52 the crew started the right engine. At 1757:32 the captain conducted a takeoff briefing with the first officer, including a review of the procedures for a rejected takeoff. Air traffic control then cleared the flight for takeoff at 1758:36.

The first officer was performing the flying pilot duties for this flight and therefore handled the flight controls during the takeoff roll. However, the airline's procedures required the captain to handle the throttles during the takeoff roll and prescribed that only the captain could decide whether to reject a takeoff, in which event the captain would also take over as the flying pilot and execute the rejected takeoff procedure.

As the aircraft accelerated the captain noticed that his airspeed indicator appeared to be operating erratically; he cross-checked the first officer's airspeed indicator, which also appeared to be giving erratic readings, and then commanded that the takeoff be aborted. By this time the aircraft had reached 145 knots,[1] and even though the crew correctly executed the rejected takeoff procedures they were unable to stop the airplane within the confines of the runway.

The National Transportation Safety Board determined that the probable causes of this accident were:

> ... the failure of the flight crew to comply with checklist procedures to turn on an operable pitot-static heat system, resulting in ice and/or snow blockage of the pitot tubes that produced erroneous airspeed indications, and the flight crew's untimely response to anomalous airspeed indications with the consequent rejection of takeoff at an actual speed of 5 knots above V1 (NTSB, 1995b, p. v).

Significant events and issues

1. Crew did not turn on pitot heat when performing the Before Pushback/Before Start checklist

The 30-minute loop of the cockpit voice recording began during startup of the first engine at the ramp, so it did not record the crew's execution of the Before Pushback/Before Start checklist. One of the eight steps of this checklist was turning on the pitot-static system heating elements. The company's standard procedures for this checklist required the first officer to call out the pitot heat item and the captain to respond by positioning a pitot/stall heat rotary switch on the overhead panel from the "Off" to the "Capt" position. The captain was then required to verify that current was flowing to the heating elements by noting a positive indication on an ammeter that was located next to the switch. The first officer was supposed to verify that the captain had performed these actions.

Interviewed after the accident, the captain recalled that he had turned on the pitot heat during this step of the checklist. The switch was found in the "Capt" position when the cockpit was documented[2] on the day after the accident. However, the NTSB noted that switch positions may be altered during aircraft recovery. Further, based on FDR data and post-accident functional tests of the pitot heating equipment, the NTSB concluded that the captain did not turn on the switch during execution of the checklist or at any time prior to takeoff. Investigators attributed the anomalous indications that appeared on both pilots' airspeed indicators during takeoff to snow and slush entering the unheated pitot tubes.

Without CVR information for the time that the crew executed the Before Pushback/Before Start checklist the NTSB could not ascertain and we will never be certain why the crew did not turn on the heat switch. Certainly post-accident crew interviews conducted by investigators did not provide any understanding of the event, because the pilots stated that they had turned on the heat. We suggest two possible explanations for this event: the pilots may have performed the checklist step incompletely, or they may have inadvertently omitted the step entirely.

Regarding the first possibility, we note that investigators found that the pitot heat switch was poorly aligned relative to the legend printed on the instrument panel. As a result, when the switch was turned off, its pointer was aligned one third of the distance toward the "Capt" position. Conceivably this poor alignment may have misled the crew. It is possible that the first officer called out the pitot heat checklist item properly and that the captain looked at the heat switch, but with the misalignment of the legend believed that the switch was already turned on. If this was the case, though, the error should have been caught by the portion of the checklist step that required the captain to verify heater operation by noting a current draw on the ammeter located next to the pitot heat switch.

We suggest that if this scenario did occur, the failure of the verification step (checking the reading of the ammeter) may have been related to the limited reliability of human monitoring and detection, especially when monitoring an inherently reliable system (Parasuraman, Molloy, and Singh, 1993) such as pitot heat. The captain had performed this checklist step thousands of times in his career; undoubtedly, he would have seen the proper current draw on almost or even all occasions. With this repeated experience, the quality of the captain's verification of the ammeter reading may have degraded over time without becoming apparent to him. Perception is strongly influenced by expectation – we are biased to see what we expect to see, and this bias is probably stronger when visual inspection consists only of a fleeting glance (Austen and Enns, 2003). A related phenomenon is "change blindness", in which individuals do not notice unexpected changes in visual scenes and "inattention blindness", in which individuals do not notice a visible but unexpected stimulus because their attention is focused on another aspect of the viewed display (Simons and Rensink, 2003).

It may also be relevant that visual sampling of the environment is driven by the rate at which the item sampled typically changes,[3] along with several other variables (Wickens, Goh, Helleberg, Horrey, and Talleur, 2003). An instrument display that rarely if ever changes provides little new information; thus, unless the individual exerts considerable discipline to consciously force checking, monitoring of a rarely changing instrument is likely to become ineffective. Because this deterioration is subtle and because the instrument normally reads the expected value, individuals may be unaware that their monitoring has become ineffective.

Thus, without strong efforts by pilots to resist the tendency to be lulled by a very reliable system, a two-step procedure that includes a control action followed by verification may collapse into only a single control action step. The verification function will no longer be reliable and cannot be depended upon to catch human errors or aircraft system malfunctions.

The other possibility we suggested was omission of the entire step of the checklist that involved turning on the pitot heat. In this case a double omission may have occurred, because NTSB investigators were told by seven of the airline's MD-80 pilots that they routinely performed their before-start procedures by first "flowing the panel", setting switches appropriately, and then reading the checklist to ensure that all critical items have been set. This common technique has the advantage of providing a double-check of critical items: the initial setting of each item by memory is followed by an explicit re-check read from the checklist. (At this time company procedures did not require a flow-then-check procedure for this checklist.)

However, even with the flow-then-check technique, checklist procedures are more vulnerable to error than may be apparent. During the re-check with the printed checklist, pilots are checking their own actions from a few seconds or minutes earlier during the flow check of the panel. But when they perform the checklist, they naturally expect that the checklist items are already complete because they remember performing them only moments before, and expectation strongly biases what individuals perceive.

A further complication is the inherent cognitive vulnerability to be confused whether an action was taken recently if that action has been performed many times recently – a phenomenon called "source memory" confusion (Johnson et al., 1993). Because the many episodes of performing an action are quite similar, little is recorded in memory to distinguish one episode from another. Also, for much the same reason, individuals may unwittingly confuse having thought about performing an action with actually having performed it. (Also see discussion in Chapter 9.)

We also note that interruptions and distractions during the before-start period when the panel is being flowed are commonplace and are frequently reported causes of omitted procedural steps (Loukopoulos et al., 2006). Interruptions and distractions force pilots to suspend a procedure temporarily, and when they resume they may think they have completed the last step they were thinking about. (See again discussion in Chapter 9.)

Reading the checklist aloud is an effective safeguard for these vulnerabilities only if crews very deliberately verify the status of each item. Execution of checklists is vulnerable to problems similar to those experienced when checking the pitot heat ammeter. After a pilot has performed a particular checklist many times, execution of the checklist tends to become highly automatic. The pilot's verbal response to each item challenged is generated automatically, rather than deliberately, even before the pilot has time to direct his or her gaze to the item to be checked. Pilots can overcome this automatization only by consciously slowing down and examining each item in a deliberate manner. (This is further discussed in the concluding section of this chapter.)

We have no information on whether this crew was rushing during cockpit preparations, but it is worth noting that rushing would exacerbate the cognitive vulnerabilities we have been discussing. Some phases of airline operations, such as preparations for starting the aircraft, pushback, and taxi for departure, are at times subject to time pressure. Delays may cause crews to lose their time slot for departure, which in some cases causes considerable inconvenience to passengers. Even though these time pressures are not always present, they may undermine attempts to establish habits of executing procedural flows and checklists in a deliberate manner.

NTSB investigators obtained information bearing on the typical checklist performance by the crew of flight 795 and by other crews within the airline. Information regarding the crew of flight 795 was conflicting. A first officer who frequently flew with the captain described him as a "perfectionist performing checklists" (NTSB, 1995b, p. 6). Other captains who flew with the first officer described him as "methodical in his checklist execution" (NTSB, 1995b, p. 8). However, the crew's performance on checklists during the portions of flight 795 that were recorded by the CVR revealed several deviations from formal procedures: the crew were inconsistent in calling for these checklists to be initiated, rarely called out that the checklists were complete, responded to several challenges with responses not specified by company procedures, and omitted several checklist items.[4] These deviations suggest that this crew's normal manner of executing checklists may have increased their vulnerability to errors such as failing to notice that pitot heat had not been turned on.

The NTSB investigation found evidence of systemic problems with poor checklist discipline and compliance at this airline. Investigators focused on the results of a 3-week inspection of the company conducted by the FAA two months before the accident, which found that "some pilots were not following the checklists and standard operating procedures". The NTSB concluded that the results of the FAA inspection "suggest that the problems identified in this accident regarding improper checklist procedures were systemic" at the airline (NTSB, 1995b, p. 58). We note that subsequent to the accident, this airline has strongly emphasized checklist and standard operating procedures compliance, has conducted several audits of line operations to monitor progress on safety issues, and has become an industry leader in using line safety audits (FSF, 2005).

Close-knit groups, such as an airline's pilots, readily develop common attitudes and ways of operating as part of their culture. If deviation from the company's formal procedures becomes common, individual pilots and crews are strongly influenced. Deviation becomes regarded as acceptable and normal (Snook, 2000, Chapter 6). The trend toward deviation may be especially powerful in the case of checklists because the formally prescribed methods of performing checklists are typically more time-consuming and effortful than automatic execution. Pilots who attempt to stick with the formal method may experience subtle or not-so-subtle social pressure from peers, especially if the operation is slowed. Deviation becomes normal for diverse reasons: for example, there may be production pressures such as on-time performance; lack of emphasis on compliance by company managers, instructors, and checkpilots; and failure to fully explain to pilots the benefits of the more laborious way of executing procedures (Karwal, Verkaik, and Jansen, 2000). Without explanation pilots may not recognize that features such as formal calls to initiate checklists, the format for challenge and response, and calling completion of checklists are designed to guide attention and protect against cognitive vulnerabilities to error.

2. Rushing to complete the Before Takeoff checklist, the crew did not notice an annunciator light indicating that the pitot/stall heaters were turned off

During pushback at 1730:13, just after the left engine was successfully started, ramp personnel told the flight crew by interphone that the right engine was clear for starting. The first officer asked the captain: "You want to, ah, go on two or just one [engine]?" The captain replied: "I think just one".

A single-engine taxi operation, commonly performed as a fuel conservation measure when pilots expect a long taxi duration, was consistent with the airline's standard operating procedures in most conditions, but not in winter weather with snow-contaminated surface conditions. (In these conditions, single-engine taxi operations can lead to steering problems or engine damage.) We note, though, that ground delays prompting single-engine taxiing occur frequently, while operations in snow and icing conditions that are supposed to preclude it are much more rare. We do not know how thoroughly the injunction not to use single-engine taxi in contaminated surface conditions was taught and checked, but we do know that airline pilots normally try to conserve fuel, both because of costs and because of the safety margin provided by extra fuel.

Flight 795's taxi-out to the runway lasted approximately 28 minutes. Near the end of this period, the single-engine taxi operation added to the time pressure on the crew as they prepared for takeoff. At 1742:34, about 11 minutes into the taxi, the first officer asked the captain, "Well, what's your best guess we crank it up [start the second engine] or – we gonna be number five or six to go." The captain replied that he estimated ten or more minutes before they would be the number one airplane for departure, and then he changed the subject of the crew's conversation to the pre-takeoff wing contamination check that the first officer had to perform from the passenger cabin before departure.[5] The captain decided that the first officer should perform the check later, when the flight was in the number one position for departure.

At 1754:44 the first officer returned to the cockpit after performing the icing inspection, telling the captain: "Looks okay to me". The captain acknowledged and, at 1754:53, told the first officer to start the right engine. At 1756:05 the CVR recorded the first officer beginning the Taxi checklist.[6] His recitation of the Taxi checklist items continued directly into the Before Takeoff checklist items, with the flight cleared into position on the runway while these checklists were still being performed at 1757:02. At 1757:32 the captain conducted a takeoff briefing that included a review of rejected takeoff procedures (this was part of the Taxi checklist that the first officer was still executing). At 1758:01 the captain turned over control of the airplane to the first officer, with the airplane stopped on the runway and the brakes set.

Immediately after this, the first officer continued with the items of the Before Takeoff checklist, which company procedures specified that the first officer should perform while the captain was taxiing onto the runway. One item on that checklist was a review of the annunciator panel. According to procedures for the annunciator panel check outlined in the company's MD-80 flight manual, when the airplane is ready for takeoff "the rudder unrestricted [blue advisory] light must be on … [a]ll other panel lights should be out, except those of an advisory nature" (NTSB, 1995b, p. 39). At 1758:11, during his recitation of the Before Takeoff checklist items, the first officer stated: "Annunciator panel's checked …"

The basic design of the MD-80 included a warning system for pitot-static heat. The cockpit annunciator panel would display an amber "Pitot/Stall Heater Off" light if the heat switch was turned off, or if the switch was on and power was not being applied to the heaters because of a malfunction.[7] This suggests that on flight 795 the "Pitot/Stall Heater Off" light probably was illuminated during the Before Takeoff check but was not noticed by either crewmember.

Based on aircraft design and company operating procedures, MD-80 pilots would see only blue (advisory) lights illuminated on the annunciator panel during most takeoffs, and the illumination of any of the amber lights during the Before Takeoff check of the panel would signal an abnormality. However, in the less common situation of a departure on an ice- or snow-contaminated runway, it was appropriate to leave the tail-mounted auxiliary power unit (APU) running during takeoff. In that event, the annunciator panel would also display an amber caution light signifying that the APU electric generator was running but off-line. The rule provided in the company procedures (only blue lights should be illuminated for takeoff) therefore was applicable to most, but not all, flights. The crew of flight 795 had the APU running for takeoff and so would have seen an amber light on the annunciator panel for the APU generator in addition to the amber light indicating that the pitot/stall heaters were off. We suggest that because the crew expected to see an amber light for the APU they may have been less likely to notice the additional amber light in a quick scan before opening the throttles. Thus, even though the "only blue light" rule in principle provides a useful last quick check that the aircraft is properly configured for takeoff, in practice it may be undercut. On flight 795, with the Taxi and Before Takeoff checklists compressed into the final two minutes of a long taxi operation, and with the annunciator panel not checked until the airplane had already been aligned with the runway for takeoff and control of the airplane turned over to the first officer, the crew's check of the annunciator panel may have been rushed. This would have made it even less likely for the crew to detect the additional amber caution light.

We suggest that the first officer's earlier query about starting the second engine may have been an indirect hint that he was anticipating the substantial workload that remained after starting the engine and that he would have preferred not to wait longer. The captain, declining this suggestion, had overall control over the pace of the flight by deciding when to accept clearance into position on the runway and then with the speed with which he taxied onto and aligned the airplane with the runway centerline. Ideally, when the first officer's workload began to mount during this period the captain would have recognized the first officer's rush to complete his procedures. The captain could then have asked the first officer if he needed more time or could have taken the initiative to slow down his taxiing onto the runway and his transfer of control to the first officer. Thus, the captain exercised poor time and workload management during the taxi to the active runway, which contributed to an intense workload (especially for the first officer) just prior to takeoff and at the time when the annunciator panel check was performed. The first officer could have asked the captain for more time to complete the checklists, but junior flight officers are more likely to rush their procedures to keep up with the pace set by the captain than to admit falling behind.

The icing check, engine start, configuration of the airplane for takeoff, and multiple checklists could not be accomplished with reliable accuracy by a first officer in the time that the captain of flight 795 provided. Further, the checklist procedures established by the airline did not help the captain manage this situation well – in fact, by specifying that the second half of the Taxi checklist be performed when the airplane was approaching the departure runway, the company's procedures fostered time and workload compression at this critical time. Also, we are not aware of any airline-provided guidance to pilots about how to manage the workload of a single-engine taxi and the timing of startup of the second engine. We note that a previous accident (Delta flight 1141, B727, Dallas/Fort Worth, August 1988 – NTSB, 1989), involved time compression and rushed takeoff preparations resulting from crews delaying the startup of the second engine. This suggests that commonly issued company guidance encouraging single-engine taxiing should be accompanied with guidance about timing and workload management.

3. Captain rejected the takeoff at 143 knots, 5 knots faster than the calculated V1 takeoff decision speed

Cleared for takeoff at 1758:36, the flight accelerated down the runway. The captain later recalled to investigators that the airspeed appeared to stop increasing at approximately 60 knots indicated airspeed. The airspeed needle then indicated 80 knots, after which it returned to 60 knots. The captain said that he cross-checked the first officer's airspeed indicator and noted 60 knots on that instrument as well.

These airspeed indications were erroneous; the NTSB determined that the airplane actually accelerated normally during the takeoff and had exceeded V1 speed by the time the captain rejected the takeoff. The NTSB found that the readings on the captain's and first officer's airspeed indicators were inaccurate because of ice and snow plugging the unheated pitot tubes, and investigators calculated that approximately 20 seconds elapsed between the time that the airplane first accelerated through 60 knots and the captain's rejection of the takeoff.

The NTSB concluded that the captain's decision to reject the takeoff "[could] not be faulted under the circumstances" (NTSB, 1995b, p. 51), suggesting that the information the captain saw on his airspeed indicator and in his cross-check of the first officer's airspeed indicator was problematic enough to warrant rejecting the takeoff. However, investigators also concluded that the captain was not adequately attentive to airspeed indications during the takeoff roll, because of the 20 seconds that elapsed between the apparent beginning of the airspeed indication fault and the captain's decision to reject the takeoff. However, for several reasons, we suggest that it is not surprising that the captain required 20 seconds to begin rejecting the takeoff.

The NTSB noted that the captain had a greater than normal monitoring workload on this takeoff because of the slippery runway, crosswind, low visibility, and the need to monitor all of these environmental factors through the windshield as well as the first officer's handling of them. Moreover, as part of the normal workload of every takeoff, the monitoring pilot must check the throttle settings and engine instruments, attend to the outside visual scene to ensure that the aircraft is tracking properly, and make several airspeed calls in succession. This requires moving his or her visual gaze back and forth among targets frequently until the airplane is airborne.

In many cases the first airspeed call required for the monitoring pilot is 80 or 100 knots, and no standard exists for when first to check the airspeed in anticipation of this callout. Pilots probably develop a habit of starting to check the airspeed periodically at about the time movement of the airspeed indicator typically becomes apparent. The "round-dial" airspeed indicator of older aircraft is not linear at low speeds; the first tick mark is at around 60 knots, essentially the first point at which a pilot is likely to be able to discern movement. FDR data for flight 795 showed that the indicated airspeed stopped rising just below 50 knots, dropped to 0 momentarily and returned to about 45, slowly declined, and then dropped back to 0 and stayed, at which point the aircraft was actually traveling at approximately 143 knots. (Because they shared a data source, the FDR airspeed information may be equivalent to the speeds displayed on the first officer's airspeed indicator.) Thus it may be that the captain periodically monitored the airspeed indicator in a completely normal way, waiting for the needle to reach the first tick mark, and in the meantime all other cues (engine instruments readings, sounds, acceleration, and outside visual cues) appeared normal and in no way suggested a malfunction.

The captain was not alerted to a malfunction until an obvious airspeed indicator fluctuation occurred or it became apparent from the outside visual scene that the aircraft was traveling much faster than indicated. His recollection was that he noticed a fluctuation at 60 knots indicated, but we do not know how fast the aircraft was actually traveling at this point. We note that the captain had no direct way, throughout this period, of knowing the aircraft's actual speed, and he could only form a rough impression from estimating time elapsed and runway remaining. Individuals' time estimations are crude, at best, when occupied with other tasks, and the nighttime and poor visibility conditions would have hampered estimating the amount of runway remaining and the rate at which the airplane was consuming it.

For these reasons, we would not expect pilots in this situation to reliably detect the inaccurate airspeed indication until well past the 60-knot point. In addition to the detection process, the diagnostic process was also complex. The NTSB investigation found that the captain reported cross-checking the first officer's airspeed indicator, which apparently read about the same as the captain's. In general it is challenging for humans to quickly diagnose a gradually evolving discrepancy between conflicting cues and to make an appropriate decision on what action to take, especially if the anomaly is a very rare event. Pilots may go through an entire career, making tens of thousands of takeoffs, without an airspeed indicator malfunction; a dual airspeed indicator malfunction is even more rare.

In this situation, only gradually would a conflict become apparent between normally highly reliable airspeed indicator readings and the more subtle cues of normal acceleration, such as the sounds and feeling of the landing gear passing over runway bumps and expansion joints. We suggest that most pilots, noticing a discrepancy, would cross-check the other airspeed indicator, and then would require several more seconds to interpret the problem, decide to reject the takeoff, and initiate the rejection. Complicating and perhaps further slowing the decision was that the captain had no way of accurately determining the aircraft's speed but had to decide whether it was past V1 (the normal maximum speed for rejection) and whether it would be safer to reject the takeoff or continue without airspeed information.

4. After bringing the airplane to a stop, the crew mistakenly left the engines running and turned off the cabin emergency lighting during the emergency evacuation

The captain stated that he applied maximum braking and reverse thrust during the rejected takeoff. However, because the airplane was traveling faster than V1 when the captain began the rejected takeoff and the pavement was slippery, the airplane could not be stopped on the remaining runway. It came to rest atop a dike located just beyond the departure end of the runway with the nose resting on a mudflat (the nose became partially submerged later when the tides rose in Flushing Bay). Then, at 1800:00, with multiple alarm systems sounding loudly, the first officer asked the captain: "Okay, what do you want me to do?" The captain told the first officer to radio the company operations facility. At 1800:24 the captain told the first officer: "Alright let's shut the eng – shut all the electrical down … get the ah – speed brake … where's the checklist? … the abort checklist?" At 1800:41 the captain commanded an evacuation over the cabin public address system. He stated: "Easy victor easy victor [evacuation command to flight attendants], we see no fire we see no fire, be careful and go to the rear of the airplane, go to the rear of the airplane after you exit the aircraft". At 1801:08 the captain repeated: "Where's the abort checklist?" At 1801:25 the CVR recorded a fireman's voice repeating four times, "Cut the engines." The captain replied: "The engines are off, the engines are down". The first officer added: "Naw, they weren't … did you pull the fire handle?" The captain, apparently pulling the fire handles (emergency engine shutoffs) at this time, replied: "Now they're down".

This CVR information reveals that the captain's first action in the wake of the rejected takeoff and accident was to issue a flurry of commands to the first officer. We suggest that he might have generated a better-organized and more thorough response if he had immediately called for the Rejected Takeoff checklist (which he referred to as the abort checklist) instead of the list of commands. The captain did subsequently ask about the checklist twice but his query was not framed as a direct command and no response from the first officer was recorded on the CVR. Further, the captain did not pause for the checklist before ordering the passenger evacuation.

Although the captain later recalled that he had shut down the engines by closing the fuel shutoff levers (the normal method for engine shutdown), rescue crews found that the right engine was still running while passengers were evacuating. It is possible that the captain incorrectly recalled shutting down the engines prior to ordering the evacuation, but conceivably he may have attempted to shut down the engines using the normal method. If so, the attempt was unsuccessful – perhaps one or both of the shutoff levers were rendered inoperative by crash damage.

Company procedures required the captain to call for the Emergency Evacuation checklist before ordering passenger evacuation. We note that in addition to specifying that the engines should be shut down with the fuel shutoff levers, the checklist also specified pulling the engine fire handles, an effective alternate method for shutting down the engines. The crew of flight 795 did not pull the engine fire handles until prompted by the rescue crews. Also, passengers reported that the emergency lights in the cabin, which came on automatically after the crash, subsequently extinguished when both engines were shut down. One item of the Emergency Evacuation checklist would have prompted the crew to switch the cabin lighting to battery power, and if this step had been accomplished the lights would have remained on after engine shutdown. These events suggest that the crew did not execute the Emergency Evacuation checklist, and with the passengers evacuating through a dark cabin and then toward an operating engine, the risk of serious injury was increased.

In the stress and confusion immediately following an accident individuals are quite vulnerable to disorganized responses and to omitting procedural steps because of acute stress reaction (Burian and Barshi, 2003), and it is hardly surprising if this crew was at least momentarily stunned and overwhelmed by what had just happened. Other crews have shown disorganized responses similar to those of this crew after a crash landing (see for example, the Federal Express in-flight fire and emergency landing – Federal Express flight 1406, Newburgh, New York, September 1996 – NTSB, 1998b). Stress narrows attention span and reduces the availability of working memory capacity, two cognitive functions essential for assessing unfamiliar situations and making appropriate decisions (see Chapter 1). In addition to the stress and confusion from the crash itself, the pilots of flight 795 were subjected to continuous loud cockpit warning alerts as they tried to communicate after the airplane came to rest. These loud sounds probably seriously impaired the pilots' efforts to organize their thoughts and decide what to do next.

Pilots are trained to follow the Rejected Takeoff checklist and the Emergency Evacuation checklist but receive only infrequent and brief practice (at most every six months for captains and 12 months for first officers, and this recurrent training often does not include emergency evacuation). This level of practice is not sufficient to develop automatic responses engrained deeply enough to be highly reliable when pilots are in a state of psychological shock and confusion. Because emergency evacuations demand reliable human performance under the most difficult circumstances, we suggest that more work is required to incorporate knowledge of how humans perform under high stress into the design of emergency procedures and checklists and into the training of flight crews.[8]

Concluding discussion

The NTSB attributed this accident primarily to the crew's poor use of checklist procedures and failure to detect the erroneous airspeed indications quickly enough to reject the takeoff at a safe speed. Checklists and other standard operating procedures are vital ingredients of aviation safety; however, these procedures have weaknesses that must be understood if they are to be used effectively. Checking procedures take time and effort, and these procedures can deteriorate as the human tendency toward automaticity in routine situations leads pilots to look without seeing and check without checking. These habits may develop and persist without immediate negative consequence; thus companies and individual pilots must exert great discipline to maintain high standards in order to avoid the eventual consequences.

Paradoxically, the reliability of monitoring and detection of system faults tends to decline when the monitored system is so reliable that faults rarely occur. Also, limitations in human memory can lead individuals to confuse memory of performing a task many times previously or memory of having recently thought about performing the task with actually having performed the task currently. Further, in typical line operations crews are constantly interrupted during pre-start procedures, and humans are inherently vulnerable to forgetting to perform procedural steps when interrupted or forced to perform steps out of normal sequence (Reason, 1990, p. 71; Loukopoulos et al., 2006). Both pilots and airline managers may underestimate the depth of these vulnerabilities, and it is not clear how well airlines educate pilots about the associated dangers.

In this accident it appears that both the company and the crew fell short of adequate standards for adhering to procedures. However, the airline industry as a whole has not dealt adequately with factors that often undermine the effectiveness of checking procedures. Similarly, we suggest that the industry may not have adequately recognized that its own norms accept rushing, and thus may not have confronted the ways in which rushing can undermine defenses against error. Checklists are an important defense, but to be fully effective they must be performed in a deliberately paced, controlled fashion in which attention is focused on each item long enough for full cognitive processing. Pointing to or touching each item checked is one way to support this processing. A downside of performing checklists and flow of procedures in this deliberate fashion is that pace of operations will slow down, though we argue that the amount of time lost is actually quite small, much smaller than the subjective sense of slowing down might suggest. But because individuals find it quite natural to perform highly practised tasks at a brisk rate, pilots are unlikely to slow down their execution of procedures unless they are well educated about why this is needed and companies reinforce standards through checking and recurrent training.

Design of checklists can be tailored to enhance reliability under typical operating conditions. For example, instead of combining selecting a switch position with verifying the proper operation of the selected system (as the checklist for pitot heat in this accident required), the selection and verification steps could be separated into two different challenge/response items. This design would make it less likely for crews to inadvertently skip the verification portion of the check. Also, the crew response for an item that requires verifying an instrument reading should state the specific indication on the instrument; for example, "60 amps" rather than "Checked". Requiring the crewmember to verbalize a specific reading can help counter the tendency to respond automatically without consciously processing the instrument reading and its significance.

Flight 795 also illustrates several ways in which air carrier warning systems, operating procedures, and training are often designed with unrealistic assumptions about human information-processing characteristics. The equipment and procedures used in flight 795 were designed with the implicit assumption that crews would reliably detect an amber caution light for pitot/stall heaters when scanning the annunciator panel, even in a situation in which another amber caution light was on (appropriately) and with the assumption that crews would reliably detect an airspeed indication anomaly immediately after indicator movement became detectable. Unfortunately, these assumptions are unrealistic, given the workload and competing task demands at the moment detection is required and given the delays inherent in processing information from unexpected and confusing events.

Similarly, implicit in the training programs to which the crew of flight 795 were exposed, typical of all air carrier training, was the assumption that infrequent practice in emergency procedures is adequate to ensure that crews will reliably initiate and execute an evacuation checklist in the shock, stress, and confusion immediately following an accident. However, the variable performance of many crews following a crashed landing reveals that this assumption is clearly wrong.

For these reasons we argue that many of the errors committed by highly experienced airline pilots should be considered the manifestation of system failures rather than idiosyncratic shortcomings of the individual pilots. Our view of this accident is that the initiating error (not turning on the pitot heat) was inadvertent and that similar errors occur frequently but are either caught or happen not to combine with other circumstances to cause an accident. In this accident the initiating error was not trapped and ultimately led to a bad outcome because the procedural defenses against such errors were weakened by inherent vulnerabilities of monitoring and checklist execution, worsened by line norms allowing relaxed checklist compliance and discipline. Like other commentators (for example, Perrow, 1999; Reason, 1990; Cook, Woods, and Miller, 1998), we argue that safety cannot be maintained, much less advanced, unless the industry adopts this systems perspective on human error.

In its recommendations for safety improvements (Safety Recommendation A-95-21) based on the accident, the NTSB recognized that requiring crews to turn on pitot-static heaters on each flight instead of having the heaters come on automatically unnecessarily exposes the flight to the danger of omission (NTSB, 1995b, p. 63). In cases such as this a simple solution exists – many modern aircraft activate the pitot-static heaters automatically. Admittedly, however, many vulnerabilities to system failure, manifested as "crew error", cannot be remedied so easily. It is not possible to design a system in which errors never occur, and the airline industry has already reached high levels of reliability through generally good design practices. Further improvement will require focusing on the conditions that underlie vulnerability to error and providing better ways to detect and correct errors, rather than blaming those who inadvertently commit errors.

Notes

1   Takeoff decision speed (V1) was 138 knots.
2   After an accident, depending of course on the availability and condition of aircraft wreckage, investigators transcribe the exact position of all levers and switches and the readings indicated by all gauges in the cockpit.
3   Strictly speaking, this phenomenon has been studied only as the frequency of sampling of a display, but the same relationship may hold between quality of sampling and rate of change of what is displayed.
4   In its accident investigation report the NTSB noted the following deviations by the accident crew from standard operating procedures:

   • the crew did not call the After-Start checklist complete;
   • the Delayed Engine Start procedure should not have been used in icing conditions;
   • the first officer started the second engine without calling for/performing the Delayed Engine Start checklist;
   • the captain did not call for the Taxi checklist, and it was then self-initiated by the first officer one minute before the flight entered the departure runway;
   • the first officer self-initiated the After (Delayed) Engine Start checklist on the runway, omitted items, and did not call the checklist complete;
   • the captain did not call to initiate the Before Takeoff checklist, and the first officer self-initiated the checklist and did not call it complete.

5   Regulations specified that the pre-takeoff inspection be performed no more than five minutes before takeoff.
6   According to the NTSB accident investigation report (1995b, pp. 37–8), the company's procedures for executing the taxi checklist specified that the first officer should perform the first five steps of the checklist at the beginning of the taxi, then interrupt the procedure to perform the Delayed Engine Start checklist (if taxiing on a single engine), then wait until the airplane has arrived at the departure runway to resume the Taxi checklist with flap/slat extension and the remaining items. Of seven company pilots interviewed by the NTSB, all but one stated that the norm in line operations was to perform the entire Taxi checklist when the time came to position the flaps (shortly before taxiing onto the runway).
7   The warning system would also illuminate an amber master caution light on the pilots' forward panels. According to MD-80 pilots interviewed by the NTSB, it was normal for several systems to trigger a master caution light prior to and during engine start; as a result,

it was likely that after engine start pilots would automatically cancel a master caution light generated by unpowered pitot/stall heat. Thus it is likely that the accident aircraft displayed the "Pitot/Stall Heater Off" warning light but not the more conspicuous master caution warning light when the first officer performed the Before Takeoff checklist.

Chapter 12

USAir 405 – Snowy Night at LaGuardia

Introduction

On March 22, 1992 at 2135 eastern standard time, USAir flight 405, a Fokker F-28 jet, rolled uncontrollably to the left and crashed while taking off on runway 13 at LaGuardia Airport in Flushing, New York. The airplane broke apart and partially submerged in Flushing Bay. Of the 51 persons aboard, the captain, one flight attendant, and 25 passengers were killed in the accident.

Flight 405 originated in Jacksonville, Florida earlier in the day and was bound from New York to Cleveland, Ohio when the accident occurred. This was the crew's fourth flight leg on the day of the accident, which was the third day of a scheduled four-day trip together. It was snowing lightly at LaGuardia Airport as the captain and first officer prepared for departure, and snow continued during the flight's taxi to the runway. Flight 405 was operating almost two hours behind schedule because of delays on previous legs, heavy evening departure traffic at LaGuardia, and deicing operations. The captain, who had three years of experience and 1,400 hours as a pilot-in-command in the F-28, was the flying pilot. The first officer was newly upgraded and assigned to the F-28. He had served as a flight engineer at the airline for more than two years before qualifying in the right seat of the F-28. The 29 hours that he had accumulated in the F-28 during the month preceding the accident constituted his only flight experience in a transport category jet.

The NTSB investigation found that the airplane stalled during takeoff rotation, which prevented it from accelerating or climbing and also led to the uncommanded roll. The wing stalled at a lower than normal angle of attack because its upper surface was contaminated, probably with a thin, rough layer of snow or ice. The agency found that the takeoff occurred with a contaminated wing because the crew of flight 405, as well as other airline crews, had not been provided adequate procedures and equipment to detect upper wing icing reliably. The NTSB also found that the crew rotated for takeoff at a slower airspeed than specified for the airplane's loading and operating conditions, which may have been a factor in the stall, poor climb performance, and uncommanded roll.

The NTSB determined that the probable causes of this accident were:

> ... the failure of the airline industry and the FAA to provide flight crews with procedures, requirements, and criteria compatible with departure delays in conditions conducive to airframe icing and the decision by the flight crew to take off without positive assurance that the airplane's wings were free of ice accumulation after 35 minutes of exposure to precipitation following deicing.

The NTSB also cited, as contributing to the cause of the accident, "the inappropriate procedures used by, and inadequate coordination between, the flight crew that led to a takeoff rotation at a lower than prescribed airspeed" (NTSB, 1993b, p. vi).

Significant events and issues

1. The captain chose to reduce the V1 (takeoff decision) speed below the calculated value

Interviewed after the accident, the first officer recalled noting while he was seated in the airplane prior to pushback that the snow was not falling heavily. He also recalled that "the airplane's nose had a watery layer as far as his arm could reach out the window" (NTSB, 1993b, p. 2). During flight 405's ground time at LaGuardia the captain and first officer did not perform an exterior inspection of the airplane, nor did the airline's procedures require the crew to perform an external inspection in this situation. However, the crew did request that company ground personnel deice the airplane. Also, when it became apparent that the flight's departure from the gate would be further delayed, the captain requested a second application of deicing fluid. The flight was pushed back from the gate to facilitate the second deicing operation, which was completed around 2100.

Although it may have been prudent for one of the crewmembers to conduct an exterior inspection of the airplane because of these weather conditions, we suggest that the crew took all of the necessary precautions prior to pushback, including ordering the two applications of deicing fluid. The deicing procedures included inspections of the wings by maintenance personnel from the elevated vantage point of a deicing vehicle, which provided a better view of the upper wing surface than a pilot could obtain either from the ground level or from the cabin. Further, the pilots' request for a second application of deicing fluid indicates that they were aware that the deicing application would be effective only for a limited time during snowfall (the "holdover time"). The crew's request suggests that they intended to comply with regulations about ensuring a "clean wing" for takeoff and were willing to make conservative decisions about icing, even at the expense of an additional departure delay.

After the flight was cleared to taxi at 2105, the captain took several additional steps related to operating in icing conditions. He delayed extending the flaps during the taxi (placing a coffee cup over the flap handle to remind the crew to set the flaps later) and then used a greater flap deflection than normal, which was appropriate for the existing snow-contaminated taxiways and runways. He avoided taxiing close behind the preceding flight, briefing the first officer on the importance of avoiding the melting/refreezing cycle that can result from taxiing into jet exhaust. Further, he told the first officer to set a reduced airspeed for V1, the takeoff decision speed. The calculated V1 speed for this takeoff that the crew derived from their flight papers was 124 knots, but the captain established V1 as 110 knots, instead. Reducing V1 was not an approved procedure at this airline at the time of the accident, but it was sometimes used at other airlines for taking off on a slippery runway. The captain's use of an unapproved V1 reduction was probably a response to recently publicized concerns about the hazards of rejecting takeoff on a snowy runway. The reduced V1 speed would compensate for the poor braking effectiveness that flight 405 would experience if a rejected takeoff became necessary on the slippery pavement.

The crew's discussion recorded by the CVR during this period suggests the first officer understood that the V1 speed would be reduced from 124 knots to 110 knots. The calculated rotation speed (Vr) for this takeoff, also 124 knots, was not affected by the reduction of V1 to 110 knots. The accident investigation revealed that it was typical of F-28 operations for V1 and Vr to be the same, or nearly the same, airspeed. Consequently the crew of flight 405 would have been accustomed to calling for and performing the takeoff rotation immediately after attaining V1 speed. The crew did not explicitly discuss that, on this takeoff, V1 and Vr would differ and the airplane thus would have to accelerate for some period after attaining V1 before reaching Vr. Thus, the captain's decision to reduce V1 introduced a change to the normal takeoff routine for which the crew had apparently not been specifically trained, and the captain did not explicitly brief the first officer on the implications of this change for the timing of events during the takeoff roll.

Later in this chapter we will discuss the consequences of this change to the normal routine, but for now we note that the captain's reduction of V1, clearly motivated by the desire to build a conservative bias into the operation by avoiding the hazards of a high speed rejected takeoff, nonetheless increased vulnerability to errors involving the callout and execution of the takeoff rotation. Pilots, like other experts, often fail to identify all potential risk factors when they deviate from standard operating procedures, especially when they deviate in the midst of the operation and without thoroughly discussing and briefing the idea among the entire crew. This suggests that crews should be extremely hesitant to deviate from established procedures in real time, even if the deviation appears to improve safety.

Although the captain took nearly every conceivable precaution to ensure the success of this takeoff, he apparently did not consider delaying initiation of the takeoff rotation, which is an additional conservative measure that can improve the margin of safety when wing contamination might occur. The airline had issued a memorandum four months before the accident, advising pilots to delay rotation by up to 10 knots when taking off in icing conditions (NTSB, 1993b, p. 58).[1] This memorandum was advice on "technique;"[2] at that time the airline's standard operating procedures for cold weather operations contained in its *F-28 Pilot's Handbook* did not require any change in normal rotation techniques for cold weather operations (NTSB, 1993b, p. 52).[3] The first officer also did not mention the possibility of delaying rotation; however, it is unlikely that most first officers with his limited experience would have made suggestions about technique to a captain. The company's memorandum on delaying rotation was valuable. However, the company's failure to incorporate this information into its formal standard operating procedures may have made it less likely that crews would remember and use the information when needed.

2. The flight crew commenced takeoff more than 35 minutes after deicing

Interviewed after the accident, the first officer recalled that during taxi he used the ice inspection light (which illuminates the leading edge of the wing and the black stripe painted on it to help pilots identify in-flight ice accumulation) "maybe 10 times, but at least three" (NTSB, 1993b, p. 3). He said that both pilots looked back at the wing and the black stripe as the airplane approached takeoff position, and they did not see any snow or ice on the wing. The first officer told investigators that shortly before takeoff he told the captain that the wing was clear and the black stripe was visible. (His comment as recorded by the CVR at 2129:30 was less specific: "Looks pretty good to me from what I can see"). At 2129:37, the first officer remarked to the captain, "It's pretty much stopped the precip[itation]". Air traffic control cleared the flight into position on runway 13 at 2133:50 and about one minute later cleared it for takeoff.

Despite appearances from the cockpit, the airplane's upper wing surface was contaminated with what probably was a thin layer of rough snow or ice, which degraded aerodynamic performance during the takeoff. According to company cold weather procedures in its *F-28 Pilot's Handbook* the elapsed time since deicing required the crew to conduct a "careful examination" for wing contamination before departure (NTSB, 1993b, p. 42). We suggest that the pilots of flight 405, who had been very conscientious about considering wing contamination and in taking appropriate countermeasures, probably thought that they were conducting a careful inspection by looking back at the wing and the black stripe painted on its leading edge. The pilots' repeated references to the black stripe suggest that they relied on the stripe to reveal any icing accumulation, not realizing that this is not an adequate indication of icing in ground conditions. Although in-flight icing would accumulate on the wing's leading edge where the black stripe was painted (and where the in-flight icing could be illuminated by the ice inspection light), icing from precipitation encountered on the ground accumulates on the upper surface of the wing and probably would not occur on the leading edge, including the black stripe.

The first officer recalled seeing no accumulation on the upper wing surface, but investigators found that it was impossible to obtain a good view of that part of the airplane from the cockpit without opening and leaning out of the side window. The first officer did not open the side window; however, he had most likely never been taught to do so, and probably never anticipated that the closed window impaired visual detection of wing contamination. Interviews by investigators with other company pilots and flight managers established that most F-28 pilots believed they could obtain a good view of the wing through a closed cockpit window. These findings led the NTSB to conclude that pilots had "overconfidence" in their ability to identify wing contamination from inside the cockpit (NTSB, 1993b, p. 58).

We suggest that the pilots' incorrect conclusion that the wing was uncontaminated was reinforced by the precipitation tapering off and by their earlier observations that the snow and ice were sliding off of the front surfaces of the airplane's fuselage. Together, all of this evidence would suggest to any pilot that there was no significant accumulation of snow or ice on the upper wing. However, the NTSB found that extremely thin accumulations (with the roughness of only medium-grade sandpaper) can seriously degrade the performance of a jet transport airplane. This hazard is especially great for airplanes like the F-28 that have a fixed leading edge with no leading edge slats or flaps (see further discussion of this issue in Chapter 7).[4]

The NTSB concluded that these thin accumulations could be reliably detected only by an extremely close inspection of the upper wing surface, preferably a tactile inspection.[5] At the time of this accident, neither this airline nor others provided crews with procedures or tools to closely assess the upper wing surface for possible contamination before takeoff. As a result of this accident, the FAA established a requirement for airlines operating in the most critical ground icing conditions to have one pilot leave the cockpit and visually inspect the wings from the passenger cabin. However, the NTSB's findings raise the issue of whether inspection from the cabin would be adequate to detect a thin but hazardous layer of contamination.

The NTSB concluded that one of the causes of this accident was the failure of the aviation system at large to provide flight crews with reliable means to detect and criteria with which to evaluate ice accumulations. Further, reviewing the crew's efforts to conduct a departure in snow conditions, including two applications of deicing fluid, the agency cited the system at large for failing to control the length of departure delays so as to enable flights to depart in a timely manner after deicing (that is, within the "holdover" window of time). This accident was the last in a series of contaminated-wing takeoff accidents that occurred from the 1960s through the early 1990s,[6] and it was the first of a series of accidents in which the NTSB cited systemic, industry-level factors as causal. The NTSB's identification of an industry-wide need for better procedures, criteria, and operating norms for winter operations has led to significant changes in deicing fluid types, deicing procedures, information provided to crews about holdover times, and wing inspection procedures.

The systemic nature of this problem was also shown by the activities of other airline flights departing at the same time as the accident flight. For example, two other flights were taxiing for takeoff just behind flight 405. The pilots of these flights recalled examining the accident aircraft for wing contamination, most likely in order to infer the condition of their own airplane. They saw no contamination on the accident airplane's wings and so were encouraged to continue their own operations. Investigators found that these flights had been deiced at about the same time as flight 405. The crews of these airplanes also would have attempted to take off if the airport had not subsequently closed as a result of the accident. Their situations, assessments, and decisions were quite similar to those of the accident crew. We suggest, therefore, that the mistaken assessment by the crew of flight 405 that their airplane's wing was uncontaminated probably would have been shared by many other pilots.

This accident and others discussed in this book illustrate the difficulty expert decision-makers sometimes have in recognizing whether past experience and knowledge are adequate to evaluate the current situation. Apparently experienced in winter operations, the captain of flight 405 had no way of knowing that his experience and training did not provide adequate methods to assess wing contamination. We do not know whether the flight 405 crew were reassured by aircraft in front of them appearing free of contamination, but neither pilot was likely to have been aware that their airplane, because of its wing design, may have been the most vulnerable of the airplanes in line to depart that snowy evening.

3. First officer called for rotation prior to the correct airspeed, and the captain rotated the airplane too early

At 2135:25, with the airplane accelerating down the runway, the first officer called out "V1". The first officer's callout was consistent with the captain's earlier decision to reduce the takeoff decision speed to 110 knots (from 124 knots). Less than one second later the first officer called out "Vr", which was the captain's cue to begin rotating the airplane's nose upward. Flight data recorder information indicated that the first officer called for rotation when the airplane had attained 113 knots, and the captain began rotation slightly more than one second later at 119 knots. In contrast, the correct rotation speed for the flight, which should have been unaffected by reducing the V1 speed, was 124 knots. After beginning to raise the nose when the airplane was traveling 5 knots too slowly, the captain then rotated the airplane to the normal target pitch attitude of 15 degrees. The airplane became airborne at about 2135:30.

The first officer acknowledged to investigators that he had called out "Vr" too early because rotation speed was ordinarily the same as V1 speed on the F-28. The period just before rotation is busy for both pilots, and the first officer would have had a strongly established habit of calling "V1, Vr" as a single annunciation. Individuals are normally quite vulnerable to this type of habit-capture error in time-pressured situations (Betsch, Haberstroh, Molter, and Glöckner, 2003). Also, with only 29 hours of experience, the first officer was still becoming accustomed to the aircraft and company procedures, and he was probably less likely to catch and correct his own mistake than a more experienced pilot might have been.

It is not clear whether the captain noticed that the first officer had inadvertently called Vr 11 knots early. The CVR reveals no utterances from either pilot bearing on this question, which suggests that the captain did not notice. Earlier, when the captain decided to reduce the speed for V1, he may not have thought explicitly about the fact that this change would cause the Vr speed to occur several seconds after V1, rather than immediately after. It is quite common for individuals to overlook some of the indirect consequences of changes in routine. Thus the captain may not have been primed for a delay between the V1 and Vr calls, and the close spacing between the two calls in this instance probably seemed correct, since spacing was normally close. Also, flying pilots probably are unable to cross-check airspeed reliably at the time of rotation – the aircraft is accelerating rapidly and the flying pilot must attend predominately to outside cues in order to control the aircraft. And if the captain did cross-check the airspeed indicator, the first officer's Vr call probably biased the captain to expect to see the planned rotation speed, further reducing the probability of detecting the discrepancy on the rapidly changing indicator in a brief glance.

Data from the FDR does not provide any indication that the captain performed the delayed rotation technique recommended in the memorandum as a countermeasure for possible ice contamination of the wing (see previous discussion). If the captain had used the delayed rotation technique, the target speed for rotation would have increased by 10 knots to 134 knots, or 15 knots faster than the normal rotation speed actually used on this flight. This additional airspeed would have increased the chances that the flight could safely climb away from the ground and avoid stalling. (In more technical terms, the greater airspeed would have reduced the angle of attack, providing a greater margin from the critical angle of attack at which a wing stalls.) We also suggest that, if the captain had planned to delay the rotation and had briefed the first officer about this plan, the crew probably would have thought more explicitly about the rotation speed and thus might have been less likely to rotate the airplane prematurely.

Investigators found that at the time of the accident the airline had deleted from its takeoff rotation procedures a previously established technique of pausing at the 10-degree nose-up attitude until surpassing the V2 takeoff safety speed, which is several knots faster than rotation speed (NTSB, 1993b, p. 60). In most cases an airplane would achieve V2 while still on the ground, so the takeoff rotation would be a continuous pitch-up. However, this technique would also prompt a cross-check of airspeed by the crew during rotation and thereby could provide for a greater airspeed margin, when acceleration through V2 was inadequate. The 10-degree initial pitch attitude technique was included in the procedures established by the aircraft manufacturer and had been established as the standard takeoff procedure by two of the predecessor airlines of this company that had operated the F-28.

The NTSB concluded that the company's

> ... elimination of the reference to an attitude of 10 degrees creates the practice by line pilots of rotating directly to 15 degrees [nose-up] without cross-checking airspeed .... A total reliance on a 3-degrees per second rotation rate is induced, and there is little emphasis placed on the airspeed attained until the rotation maneuver is complete (NTSB, 1993b, p. 60).

The NTSB also found that a takeoff rotation that pauses at 10 degrees until after liftoff reduces the wing's angle of attack significantly during the rotation and initial climb. However, it was not possible to determine whether using this technique would have been sufficient to influence the outcome of flight 405.

4. The airplane stalled, was unable to climb, and departed from controlled flight in a left roll

Slightly less than five seconds after rotation began, the stall warning stickshaker activated. The first officer recalled that at this time the airframe was buffeting, the airplane could not climb out of ground effect, and it rolled to the left despite the control inputs of the two pilots.

The flight simulation studies conducted as part of the investigation revealed that by this time an accident was inevitable. The early rotation had caused the angle of attack to exceed the normal post-takeoff value of 9 degrees, and wing contamination had reduced the stalling angle of attack from the normal value of 12 degrees to approximately 9 degrees. The airplane entered an aerodynamic stall, and drag from the stall prevented the airplane from climbing or even accelerating in level flight. There was insufficient runway on which to land and stop, and there was no altitude to give up in order to gain airspeed. The post-stall controllability of the airplane was poor, with a roll-off that was probably aggravated by unequal stalling of the two wings from uneven wing contamination.

The stall warning system did not alert the crew until the airplane was already in a stalled condition because the wing contamination caused the wing to stall at a lower than normal angle of attack. Aircraft certification standards require that transport airplanes provide crews with adequate warning prior to the actual stall; however, as the circumstances of this accident show (see also Chapter 5), the certification standards do not appear to provide for adequate stall detection in the event of wing contamination. If the stall warning system had activated before flight 405 entered a full stall, the crew conceivably could have reacted quickly enough to lower the nose and accelerate in ground effect to an adequate speed. However, even with this warning, the time available to respond was so short and the angle of attack was so close to the critical angle at the moment of rotation that it is not at all clear that the crew could have recovered.

It is also conceivable that some pilots in this situation might have recognized the signs of imminent stalling before the stall warning activated, through airframe buffeting; however, this is improbable. Very little time was available to interpret the unexpected and ambiguous indications of airframe buffeting. Also, air carrier pilots receive substantial training and simulator practice that causes imminent stall to be strongly associated in memory with stickshaker activation. This association might further delay recognition of airframe buffeting as a sign of imminent stalling in the absence of stickshaker activation.

Concluding discussion

Several aspects of crew performance contributed directly to this accident: the crew did not detect wing contamination, the first officer inadvertently called Vr too soon, and the captain subsequently rotated the airplane prematurely, compounding the aerodynamic impairment caused by wing contamination. Also, the airline's standard procedure for rotation was not optimal for the F-28 in icing conditions. The accident would almost certainly not have occurred if the crew had detected the wing contamination, and it might possibly have been averted if the crew had not rotated early and had employed the rotation procedures recommended by the manufacturer and used by predecessor airlines but dropped by this airline at the time of the accident.

The crew's failure to detect wing contamination resulted from a deficiency endemic to the entire aviation system: crews were not provided criteria for and means to reliably detect small but hazardous accumulation of frozen ice or snow. This was not an isolated situation; very probably many airliners took off in this era with a thin, rough layer of snow or ice adhering to the wings, their crews and passengers not knowing how small their margin of safety was. The system has since been improved and crews have been provided somewhat better information, tools, and procedures for detecting wing contamination; however, it is not certain that these improvements are adequate to ensure reliable detection of thin layers of wing contamination.

The early rotation was not a simple error; rather, it resulted from the interplay of several aspects of human vulnerability set in play by the captain's decision to use a lower V1 speed. In some respects, that decision may have seemed a reasonable response to a serious safety concern (being able to stop after a rejected takeoff in icing conditions), but the captain did not anticipate how this unpractised change in procedure would weaken normal defenses against error. Nor might most other pilots have anticipated the consequences, which is why it is seldom a good idea to modify procedures unless authorized and trained in the modification. The first officer's error in calling Vr in conjunction with V1 is entirely understandable, given the force of habit and the failure of the crew to discuss the ramifications of executing the early V1 speed. This mistake was a small, natural human slip that would have been harmless in most situations, but the chance co-occurrence with wing contamination led to disaster. It is not surprising that the busy captain did not catch the first officer's error, and almost certainly the mistaken Vr call triggered the captain's premature rotation.

When the airplane began its initial climb in a semi-stalled condition and then commenced uncommanded roll oscillations, the control task and cognitive demands on the crew were extreme. Recovery in this situation requires the crew to immediately identify the stall and to react with control inputs counter to those of a normal takeoff. For this reason crews are thoroughly trained to respond to the stickshaker cues of the stall warning system. It is not clear whether this crew or any other crew could have reliably maintained control of an airplane in the situation of flight 405, even if warned before the airplane was fully stalled. But in the absence of this warning it is unlikely any crew would have recognized that stalling was imminent, and once the stall began the accident was inevitable. The failure of aircraft certification standards to ensure that crews were provided adequate warning prior to the stall is another systemic element that we think is significant in this accident.

This accident might not have occurred in an airplane equipped with leading edge devices. The F-28 and other airliners lacking leading edge devices have an inherently reduced margin of safety when operating in conditions in which there is any possibility of taking off with wing contamination. The extreme impairment of performance of these airplanes by wing contamination was well-known, had caused several previous accidents, and had been the subject of pointed recommendations by the NTSB. Unfortunately, these issues were not heeded in time to prevent this accident. The appropriateness of operating airplanes without leading edge devices in passenger service in conditions conducive to icing is a policy issue with cost–benefit aspects going beyond the scope of this book. However, given that these aircraft are used extensively in regional jet fleets, it is especially crucial that stringent operating procedures, including those recommended by the manufacturer, be used. Also, we believe that airlines should scrutinize current cold weather operations for all types of airplanes to ensure that crews are given highly effective means to detect the presence of thin layers of wing contamination. Otherwise, the large volume of passenger operations in conditions conducive to icing may eventually lead to another accident such as this one.

Notes

1 It is interesting that this company was formed through merging with other companies that had considerable experience of operating the F-28 in winter conditions. In November 1991, the company reissued a 1984 memo written by an F-28 captain of a predecessor airline that discussed the special susceptibility of the F-28 to wing contamination effects and recommended adding as much as a 10-knot margin to the rotation speed as a compensation. The 1991 reissue of the 1984 memorandum recovered some of this valuable corporate knowledge for the benefit of flight operations in the successor company; however, the accident investigation report did not mention whether the accident captain would have seen that memo.

2 "Technique" refers to optional variations on procedures or specific ways to accomplish a procedure pilots may choose to use. In contrast, procedures are mandatory.

3 The handbook also cautioned pilots that "smooth rotation rates are essential in avoiding possible pitch-up and roll-off characteristics that may be encountered when airfoil contamination is likely" and stated that normal rotation could result in early airflow separation and control problems at liftoff if there were layers of ice on the wing. However, the manual did not provide any countermeasure besides smoothness in the rotation maneuver.

4 Most large transports with a fixed leading edge (including the F-28 and DC-9-10 series) are leaving US passenger air transportation service. However, regional jets with a fixed leading edge will be in the US airline inventory for the foreseeable future.

5 If the NTSB is correct, the current requirements for pre-takeoff wing inspections (which were developed and mandated as a result of this accident) may not reliably detect wing contamination because they permit a visual inspection of the wing from the cabin and do not go as far as requiring a tactile inspection.

6 Ozark flight 982, DC-9-15, Sioux City, Iowa, December 1968 – NTSB, 1970; Trans World flight 505, DC-9-10, Newark, New Jersey, November 1978 – NTSB, 1978; Airborne Express flight 125, DC-9-15, Philadelphia, Pennsylvania, February 1985 – NTSB, 1985; Air Florida flight 90 , Boeing 737-222, Washington DC, January 1982

– NTSB, 1982; Continental flight 1713, DC-9-14, Denver, Colorado, November 1987
– NTSB, 1988b; Ryan International flight 590, DC-9-15, Cleveland, Ohio, February
1991 – NTSB, 1991, and Chapter 7 of this book.

Chapter 13

ValuJet 558 – Two Missing Words and a Hard Landing Short of the Runway

Introduction

On January 7, 1996 at 1620 eastern standard time, ValuJet Airlines flight 558, a Douglas DC-9-32, landed hard just short of the threshold of runway 2R at Nashville, Tennessee. After the impact, which caused substantial damage to the landing gear and fuselage, the flight crew rejected the landing, circled the airport, and maneuvered the airplane to a safe landing on runway 31. Of the 88 passengers and 5 crewmembers aboard, one flight attendant and four passengers received minor injuries.

Flight 558, scheduled as a nonstop service from Atlanta, Georgia to Nashville, was the third flight of the day for the captain and first officer. The two pilots had never flown together before. Although highly experienced, both were new to their respective crew positions at this airline and in this aircraft type: the captain had 26 hours of DC-9 pilot-in-command experience (plus an additional 1,035 hours as a DC-9 second-in-command); the first officer had 205 hours of experience as a DC-9 second-in-command. The flight was operating about 1½ hours late because of delays on the airplane's previous flights. It was snowing in Atlanta during the time on the ground prior to departure. The crew planned that flight 558 would be flown by the first officer, with the captain performing the monitoring pilot duties.

Like most large aircraft, the DC-9 is equipped with sensors that detect compression of the landing gear struts, indicating whether the airplane is on the ground or in the air. In the DC-9 these sensors feed information to the ground shift mechanism, a series of relays that affect the functioning of several aircraft systems that have to perform differently when the airplane is on the ground versus in the air, including the landing gear, ground spoilers, and pressurization. The landing gear strut compression sensors are also the source of information for the landing gear anti-retraction system that physically locks the gear handle when the airplane is on the ground to prevent inadvertent retraction of the gear.

The NTSB investigation revealed that the crew of flight 558 could not move the landing gear handle to retract the gear after takeoff, probably because the nose gear strut was underinflated and thus did not signal the anti-retraction system and ground shift mechanism that the flight was airborne. Also, because the ground shift mechanism did not shift, the airplane could not be pressurized as it began its climb to cruise altitude. Then, while flight 558 was en route to Nashville, the crew used an abnormal procedures checklist that the airline had provided for dealing with this situation. As guided by this checklist, they pulled two ground control relay circuit breakers that forced the ground shift mechanism and the associated systems into their air functioning modes. That allowed the crew to retract the landing gear and pressurize the airplane. Further, the NTSB found that just prior to touchdown, the crew of flight 558 prematurely reset the ground control relay circuit breakers. As a result, the systems affected by the ground shift mechanism transitioned back to their ground functioning modes, and the ground spoiler panels, which normally extend automatically after landing to kill residual lift, deployed while flight 558 was still in the air. Loss of wing lift from the spoiler deployment resulted in the hard landing, despite the flight crew's efforts to arrest the unexpectedly steep descent with nose-up elevator and thrust inputs.

The NTSB determined that the probable cause of this accident was

> ... the flight crew's improper procedures and actions (failing to contact system operations/ dispatch, failing to use all available aircraft and company manuals, and prematurely resetting the ground control relay circuit breakers) in response to an in-flight abnormality, which resulted in the inadvertent in-flight activation of the ground spoilers during the final approach to landing and the airplane's subsequent increased descent rate and excessively hard ground impact in the runway approach light area.

The NTSB also cited the following factors as contributing to the cause of the accident:

> ValuJet's failure to incorporate cold weather nose gear servicing procedures in its operations and maintenance manuals, the incomplete procedural guidance contained in the ValuJet quick reference handbook, and the flight crew's inadequate knowledge and understanding of the aircraft systems (NTSB, 1996d, p. viii).

Significant events and issues

1. Captain did not notice abnormal nose strut inflation during the exterior preflight inspection

The captain conducted a preflight inspection of the exterior of the airplane at Atlanta, noting no discrepancies. Post-accident analysis indicated, though, that the airplane's nose landing gear strut was probably underinflated, which is a common problem in DC-9 winter operations because of the adverse effects of cold temperatures on a gas-damped strut.

The airline's aircraft operating manual (AOM) for the DC-9 instructed pilots to check the nose gear strut for inflation and leaks during the preflight inspection and further specified that proper inflation was indicated by strut extension of 2–6 inches with the airplane resting on its landing gear. However, during the investigation, the manufacturer of the DC-9 stated that flight crewmembers could not be expected to reliably detect inadequate strut inflation because strut extension also varied substantially as a function of airplane load conditions. According to the manufacturer, the verification of nose strut inflation was a maintenance, rather than a flight crew, function.

VALUJET
QUICK REFERENCE HANDBOOK
PILOT MANUAL – DC–9

UNABLE TO RAISE GEAR LEVER

NOSE STEERING WHEEL ....OPERATE   (C)

If steering wheel does NOT turn and centering
indices are aligned:

Indicates a malfunction of the anti–retraction
mechanism.

If desired, retract landing gear:

GEAR HANDLE RELEASE BUTTON ....PUSH   (PNF)

GEAR LEVER ....UP   (PNF)

If steering wheel turns:
DO NOT RETRACT THE GEAR

Indicates ground shift mechanism is still in the ground
mode.

No auto–pressurization, and takeoff warning horn will
sound when flaps/slats are retracted.

The ground control relay electrical circuits can be placed
in the flight mode by pulling the Ground Control Relay
circuit breakers (H20 and J20).

Do not exceed VLE (300 kts/M.70).

Approach and landing:
If landing gear was not retracted prior to landing,
ground spoilers must be operated manually.

AIRPLANE ...................................DEPRESSURIZE   (PNF)

ANTI–SKID SWITCH (before 30 kts) ....OFF   (PNF)

GROUND CONTROL RELAY C/Bs (if pulled)
(H20 and J20) ....RESET   (C or FO)

Figure 13.1   Cockpit Quick Reference Handbook procedure, as issued by
              ValuJet Airlines (operator), for "Unable to Raise Gear Lever"
              (NTSB, 1996d, p. 3).

The NTSB noted that, despite having received service bulletins and a DC-9 maintenance manual with a recommended cold weather servicing program from the manufacturer, the airline had not established adequate maintenance checks for the special requirements of cold weather operations. Among the checks not established were enhanced inspections of nose strut inflation by maintenance personnel; consequently, the routine monitoring of nose strut inflation had apparently devolved to the flight crews. In citing inadequate inspection procedures for cold weather conditions as a contributing factor in this accident, the NTSB effectively concurred with the manufacturer that this inspection should have been a maintenance function and that flight crews lacked the information and procedural criteria to reliably detect an underinflated nose strut. This suggests that many DC-9 pilots would not have detected the problem while performing their normal preflight inspection.

The NTSB finding illustrates a more general issue: procedures that may seem adequate when designed in the abstract sometimes fail in actual operations because of unanticipated features of the operating environment or because the procedure is not well matched to human perceptual and cognitive limitations.

2. Crew could not get the landing gear to retract after takeoff

The flight departed Atlanta at 1539. After a normal takeoff roll and rotation, with the first officer at the controls, the captain was unable to move the landing gear lever into the retract position.[1] While the first officer continued to fly the airplane, the captain referred to the company's quick reference handbook (QRH) checklist procedure entitled "Unable to Raise Gear Lever" (NTSB, 1996d, p. 3) (see Figure 13.1).

The checklist instructed the captain to "operate" the nose steering wheel to test whether the wheel could be moved from the center position. Depending on the results of that test, the checklist led crews to one of two branches. The first branch was headed: "If steering wheel does NOT turn and centering indices are aligned". It continued: "Indicates a malfunction of the anti-retraction mechanism … if desired, retract landing gear". This branch of the checklist then provided directions for overriding the anti-retraction mechanism and retracting the gear. It was essential to check that the nosewheel was centered because manually overriding and retracting a nose gear turned to the side can cause the gear to damage the wheel well or become stuck. The alternate branch of the checklist provided instructions for the other possible result of the wheel test: "If steering wheel turns: DO NOT RETRACT THE GEAR, indicates ground shift mechanism is still in the ground mode." This branch of the checklist continued with directions to force the ground shift mechanism into the air mode and provided additional information, which we will discuss later.

After executing the first step of the checklist (nose steering test), the captain determined that the nose steering wheel was centered and could not be moved. This led him to conclude that the airplane was experiencing a problem with the anti-retraction mechanism. In accordance with the checklist, the crew manually overrode the anti-retraction mechanism and retracted the landing gear. The flow of the checklist then directed the crew to skip the next steps of the checklist, which comprised the

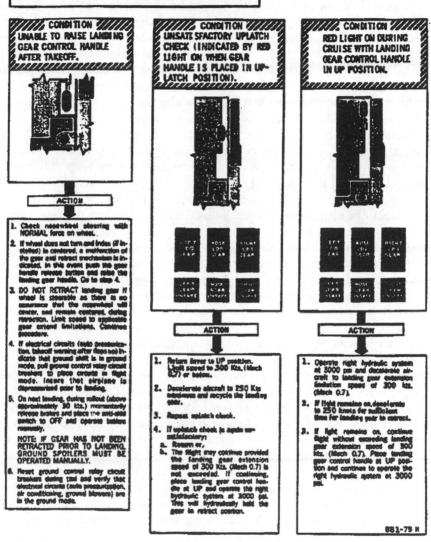

Figure 13.2   Checklist from Douglas Aircraft Company (manufacturer) for "Landing Gear – Abnormal operation" (NTSB, 1996d, p. 144).

branch pertaining to a nose steering wheel that was not centered or could be turned in flight. Because the portion of the checklist that followed these skipped steps was labeled "Approach and landing", the checklist implied that no further actions had to be taken until beginning the approach and landing phases of the flight.

We know from the post-accident investigation that the landing gear retraction problem actually was related to the ground shift mechanism rather than the anti-retraction mechanism. Therefore, although the captain apparently performed the nosewheel steering test correctly and executed the steps in the QRH checklist as designed by the airline, the checklist's diagnostics led the crew to incorrectly identify the underlying cause of the problem. However, the checklist was adequate for the crew to ascertain that it was safe to retract the landing gear.

It is not clear why the checklist was not better designed to lead the crew to the correct conclusion about the nature of the flight's landing gear problem. The NTSB did not analyze this aspect of the accident, but the logic of the company's checklist seems inconsistent with the characteristics of the landing gear and nosewheel steering systems. The diagnostic logic of the airline's checklist differed from the logic of the aircraft manufacturer's version of the same procedure (NTSB, 1996d, p. 144) (see Figure 13.2). The manufacturer's checklist used the test of turning the nose steering wheel only to diagnose whether it was safe for the crew to retract the gear. Unlike the airline's checklist, the manufacturer's checklist did not suggest that this test could distinguish the underlying cause of the gear's failure to retract. The manufacturer's checklist directed the crew, after performing the steering test, to monitor the cabin pressurization and the takeoff warning horn to ascertain whether the ground shift mechanism had remained in the ground mode. In contrast, the company's checklist directed crews to a branch that did not mention pressurization or the takeoff warning horn, so the crew of flight 558 was probably surprised shortly after completing the checklist steps when the airplane failed to pressurize and the takeoff warning horn began to sound. This shortcoming of the checklist misled the crew and added to their workload; nevertheless, they performed well as the airplane continued to climb.

During the climb, the captain took over the flight controls, and invited the first officer to review the checklist items and ensure that they had been completed properly. The exchange of the two pilots' flying and monitoring roles provided the first officer with an excellent opportunity to trap any errors that the captain may have made in assessing and reacting to the situation. When the takeoff warning horn started sounding the crew discovered that the cabin was not pressurizing; they referred again to the QRH and determined that in addition to the presumed landing gear anti-retract mechanism malfunction, the ground shift mechanism must have malfunctioned and remained in ground mode.

With the captain continuing to act as flying pilot the first officer returned to the QRH checklist and began to focus on the branch of the procedure that referred to a ground shift fault (the branch that the checklist's logic originally led them away from). (In doing so, he was obliged to skip over the admonition in that part of the checklist not to retract the landing gear, because by this time the crew had already retracted it.) As directed by the checklist, he opened two ground control relay circuit breakers, which moved the ground shift mechanism to the air mode, so that all of the systems affected by that mechanism would start behaving appropriately for an aircraft that had taken off. As a result, the takeoff warning horn stopped sounding and the cabin began pressurizing. With the checklist now complete, pending the approach and landing items, the captain returned control of the airplane to the first officer to continue the flight with the situation apparently well in hand.

To this point the crew had managed the situation quite well, under the captain's leadership. The captain appropriately distributed the workload of flying the airplane and performing the checklist, switching flying positions temporarily to allow the first officer to cross-check execution of the checklist. In spite of the problematic design of the checklist, the crew used excellent resource management to safely retract the landing gear, identify the system problem and execute the appropriate procedures.

3. En route, the crew did not contact the airline's system operations/dispatch center

Company records and the pilots' recollections reveal that they did not contact the airline's system operations/dispatch center about the landing gear and ground shift mechanism irregularities they had experienced and had apparently resolved. Had the crew done so, they would have fulfilled a requirement of the company's operations manual that "the captain shall report all incidents and/or irregularities to system operations by radio or telephone at the earliest opportunity" (NTSB, 1996d, p. 4). The manual further provided that upon notification of an irregularity the dispatcher assigned to the flight would convene technical specialists from the maintenance and flight departments to provide recommendations. Because he did not notify the system operations department, the captain did not obtain this specialized guidance.

Interviewed after the accident, the pilots explained that during the flight they believed snow and ice had contaminated the ground shift mechanism (a fairly common occurrence in winter operations) and felt they had fully coped with the situation using the QRH checklist; therefore, they thought that they needed no further assistance from ground personnel. However, with the aircraft's problems apparently under control the crew still had to decide how to conduct the remainder of the flight. One key decision was whether to turn back to Atlanta, continue to Nashville, or divert elsewhere. Although the immediate problem was resolved, the airplane was still in a non-normal situation, and the crew would continue to operate under the guidance of the QRH, which would add to their workload during approach and landing. The captain decided, without seeking guidance from dispatch, to continue the flight to its destination. We suggest that, while dispatch and maintenance personnel might have contributed information and counsel about this decision if the captain had communicated with them, it was nevertheless an appropriate decision to continue to Nashville. One of the advantages of continuing to the destination was the additional time that it provided for the crew to prepare for landing.

It is not clear why the captain thought he did not need to contact the company after having resolved the landing gear problem, given that the operations manual stated that all incidents and irregularities were to be reported. It may be relevant that the captain had very little experience as a captain at this airline, having only recently upgraded after a year as a first officer. We do not know whether the captain's upgrade training provided any specific guidance about circumstances requiring him to make radio contact with the company. The wording of the guidance in the operations manual, "… report … by radio or telephone at the earliest opportunity", might be interpreted to allow delaying a report until on the ground, especially if the captain was confident the problem was resolved.

4. The crew reset the ground control relay circuit breakers just prior to landing, causing the spoilers to deploy and the aircraft to touch down hard, short of the runway threshold

The crew used some of the time en route to Nashville to discuss the situation (among themselves) and to review the QRH checklist for "Unable to raise gear lever." The last three items on the checklist were listed under the heading, "Approach and landing". These were:

> Airplane … Depressurize
> Anti-skid switch (before 30 knots) … Off
> Ground control circuit breakers (if pulled) … Reset (NTSB, 1996d, p. 3).

Apparently concerned that the cabin may not have completely depressurized during descent, the crew decided to reset the ground control relay circuit breakers just before landing. This would cause the ground shift mechanism to revert to the ground mode and open valves in the cabin that ensure depressurization. The NTSB report does not make the crew's reasoning clear, but the captain stated that they wanted to ensure that the cabin was depressurized prior to landing, and the first officer stated that they wanted to preclude a rapid loss of cabin pressure after touchdown. The crew may have worried that since the pressurization system did not operate normally during takeoff, it might also malfunction during descent to landing. If the cabin failed to depressurize, the crew might not have been able to open the cabin doors quickly, which would have been problematic should an emergency evacuation have become necessary.

Unfortunately, the checklist provided in the airline's QRH at the time of the accident was incomplete in not clearly directing the crew to reset the ground control circuit breakers only after landing. The corresponding checklist in the manufacturer's *DC-9 Flight Crew Operating Manual* (Abnormal operations/procedures section; NTSB, 1996d, p. 144) (Figure 13.2) and the company's corresponding manual (NTSB, 1996d, p. 134) (Figure 13.3) include the words "during taxi" in the text of the step in which the ground control relay circuit breakers are reset (see Figure 13.3), but for unknown reasons the words "during taxi" were not included in the version of this procedure in the QRH, which the company had provided crews for use in the cockpit during emergency or abnormal situations. We suggest that if the company's QRH had not omitted this crucial phrase the crew would have been alerted to the proper procedure and very likely would have performed it accordingly. As it was,

PAGE: A-1 1-2
DATE: 3/13/95
REVISION: 8

VALUJET

ABNORMAL PROCEDURES
AIRCRAFT OPERATING MANUAL - DC-9

VALUJET

PAGE: A-11-.3
DATE: 3/13/95
REVISION: 8

ABNORMAL PROCEDURES
AIRCRAFT OPERATING MANUAL - DC-9

UNABLE TO RAISE GEAR LEVER

NOTE

Indicates possible malfunction of ground shift.

NOSE STEERING WHEEL....................OPERATE   (C)
- Attempt to turn nose steering wheel using
  normal force.

If steering wheel does NOT turn and centering
indices are aligned:

Indicates a malfunction of the anti-retraction mechanism.

If desired, retract landing gear:

GEAR HANDLE RELEASE BUTTON.........PUSH   (PNF)
- Bypasses anti-retraction mechanism.

GEAR LEVER...................................UP   (PNF)
- Press release button and place lever UP to retract
  the gear.

If steering wheel turns:

DO NOT RETRACT THE GEAR

Indicates ground shift mechanism is still in the ground
mode.

No auto-presaurization, and takeoff warning horn will
sound when flaps/slats are retracted.

The ground control relay electrical circuits can be
placed in the flight mode by pulling the Ground Control

Approach and landing:

If landing gear was not retracted prior to landing,
ground spoilers must be operated manually.

AIRPLANE.....................................REPRESSURIZE   (PNF)
- Ensure airplane is repressurized prior to
  landing.

ANTI-SKID SWITCH (before 30kits).............OFF   (PNF)
- During landing rollout and prior to 30 kts,
  momentarily release brakes and place Anti-skid
  switch to OFF.

GROUND CONTROL RELAY C/Bs (if pulled)
   (H2O and J20)................................RESET   (C or FO)
- Reset Ground Control Relay circuit breakers
  during taxi and verify that circuits are in the
  ground mode.

**Figure 13.3   Company Operating Manual procedure, as issued by ValuJet
Airlines (operator), for "Unable to Raise Gear Lever" (NTSB,
1996d, p. 134).**

when the captain reset the circuit breakers in the air the ground spoilers deployed,
causing a large and sudden loss of wing lift.

One could argue that the crew should have realized that the circuit breakers
should not be reset in the air. This was somewhat weakly implied in the QRH by the
fact that the step of resetting the circuit breakers followed the step of turning off the
anti-skid system "before 30 knots", which suggests actions to be taken during the
landing roll. However, we cannot expect pilots coping with abnormal situations to
reliably notice and correctly interpret such subtle implications. Failing to explicitly
state that resetting the circuit breakers must be done after landing is simply bad
checklist design. Although the NTSB stated that "there was adequate information
available [in] … the QRH for the flight to have landed uneventfully", (NTSB,
1996d, p. 37) the agency's citation of the "incomplete procedural guidance" (NTSB,
1996d, p. 45) of the QRH as a contributing factor in the accident suggests the NTSB
recognized that the incomplete phraseology of the QRH checklist contributed to the
crew's error.

In principle, the crew of flight 558 could also have determined that it was
inappropriate to reset the circuit breakers in the air by retrieving from declarative

memory their knowledge of the DC-9 ground shift mechanism and reasoning through the implications of this knowledge. They could have reasoned that resetting the breakers would place the aircraft back in the ground mode, and then further reasoned that being in ground mode would deploy the ground spoilers in the air because the spoilers were armed. The NTSB concluded that the crew's "knowledge and understanding of the aircraft systems and the effects those systems have on each other were inadequate" (NTSB, 1996d, p. 47) and cited this as a contributing factor in the accident.

However, we suggest that it is unrealistic to expect even highly experienced flight crews to reliably perform this sort of reasoning while flying an aircraft and dealing with the stress and workload of abnormal situations. (We use the term "reliably" to connote the extremely high levels of certainty expected when passengers' lives are at stake.) Experts operate largely by recognizing familiar situations and automatically retrieving directly relevant information from memory. This particular aspect of DC-9 systems knowledge is not information that pilots use regularly or are likely to encode elaborately in memory; thus retrieval would typically require deliberate search of memory for this specific information. Also, this crew was following the QRH, which did not explicitly discuss when the circuit breakers were to be reset. Consequently, nothing triggered the crew to attempt a deliberate search of memory for details of the ground/air sensor system and to reason about possible hidden pitfalls in the way the prescribed procedure should be executed. Crews are expected to rely on the QRH and to follow it to the letter in dealing with non-normal situations because these situations often involve aspects about which pilots have limited knowledge and because crews cannot be expected to think through all implications when trying to manage the increased workload, time pressure, and stress of non-normal situations.

Additional information about the "Unable to raise gear lever" procedure was available to the pilots in the company's AOM, which was aboard the aircraft. The AOM provided a more detailed version of the procedure, including the critical information that the circuit breakers should be reset during taxi. Although the crew could have consulted the version of the procedure that was in the AOM, they were already working with what appeared to be a complete listing of the procedure in the QRH. Therefore, nothing prompted them to consult the additional material in the AOM. Further, although the company's pilots apparently used the AOM as a reference during aircraft systems ground school, they were trained to use the QRH during the subsequent training in simulators. The first officer told investigators that pilots who attempted to consult the AOM during simulator training were told by their instructors to refer to the QRH instead. The airline's chief pilot told investigators that pilots "are encouraged to use the QRH as a handy initial reference manual ... but they are instructed to then refer to the ... AOM for detailed guidance" (NTSB, 1996d, p. 24). However, the chief pilot's statement was not supported in the written records or other personnel interviews obtained during the investigation. Therefore, without a specific note in the QRH procedure directing pilots to refer to the same procedure in the AOM, we would not expect pilots to take that action consistently. Further, it is highly desirable for the QRH to be a complete guide to non-normal situations, rather than forcing a crew in a demanding situation to jump back and forth between two sets of overlapping materials. (Most airlines currently design the QRH or similar media as a complete reference guide for non-normal situations.)

Investigators determined that the airline's pilots were required to perform the "Unable to raise gear lever" procedure during their initial simulator training; however, the procedure was only practised through the initial step of overriding the gear handle locking mechanism. The training scenario was not continued to landing and the end of the checklist. Thus, the crew of flight 558 did not receive simulator training on the aspects of the abnormal procedure most relevant to this accident. The crew might have been more likely to have avoided the premature resetting of the circuit breakers during the accident flight if they had practised the procedure all the way to landing in their simulation training. Also, we suggest that having practised the procedure only in its simplest form (a discrepancy in the anti-retraction mechanism rather than in the ground shift mechanism) may have biased the crew unconsciously to think that retracting the landing gear was the only critical aspect of the procedure. Additional instruction about failure of landing gear to retract situations and associated procedures in ground school class and in a procedures trainer or simulator probably would have made the accident less likely.

Although additional training might have reduced the likelihood of this accident, we note that training should never be thought of as an appropriate substitute for designing checklists (or equipment) adequately. Also, it is simply not practical for airlines to anticipate and train specifically for all possible non-normal situations.

After the accident, the airline's chief pilot told investigators that:

> If the pilots had informed system operations/dispatch of the anomaly during their departure from Atlanta, they probably would have been advised to return to Atlanta to have company maintenance personnel examine the airplane [and] ... dispatch and maintenance personnel would have reviewed the appropriate landing procedures with the flight crew before they returned to land (NTSB, 1996d, p. 37).

Based on this information, the NTSB concluded that "had the pilots adhered to [company] procedures and notified system operations/dispatch of the landing gear irregularity during their departure from Atlanta, they would probably have received sufficient maintenance advice and guidance from technical specialists to land uneventfully ..." (NTSB, 1996d, p. 37). However, while we recognize that ground personnel could have provided adequate information to prevent the accident, we suggest that it is not at all certain that either party would have thought to raise the specific issue of *when* to reset the circuit breakers, or that the crew would have been instructed to follow the procedure as described in the AOM rather than the QRH.

5. The airplane bounced back into the air, and the flight crew performed an emergency landing

After the hard landing, the airplane bounced approximately 100 feet into the air; the crew then applied engine thrust, and they found that the airplane was responding normally to thrust and to the flight controls. The captain took over the controls, and the crew began an immediate return to the airport, recognizing that the landing gear might be damaged and that additional structural damage may have occurred. The crew were unable to communicate with air traffic controllers (switch settings for their radios were changed during impact), and they had to circle at low altitude to maintain visual flight conditions below the cloud ceiling. While handling this workload, they did not brief the flight attendants to prepare the cabin for an emergency landing; just before landing the first officer recognized this omission and commented: "Should have braced them in the back".

Although it would have been desirable for the crew to initiate cabin preparations by briefing the flight attendants, their failure to accomplish this did not affect the outcome of the accident. Given the stress and workload of the situation and that no written checklist prompted the crew to brief the flight attendants, it is not surprising that they forgot to do so. Overall, the crew handled the go-around and return for landing quite well, with the exception of not telling the passengers to brace.

Concluding discussion

The crew of flight 558 was misled by a poorly designed checklist that the airline had provided for an abnormal landing gear situation. The deficient logic of the checklist caused the crew to incorrectly identify the underlying cause of the landing gear problem; as a result, they were surprised by the subsequent failures of other systems. The checklist also provided incomplete guidance about when to perform an important step. Consequently, the crew prematurely reset two circuit breakers while the airplane was on final approach, which caused the airplane to enter a high sink rate and touch down hard short of the runway.

There is no way to know or even guess what percentage of crews in the situation of this crew might have also reset the circuit breakers prematurely. The relatively low level of experience of the crew in this particular type of airplane may have made them somewhat more vulnerable. (They were highly experienced in other aircraft, though.) And, as we explained in the Introduction, the occurrence of error has a random aspect, even within individuals. If it were somehow possible to create a hundred replicas of this crew and put each replica in the same initial situation, performance would vary among the crews. Regardless, poorly designed checklists spawn errors, and with enough exposure those errors eventually lead to accidents.

It is crucial for QRHs to provide unambiguous and complete guidance to crews responding to non-normal situations. Because these situations typically involve novel aspects with which crews have had limited (if any) experience, require integration of non-normal with normal procedures, and often involve high workload, time pressure, and stress, crews cannot be expected to read between the lines of checklists or to draw subtle inferences with a high degree of reliability.

Airline operating procedures and checklists are intended to provide thorough guidance for each step crews must take to deal with specific situations. Airline training and operations strongly emphasize to crews the importance of following written procedures, especially in abnormal situations. This emphasis is highly appropriate, in part because designers have access to much more information than is available to crews and in part because of the imperfect reliability of human reasoning processes under stress, time pressure, and workload. But this approach has a downside in that following checklists step by step does not trigger pilots to systematically search their knowledge structure for subtle implications or to pull together disparate pieces of information that might help them detect pitfalls not specified in a QRH. In fact, automatic adherence to a poorly designed checklist may even inhibit crew thought processes that might otherwise overcome the deficiencies of the procedure.

Our analysis suggests two ways in which checklists and their use could be improved:

1. Checklist procedures should be rigorously evaluated for clarity and completeness for the full range of situations in which they may be used. This is best accomplished by having several individuals with extensive experience in line operations in the specific aircraft type vet draft procedures for how they may be interpreted and used in diverse situations on the line. Airlines should be extremely cautious about deleting procedural information and checklist wording provided by manufacturers, because the latter typically have more experience in writing procedures and checklists. But, conversely, airlines have substantially more experience in the diverse situations that arise in their own line operations and should carefully evaluate material received from manufacturers for clarity and completeness.

2. Pilots should be trained that even a slight uncertainty about how checklist items are to be executed in a specific situation is a red flag calling for them to buy time, discuss the situation, search memory for subtle implications, and consult all available resources.

Note

1   The 30 minutes of recording from the CVR did not start until later in the flight so the NTSB reconstructed the events described in sections 2–4 of this chapter from post-accident interviews and the FDR.

Chapter 14

Air Transport International 805 – Disorientation, Loss of Control and the Need to Intervene

Introduction

On February 15, 1992, at 0326 eastern standard time, Air Transport International flight 805, a Douglas DC-8-63 freighter, crashed near Toledo, Ohio after departing from controlled flight during a missed approach maneuver in night, instrument meteorological conditions (IMC). The airplane was destroyed, and the four persons aboard (the captain, first officer, flight engineer, and a non-revenue passenger) were killed in the accident.

The three crewmembers were highly experienced in flight operations as well as in their respective crew positions in the DC-8 aircraft type. The captain had flown approximately 2,382 hours as a pilot-in-command in the DC-8. The first officer had 1,143 hours of experience as a second-in-command in the DC-8 and an additional 1,992 hours as a DC-8 flight engineer. The flight engineer had 7,697 hours of experience in the DC-8, and he was a commercial pilot but not multiengine-rated. They had flown together numerous times before the accident trip.

In post-accident interviews, other flight crewmembers at the airline described the captain as a very good pilot. Company crews described the first officer as an average pilot, professional, adaptable, and eager. Company records indicated that he had not experienced any difficulties with training or check rides.

The crewmembers had been off duty for several days prior to beginning a trip sequence in Toledo at 0300 two nights before the accident. No information was available about their sleeping and waking schedules during their days off duty, but they probably had become accustomed to a daytime waking schedule and thus had to readjust to a daytime-sleep/nighttime-work schedule as they flew an overnight westbound operation from Toledo to the west coast and had a rest period of approximately 32 hours in Portland, Oregon. It seems likely that their bodies' circadian rhythms of wakefulness and sleepiness had not completely adjusted to the new nighttime work schedule by the time of flight 805; however, the degree to which this readjustment might have affected performance is hard to assess.

The crew began their duty in Portland at 1945 eastern standard time on the night of the accident, and flight 805 departed on time for Seattle at 2145. The trip then continued with the Seattle–Toledo segment, departing 5 minutes ahead of schedule at 2320. No anomalies were reported during the descent into the Toledo area, which began at approximately 0300. The first officer was the flying pilot as the aircraft began the instrument landing system (ILS) approach to runway 7 at Toledo.

Weather conditions on the night of the accident included overcast skies, light rain, fog, and strong southwesterly winds aloft shifting to light northeasterly winds at the surface. As a result of the winds aloft, pilots executing the ILS approach to runway 7 that night (with the final approach course oriented to the northeast) initially encountered a strong tailwind that required a greater-than-normal descent rate to track the glideslope. As the tailwind sheared to crosswind and then a headwind at lower altitudes, pilots had to adjust their heading to continue tracking the localizer and had to reduce their descent rate to stay on the glideslope. The necessary adjustments were well within the normal performance envelope of the airplane, and airline crewmembers typically would have experienced this situation numerous times. Nevertheless, the first officer of flight 805 had difficulty executing two attempts at the ILS approach, following which the captain assumed control of the airplane and executed the second of the missed approach maneuvers. The loss of control occurred approximately 1 minute 20 seconds after the captain took over the flying pilot role.

The NTSB concluded that the captain experienced spatial disorientation shortly after assuming control from the first officer. The agency suggested that failure of one of the primary attitude indicators on the instrument panel could have made disorientation more likely, although there was no conclusive evidence that such a failure occurred. The first officer took control of the airplane after the captain lost control. Based on its evaluation of recorded data, the agency found that the crew could have recovered control and prevented the accident if the first officer had intervened on the controls more quickly and used more of the roll and pitch control authority that was available from the airplane. The NTSB determined that the probable cause of the accident was "the failure of the flight crew to properly recognize or recover in a timely manner from the unusual aircraft attitude that resulted from the captain's apparent spatial disorientation, resulting from physiological factors and/or a failed attitude director indicator" (NTSB, 1992b, p. vi).

Significant events and issues

1. The first officer slowed the airplane without calling for configuration of the flaps, and he could not track the localizer or glideslope courses during two attempts at the ILS approach

The crew began the Descent checklist as the flight descended through 18,000 feet. According to the cockpit voice recording, at 0300:34 the flight engineer initiated the final item of that checklist: "Crew briefing". The first officer responded: "[Unintelligible] ILS runway 7 at Toledo." At 0304:20, flight 805 received air traffic control vectors to the final approach course. At 0311:43 the first officer stated: "Gear down, before landing check", a standard procedural call during this approach phase. The captain stated, almost simultaneously: "Need some more flaps". The CVR then recorded the sounds of flap lever movement (apparently the captain moved the flap lever without waiting for the first officer to call for flap extension) followed by the crew performing the Before Landing checklist. At 0312:23 the captain once again expressed his discomfort with the airspeed and flap configuration, stating: "If you're gonna fly that slow you gotta have more flaps". The first officer responded by requesting flap extension to 35 degrees. However, the captain remained uncomfortable with the flight's airspeed, configuration, and approach profile. He continued: "... Still don't have enough flaps for this speed ... add power ... you're not on the glidepath ... bring it up to the glidepath ... you're not even on the [expletive] [expletive] localizer at all".

At 0313:10, with the airplane descending through approximately 2,500 feet MSL, the captain told the first officer: "Okay, we're gonna have to go around 'cause we're not anywhere near the localizer ... anywhere near it". The crew executed a missed approach and received vectors for a second attempt at the ILS approach to runway 7. During this period, the captain attempted to prepare the first officer for the task of re-intercepting and tracking the approach course in the strong winds aloft. The captain stated: "We're gonna have trouble with the right drift here ... let's see what it looks like ... It's gonna take quite a bit of drift there because you got 14 degrees of left drift ... it takes a lot. The wind's blowing like a [expletive] up here".

While flight 805 was descending and being vectored to the final approach course for the second approach attempt, the CVR transcript included several instances in which the airplane's altitude alerter activated. The NTSB's correlation of these alerts with the airplane's recorded altitudes at the same time indicated that, although the crew were adhering to their assigned altitude throughout, they failed several times to reset the alerter to the next assigned altitude. At 0323:25 the captain checked his understanding of the wind situation by confirming the light easterly surface winds with the air traffic controller. He then transmitted to the controller: "Okay, up here on the final approach course you got winds at 180 at about 35 knots".

The first officer successfully configured the airplane for this second approach attempt; but the captain continued to coach him about the task of tracking the localizer throughout the approach. Beginning at 0324:02, the airplane's ground proximity warning system activated with a series of below-glideslope and sink rate warnings. At 0324:08 the captain stated: "Push the power, get it back up to the glidepath". The CVR recorded the sounds of power increasing. The captain continued to coach the first officer through the recovery from the below-glideslope deviation, stating: "Okay, now take it back off ... stay with it".

We are not certain why the first officer was experiencing these problems with his two attempts at the ILS approach. Because of the prevailing wind situation, the approach was more difficult to fly than usual, requiring the first officer to establish greater-than-normal descent rates to track the glideslope and to maintain wind correction (crab) angles to track the localizer, and then to readjust descent rate and crab angle continually as the winds aloft changed direction and decreased during the descent. However, with substantial experience in the DC-8 and in other aircraft, the first officer very likely had previous experience flying ILS approaches in a tailwind aloft. His record of performance on previous check rides and his reputation suggest that the first officer was a competent pilot. The airplane's flight instruments would have informed him quite clearly about the required descent rates and headings, so the tasks of tracking the localizer and glideslope should have been within the first officer's capabilities, especially during the second attempt when his recent experience and the captain's coaching would have helped him anticipate the effects of the changing winds.

Apparently factors beyond the challenge of correcting for shifting winds played a role in the first officer's difficulties with the ILS approaches on the night of the accident. One possibility is fatigue – as we have suggested, the crew had probably not yet completely adapted to a nighttime waking schedule, and thus the approaches were being flown during the crewmembers' circadian low period. The NTSB noted, "… the accident occurred during the second day of [a] disrupted sleep cycle during the early morning hours, a time of day associated with diminished capacity to function effectively … during such times, the human ability to obtain, assimilate, and analyze information … may be diminished" (NTSB, 1992b, p. 50). The NTSB also noted that several aspects of crew performance, including the first officer's failure to maintain a safe airspeed for the existing flap configuration during the first approach and the crew's apparent failure to use the altitude alerter during the second approach, were consistent with known effects of fatigue.

2. Shortly after assuming the flying pilot role, the captain became disoriented and lost control of the airplane

At 0324:17 the captain stated, in what the NTSB described as "a frustrated or disgusted tone of voice" (NTSB, 1992b, p. 49), "Oh [expletive], I've got it". He commanded "Flaps 25" to begin the go-around procedure, and the first officer relinquished control to the captain and immediately took on the monitoring pilot's task of radio communication. Air traffic control cleared the flight to climb to 3,000 feet. According to recorded radar data, the flight briefly exceeded the assigned altitude while leveling off (reaching 3,200 feet), then returned to 3,000 feet.

While the aircraft was leveling, ATC instructed flight 805 to turn left, beginning vectors for a third approach. At 0325:36 the first officer acknowledged the new assigned heading. Radar and flight data recorder data showed the airplane beginning a left turn in response to the clearance. At 0325:39 the captain stated: "[expletive] [expletive] what's the matter?" At 0325:43 he followed this with "What the [expletive]'s the matter here?" Five seconds later he asked the first officer, "You got it?" apparently indicating either that the first officer was taking the controls or the captain wanted him to take the controls. During its investigation the NTSB used recorded data to recreate the path of the airplane in a flight simulator. This simulation revealed that the airplane rolled sharply to the left during this period, the angle of bank increased to 80 degrees left wing down, and the airplane began a rapid descent. The NTSB estimated that 1 minute 22 seconds elapsed from the captain's assumption of control of the airplane to his first "what's the matter" statement.

The captain's expressions of confusion and concern, as well as the bank angle becoming excessive, suggest that he was struggling to control the airplane. However, only a few seconds later the first officer was able to roll the airplane toward recovery, which indicates that the basic flight controls were functioning properly. Apparently the captain became disoriented as he began the left turn and unwittingly rolled the airplane into the steep left-wing-down attitude.

What went wrong during the turn? The NTSB suggested two possibilities, one of which was failure of the captain's primary flight instrument, the attitude director indicator (ADI) positioned directly in front of him on the instrument panel. The night was dark and cloudy, which would have led the captain to rely primarily on the ADI to maintain correct orientation of the airplane with respect to the ground. The NTSB suggested that an ADI malfunction would have been particularly problematic if the instrument failed in a subtle manner, such as freezing the roll indication so that the airplane seemed to be wings-level even as its bank became increasingly steep.

In principle it was possible for the captain to cross-check the accuracy of his ADI with two other sources of attitude information present in the cockpit: the first officer's ADI located on the right-hand instrument panel (across the cockpit from the captain's seat), and the standby artificial horizon located on the center instrument panel.[1] Cross-checking the three attitude instruments would have revealed whether the captain's ADI was working properly, and if it were not the captain could have flown using the other two instruments for guidance. However, failure of the primary ADI is rare, and pilots seldom practise responding to such failures in training. Thus, we would not expect pilots to reliably detect a failure immediately (Beringer and Harris, 1999), especially when fatigued and conducting a second missed approach, though given enough time pilots would no doubt sort out the problem. No data exist to indicate what percentage of crews in the situation of flight 805 might detect an ADI failure and interpret the situation quickly enough to maintain control of the airplane. (And we expect the performance of any given pilot would vary substantially as a function of fine-grained details of the situation and the pilot's physiological and mental state at the moment.)

Although the captain's confusion and disorientation are quite consistent with the possibility that his ADI failed, the NTSB found no physical evidence to confirm or disconfirm ADI failure. However, the NTSB included the possibility of ADI failure in the probable cause statement of the accident investigation report, which suggests that the agency suspected this was a factor in the accident but did not have adequate information to draw a firm conclusion.

The second possibility that the NTSB suggested for the loss of control in the turn was that the captain may become spatially disoriented as a result of a vestibular illusion. The dark night and cloudy conditions would have required the captain to rely primarily on instrument references when he pushed the nose down to recover from overshooting the assigned altitude and about the same time entered a left turn to comply with ATC instructions. When executing maneuvers involving a combined pushover and turn without clear visual reference to the actual horizon, all pilots are vulnerable to several vestibular illusions[2] that might cause them to roll the airplane in the wrong direction (that is, deeper into the turn when attempting to recover to wings-level) and to push the nose down when attempting to maintain level flight.

Pilots are also vulnerable to spatial disorientation when they fly through layers of clouds, especially on dark nights. Between clouds it is natural to try to maintain orientation by looking out of the cockpit, but when the airplane passes into a cloud that orientation is lost. The airplane may pass in and out of clouds too rapidly for the pilot to adjust between using outside visual references and using the flight instruments inside the cockpit. Also, cloud layers are sometimes not entirely parallel to the true horizon, creating a misleading impression if the true horizon is not visible. The safeguard against this source of disorientation is to direct one's gaze only to the flight instruments, but this requires practice and discipline that are difficult when a pilot is fatigued.

The NTSB noted that fatigue exacerbates vulnerability to disorientation. We agree and suggest that, even if the captain's ADI did not fail, conditions during the second missed approach – fatigue, climbing through clouds on a dark night, and the combination of pushover and roll-in to a turn – would make any pilot vulnerable to spatial disorientation. Pilots' training in responding to conflicts between visual and vestibular cues is limited mainly to their initial instrument training in small airplanes. Although airline pilots do a great deal of flying in instrument conditions, much of that flying is in benign, unaccelerated flight and only occasionally do most airline pilots experience the combination of factors present during flight 805's missed approach. The captain of flight 805 may never have experienced disorientation from these vestibular illusions, and it is likewise possible that most other air carrier pilots have not experienced an actual episode of spatial disorientation.

3. The first officer took control of the airplane but did not complete the recovery before impact

At 0325:50, the first officer stated: "I've got it", signifying that he had taken control of the airplane from the captain. The NTSB's comparison of recorded data about flight 805's path with flight simulation data indicated that the airplane began to decrease its nose-down and rolling motions at this time, suggesting that the first officer applied control inputs to recover from the steep left bank and nose-down attitude of the airplane. However, 11 seconds later the airplane crashed, before recovery was complete.

The timing of the first officer's intervention was critical. He apparently took control of the airplane about 11 seconds after the captain first voiced his confusion and discomfort with the situation. The NTSB's performance analysis led the agency to conclude that the first officer could have recovered the airplane if he had intervened earlier (or used greater control inputs, which we will also discuss). We suggest that several factors made it difficult for the first officer to quickly recognize the need to intervene and to take control of the airplane.

Surprise was probably a factor initially. Disorientation by the flying pilot, leading to an upset attitude requiring transfer of control, is a very rare event that the first officer had probably never practised and almost certainly never experienced. Individuals suddenly confronted with a totally unexpected anomaly with which they have no experience typically require at least a few seconds to recognize and evaluate the situation and decide on an appropriate response, and even longer if the anomaly is subtle (Beringer and Harris, 1999; Summala, 2000). Reaction is likely to be even more delayed when the individual is tired and busy with other tasks. The first officer was performing the duties of monitoring pilot, and his difficulty with the two approaches strongly suggests he was fatigued. He was also subject to the same vestibular illusions as the captain, although his performance indicates that if he too experienced spatial disorientation he overcame it.

Monitoring and challenging the performance of other crewmembers while performing other tasks oneself is more difficult than may be obvious. The NTSB found monitoring and/or challenging errors in the great majority of the accidents reviewed in its 1994 safety study (NTSB, 1994a). Recognizing the subtle incapacitation of another crewmember may be the most difficult of monitoring tasks because it is often not immediately obvious whether the other crewmember's actions or inaction are deliberate or the result of impairment. The captain's initial actions to lower the nose and bank left were consistent with ATC instructions and would have seemed normal to the first officer. The first hint of trouble was the captain's ambiguous statement of confusion: "... What's the matter?" at 0325:39, followed 2 seconds later by the bank angle beginning to exceed 30 degrees, the steepest bank normally used in air carrier operations. These hints may have caught the first officer's attention but we would not expect him to intervene at this point because he would not know whether the captain was able to sort out the problem and reduce the bank angle. It would have been appropriate for the first officer to ask the captain what was wrong, but this would have required waiting for a reply that may have been slow coming because of the captain's confusion. Also the first officer may have been reluctant to distract the captain with a question at this critical moment.

That the situation was degenerating became more apparent over the next few seconds as the airplane began a steeply banked spiral dive and the captain again expressed confusion: "What's the ... matter here?" at 0325:43. During this period the first officer was probably trying to assess the nature and magnitude of the problem, whether the captain had a legitimate reason for the unusual maneuver or had lost control, and whether the captain was able to correct the problem. At 0325:48.8 the captain said: "You got it?" which suggests that the first officer was coming on the controls to correct the situation at this time.

Several psychosocial factors also may have contributed to the first officer's delay in taking over the controls. The inherent gradients in experience and in authority between captains and junior officers (first officers and flight engineers) make junior officers hesitant in varying degrees to directly challenge the decisions and flying performance of captains (Fischer and Orasanu, 2000). Taking the controls from the captain without a direct request is perhaps the most extreme form of intervention a first officer can take, and one that may incur the most hesitancy. Many airlines provide junior officers with CRM training to help them know when and how to challenge the captain, and some carriers have formal procedures to help monitoring pilots challenge deviations from appropriate flightpath and attitude. For example, the monitoring pilot might be taught to call out "Bank angle" if the angle of bank exceeds 30 degrees and to repeat the challenge if necessary. If the flying pilot does not respond to the second challenge, some airlines call for the monitoring pilot to state something like: "Assumed incapacitation" and take control of the airplane. We do not know what training, if any, the first officer of flight 805 received for taking control in this situation. Note that the process of making two challenges and evaluating whether the flying pilot is responding adequately would take several seconds, in some situations enough for an upset to progress to the point that recovery would be extremely challenging.

Beyond the gradients in experience and authority inherent among almost all crews, the situation of flight 805 during the missed approaches involved another psychosocial factor that may have altered the normal roles of the captain and first officer substantially. The NTSB noted that the captain of flight 805 "increasingly assumed an instructional role" (NTSB, 1992b, p. 51) during the first officer's attempts to execute the instrument approach during the period immediately preceding the loss of control. The instructor–student relationship is quite different from a captain–first officer relationship. Typically the instructor guides the student's actions and the student is very likely to believe that the instructor knows more about each flight situation and is taking the correct action. This instructor–student dynamic is not conducive to monitoring and challenging by the flight crewmember in the "student" role. In contrast, the captain–first officer relationship, though characterized by disparate authority levels, is more balanced in terms of technical knowledge and in assigned responsibilities. When the captain in this accident began to behave increasingly like an instructor (triggered by the first officer's inadequate performance on the approaches), the first officer may have unwittingly slipped into a student mind-set that may have hampered his monitoring and challenging of the captain when the airplane began to exceed normal operating parameters.

Also, the first officer's inadequate performance during the two failed approaches may have broken his confidence in his own abilities and slowed his challenge of the captain's performance. The first officer was probably frustrated and embarrassed by his own performance, and these negative feelings may have continued through the time when he had to override the captain, less than two minutes later. And just as fatigue may have impaired his performance on the failed approaches, it may also have made it more difficult to quickly assess the captain's performance and to decide to take control.

Although the first officer's intervention was delayed, the NTSB's simulation study revealed that he could have recovered control of the airplane successfully if he had used larger roll and pitch control inputs. The airplane's flight control system allowed more rapid roll to wings-level than he used, and the nose could have been pulled up more quickly without exceeding structural load limits. However, the first officer had not been trained in recovering from a steeply banked, nose-low upset in a heavy jet transport. Further, the simulation training that airline pilots receive does not provide a true sense of the amount of g-force developed in actual flight when control inputs are made beyond those normally used in line operations. We would not expect any pilot in an upset situation to be able to reliably exploit all of the available control authority without relevant training and realistic practice.

Concluding discussion

In this accident the first officer's difficulty in managing a moderately challenging approach led the captain to take control and conduct a second missed approach, during which he became spatially disoriented. Several factors apparently exacerbated the crew's difficulties and undercut their ability to manage the situation; these factors included fatigue, frustration, and the authority gradient inherent between captains and first officers.

Even without these exacerbating factors, spatial disorientation resulting in an upset attitude is a major challenge for any crew to manage. All pilots are subject to vestibular illusions in the conditions present during the missed approach; these illusions easily lead to spatial disorientation, and when the airplane is being flown manually this disorientation can quickly result in an upset attitude – in this case a spiral dive. If, as the NTSB suspected, the captain's ADI failed, it is not at all surprising that he became disoriented and confused. Fatigue amplifies vulnerability to spatial disorientation and can impair the monitoring pilot's ability to recognize the situation quickly and choose the correct intervention.

Only prompt, accurate, and aggressive intervention by the first officer could have saved the flight after the captain lost control. This accident illustrates both that monitoring and challenging are essential safeguards and that effective monitoring and challenging is difficult. In this accident the first officer had to recognize and interpret initially ambiguous cues that the captain was becoming disoriented, then decide on the appropriate course of action and take control away from the captain in the face of the authority gradient and other countervailing psychosocial factors.

We argue that monitoring and challenging should be emphasized in both initial and recurrent training of airline pilots (Sumwalt et al., 2002; 2003). In particular, pilots need specific decision rules for how to intervene if the flying pilot does not respond or the monitoring pilot suspects incapacitation. This guidance is especially important for first officers, to help them overcome the authority gradient when necessary. The two-challenge rule, discussed earlier in this chapter, is one example of a decision rule for this situation. Also, Besco (1994) has proposed specific guidelines that help the monitoring pilot choose an appropriate level of assertiveness and use a series of escalating challenges to alert the flying pilot to problems. These guidelines also help the monitoring pilot decide whether the flying pilot is incapacitated. Whatever training in monitoring and challenging is given should realistically take into account the actual conditions that occur in line operations, including high workload, limited time to respond, fatigue and psychosocial factors.

Loss of control is one of the largest accident categories in airline operations. Diverse events have initiated these accidents, including spatial disorientation, instrument failure, weather conditions, and flight control malfunctions. What many of these accidents have in common is that it was in principle possible to recover, if the crew had completely understood the situation (often difficult except in hindsight) and had executed the appropriate recovery response optimally. Realistic and thorough training in upset recovery might have prevented some of these accidents. The NTSB has several times recommended this type of training, and many airlines now provide at least an introduction to upset attitude recovery.

We suggest that upset recovery performance could also be improved with better displays of critical information such as total energy available for recovery and angle of attack and by providing flight director commands for recovery. Aircraft automation can also be designed to assist recovery. For example, fly-by-wire flight control systems can allow pilots to apply full control inputs and obtain optimum recovery performance without overstressing the aircraft. This design simplifies the flying pilot's recovery task, which should, in turn, enable more reliable performance.

We see no evidence that the captain's spatial disorientation and loss of control, and the crew's failure to adequately execute recovery procedures were related to characteristics of these two pilots rather than to the vulnerabilities of all flight crewmembers operating in these conditions. No studies have been conducted that would reveal how many of a large population of airline crews exposed to all of the conditions of flight 805 would have recovered after the captain became spatially disoriented. We suggest that performance of this population of crews might be quite variable, depending as much on the dynamic interplay and timing of the many factors operating in this situation as on the skill of the pilots. In this book we repeatedly emphasize our view (shared by many who do research on human factors in accidents) that the occurrence of accidents has a large random aspect – that is, chance combinations of multiple factors interacting dynamically make the outcome of situations largely probabilistic rather than deterministic[3] (somewhat analogous to modern physicists' views of causality). Diverse factors influence the probability of an accident on any given flight, and those factors combine in ways that are largely random, though sometimes systematic. (By systematic we mean that the presence or influence of some factors is modulated by some of the other factors.) Effective training and appropriate design of equipment and procedures can reduce the probability of accidents substantially, but never to zero. The level of probability to accept and the corresponding level of investment in training, procedures, and equipment should be a matter of public policy.

Notes

1   The standby horizon became a requirement for transport jets as a result of previous accidents involving upsets after failure of one or more of the ADIs. In its accident investigation report on this accident the NTSB discussed a Zantop Airlines accident in Chalk Hill, Pennsylvania that led to the requirement for the third attitude instrument. See NTSB, 1992b, p. 37.

2 "'The leans' – A banked attitude, to the left for example, may be entered too slowly to set in motion the fluid in the "roll" semicircular [ear canal] tubes. An abrupt correction of this attitude can now set the fluid in motion and so create the illusion of a banked attitude to the right. The disoriented pilot may make the error of rolling the aircraft back into the original left-banked attitude … 'Inversion illusion' – An abrupt change from climb to straight and level flight can excessively stimulate the sensory organs for gravity and linear acceleration, creating the illusion of tumbling backwards. The disoriented pilot may push the aircraft abruptly into a nose-low attitude, possibly intensifying this illusion" (US DOT FAA, 1980, p. 9).

3 In several accident investigations the NTSB has recognized the probabilistic nature of recovering from aircraft upsets, especially when surprise and flight control problems or malfunctions occurred. In these accidents the crew could in principle have recovered if they had executed recovery procedures optimally, yet the agency did not cite crew performance shortcomings as a cause or contributing factor. We infer from the decision not to cite the crew in these accidents that the NTSB concluded that crews cannot be expected to perform optimally under these circumstances and that many crews in the same situation would not have recovered. (See, for example Emery Worldwide flight 17, DC-8-71F, Rancho Cordova, California, February 2000 – NTSB, 2003; Fine flight 101, DC-8-61, Miami, Florida, August 1997 – NTSB, 1998c; United flight 585, Boeing 737-200, Colorado Springs, Colorado March 1991 – NTSB, 2001k; USAir flight 427, Boeing 737-300, near Aliquippa, Pennsylvania, September 1994 – NTSB, 1999; Simmons (d/b/a American Eagle) flight 4184, ATR 72-212, Roselawn, Indiana, October 1994 – NTSB, 1996b). However the NTSB did cite the performance of the crew of flight 805 as a causal factor, presumably suggesting that the NTSB concluded that it would be reasonable to expect crews to recover in the conditions of this flight. Scientific knowledge is not yet sufficient to ascertain what percentage of crews might be able to recover in the situation of a particular accident flight, and we are not aware of any consensus among experts of how to decide whether to cite crew performance as causal. See our discussion of causality in the final chapter of this book.

Chapter 15

American 903 – Loss of Control at Altitude

Introduction

On May 12, 1997 at 1529 eastern daylight time, American Airlines flight 903, an Airbus 300-600, entered a series of uncontrolled roll and pitch oscillations and a steep descent while operating at 16,000 feet in the vicinity of West Palm Beach, Florida. Of the two pilots, seven flight attendants, and 156 passengers aboard, one passenger received serious injuries and one flight attendant received minor injuries during the loss of control and recovery. The airplane sustained minor damage.

Flight 903 had departed from Boston, Massachusetts 2 hours 16 minutes before the upset event; the flight was bound for Miami. While traveling over northern Florida, the crew received reports of severe thunderstorms in the Miami area and discussed the weather and possible diversion options with the company flight dispatcher, using onboard datalink equipment. Flight 903 completed a 30-minute period of holding over Ormond Beach, Florida. The flight then continued routinely until arriving in the vicinity of the HEATT intersection, an arrival fix for the Miami International Airport. At 1518:03, approaching HEATT, the crew requested to slow the airplane as a precaution for penetrating turbulence and conserving fuel. Air traffic control instructed the flight to slow to 230 knots.[1] The airplane was then cleared to descend to 16,000 feet and hold at the HEATT intersection. Concerned about indications on their weather radar displays that a thunderstorm cell was nearing HEATT, the crew requested to hold 10 miles northeast of the fix. Air traffic control approved the request.

During this period the first officer, who was performing the flying pilot duties, operated the airplane using the autopilot and autothrottle systems. In the automation modes that he had selected for the descent, the autopilot was programmed to a "vertical speed" mode that would adjust the airplane's pitch attitude to maintain a selected descent rate until reaching 16,000 feet, then pitch the airplane up to level off. The autothrottle was programmed to adjust engine thrust to maintain a selected airspeed during the descent, then add thrust to maintain that airspeed during the level-off at 16,000 feet. However, during the descent the autothrottle disconnected without the crew being aware of this.

Flight 903 leveled at 16,000 feet just as it arrived over the holding fix, and the first officer commanded a right turn to enter the holding pattern. During this turn, the autopilot made pitch-up inputs to maintain altitude; with the autothrottle disengaged, the airspeed gradually decreased to 177 knots and the airplane entered an aerodynamic stall. The stall caused the airplane to roll sharply right, the autopilot disconnected, and a series of uncontrolled roll and pitch oscillations ensued. The airplane descended several thousand feet while the crew struggled to regain control, and the maneuvering loads that occurred during the loss of control and recovery caused the injuries suffered by the passenger and flight attendant. After arresting the uncontrolled descent at 13,000 feet, the pilots performed an uneventful emergency landing at Miami.

The NTSB determined that the probable cause of this accident was "the flight crew's failure to maintain adequate airspeed during level-off which led to an inadvertent stall, and their subsequent failure to use proper stall recovery techniques". The agency also cited "the flight crew's failure to properly use the autothrottle" as a contributing factor in the accident (NTSB, 2000b, p. 2).[2]

Significant events and issues

1. The autothrottle system disconnected during the descent to 16,000 feet without being noticed or remembered by the crew

According to information obtained from the flight data recorder (FDR), at 1523:44, while the airplane was descending to 16,000 feet and approaching HEATT, the engine throttles moved aft to the position consistent with the minimum (idle) power that the autothrottle system could command. At 1525:55, the throttles moved slightly farther aft to a lower idle position at the mechanical stops in the throttle quadrant, a position attainable only by a pilot physically retarding the throttles. The autopilot captured the target altitude at 1527:59, and airspeed began to bleed off slowly, eventually going well below the 210 knots the pilots later stated they had selected for holding. This loss of airspeed led the NTSB to conclude that the autothrottle disconnected at some point during the descent.[3] In principle the disconnection may have occurred either because of a malfunction or crew action; however, the NTSB was not able to resolve which of these alternatives actually happened.

The autothrottle system was designed to disconnect itself under various abnormal and system failure conditions. Post-accident testing found no evidence of malfunction; however, an intermittent problem would not necessarily have been detected by these tests. The possibility of flight 903's autothrottle disconnecting itself was supported by investigators' interview with an A-300 captain, not involved in the accident, who had experienced an uncommanded disconnection of the autothrottle system in flight without warning.

Alternatively, one of the pilots may have inadvertently disconnected the autothrottle without noticing it. Although the autothrottle can be disconnected in several ways, the most common method is to use a thumb to press a button on the side of the throttles. Pilots commonly keep their hands on the throttles to check that the autothrottles are reducing thrust during a descent; this allows them to monitor the throttles without having to divert their eyes from whatever they are doing at the moment. A-300 pilots also frequently move the throttles past the autothrottle idle thrust position to the throttle control lever mechanical stops because this allows the aircraft to descend or slow down a bit more quickly without disengaging the autothrottle. FDR throttle position data suggest that the first officer of flight 903 performed this manual thrust reduction to the mechanical stop. It is conceivable, though purely speculation, that the first officer inadvertently pressed the autothrottle disconnect button while moving the throttles to the mechanical stop.

Regardless of how the autothrottle became disconnected, it is apparent from the pilots' recollections in post-accident interviews and from their actions at the time of the level-off at 16,000 feet they were not aware that the autothrottle system was no longer engaged. Two cockpit indicators installed on the A-300 instrument panels display the status of the autothrottle system. When the autothrottle disconnects, a flight mode annunciation (a portion of a line of alphanumerics on the primary flight display in front of each pilot) switches from a green "Speed" to an amber "Man" (manual) indication. Also, three small lighted green bars extinguish within the autothrottle mode selection pushbutton located on the flight control unit, which is mounted on the glareshield in front of the pilots and contains most of the autoflight system and display controls. It is natural, therefore, to question why the two pilots did not detect the disconnection of the autothrottle. We suggest that these cues arc not highly salient and are unlikely to be noticed unless a pilot looks for them specifically. No aural warning is provided on the A-300 to draw the crew's attention to autothrottle disconnection, and the airplane's master caution warning system does not activate.

The A-300 captain who reported an uncommanded autothrottle disconnect in a previous incident stated that she noticed the problem only because she happened to hear a click caused by the magnetic autothrottle arming switch on the overhead panel dropping to the "Off" position. Several studies in recent years reveal that pilots of automated aircraft have difficulty maintaining automation mode awareness and often fail to anticipate or note a change in the mode in which the automation is operating (Sarter and Woods, 1997). Mumaw and coworkers (Mumaw, Sarter, Wickens, Kimball, Nikolic, Marsh et al., 2000) found that pilots highly experienced in an automated aircraft often failed to detect unexpected changes in automation mode. Crews are trained to attend closely to flight mode annunciations while selecting a new mode or while expecting an automated mode transition; however, with changes on the flight mode annunciators being rather subtle and so many other displays to attend to during flight, crews are much less likely to notice uncommanded mode changes without supplementary, highly salient cues such as an aural warning or illumination of a master caution light.

A large factor in this vulnerability is the automation interface, which in some cockpit systems does not adequately support the complex monitoring processes required of pilots supervising automated systems. When pilots fly aircraft manually they are forced to continuously monitor parameters that provide information necessary to maintain moment-to-moment control. However, in automated aircraft, pilots must shift into the role of supervisors of systems that they set in operation and then monitor periodically. Unfortunately it is inherently difficult for humans to maintain vigilant monitoring of normally reliable systems that they are not actively controlling; consequently it is unrealistic to expect pilots to perform this monitoring function reliably without salient alerting systems.

Thus, in the absence of a highly salient warning for a rare and unexpected event, it is not at all surprising that the crew of flight 903 did not notice the disconnection of the autothrottles. Concerned by the risk that crews may not notice autothrottle disconnection, the NTSB sent a safety recommendation letter to the FAA administrator after the flight 903 accident, pointing out that other transport-category airplanes similar to the A-300 use much more salient indications, such as a flashing red light that stops only when a crewmember presses the disconnect button a second time. The NTSB recommended that the FAA compare different aircraft types to ascertain whether the A-300 display should be redesigned (NTSB, 1998d).

It seems likely that most crews in the situation of flight 903 would be vulnerable to some degree to not noticing autothrottle disconnection in time to prevent loss of airspeed, possibly to the extent that the airplane would stall. We note that aircraft certification rules do not treat autothrottle disconnection as a failure mode that must be protected against by system redundancies; thus it appears that certification authorities assume that pilots will reliably notice a disconnection and intervene quickly enough to prevent problems. The events of this accident suggest that this assumption is unrealistic.

2. The airplane stalled and entered uncontrolled flight

Because the autothrottle was disconnected and the throttles were at idle, airspeed began dissipating as soon as the autopilot leveled the airplane at 16,000 feet; then, to hold the aircraft level at 16,000 feet, the autopilot continuously increased the airplane's pitch attitude and angle of attack, causing flight 903's airspeed to dissipate further. At 1528:22 the airspeed was falling through 227 knots; 12 seconds later airspeed had decreased to 209 knots and the airplane began a roll to the right that was commanded by the first officer as he entered the holding pattern negotiated with ATC earlier.

Having entered the holding pattern at HEATT, flight 903 was authorized to slow from the previously assigned speed of 230 knots to its holding or maneuvering speed. Although the target holding or minimum maneuvering speeds for the flight were not provided in the NTSB's records, the pilots stated in interviews with investigators that they noted the airspeed was in the "200 range" and that this was near the "hook" in the airspeed display that denoted minimum maneuvering speed for the existing weight and flaps-up wing configuration. However, the airplane continued to slow down. Consequently, we can conclude that beginning at about this time the airplane, unbeknownst to them, was operating slower than the airspeed that the pilots desired for maneuvering in the holding pattern.

In post-accident interviews the pilots said that the airplane entered a cloud deck just before the loss of control. As the airplane leveled they noticed the airspeed dropping below 210 knots. The captain recalled the first officer apologizing for the loss of airspeed and said that the first officer began to roll out of the turn; however, the captain was concerned about the weather area ahead of the airplane, and he encouraged the first officer to continue the right turn. These recollections are reflected in the events recorded on the FDR, which indicate that the airplane temporarily rolled out of the turn (at 1528:54) but rolled back to the right 9 seconds later. Meanwhile, airspeed continued to decrease through 186 knots.

At 1529:08 the FDR showed that the throttles moved forward quickly as the first officer manually added thrust (likely in order to compensate for the loss of speed), and the airspeed stabilized at slightly less than 180 knots. However, the airplane was beginning to enter an aerodynamic stall, and the airplane rolled more steeply to the right despite the autopilot applying left-wing-down roll control inputs. In quick succession, the autopilot then disconnected itself (most likely because it had reached a control input limit), the stall warning stickshaker activated, and the airplane continued to roll to the right despite full left wheel and left rudder inputs from the crew. At 15:29:16, when the autopilot disconnected and the stickshaker began, the airplane was rolling through 53 degrees of right bank, and its nose was pitched up to 13 degrees above the horizon because of the autopilot's preceding attempts to hold altitude. At this time the first officer moved the throttles forward again, commanding greater thrust, and he began a nose-down elevator input. Despite his addition of thrust the airplane did not accelerate, because by now it was in a high drag state from the increasing angle of attack that the autopilot had commanded. The airplane then entered uncontrolled roll, pitch, and yaw excursions for the next 34 seconds, while rapidly losing altitude.

This pattern of events reveals that the pilots relied on the autothrottle to maintain proper airspeed when they entered the holding pattern and did not realize that the autothrottle was disconnected until the airplane began to stall. Several factors may have delayed the crew's recognition that the autothrottle was disconnected. We do not know what speed the autothrottle was set to capture in holding, but it was presumably less than the 230 knots in descent (the "green dot" speed suggests the crew may have set the autothrottle to about 210 knots). Consequently the crew would have expected the speed to bleed down as the airplane leveled at 16,000 feet. As they leveled off and entered a holding turn the pilots noted the speed was in the "200 range", which apparently was near the minimum maneuvering speed for the plane's weight and configuration.

The continued decrease in airspeed after the flight entered the holding pattern was a cue that might alerted the crew that the autothrottle was disconnected. However, the other A-300 line captain interviewed by investigators revealed that the A-300 autothrottle system sometimes allowed airspeed to decrease 10–15 knots below the crew-selected value in turbulence. In fact, the A-300 autothrottle was slower to adjust back to the desired airspeed than the autothrottle installed in the MD-80, in which both she and the accident captain had substantial experience. We suggest that the accident captain's prior experience in the MD-80 may have influenced his initial interpretation of the loss of airspeed when the flight entered holding. The nature of human memory is to retrieve first the most typical explanation for an event (described as "representativeness bias" by Tversky and Kahneman, 1974). In this case, the most typical explanation that would come to mind was an autothrottle undershoot that would self-correct, and only after this explanation proved wrong was the less typical but correct explanation (autothrottle disconnection) likely to occur to the pilots. Thus, the crew may have initially interpreted their observations that the aircraft had slowed below 200 knots as a normal characteristic and assumed that the autothrottle would correct the airspeed to the expected value as the aircraft stabilized. In theory, it would have been appropriate for the crew to confirm this initial interpretation by checking the autothrottle mode annunciation, but apparently they did not do so, perhaps because routine cross-checking of mode annunciations for unexpected changes in automation status is not a strongly developed habit among pilots.

According to FDR data, 23 seconds elapsed as the airspeed decreased from 200 knots to 186 knots, at which point the crew first reacted to the airspeed loss by advancing the throttles. Some of the crew's delay in responding may have been accounted for by their initial expectation that the autothrottle would add the required thrust, the time required to recognize and react to the autothrottle's failure to perform as expected, and the possible complicating factor of having become habituated to the autothrottle initially undershooting the desired airspeed. However, it is likely that some of the 23-second delay also derived from the crew's degraded monitoring of airspeed. We do not know how often the pilots looked at their airspeed indicators, but we suggest that crew monitoring of airspeed may become less thorough when airplanes are controlled predominantly through automation. When pilots control the aircraft manually (which was always necessary before cockpits became automated), they must frequently check airspeed indicators to guide their control inputs. But when automation is used, checking airspeed is not necessary for aircraft control. In principle, pilots must still monitor airspeed to insure the automation is working properly, but humans are not very reliable in monitoring vigilantly for very low-probability events. The extremely high reliability of cockpit automated systems makes the role of pilots as monitors problematic, an issue with which the aviation industry continues to struggle (Parasuraman, Molloy, and Singh, 1993). Thus it is not surprising that the crew of flight 903 were slow to notice that airspeed continued to decay.

An air carrier industry association human factors subcommittee on automation discussed mode selection and annunciation monitoring errors, observing that:

> … ongoing monitoring is required, not simply selection and confirmation. A number of data sources identify situations where pilots failed to monitor or control the actions of an autoflight system in a timely manner. This may reflect both an inappropriate level of trust in the autopilot during critical flight modes such as altitude level-off and a tendency to "fly the aircraft through" a flight guidance or flight management system. These events often reflect a failure to continue scanning the performance of the aircraft following selection and confirmation of an autoflight mode. The subcommittee noted that policy and procedural guidance on this issue remain limited (ATA, 1998, p. 5).

The subcommittee concluded that "a low-probability, high-criticality error is exactly the one that must be caught and corrected" and proposed, in response, that air carriers "should assess and emphasize [monitoring] skills" (ATA, 1998, p. 14). The proposal to emphasize monitoring functions and skills is well directed, because monitoring has not been emphasized adequately in air carrier procedures and training programs. However, we suggest that the tendency toward degraded monitoring in the conditions of flight 903 is rooted in basic human cognitive vulnerabilities and that simply cautioning pilots to monitor frequently will not by itself greatly reduce vulnerability. The best solution currently available is to provide highly salient warnings whenever an automated system changes modes; however, designers must struggle with the trade-off of cluttering the cockpit with frequent warnings to which pilots may habituate and which may prove distracting at crucial moments (Bliss, Freeland, and Millard, 1999; Staal, 2004, pp. 88–92). We also suggest that research is required to determine whether it is possible to train pilots in specific techniques they can practise to maintain monitoring (Sumwalt et al., 2003).

3. The captain joined the first officer on the flight controls, and the pilots used large rudder inputs in an attempt to control the airplane's bank attitude

As the right bank steepened the first officer applied left rudder. The captain recalled in interviews that the ailerons were "not working" so he, too, used the rudder. The captain did not tell the first officer that he had taken control, so both pilots were applying wheel and rudder control inputs at the same time.

The airline's "Cockpit Management" procedures required that "when control is transferred between pilots, the pilot surrendering control will do so with a clearly audible statement that must be acknowledged by the pilot accepting control" (NTSB, 1998e, Section 4, p. 1). The captain stated afterwards that he came on the controls with the first officer, apparently without notifying him. Control input forces were not included in the recorded data, so we do not know how long the two pilots were on the controls together or whether they made conflicting inputs that might have impeded recovery. This incident demonstrates that stress and time pressure can disrupt even trained routine procedures, such as announcing transfer of control.

The investigation revealed that the airplane's roll oscillations were worsened by the large rudder inputs made by the pilots. Both pilots had received training from the airline in recovering from upsets (the American Airlines Advanced Maneuvering Program, or AAMP) that combined presentations on aerodynamics with simulator practice in recovering from upset attitudes. Review of the AAMP program materials suggests that the program stressed the need for pilots to consider using the rudder, in addition to the wheel (ailerons and spoilers), to recover from roll upsets.[4] Pilots were informed that at a high angle of attack (the condition of the accident airplane) the rudder remains highly effective even though normal roll controls become less effective. Unfortunately, however, the very effectiveness of the rudder at high angles of attack makes overcontrol and roll oscillations more likely.

The potential hazards of large rudder inputs may not have been stressed during early versions of AAMP training, possibly including the training that the crew of flight 903 received; a company flight manager interviewed after the accident told investigators that the airline "did not emphasize to pilots the concerns of overuse of the rudder", explaining that "a pilot who is in an unusual attitude is already at risk" and the airline did not want to "add confusing information to a person under stress". He suggested that the emphasis on rudder usage was reduced in later versions of the course, stating that "rudder use was overemphasized in AAMP at first; now they are saying: 'Don't forget the rudder'" (NTSB, 1998f, p. 23). Further, he acknowledged that flight training simulators used for AAMP may not reproduce with great fidelity the actual yaw/roll coupling characteristics of airplanes in high angle of attack and sideslip conditions (the accident conditions). The investigation record did not reveal which version of the upset recovery course the accident pilots had received or how the simulator handling that they experienced may have differed from the handling of the actual airplane.[5]

4. The pilots' primary flight display screens blanked out for 2–3 seconds during the recovery

Both pilots recalled the temporary loss of the two primary flight display screens during the period of oscillations, which removed information about the airplane's attitude, airspeed, and altitude as the crew attempted to bring the airplane under control. Investigation revealed that the designers of these displays and the associated computer processors had programmed their equipment to interpret extreme or rapidly changing attitudes as error conditions; also the designers were concerned that rapid attitude changes might overwhelm the refresh rate of the processors and displays. The displays were blanked by design, in these situations, to avoid providing false information to the pilots.

We recognize that providing false information to pilots is highly likely to lead them to apply incorrect control inputs; if attitude sensing and display equipment cannot be designed to provide valid information in all conceivable flight situations, it may be better to suppress the false information by blanking the displays. Despite these understandable system programming considerations, we suggest that the loss of basic attitude, airspeed, and altitude information could have caused a much more severe accident. Fortunately the crew were able to transfer their attention to standby instruments during the display outage. Implicitly, by defining extreme or rapidly changing attitudes as error conditions for primary flight displays, the designers had assumed that the airplane would never actually be operated at these attitudes. The adverse consequence of this incorrect assumption was, in this case, removal of the most critical flight instrumentation at the time when the crew needed it most critically.

5. The pilots delayed reducing the angle of attack, which worsened the airplane's roll oscillations and altitude loss as it continued in a steep descent

FDR data indicated that the crew applied varying pitch inputs, including nose-down inputs at times, as the airplane entered a steep descent and as it continued to roll left and right. However, the crew's nose-down pitch inputs were insufficient to reduce the airplane's angle of attack, and the airplane remained stalled until thousands of feet of altitude were lost.

In post-accident interviews both pilots stated that they interpreted the sudden deterioration of airplane performance as an indication that they had encountered a windshear (turbulence from a thunderstorm cell). The captain recalled that as they attempted to recover from the pitch/roll oscillations and the steep descent he called out: "20 degrees up [pitch attitude], 20 degrees up, firewall [maximum thrust]". These instructions indicate that the captain was commanding a windshear escape or recovery maneuver, which stresses maintaining a nose-high target pitch attitude and accepting intermittent stall warning stickshaker activation, as prescribed by the Windshear/Microburst Escape Procedure in the company's *A-300 Operating Manual* (NTSB, 1998g). The FDR data seem consistent with the crew attempting (at least initially) to hold a constant nose-up pitch attitude, consistent with the pitch targets of windshear recovery. In contrast, the procedures established for stall recoveries stressed reducing pitch attitude to decrease the angle of attack below the critical stall value and silence the stall warning stickshaker. In fact, there was no windshear, and the airplane had stalled. The stall occurred at a lower angle of attack than its design criterion (the NTSB was unable to determine the reason); consequently, the stall warning stickshaker system did not activate until after the airplane had already departed from controlled flight.

Continued application of the windshear recovery procedure, especially when combined with the stickshaker system's failure to provide warning of the stall before it occurred, would have worsened the oscillations and altitude loss and delayed the recovery to controlled flight. In fact, the flight might not have recovered at all; holding the airplane nose-high in a semi-stalled condition could have caused the airplane to descend continuously all the way to the ground. Fortunately, the crew used maximum engine thrust and apparently reduced elevator input enough at some point to allow the angle of attack to decrease below the critical value. After the airplane descended out of control for more than 30 seconds the crew was able to regain control. Apparently the injuries to the passenger and flight attendant occurred as a result of what the NTSB described as "a series of violent oscillations" (NTSB, 1998h, p. 8) during this period.

We suggest that several factors probably combined to bias the crew to interpret the airplane's performance in terms of windshear rather than stall. The pilots were aware of a line of thunderstorm cells in their vicinity and discussed the implications of the weather for their holding fix and for fuel status and diversion options. This discussion would have primed them to think about possible consequences of the weather, such as windshear, and would have facilitated retrieval from memory of windshear recovery techniques (described as "availability heuristic" by Tversky and Kahneman, 1974). Research on human memory has shown that the way individuals conceptually frame their current situation substantially biases what information is retrieved from memory and how that information is interpreted (Tversky and Kahneman, 1981; Loft, Humphreys, and Neal, 2004).

The aircraft motions that the pilots perceived as light-to-moderate turbulence on flying into the clouds shortly before entering the holding pattern may have further primed them to interpret what was actually pre-stall buffet as an atmospheric phenomenon rather than the indications of an imminent stall. As the airplane slowed, the separation of airflow from the wing upper surfaces resulted in an increasingly strong buffet, with a rumbling vibration of increasing intensity and sound that was even audible in the cockpit. An off-duty pilot riding in the cabin recognized the rumbling sounds and vibrations as stall buffet; however, the pilots of flight 903 interpreted these sounds and sensations as turbulence related to the clouds that the flight had just entered. In post-accident interviews the captain told investigators that the airplane encountered light chop or turbulence and then "took a jolt" as the airplane rolled to the right. The first officer recalled at this time that there was a "rumble or something" that "sounded like a wind load, an external force, a rumble". The captain stated that the sensation was one of an airplane on the fringes of turbulence and he "felt rumbling building and building".

The pilots' interpretation of the worsening vibrations as the airplane continued to slow may have been driven by their attribution of the initial vibrations to atmospheric turbulence; once a person settles on an interpretation of a situation, their mind-set or mental model can strongly influence interpretation of new information (Adams et al., 1995). Even after the accident, neither pilot characterized the rumbling as a stall buffet. Few pilots have experienced stalling in a large transport airplane in actual flight, but the first officer recalled experiencing stall buffet in the simulator, and he said that the sounds and sensations of the actual event were different. Based on his experience in the simulator, he said that "you would not hear the outside noise, the airspeed would be way down, and the noise would be more of a rumbling flutter". Thus the pilots' previous experience in the A-300 simulator, with its low-fidelity reproduction of buffet sound and vibration, may have further biased them to misinterpret the vibration cues they encountered in actual flight.

All airline crews, including the pilots of flight 903, receive recurring simulator training on windshear cues and recovery procedures. Conceivably this recurring training, coupled with knowledge of highly publicized airline accidents caused by windshear, may bias pilots to interpret ambiguous cues as indications of windshear. The crew of flight 903 encountered weather conditions and aircraft performance cues that could be misinterpreted as windshear; however, they were operating at a much higher altitude than was appropriate for the windshear recovery maneuver, which is designed to avoid imminent contact with the ground. We suggest that if pilots confronting the situation of flight 903 were given the time and opportunity to think about their situation, they almost certainly would realize the inapplicability of the windshear recovery technique; however, surprise, confusion, stress, and the need to respond quickly impair deliberate cognitive processing. Experts, such as airline pilots, are usually able to respond appropriately and quickly to a wide range of situations within their domain of expertise, through cognitive processes Klein (1997) has described as recognition-primed decision-making. However, it appears that these cognitive processes are vulnerable to error when the current situation only partly matches previous experience and when surprise and time pressure are present.

The failure of the stall warning stickshaker system to activate during the pre-stall buffet may have contributed substantially to the crew's misinterpretation of their situation and inappropriate response. In all of the crew's airline training in stall recovery, they would have experienced the unmistakably forceful stickshaker as the pre-eminent indication of approaching stall. Absence of this normal cue would slow recognition of pre-stall conditions significantly. Further, airline pilots are taught to recover immediately at the onset of stickshaker activation and not wait for full aerodynamic stall to develop. Typically, airline training does not provide experience with the actual stall characteristics of the airplane; thus, the pilots of flight 903 had not experienced the behavior of an A-300 after it departs from controlled flight, including the proclivity to roll oscillations. In contrast, if the pilots had experienced the A-300's stall behavior and cues in training, they would have been more likely to recognize the full stall and correct their erroneous initial interpretation.

Also, after the airplane departed from controlled flight the stickshaker activated only intermittently, and the pilots may have interpreted this intermittent activation as the result of their deliberate attempts to hold the nose up to the boundary of stickshaker activation. In an actual windshear encounter momentary activation of the stickshaker can indicate that the pilots are successfully controlling the airplane's pitch attitude to obtain the maximum climb performance. However, the delayed activation of the stickshaker in flight 903 may have caused them to have hold pitch higher than is appropriate for windshear recovery, keeping the airplane stalled rather than just short of stall as intended. Thus, in several ways the pattern of stickshaker activation in this accident may have reinforced the crew's misinterpretation of what was happening to the airplane rather than correcting it.

The crew's inappropriate management of pitch control during the stall may have been influenced by the way the airlines train stall recovery, following FAA guidance. Stall recovery procedures and training focus on recovering with minimum loss of altitude, which requires using minimum reduction in pitch necessary to break the stall. This technique is appropriate for stalls that occur close to the ground, which are the most dangerous, but stall recovery at higher altitudes may require greater reduction in pitch that airline pilots have the opportunity to practise in flight simulation training.[6] Also, a fully developed stall, such as the one that flight 903 entered, requires substantially greater pitch reduction than does the pre-stall condition in which airline pilots practise recovery. Thus, airline stall recovery training focuses on the most hazardous stall situations – stalls close to the ground during takeoff, landing, or go-around, which may also be the most common situations – but this training may not adequately prepare pilots for stalls at higher altitudes.

During the stall the airspeed indicators provided crucial information that in principle could have helped the crew reinterpret their situation. However, the crew focused on the attitude director indicators (ADI) directly at the center of the primary flight displays directly in front of each pilot. The captain stated afterward that he did not recall airspeed during this period and that he was "focused on the ADI." The first officer also did not notice airspeed, stating that "the sky pointer [bank angle index on the ADI] and attitude indicator was everything." Given that the ADI is the primary instrument reference for controlling attitude, it is not surprising that the pilots focused on it as they desperately tried to control attitude. In principle the pilots should have concurrently monitored other displays, especially airspeed; however, stress is well known to narrow the field of attention (Stokes and Kite, 1994, Chapter 3), and the high workload during the stall may have exacerbated this effect.

Even if the pilots had noticed airspeed, interpreting its significance under stress and workload would not have been easy. Airspeed varied throughout the period of loss of control, and interpreting dynamic changes in airspeed is not simple when an airplane is operating close to the stall angle of attack and under the varying loads imposed by turbulence and the pilots' control inputs. Some parties within the airline industry advocate displaying angle of attack information in the cockpit, and some airlines and aircraft manufacturers have installed angle of attack indicators as a separate instrument reading on the primary flight display. Compared to the airspeed information that is currently presented, angle of attack information would be more directly useful in recovering from a stall.

Recent research suggests that vulnerability to misinterpreting stall cues as windshear and failing to execute the appropriate recovery procedure may be widespread among airline pilots in situations similar to that of flight 903. A study of newly hired airline pilots' performance in recovering from several types of airplane upset found that almost all pilots recovered from a windshear upset but were far less successful in recovering from stalls and other situations involving roll and pitch excursions, especially when no stall warning occurred (Gawron, Berman, Dismukes, and Peer, 2003).

6. The crew recovered control of the airplane and performed a successful emergency landing in Miami

After the airplane descended from 16,000 to 13,000 feet, the pilots started to regain roll and pitch control and to recover from the stall. Apparently a nose-up excursion then occurred during the latter stages of recovery, and the airplane climbed back up to 17,500 feet. The pilots then stabilized the airplane, declared an emergency, and began a controlled descent back to 13,000 feet, following ATC instructions. With the captain performing the flying pilot duties for the remainder of the flight, the airplane landed safely at its Miami destination at 1604.

Concluding discussion

It may seem surprising at first that the crew of flight 903 did not recognize that the autothrottle disconnected, did not correctly interpret the signs of an incipient stall until after the airplane had departed controlled flight, mistook the stall itself for windshear, and then were slow to reduce the airplane's angle of attack. However, the crew's perceptions and reactions become far less surprising with careful analysis of human limitations in monitoring automation for unexpected changes, situational factors biasing the crew toward thinking of windshear, unintended effects of the way pilots are trained to recover from windshear and from stalls, inadequate information from several of the airplane's systems, task demands during the loss of control, and cognitive vulnerabilities such as confirmation bias and narrowing of attention under stress.

The accident sequence began when the autothrottle disconnected without being noticed by the crew. This event had no immediate consequences until the airplane began to level at 16,000 feet under autopilot control with inadequate thrust to maintain safe airspeed in level flight. The autothrottle is not a required system, which is probably why FAA and certification authorities in other countries do not require autothrottle functions and malfunctions to be annunciated by highly salient cues. In contrast, highly salient cues are mandated for systems considered safety-critical – for example, engine fire or stall warning systems. A well-publicized previous accident (Eastern Air Lines flight 401 in 1972 – see NTSB, 1973) drew attention to the dangers of autopilots disconnecting without conspicuous warning; as a result, autopilot disconnection is now clearly annunciated by visual and aural warnings that require positive pilot action to cancel and silence. Although not mandated by certification authorities, autothrottle disconnection is saliently annunciated in many modern aircraft cockpits, presumably because the designers of these cockpits recognized that crews might be vulnerable in some situations to not noticing an unintended disconnection.

In additional to the autothrottle system, two other equipment systems failed to provide the crew of flight 903 with essential information at critical moments: the stall warning system, which did not activate until the airplane was fully stalled, and the primary flight displays, which blanked out for 2–3 seconds during the stall. Designers of cockpit systems and certification authorities face a formidable task because it is not possible to anticipate every possible abnormal situation crews may encounter. Nevertheless, it is crucial to try to anticipate as wide a range of situations as possible and to carefully analyze how the characteristics and limitations of human perception and cognition will affect crew responses to those situations. This analysis should guide decisions about what information to provide the crew and in what manner. Similar issues apply to the design of cockpit operating procedures and to the form of training for these procedures, as was illustrated by this crew's confusion between stall and windshear situations. Designers should realistically assess how crews will be affected by surprise, confusion, stress, and workload when they suddenly encounter unexpected and non-normal situations, and procedures and training should be built around this assessment.

This, like almost all accidents, resulted from confluence of multiple factors. The airline industry has developed many safeguards to prevent human error from escalating into accidents, and these safeguards work to a very large degree; however, on this flight the safeguards were breached. The devices and operating procedures designed to prevent human error and trap errors once committed cannot be expected to be perfect safeguards. In part because opportunities for error are almost limitless, occasional errors slip through in a somewhat random fashion. An insidious aspect of many accidents is that once an error slips through defenses it can undermine other defenses downstream. For example, the initial error of not noticing that the autothrottle system disconnected combined with inherent cognitive vulnerabilities and features of the situation to set the stage for misinterpreting the decay of airspeed, and this second error then combined with other cognitive vulnerabilities and situation features to set the stage for misinterpreting the stall buffet and ensuing stall.

The concept of using multiple defenses against human error and system failures is crucial to safety; any one defense has a finite probability of working, but a series of overlapping defenses can reduce risk to extremely low levels because an event that slips through one defense will probably be caught by one of the other defenses (Reason, 1990). But this concept works only to the extent that each defense operates as envisioned and is independent of the other defenses. Careful analysis of the accidents in this book reveals that defenses have sometimes failed to work because designers did not anticipate aspects of the situations in which their systems would operate and because multiple defenses were not fully independent. Designers of equipment and operating procedures face enormous challenges because the universe of potential failure modes is almost boundless when all possible combinations and permutations are considered. However, although perfect defenses will never be possible, considerable improvement can be achieved through research on skilled human performance in typical operating situations and by thorough analysis of human performance demands and vulnerabilities early in the design process of equipment and operating procedures. The sometimes random ways in which errors and system failures and deficiencies combine should be central to this analysis.

Notes

1   Interviewed after the accident, the pilots stated that air traffic controllers subsequently instructed the flight to slow to 210 knots. However, review of the air traffic control transcript did not reveal evidence of an instruction to slow to 210 knots.

2   The NTSB conducted a major investigation of this accident but did not produce a major accident investigation report. The information for this review was obtained from the NTSB (2000b) Brief of Accident and the public docket for the investigation. The docket elements that we examined were the NTSB Operations Group Chairman's Factual Report, Flight Data Recorder Group Chairman's Factual Report, and Aircraft Performance Group Chairman's Factual Report. The investigation did not obtain useful information about

communication within the cockpit because the CVR continued to run after the airplane returned to controlled flight; as a result, the recording of the period leading up to the loss of control was overwritten by the recording of the subsequent approach and landing in Miami. The lack of CVR data limited our ability to assess the human factors issues. The only available communication transcript was from the ATC recorder, which provided us with limited information on exchanges between the accident aircraft and ATC.

3   This issue is discussed by the NTSB in a January 21, 1998 letter from NTSB Chairman Jim Hall to FAA Administrator Jane F. Garvey, in which the NTSB issued *Safety Recommendations (A-98-3 through 5)* as a result of this accident (NTSB, 1998d).

4   The AAMP also stressed reducing angle of attack in nose-high scenarios to restore control effectiveness. FDR data indicate elevator control inputs from the crew during the period of extreme roll oscillations varied back and forth as the crew tried to control pitch and roll oscillations. However, the pilots did not reduce angle of attack sufficiently to break the stall (apparently because they misinterpreted the situation as a microburst/windshear encounter; see later discussion).

5   We note that after the accident and investigation of flight 903 the attention of the entire airline industry became increasingly focused on problems associated with excessive use of rudder following the crash of American Airlines flight 587 (A300-605R , New York, November 2001 – NTSB, 2004). That accident raised issues about the susceptibility of transport jet aircraft to overcontrol of the rudder by the pilots leading to overstress and structural failure. The investigation further found that pilots' tendencies to overcontrol the rudder can be compounded by the light rudder pedal forces and minimal pedal travel that commands full rudder input on some aircraft types, and can be influenced by the training many pilots receive for recovering from upset attitudes.

6   Aircraft operating at altitude have a narrower margin of thrust in excess of drag, and consequently may have little or no capability to accelerate out of a stall condition without trading altitude for airspeed. In contrast, at low altitude a typical twin-engine transport jet with both engines operating will have large thrust margins and may be capable of "powering out" of a stall with little or no reduction of pitch attitude. Most air carrier pilot training concentrates on the low altitude stall recovery; further, pilots are taught to effect the stall recovery with the minimum necessary pitch reduction, in order to minimize altitude loss as would be appropriate for recovering from a stall at low altitude.

Chapter 16

Simmons 3641 – Over the Gates and into Forbidden Territory

Introduction

On February 1, 1994, Simmons Airlines flight 3641, a Saab 340B turboprop operating as a scheduled Part 121 air carrier flight, experienced a dual engine flame-out and performed an emergency, power-out landing at False River Air Park, New Roads, Louisiana. Flight 3641 had departed from the Dallas/Fort Worth International Airport in Texas and was bound for Baton Rouge, Louisiana. The dual engine failure occurred while the flight was descending toward its destination. The airplane was substantially damaged when it departed the paved runway surface during the forced landing in New Roads. There were 23 passengers, two pilots, and one flight attendant aboard. The flight attendant received a minor injury during the post-crash evacuation, but no one else was injured.

The captain of flight 3641 was highly experienced, with more than 20,000 hours of flying time. However, he was relatively new to the Saab 340, having accumulated only 300 hours since transitioning from the Jetstream 31 and Shorts 360, also operated by this airline, less than one year earlier. The first officer, too, was highly experienced, with 6,500 total flight hours and 1,700 hours of experience in the Saab 340. He was qualified as a Saab 340 captain and had operated two flights earlier on the day of the accident in that capacity.

As the flight entered the Baton Rouge terminal area it was projected to arrive within 5 minutes of its scheduled time. The captain was the flying pilot, and the first officer was performing the monitoring pilot duties. The operation had been routine as Houston Air Route Traffic Control Center cleared flight 3641 to descend to 11,000 feet and the crew reported leaving the cruise altitude of 21,000 feet.

The investigation revealed that during this descent both engines were placed in an overspeed condition that damaged their power turbine sections, causing a complete loss of power and forcing the crew to glide the airplane down to an airport that was fortuitously located below them. The airplane's power levers (used by the pilots to adjust engine power and propeller pitch) commanded the overspeed condition when they were placed below flight idle, the lowest power setting approved for use in flight, and into the beta, or ground operating, range. The NTSB determined that the probable causes of this accident were:

... the captain's movement of the power levers below flight idle in flight, the inadequate certification requirements and consequent design of the airplane's power levers that permitted them to be moved below the flight idle position into the beta range, either intentionally or inadvertently, while in flight, and the inadequate action taken to require a positive means to prevent beta operation on airplanes for which such operation is prohibited (NTSB, 1994e, p. v).

Significant events and issues

1. The captain requested a straight-in approach to runway 13 in order to expedite the flight's arrival

The automatic terminal information service (ATIS) broadcast that the flight crew obtained upon entering the Baton Rouge area informed them that the active runways for landing were runways 22R and 31, and that surface winds were light and variable. At 2120:09, while the first officer was listening to the ATIS information and the captain was descending the airplane, the cockpit voice recorder captured the sounds of the aural warning system indicating that the airplane was exceeding maximum operating indicated airspeed (Vmo). This warning continued for 13 seconds.

Arriving from the northwest, the pilots could expedite the flight's arrival by maneuvering straight-in to runway 13, the opposite direction of the active runway announced on the ATIS. The captain apparently noted the operational advantages of runway 13 and that surface winds favored that runway as much as any other. At 2121:11 he said to the first officer: "Well, what the heck's wrong with the ILS to runway 13?" The first officer replied: "Nothing – they'll probably give it to us". The captain replied: "That's what I would ... believe I'd like to have".

The captain's request for the straight-in approach to runway 13 suggests he had evaluated that the flight would be able to descend rapidly enough to reach the runway without exceeding normal operating parameters. However, at 2122:10 the captain, most likely noting the flight's high ground speed resulting from the maximum indicated airspeed and the existing tailwind conditions, said: "Man, we're almost the speed of heat here ...". It turned out that the flight's altitude and distance from the destination runway, combined with high airspeed and tailwind, gave the captain little flexibility for slowing the airplane without overshooting the runway on a straight-in approach. This was a maximum performance descent requiring the best flying technique from the crew to simultaneously slow and descend the airplane.

Crews do not have good information for projecting their ultimate touchdown and stopping point based on the variables of position, altitude, and winds that determine the outcome of an approach; instead, they use rules of thumb and judge from experience. Normal visual approaches are highly practised by crewmembers and there is usually latitude for recovering from a high and/or fast situation; however, airline operating pressures, air traffic control procedures, and (as in the case of flight 3641) the pilots' own desire to expedite their operation sometimes put crews in situations that require maximum performance descents. Setting up such a descent requires fine judgment about whether the approach can be stabilized before touchdown and the airplane can be stopped properly on the runway, and, not surprisingly, crews sometimes misjudge, in which case the approach must be abandoned and the crew must maneuver around for another approach. Perceptual cues revealing whether the airplane can be stabilized at the normal point before landing (typically by 500 feet above ground) gradually become more apparent as the airplane continues its descent. Thus, at some point during a maximum performance approach, the crew may recognize that the approach is not working out. The comments made by the captain of flight 3641 about traveling "at the speed of heat" suggest that the captain was uncomfortable with the approach situation, even when the flight was still several miles from the airport and higher than 10,000 feet.

2. The airplane entered turbulence that required slowing down, and the captain placed the power levers in the beta range

Interviewed after the accident, the captain and first officer recalled that the flight encountered increasing turbulence as it descended from 12,000 to 10,000 feet. At 2127:19, the captain noted to the first officer: "A little bouncy here". The turbulence encouraged the captain to slow the airplane down to stay within safe operating limits and improve the ride comfort for the passengers, but this presented a dilemma. FDR data confirmed post-accident statements by the captain that he had already positioned the power levers at the flight idle stops well before encountering the turbulence. Now, because the airplane's speed and proximity to the runway left him little flexibility to slow the airplane without becoming high on the approach, the captain would have to choose between increasing the airplane's drag (to slow the airplane while maintaining the desired descent rate) and obtaining more time and distance to descend (by requesting vectors off the straight-in approach or by requesting a different runway). The airplane was traveling too fast to extend the landing gear and flaps, which are the normally available and approved drag devices. The alternative of taking vectors off the straight-in approach would have required the captain to admit (to himself, the first officer, and air traffic control) having misjudged the approach.

Many people find it difficult to reveal their misjudgment, especially involving professional skill. Also, as we have noted in the discussions of several other accidents, humans have a strong bias to continue their current plan of action even when changed circumstances make the plan unworkable. Pilots, like other highly skilled professionals, use their skills to manage whatever situation confronts them so that their planned course of action works out. This, however, can easily make pilots vulnerable to continuing the original plan past the point at which it becomes inappropriate. Given that a maximum performance approach is hard to judge with high reliability, the reluctance to abandon an approach can become very dangerous if pilots allow the approach to continue in an unstabilized state (flying too fast or above the normal descent gradient – see Chapter 5). However, the captain of flight 3641 apparently performed an even more dangerous action in his attempt to salvage this highly unstabilized approach – using the ground operating (beta) range of propeller pitch control to increase the airplane's drag and slow it down.

In-flight operation in the beta range is prohibited for the Saab 340, and the power lever design includes a hard stop, or gate, at the flight idle position (just above the beta range) to inhibit inadvertent selection of beta, with triggers provided to override the gate once the airplane is on the ground. The triggers are spring-loaded and require a combined force of 12 pounds to release the gate and allow the power levers to be moved into the beta range, for the purpose of slowing the airplane down after landing or while taxiing. Pilots use the triggers to release the gate on the power quadrant and move the power levers back into the beta range after every landing, and frequently also during taxi operations. At the beginning of the beta range, just below the flight idle gate, the propeller blades begin to flatten out, and drag from the propellers increases significantly as the power levers reach the ground idle position. Deeper into the beta range, below the detent for the ground idle position, the power levers command the propeller blades to twist into reverse pitch. This provides even greater drag and stopping power for use during the landing roll. But if the power levers are moved into the beta range while the airplane is in flight the drag created by the flat or reverse propeller blade pitch can cause the airplane to descend or roll uncontrollably, and the flat blade pitch can also overwhelm the engine's speed governors and cause the engines to overspeed; hence the prohibition on in-flight beta operation.

At 2127:41, the captain stated: "Yeah, we'll just slow this baby up a little bit". According to FDR data, at this time the airplane was descending through approximately 9,300 feet and traveling at 226 knots. The recorded data for power lever position indicated that the levers moved below the flight idle gate (into the beta range) beginning at 2127:43. The power levers reached the ground idle position 8.5 seconds after first moving below flight idle. At 2127:52, the power levers were positioned approximately 4 inches below the flight idle gate, slightly below the ground idle detent. At this time the propellers began to increase their rotational speed to greater than the maximum allowable RPM value of 1,225 RPM (as revealed by the propeller sound spectrum recorded on the CVR and confirmed by FDR data showing propeller speed above the maximum recordable value of 1,500 RPM). The power levers abruptly returned above the flight idle position within one second after the propeller and engine RPM started to increase. Despite the levers being restored above flight idle, however, both engines continued to operate well above maximum RPM. At 2127:56, the master caution warning was recorded by the FDR and the first officer questioned, "What happened?" The captain stated: "What the [expletive]?" Six seconds after the overspeed began, the left and right engines flamed out because of the damage that excessive RPM had caused to their power turbine section.

The NTSB concluded from these data that the captain released the flight idle gate using the triggers and moved the power levers below flight idle immediately prior to the engine flameouts. Both pilots stated in post-accident interviews that they had not intentionally moved the power levers below the flight idle gate. Also, neither pilot was aware of unintentionally raising the triggers that would permit movement of the power levers into the beta range. The recorded data indicated that the power levers were positioned below flight idle, but consistent with the crew's lack of recall, investigators could not exclude the possibility that the captain may have moved the power levers to the beta range inadvertently or unconsciously. It is conceivable that the captain performed the actions of releasing the flight idle gate and selecting the beta range unwittingly. These actions were well-ingrained habits from ground operation and he might have reflexively performed them in flight when he recognized the need to slow the airplane substantially (see Chapter 3 for a discussion of habit capture). However, the NTSB suggested that the slow rate at which the power levers moved below flight idle, combined with their quick restoration above flight idle when the engines and propellers began to overspeed, implied deliberate action by the captain, presumably to slow the airplane.

The NTSB expressed concern that the captain of flight 3641, as well as other pilots, might have developed a technique of moving the power levers somewhat below flight idle in order to obtain extra drag when needed to slow down. Apparently pilots could get by with this technique even if they moved the power levers well into the beta range but avoided selecting a position below ground idle. (Moving the power levers below ground idle, as the captain of the flight 3641 did, was almost certainly unintentional.) The NTSB's concern was purely inferential – the investigation did not present any evidence about techniques used by the crew of flight 3641, or by other pilots.

If, in fact, the captain's action was deliberate, several factors may have predisposed him to this action that violated his training and the company's standard operating procedures. One factor, already mentioned, is the inherent cognitive bias to continue a planned course of action without fully examining implications of changed circumstances. Slowing the airplane with beta pitch, although prohibited, would allow the captain to continue the straight-in approach he had requested. Another possible factor is the incompleteness of the company's guidance about subtle aspects of the consequences of operating the engines in the beta range. The Saab 340B aircraft flight manual (AFM) provided to the captain stated: "It is prohibited to move the power lever below FLIGHT IDLE when airborne. If the power lever is moved below FLIGHT IDLE when airborne, the propeller will go into low pitch angle, the propeller speed will increase uncontrolled with consequential extremely high drag and uncontrolled flight" (NTSB, 1994e, p. 23). This information should have made the captain very hesitant to place the power levers in the beta range in flight; however, the information was incomplete and not entirely accurate. The airplane did not, in fact, develop uncontrolled flight from high drag in beta mode (the AFM information was probably based on accidents of a different type of turboprop airliner, which did become uncontrollable in the beta range). Further, the AFM did not inform pilots that, although the engine/propeller would continue to operate within RPM limits over a broad area of the beta range, just below this range the propeller would rapidly overspeed without warning and probably destroy the engine. Thus, if the captain and other pilots had previously experimented with using beta settings, they may have found that these settings provided a useful advantage in line operations, but not have recognized how close they were to sudden, uncontrollable propeller/engine overspeed. If this did occur, we can imagine how this experimentation may have become a routine practice, until an over-confident captain, encountering turbulence, deliberately or inadvertently applied slightly more beta than usual and destroyed both engines.

One way in which companies can improve compliance with mandated procedures is to fully explain the reasons for those procedures. Regulations, operating limitations, required procedures, and similar rules are essential in commercial aviation, of course, but they are more likely to be effective if pilots are well informed about the background, rationale, and vulnerabilities to risk that underlie the rules.

3. The crew performed abnormal/emergency checklists to attempt engine restarts and, when these were not successful, maneuvered for an emergency landing

Immediately after the dual engine failures occurred the first officer confirmed the failures to the captain, stating: "Both engines flamed out", and immediately adding: "You've got an airport right beneath you". The first officer had sighted the False River Airpark below the airplane. Over the next 30 seconds he repeatedly pointed the airport out to the captain. Then, following the captain's command, at 2128:43 the first officer declared an emergency with air traffic control. At 2128:58 the captain called out: "Okay checklist", and the first officer responded by running the Engine Failure checklist. He also reminded the captain several times during this period to continue controlling the airplane along the desired circling descent path.

After restarting the gas generator section of both engines, the pilots correctly identified that neither engine was producing power. At 2130:47 the first officer began a second checklist, the Both Engines Flamed Out procedure, while the captain continued to maneuver the airplane in a descending circle around the False River Airpark. This second procedure also failed to restore power because of damage to the engines.

Throughout this period, the pilots communicated and coordinated effectively in the aftermath of the dual engine failure. Based on the available information, they apparently did everything possible to restore engine power. Their recorded conversations suggest that the pilots managed the emergency descent well and placed the airplane in a position for a successful engine-out landing at the False River Airpark.

4. The first officer's briefing to the passengers and flight attendant to prepare them for the emergency landing was broadcast over the air traffic control frequency rather than the cabin public address system

At 2132:20 the captain stated: "Okay, better warn the flight attendant". The first officer responded by briefing the flight attendant and passengers about the impending emergency landing. However, instead of sending his briefing over the cabin public address system as intended, the first officer transmitted the message over the radio to air traffic control. The controller attempted to inform the first officer that his briefing had been misdirected ("Okay and that was on Baton Rouge Approach"), but the first officer did not respond to the controller's transmission.

The first officer's failures to switch his audio control panel to the public address position and to notice the controller's correction are quite typical of the kinds of error individuals frequently make in conditions of stress and high workload. In addition to the stress of the emergency, the first officer was busy running checklists, monitoring the flightpath, advising the captain on the location of the airport and the flight's descent path, communicating with controllers, and responding to the captain's command to extend the landing gear (using the emergency gear extension procedure, which is more complex than the normal procedure). The air traffic controller's response to receiving the first officer's public address announcement as a radio transmission was not sufficiently direct to cause the first officer to realize his mistake. Fortunately, in this case, no passengers were injured in the emergency landing and evacuation, even though they were not briefed on what to do.

5. The airplane landed fast and close to the far end of the runway, continued off the end of the runway, traveled through a grassy area, received damage crossing a ditch and fence line, and stopped in a sugar cane field

The CVR recorded the sounds of touchdown at 2133:59. The pilots commented during the landing roll that the brakes were ineffective (this was a result of tire failure). Although the airplane touched down fast and well beyond the runway threshold and then overshot the pavement as a result, the crew successfully completed the emergency landing without injury to the occupants. We suggest that overshooting the runway is not surprising in conditions like these, considering the difficulty of an engine-out approach and that air carrier pilots receive little or no training or practice in performing this maneuver all the way to a touchdown.

Concluding discussion

This accident was proximally caused by propeller/engine overspeed when the power levers were moved into the beta range of operation. The NTSB inferred that the captain deliberately used the beta range to slow the aircraft, although it could not eliminate the possibility that his action was inadvertent. The captain's level of intentionality and consciousness in performing this action is uncertain; however, it occurred when he had just realized that the airplane had to be slowed substantially, and it may have been apparent that normal methods of slowing would delay the flight's arrival. These considerations may have interacted with the human tendency to persist with an existing plan, especially if the captain did not take time to analyze the situation explicitly – a quick reaction to maintain the profile for a straight-in approach may have been the captain's mode of evaluation. The NTSB also inferred that other pilots may have been using beta in flight, although it was explicitly prohibited. It may be that some turboprop pilots had experimented with using beta and found that it provided an operational advantage. Not realizing how close they were operating to disaster, these pilots would have been reinforced by their success and may have come to use beta thrust routinely, underestimating the threat to safety.

Beyond the specific circumstances of this accident, intentional deviations from established operating procedures pose a serious challenge to safety in airline operations. Undoubtedly, many factors contribute to these intentional deviations. One of those factors may be that pilots do not fully understand the reasons underlying some procedures that seem cumbersome, and consequently these pilots succumb to the temptation to deviate, either for convenience or to maintain on-time performance, which is heavily emphasized in the airline industry. We suggest that pilots are more likely to adhere to aircraft operating limitations and to well-designed operating procedures when system functions, inherent risks, and reasons for specific procedures are explained clearly and thoroughly. Also, it is difficult for pilots to anticipate all of the possible downstream consequences of actions they improvise. Proceduralization of airline flight operations is a major safety measure because it allows potential consequences to be explored thoughtfully in advance. Well-developed procedures obviate the need for pilots to improvise, in most cases, and a company culture of adherence to procedures can further inhibit improvisation when it is not necessitated by circumstances. We suggest that if pilots develop a greater awareness of their vulnerability to unanticipated adverse consequences of improvising during flight they will be less likely to intentionally deviate from procedures.

If the captain's use of the beta range in flight was inadvertent, the human tendency to act automatically may have contributed to the error. With high levels of practice, an initially complex motor action typically becomes simple and automatic, requiring minimal conscious effort (think of driving a car). Our ability to perform automatically generally serves well, as it frees up attention resources and executive control for other tasks. A complex and dynamic activity such as piloting an airplane would probably be impossible if most tasks could not be performed automatically to some degree. However, automatization can make us vulnerable to errors in which we automatically execute a response to a situation that resembles – but only superficially – other situations in which the response *is* appropriate. In this case, the flight idle gate, with its integral trigger locks that require a rather complex motor action to disengage, was designed to inhibit inadvertent selection of the beta range by providing a positive detent to interrupt power reduction at flight idle, and by requiring a unique and greater effort to select power lever positions below flight idle. However, all Saab 340 pilots, including the captain of flight 3641, become habituated to lifting the trigger locks on the power levers to override the flight idle gate by performing this action at least once per flight to slow the airplane down after landing. Given that this movement is so highly practised, pilots may inadvertently respond automatically to in-flight cues to slow down by applying an action that is appropriate only for slowing on the ground. Thus, the flight idle gate may not be as effective as assumed in preventing inadvertent selection of beta range in flight, and certainly it does not prevent deliberate selection.

The NTSB concluded from this accident that existing guidance, training, and equipment design features on several turboprop aircraft types were not adequate to ensure that the beta range would not be used in flight. Noting a long history of turboprop accidents involving airborne use of beta, whether deliberate or inadvertent, the NTSB reiterated a previous request to the FAA to change aircraft certification standards so that power levers would be electrically locked out of the beta range while the airplane was in flight. This is an appropriate system-level response to a systemic vulnerability of turboprop aircraft engine controls to inadvertent or intentional misuse with severe consequences.

Chapter 17

American 1340 – Autopilot Deviation Just Prior to Landing

Introduction

On February 9, 1998 at 0954 central standard time, American Airlines flight 1340, a Boeing 727, crashed short of the threshold of runway 14R at O'Hare International Airport, Chicago, Illinois, after deviating below the glideslope while conducting an autopilot-coupled instrument landing system (ILS) approach. The airplane struck the ground hard, shearing off its landing gear and damaging the fuselage and wings. It bounced onto the runway surface, then slid off the right side of the runway and came to a stop in the grass. The airplane was destroyed in the accident. Of the 116 passengers and six crewmembers aboard, 22 passengers and one flight attendant received minor injuries.

The weather at O'Hare at the time of the accident was ½-mile visibility in freezing fog and a 100-foot overcast cloud ceiling; both temperature and dewpoint were 28 degrees Fahrenheit. Winds were calm. The runway visual range (RVR) for runway 14R was variable between 1,400 and 1,800 feet.

Both pilots were highly experienced, but the captain had qualified as a Boeing 727 pilot-in-command only within the past year and accumulated 424 hours in that position. The first officer had been flying the 727 for seven years and had 3,731 hours of second-in-command experience in that aircraft type. The flight engineer, too, was well experienced in his role, with five years and 1,550 hours as a 727 flight engineer at the airline.

After experiencing a gate hold because of air traffic in Chicago, flight 1340 departed from Kansas City, Missouri nearly one hour behind schedule. The flight was routine through the en route portion and descent into the Chicago area. The first officer was the flying pilot and the captain was performing the monitoring pilot duties. The weather in Chicago continued to be poor as the flight arrived in the area, with visibility below the standard (Category I) ILS minimum of 1,800 feet RVR. Consequently, the crew chose to perform a Category II ILS approach, which requires special ground facilities, cockpit equipment, and crew training in order to use lower weather minimums for landing (1,200 feet RVR). In this case, a Category II approach required the crew to operate the airplane under autopilot control at least until they could see the runway environment (the runway surface, lighting, and approach light systems).

The flight proceeded normally as the airplane was vectored onto the final approach course. Analysis of radar and FDR data by the NTSB revealed that the flight then proceeded along the centerlines of the localizer and glideslope courses until reaching approximately 200 feet above ground, ½ mile from the runway. At that point, the autopilot caused the airplane to deviate increasingly above and below the proper glidepath to the runway. Comparing flight simulations with the actual descent path of flight 1340, the NTSB found that these deviations were consistent with an excessively sensitive response by the autopilot to the glideslope signal.

The autopilot-induced oscillations caused the airplane to enter a steep descent when it was very close to the ground. In the last seconds before impact the crew noticed that the airplane was descending toward the approach lights and attempted to recover, but the airplane struck the ground short of the runway. Concluding that the crew should have been able to prevent this undershoot of the runway, the NTSB determined that the probable cause of the accident was "the failure of the flight crew to maintain a proper pitch attitude for a successful landing or go-around". Contributing to the cause of the accident were "the divergent pitch oscillations of the airplane, which occurred during the final approach and were the result of an improper autopilot desensitization rate" (NTSB, 2001i, p. 26).[1]

Significant events and issues

1. The crew prepared for a Category II ILS approach

Beginning at 0923:52, while the airplane was at cruise altitude and entering the Chicago area, the captain conducted a thorough briefing about the ILS approach to runway 14R and the Category II procedures that the weather conditions necessitated. According to the company's Category II guidelines, this type of approach must be flown by the first officer using the autopilot. When the airplane nears the decision height, 110 feet above runway elevation in this case, the captain attempts to acquire visual contact with the runway environment. If the captain is able to identify the required visual cues prior to decision height, he or she announces: "I've got it" and displaces the first officer's hand from the throttles and lands the airplane. If the captain does not make this call by the time the airplane reaches decision height, the first officer disengages the autopilot and executes a missed approach. Consistent with the company's Category II procedures and 727 operating limitations, the captain briefed the crew that after taking over the flying pilot duties he planned to use the autopilot to continue the descent until slightly below decision height. He would disconnect the autopilot, in accordance with the company-established minimum altitude for autopilot use under the existing conditions, prior to reaching 80 feet above the ground.

At 0936:51 the flight crew contacted the arrival controller, who advised them to expect the ILS approach to runway 14R and that the RVR was 1,600 feet. This RVR observation confirmed to the crew that the visibility was too low for Category

I approaches but adequate for Category II. At 0948:32, when flight 1340 was 18 miles from the airport, the controller cleared the flight for the ILS approach. With the autopilot engaged, the flight intercepted and tracked both the localizer and glideslope courses. The flight had been operating in clear skies above a solid layer of clouds that obscured the ground. At this time the crew noted that some of Chicago's tall buildings were visible above the clouds, suggesting that the tops of the obscuration were low. As the descent continued through 500 feet above the ground (less than one minute from the planned touchdown), the airplane entered the clouds and the first officer removed his sunglasses. The captain, who was monitoring the first officer's execution of the approach and the autopilot's control of flight parameters at this time, continued to wear his sunglasses. The crew later reported that the autopilot was tracking the localizer and glideslope courses perfectly as the descent continued through 500 feet. FDR data indicated that the approach was normal until the airplane descended below approximately 200 feet, 9 seconds prior to impact.

2. Under autopilot control the airplane oscillated slightly below, then slightly above the glideslope

According to FDR and radar data the airplane began to deviate about ½ dot (one quarter scale) below the glideslope at approximately 170 feet above runway elevation. The autopilot then increased the airplane's pitch attitude by more than 3 degrees, causing the airplane to fly up to and then above the glideslope, following which the autopilot began to decrease the airplane's pitch attitude in response to the fly-down indications of the glideslope signal. At about 5 seconds before impact the airplane was ½ dot above glideslope, 136 feet above the ground, and pitching down through 2 degrees below the horizon. In contrast, the normal pitch attitude for a steady descent on an ILS glideslope would have been slightly above the horizon.

The CVR did not record any comments from the crewmembers on these excursions below and above the glideslope, and it is not known whether they noticed the excursions initially. Company procedures for the Category II ILS approach required the captain to monitor outside the cockpit for the first visual indications of the runway environment while the aircraft approached decision height, so there is a good chance that he would not notice small transient excursions from the glideslope during this period. As flying pilot, the first officer was responsible for monitoring the instruments and making callouts of altitudes, flight parameters, and course deviations. The first officer in fact made the required callout at 500 feet for altitude, sink rate and airspeed, and he continued to call altitude at 100-foot intervals as required.

We do not know whether the first officer noticed the deviations from the glideslope that occurred after he made the 500-foot callout, or whether he would have found them remarkable without foreknowledge of what was to happen in the seconds that followed. After the accident he did not recall these initial deviations that remained within ½ dot. Review of the airline's manuals and procedures suggests that the company had not established specific limits for glideslope deviation that would require either a verbal challenge from the pilots or a missed approach. Company pilots interviewed after the accident verified that there were no specific limits for continuing the approach or calling out deviations; however, a company check airman told investigators that he had been trained to execute a missed approach if a glideslope deviation of greater than ½ dot occurred. A company line pilot who was interviewed stated that a ½-dot glideslope deviation should result in a verbal challenge from monitoring pilots. But the company's Category II Operations Study Guide from the *B727 Flight Training Manual* suggested a greater deviation limit: "Normally a landing can be made if the aircraft is displaced ... no more than one dot from the center of the glideslope" (reproduced in NTSB, 1995c). Thus it appears that the initial glideslope excursions of flight 1340 bordered on values that warranted action; however, it is not clear what the company expected of pilots in this situation or what significance pilots would attach to deviations of this magnitude.

The pitch excursions from 3 degrees above the horizon to more than 2 degrees below the horizon during this period also provided a cue, reflected on the pilots' attitude indicators, that something might be amiss; however, this airline, like most others, did not provide pilots with guidance to use pitch excursions of this magnitude as a criterion for discontinuing an autopilot-coupled approach. Because the first officer was probably actively monitoring the autopilot's execution of the approach, he may have noticed the glideslope course and pitch deviations that began below 200 feet but found them unremarkable, in which case he would have had no reason to mention them at the time or to recall them later.

3. The captain saw the approach light sequence flashers and took control of the airplane, keeping the autopilot engaged; the airplane then deviated well below the glideslope

At 0953:49 (5 seconds before impact) the captain stated: "I got it", indicating that he had acquired visual contact with the runway environment and, per procedure, was taking over the role of the flying pilot (he later recalled seeing the sequence flashers of the approach light system on the ground at this point). The first officer confirmed relinquishing flying responsibility to the captain by stating: "You got it". The captain continued the descent with the autopilot engaged, while he focused on the view through his windshield. According to company procedures the first officer (now performing the monitoring pilot role) was required to continue monitoring the autopilot and the cockpit instruments for any system malfunctions or flightpath deviations.

When the captain took control of the airplane it was descending through approximately 25 feet above decision height (135 feet above ground level), positioned ½ dot above the glideslope centerline, and pitching down to 2 degrees below the horizon as the autopilot attempted to bring the airplane back to the center of the glidepath. During the next 2 seconds, the airplane continued pitching down to 6 degrees below the horizon and began to sink rapidly below the glideslope. Investigators later determined that the autopilot commanded this large pitch-down because it was oversensitive to glideslope signals and was overcorrecting for the small oscillations it had created moments before. At the time of the accident this airline, and others, had not implemented a service bulletin that the aircraft manufacturer previously issued that would have desensitized the autopilot's response to glideslope deviations.[2]

It was around this time that the first officer recalled feeling "a pitch-down". He told investigators that he glanced up from the radar altimeter, which he had been focusing on in preparation for calling out the decision height to the captain, and he saw the approach lights through the windshield and the "nose pointed short of the runway". The CVR did not record any verbal utterance by the first officer at this time. The flight engineer recalled that the airplane "nosed over" at about 150 feet. He saw the "windshield full of approach lights". He recalled that about 1 second elapsed after seeing the lights before he could tell that the airplane was in an incorrect attitude and position. At 0953:51, the CVR recorded the flight engineer stating: "Oooh, nose uh". In the captain's post-accident interviews he recalled that "in a heartbeat", his view of the approach lights went from "normal" to "all around us".

The flight lasted only 2 seconds longer. FDR and CVR data indicate that at 0953:52 the autopilot disengaged. The captain did not recall disengaging the autopilot, but he did recall positioning his finger next to the disengage button earlier; thus it is possible that he disengaged the autopilot in response to the aircraft's pitch-down motion, which would have been appropriate. At this time the first officer called out: "100 feet", the airplane's ground proximity warning system annunciated: "Sink rate", and the flight engineer said: "Nose up, nose up". At approximately the same time, the captain added a substantial amount of thrust (he later described his throttle inputs as "cobb[ing] the power", a "healthy fist worth") and pulled back on the elevator control.[3] The airplane responded to the captain's elevator and power inputs, and its pitch attitude increased to 5 degrees above the horizon. However, the steeply descending flightpath could not be arrested quickly enough. At 0953:54, the airplane struck the ground 314 feet short of the runway threshold at a sink rate of 1,260 feet per minute.

The NTSB concluded that "... the flight crew did not react in a proper and timely manner to excessive pitch deviations and descent rates by either initiating a go-around or adjusting the pitch attitude and thrust to ensure a successful landing ..." (NTSB, 2001i, p. 24). At issue here is how quickly airline pilots might be expected to react reliably and appropriately to the indications available to the crew of flight 1340. At 0953:51 – 2 seconds after the captain took control and 3 seconds before impact – the airplane was approximately on the center of the glideslope; however, the abnormal pitch attitude and the rapid rate of nose-down attitude change revealed by the outside visual scene alerted the captain to the danger. His responses to correct the situation (adding power and pulling back the yoke) occurred about 1 second later, which is consistent with the range of normal response times for humans to initiate a complex response to an unexpected stimulus (see, for example, Summala, 2000). (In general, humans can respond much more quickly to an expected stimulus than to an unexpected one, and they can respond more quickly to a simple stimulus than to a changing complex stimulus that requires interpretation: for a review of the reaction time literature, see Wickens and Hollands, 2000, pp. 340–9). Thus, the captain's reactions after recognizing the problem were what would be expected of a skilled pilot.

Is it reasonable to expect airline pilots to reliably recognize an abnormal pitch-down attitude more quickly than this captain did? No data exist to address this question directly. Only 2 seconds elapsed between the captain assuming the controls, at which time the flightpath seemed to be within acceptable limits, and the time at which the crew recognized that the pitch attitude had become dangerous. During this brief period the captain was shifting his attention from the cockpit instruments to the outside world to acquire visual reference to the runway. Generally, appreciable time is required to make this transition to using outside visual references to control the airplane's flightpath and attitude, and this period of adjustment increases if the available visual cues are incomplete or ambiguous because of weather, as in this case. Further, the outside visual cues first noticed by the captain were the approach light system's sequence flashers, which provide no direct information about the aircraft's attitude or descent path. In fact, there is a visual illusion that is known to occur in which pilots tend to descend into approach lights because of the absence of visual cues to the horizon – in effect the brain incorrectly treats the approach lights as the horizon line (this was dubbed the "black-hole approach" by Gillingham and Previc, 1996).

We have no way of knowing how much time elapsed before better visual cues emerged from the fog to allow the captain to judge attitude and flightpath. The NTSB noted that the captain was at increased risk of visual illusions from reduced visibility because he did not remove his sunglasses when the airplane entered the clouds; however, it cannot be determined whether this appreciably slowed the captain's recognition of the airplane's flightpath deviation.

Considering the inherent limitations of human reaction time to unexpected events that require recognition, analysis, and response selection, the rapidity of the large pitch-down at the moment the captain was transitioning to outside visual references, and the initial incompleteness of visual information available from the runway environment, it is not at all surprising that the captain did not respond quickly enough to prevent the accident. Although pilots might sometimes respond quickly enough to such a sudden deviation from flightpath, it is unrealistic to assume that this would happen reliably.

CVR, FDR, and post-accident flight crew interview data indicate that the first officer did not challenge the airplane's steeply descending flightpath after the captain took control. The airline's procedures required the first officer to continue monitoring the instruments after transfer of control and to call out decision height (which he did) as well as any significant deviation from glidepath (interpreted by some company training personnel to be greater than ½-dot deviation from the glideslope centerline). However, the final glideslope deviation did not reach ½ dot below centerline until about two seconds before impact, at which time the captain was already attempting to recover. Therefore, glideslope indications would not have enabled the first officer to warn the captain quickly enough to hasten his response.

During this period the first officer would have been monitoring several instruments on his panel, but some of the information from those instruments was misleading or incomplete. Sink rate, in principle, might have provided the first officer with an indication of the problem sooner than the glideslope deviation information; however, this aircraft was equipped with a non-instantaneous vertical speed indicator that lagged the actual sink rate. In post-accident interviews the first officer partially attributed his delay in challenging the flightpath deviation to the inherent lags in the instrument's indications.[4] Also, pitch changes displayed on the attitude indicator provided a nearly instantaneous indication of the developing problem. However, without specific attitude targets to help pilots judge what they see on the indicator, attitude data require more interpretation, thereby increasing response times. More important, we suggest that monitoring pilots generally scan the radar altimeter, barometric altimeter, glideslope deviation indicator, vertical speed indicator, and airspeed indicator during the final stages of an instrument approach, but in the very last seconds of the approach they devote substantial attention to the radar altimeter because that instrument is necessary to determine when decision height is reached. It is likely that during the 1-second period before flight 1340 reached decision height the first officer was concentrating mainly on the radar altimeter in order to be able to make his required callout at that altitude. The large pitch-down occurred during this same period, and the first officer probably was not able to monitor the attitude indicator frequently enough to catch the pitch-down indication instantly. In fact, we doubt that other pilots in this situation would perform differently, other than by chance, with high reliability. After the accident the first officer recalled that he was first alerted to the large pitch-down by his body's vestibular responses, which caused him to look outside and see that the aircraft was descending short of the runway; by that time, though, a verbal callout would have been too late. Thus, as with the captain, it is unrealistic to assume that pilots in the situation of the first officer can reliably intervene quickly enough to prevent an accident if an autopilot quickly pitches down so close to the ground.

Company records indicate that the pilots of flight 1340 were trained and qualified to perform the Category II ILS procedure. Training included a study guide, ground school, and simulator training. Crews were also required to demonstrate Category II ILS procedures during qualification check rides, including both landings and missed approaches. In the simulator pilots experienced system malfunctions such as failure of the autopilot to arm, but they were not exposed to pitch oscillations at low altitude on short final. Instructors demonstrated below-minimum visibility conditions and demonstrated the appearance of the approach lights on a normal Category II approach. Apparently they did not demonstrate how the approach lights appear if the airplane is not on the glideslope or at the proper pitch attitude.[5] We also note that while crews were trained in the flying pilot functions for the Category II approach (including the transfer of control from the first officer to the captain prior to reaching decision height), there was no evidence of specific training for the instrument and flightpath monitoring functions required of both the flying and non-flying pilot in this type of approach. Such training, which would help pilots respond in the situation of this accident, might include practice in effective scan patterns, practice in identifying hazardous malfunctions, and realistic experience with the pace of events and inherent time pressure of monitoring the critical phases of the approach.

Company pilots told investigators that they typically performed only one or two Category II approaches per year in regular line operations. We also note that, although the captain of flight 1340 was a highly experienced pilot, he was a relatively new 727 captain, and the accident flight was his first actual Category II approach in this aircraft type. Thus although airline crews are trained to monitor for certain types of equipment malfunctions on instrument approaches, this captain had not encountered or been trained for an autopilot-induced flightpath deviation of the type that occurred. When the airplane abruptly pitched down 2 seconds after the captain took control, it presented him with a picture that did not match anything in his previous experience. It is possible that previous exposure to this situation in a simulator might have allowed the captain to react more quickly, although as we have noted the captain's response was rapid compared to the expected human response time to react to an unexpected event. Similarly, if the first officer had encountered pitch oscillations during Category II training he perhaps would have been better primed to recognize and call attention to a potential threat. However, airlines obviously cannot anticipate and train for all possible malfunctions, and even a thoroughly trained crew would remain subject to the cognitive limitations and vulnerabilities that we have discussed.

The investigation revealed that several company 727 pilots had experienced pitch oscillations on instrument approaches before the accident. A check airman who had trained the captain of flight 1340 told investigators that he had experienced an autopilot-induced pitch oscillation at 300 feet above ground. He also related that in his experience, as a test pilot conducting post-maintenance functional evaluation flights, approximately three quarters of 727s leaving the company's heavy maintenance base required adjustments to correct for autopilot pitch oscillations. Another line captain reported that he had experienced "porpoising" on a Category I approach with the autopilot engaged. He noticed the pitch oscillations below 1,000 feet and addressed the problem by disconnecting the autopilot in order to stop the oscillations. At the time he assumed that the oscillations were caused by a vehicle or other aircraft violating the ILS protected area on the airport surface. Neither he, nor any other line pilot interviewed by investigators, was aware of the company test pilots' seemingly routine experiences with autopilot pitch oscillations following maintenance. We note that all of these instances of pitch oscillation occurred at higher altitudes than those of flight 1340. Thus these other flight crews had the benefit of much more time and space to recover.

Apparently, the information about pilots' experiences with 727 autopilot-induced pitch oscillations was not widely disseminated among line pilots at this time. We suggest that if this information had been common knowledge, it might have prompted the crew of flight 1340 to be more skeptical about autopilot reliability, which in turn might have made them more likely to notice and respond to the small initial glideslope deviations on this flight. Better dissemination of information about the problem of autopilot-induced pitch oscillation might also have led the airline, manufacturer, and regulator to address the problem before it led to this accident.

Concluding discussion

This accident situation allowed the crew only a few seconds to recognize and respond to a situation they had never encountered previously or been trained for – at a time when their attention was focused on the demands of executing a Category II ILS approach. Under Category II, approaches may be flown with lower cloud ceilings (decision height is as little as 100 feet above the runway, in contrast to the 200 feet of Category I approaches) and lower visibility (minimum RVR is 1,000–1,200 feet, in contrast to 1,800 feet for Category I approaches). Deviation tolerances for airplane attitude and flightpath are quite small, and when an airplane breaks out of the clouds at 100 foot minimums, the crew has only seconds to decide whether the airplane is in a position to land or to recognize deviations or malfunctions. Recognizing that Category II operations are by default challenging, with narrow margins for equipment failure or human error, the FAA requires special equipment, training, and performance capabilities for Category II. This accident illustrates those narrow margins. Under the much more frequently flown Category I procedures, the crew of flight 1340 would have already established full visual contact with the runway by the time the autopilot pitched the nose down; or, in the weather conditions that existed on the day of the accident, the flight would not have been allowed to attempt to land and would have been executing a missed approach.

The NTSB cited the cause of the accident as the crew's failure to maintain proper pitch attitude following the autopilot malfunction. However, in its report on this accident, the agency did not provide a rationale for whether and how crews might be expected to reliably react in time to correct the situation that the crew faced in the critical moments after they reached decision height. We suggest that it is unreasonable to assume that airline pilots, no matter how skilled and conscientious, can respond quickly and accurately enough to this situation to avert an accident with the level of reliability required for passenger operations. Although no data are available on airline pilots' responses in this exact situation, it is well known that humans cannot instantly detect, interpret, and respond appropriately to an unfamiliar and extremely rare perturbation of a normal visual scene. Therefore, although the flight crew's inability to recover in time was the most proximate cause of the crash, we argue that this is a classic "systems accident", caused by a known equipment deficiency, organizational failure to correct the deficiency and disseminate information about it, and unrealistic assumptions about human performance capabilities.

Modern autopilot systems developed after the 727 have dual- and triple-redundant autopilots in which the individual systems monitor each other, reject incorrect control inputs, or disengage safely in the event of a malfunction of one of the autopilots. They are much more reliable, and when these modern systems fail they do so in ways that are easier for pilots to manage. Yet these advanced systems are currently required only for the even more demanding Category III autopilot-coupled operations; the less reliable autopilots such as those installed on flight 1340 can still be used for Category II operations, although the older equipment involved in this accident is being phased out in most US airline fleets. The vulnerability revealed by flight 1340 suggests that the industry should systematically review adverse interactions between equipment malfunctions in Category II operations and human perceptual and cognitive limitations in responding to these malfunctions. More broadly, it would be useful for the airline industry to carefully review all critical operating situations in which tolerances for equipment failures and human error are small to ferret out unrealistic assumptions about human performance embedded in the design of operating procedures and equipment. Although safeguards in the airline industry for the most part work extremely well, periodic reviews of this sort are essential to uncover latent threats to safety before they eventually cause accidents.

Notes

1   The NTSB conducted a major investigation of this accident but did not produce a major accident report. A summary of factual information and analysis were published in an Aircraft Accident Brief (NTSB, 2001a). We obtained information for this review from that report and the following elements of the public docket: Operations/Human Performance Group Chairman's Factual Report (November 24, 1998), Aircraft Performance Group Chairman's Factual Report and Addendum 1 (February 5, 2001), Flight Data Recorder Group Chairman's Factual Report (May 26, 1998) and Cockpit Voice Recorder Group Chairman's Factual Report (March 1, 1998).

2   Under FAA procedures and terminology, operator compliance is optional for a manufacturer-issued service bulletin (SB) but mandatory for an FAA-issued Airworthiness Directive (AD). No AD was issued in this instance. Typically, air carrier engineering departments evaluate each SB to ascertain whether the carrier will comply with the bulletin and, if so, the timing for compliance.

3   The exact instant of the captain's responses to the excessive pitch-down is difficult to determine. The FDR did not provide usable data for the elevator position. Engine pressure ratios (EPR), which slightly lag throttle inputs, began to rise, and pitch attitude began to increase about 2 seconds before impact.

4   The NTSB did not evaluate the potential effects of lags in vertical speed indication in this accident, but NTSB investigators did raise this issue in a later accident (see Chapter 18) involving a below-glideslope excursion.

5   The FAA does not require this to be included in training, but some other air carriers do include it in their Category II ILS training program. One instructor at this airline told investigators that he exposed students to a situation in the simulator in which an increasing crosswind moved the airplane beyond the lateral deviation limits for a Category II operation, prompting the students to execute a missed approach. However, this was not a required simulator scenario so not all students at the airline might have received it, and the scenario also did not involve glidepath deviations.

Chapter 18

Delta 554 –
Undershot Landing at LaGuardia

Introduction

On October 19, 1996 at 1638 eastern daylight time, Delta Air Lines flight 554, a McDonnell Douglas MD-88, struck the approach light system and runway deck structures while landing on runway 13 at LaGuardia Airport in Flushing, New York. The main landing gear separated on impact, and the airplane slid down the runway on its fuselage belly. The airplane was substantially damaged in the accident. Of the 58 passengers and five crewmembers aboard, three passengers suffered minor injuries during the ensuing evacuation. The accident occurred in daylight, IMC.

The flight from Atlanta was operating on schedule and proceeded normally through its descent into the New York terminal area. The captain was the flying pilot, and the first officer was performing the monitoring pilot duties. The accident flight was the first leg of a planned 3-day trip for the pilots. They had flown another trip together nine months earlier. Both the captain and the first officer were highly experienced in the MD-88 aircraft and in their respective crew positions.

The National Transportation Safety Board determined that the probable cause of this accident was:

> ... the inability of the captain, because of his use of monovision contact lenses, to overcome his misperception of the airplane's position relative to the runway during the visual portion of the approach. This misperception occurred because of visual illusions produced by the approach over water in limited light conditions, the absence of visible ground features, the rain and fog, and the irregular spacing of the runway lights (NTSB, 1997b, p. vii).

Significant events

1. The crew thoroughly discussed the challenging aspects of the approach and demonstrated good awareness of the changing weather conditions during the approach

As the flight descended towards LaGuardia Airport, the captain briefed the first officer about several aspects of the approach that would be challenging. He mentioned that the localizer course was offset from the runway, requiring a late alignment with the runway centerline if the approach were to be flown to minimums. Also, the captain mentioned that the glideslope signal was unusable below 200 feet above the ground (a somewhat unusual technical limitation of the system installed on that runway), so the crew would have to disengage the autopilot and also ignore electronic glideslope indications below that altitude.

Later in the flight, the captain noted that the runway visual range values reported by air traffic control for runway 13 were decreasing (visibility was going down), and he inferred, during a discussion with the first officer, that it must be raining heavily at the airport. As the airplane descended on the glideslope, the crew found that the winds were steady and turbulence was decreasing, despite an earlier report of low-level windshear. The captain also noted that the cloud ceiling was lower than the reported 1,300 feet.

These recorded comments suggest that the crew did a thorough job of preparing for the approach. Further, the crew was keeping abreast of developments when the weather deteriorated from the conditions that had been reported. The comments recorded by the CVR suggest (by both the number of comments and their content) that the captain and first officer were not only planning and preparing, but also communicating effectively as a crew. Planning and communication are behavioral characteristics that researchers have associated with effective crew performance (Foushee and Manos, 1981).

2. The aircraft departing ahead of flight 554's arrival rejected its takeoff, and the captain of flight 554 prepared for the possibility of a missed approach, resulting in a deviation above the glideslope

At 1637:29, while flight 554 was about 2 miles (approximately 1 minute of flying time) from the threshold of runway 13 and still operating in instrument meteorological conditions, another airliner that had been cleared for takeoff on the same runway transmitted that it had rejected its takeoff and would be exiting the runway.

The captain of flight 554, preparing for a possible missed approach, responded by disengaging the autopilot at 1637:33 so that he could manually control the attitude of the airplane with the control column. Flight 554 was descending through approximately 700 feet at that time. The crew monitored a radio conversation between ATC and the other flight about whether that airplane could clear the runway soon enough for flight 554 to avoid having to go around. At 1637:52, the captain of flight 554 uttered an expletive and began to decrease the airplane's descent rate by pulling back on the control column – suggesting that he had began to feel uncertain that the aircraft on the ground would depart the runway in time. As a result of the captain's action on the control column, at about 400 feet above the ground, the flight began to deviate above the glideslope. Additional radio transmissions from ATC to the other flight, urging that airplane to clear the runway, were recorded in the cockpit of flight 554. At 1638:07, the captain stated: "No contact yet". This comment suggests that, some 15 seconds after beginning to deviate above the glideslope, he had not yet acquired visual contact with the runway environment and was continuing the approach using instrument references. (The flight had not yet arrived at the decision altitude, so operation under instrument references was appropriate.)

At 1638:10, the first officer stated: "100 [feet] above [minimums]". At that time, the airplane was 350 feet above the ground, it was deviating further above the glideslope, and the autothrottle system was adding power in an attempt to maintain the selected airspeed.[1] One second later the captain stated: "I got the … approach lights in sight". According to FDR data, flight 554 was continuing to descend throughout this period of above-glideslope deviation; however, the flight's descent gradient was more shallow than the 3-degree gradient of the glideslope so its angular displacement from the center of the desired glidepath to the runway was increasing. This would have been displayed to the crew as an increasing fly-down indication on the glideslope displays.

Although the NTSB did not explicitly analyze the issue, we note that the company's procedures did not provide for continuing an ILS approach under manual control in the low-visibility conditions that existed at the time of the accident (the touchdown zone runway visual range was 3,000 feet, and the airline's procedures specified that ILS approaches were to be flown with the autopilot engaged when the RVR was reported less than 4,000 feet). In these conditions, company procedures outlined in the flight operations manual authorized disengaging the autopilot only after the runway was in sight (NTSB, 1997b, p. 34).

We cannot determine with certainty why the captain deviated from the air carrier's requirement to use the autopilot on low-visibility approaches and then attempted to continue the instrument approach after deviating above the glideslope. It is clear that both actions were triggered by the somewhat unusual and undesirable possibility of having to execute a go-around because of the departing aircraft's rejected takeoff. It seems that in taking manual control of the aircraft, the captain was readying himself to either execute a go-around as quickly as possible, should it become necessary, or to continue the approach. The MD-88 aircraft required the autopilot to be disengaged for a go-around; further, once above the glideslope, a pilot desiring to continue the approach may anticipate that it would be smoother to rejoin the glideslope under manual control.

It is not surprising that the captain reduced his airplane's descent rate in reaction to the information that he was receiving about the other airplane on the runway. He could not see the threat on the runway surface, yet his own airplane was quite close to touchdown. His adjustment of the descent rate may have been an automatic, rather than deliberate, reaction to increase the physical separation from the airplane on the runway and to increase the time available for that airplane to clear the runway. Further, although the captain's physical control inputs caused the airplane to continue to descend while he waited for the traffic situation on the runway to resolve itself, disconnecting the autopilot and reducing the descent rate suggest that his plans and goals may have been in transition from continuing the approach to beginning a missed approach.

After the captain reported the approach lights in sight at 1638:22, flight 554 entered the visual segment that concludes every instrument approach that is continued below a defined altitude for deciding whether to continue or to execute a missed approach. During this portion of the approach, according to company procedures, the flying pilot (the captain in this case) maneuvers to a touchdown point approximately 1,000 feet beyond the runway threshold, using the view outside through the windshield, with occasional glances inside at the flight instruments. The monitoring pilot (the first officer, in this case) concentrates mostly on the flight instruments to identify and call out flightpath deviations.

One reason to use the autopilot in low-visibility conditions is to ensure that this visual segment of the approach begins with the airplane stabilized on the proper glidepath to the desired touchdown point on the runway; with the exception noted in the preceding chapter, autopilot-coupled approaches such as this usually track the centerline of the electronic glideslope reliably during the instrument portion of the approach. When a flight begins the visual segment of an approach on the proper glidepath, its crew experiences lower workload and has less risk of making control inputs that destabilize the flightpath than a crew that must quickly correct the flightpath, especially when visibility is limited. The latter, of course, is the difficult situation in which the crew of flight 554 found themselves.

3. The captain continued the approach, reducing pitch and power in an attempt to descend back onto the glideslope, and the airplane descended below the glidepath to the runway

The NTSB analyzed the situation of flight 554 and concluded that the approach was adequately stabilized until approximately 1 second before the captain reported the approach lights in sight (NTSB, 1997b, p. 61). However, the deviation above glideslope continued to increase as the flight entered visual conditions and for the next several seconds. At 1638:13, the first officer stated: "You're getting a little bit high". At 1638:15, he added: "A little bit above glideslope". By this time the captain was applying nose-down control column (elevator) input, and the airplane began to accelerate downward. The autothrottle reduced engine thrust to maintain the selected airspeed, then stabilized the thrust. At this time, the other aircraft finished taxiing off the runway, and the LaGuardia Tower controller cleared flight 554 to land.

As long as the other aircraft was on the runway, the captain of flight 554 may have sensed an increasing likelihood of needing to execute a missed approach. Then, when the runway became clear, the flight's new situation combined permission to land with a worsening above-glideslope deviation. We know that the captain was aware of the above-glideslope condition because the FDR recorded his corrective pitch inputs. Also, the first officer recalled that even as he was alerting the captain that the flight was too high, the captain was already correcting for the condition.

Whether it is best in this situation to discontinue the approach or to make corrections and continue the approach is a complex issue that hinges on the combination of the specific details of the situation. Expert pilots would probably vary in choosing between these alternatives at this point according to their feel for the situation. In general a pilot might feel safe continuing the approach while correcting for an above-glideslope deviation because a deviation on the high side of the glideslope, in general, maintains safe obstacle clearances whereas a below-glideslope deviation may appear to be a riskier condition because it reduces clearance from the ground and obstacles. In reality though, in choosing to continue the approach to landing when coming in above the glideslope, the pilot is required to make a considerable downward change in the airplane's descent path in order to regain the normal profile and touchdown point. This kind of recovery with a large corrective descent rate is a critical maneuver at low altitude. Unless the descent rate is decreased at precisely the correct time, an above-glideslope deviation can quickly become a more hazardous situation with a below-glideslope deviation accompanied by high sink rate. Thus the above-glideslope condition exposes flights to risk and may not be as benign as it appears. Furthermore, making the precise control inputs required to adjust the flightpath so close to the ground depends heavily on the flying pilot's perception of the visual environment outside the cockpit. This visual judgment is significantly more challenging when visibility is degraded by weather, as was the case this day.

The strong tendency of even experienced pilots to attempt to salvage an approach has often been noted (a form of plan continuation bias) though the underlying causes are poorly understood. Several cognitive and social factors probably contribute to this proclivity. In every approach flown manually the flying pilot makes continuous small adjustments to the flightpath. These small corrections are necessary and do not normally pose risk; however, it may be difficult for pilots to judge exactly how large an adjustment can be made safely, especially under high workload and time pressure, and pilots may become entrained in the mode of making corrections and be slow to recognize the need to break off the approach. Situations that evolve over time may draw pilots into reacting first to one change and then to another, serially managing each event that occurs without fully recognizing the implications of the sum of all the changes. High workload exacerbates this tendency. Furthermore, completing an approach is intrinsically more rewarding to most pilots than executing a go-around, and this may be strongly reinforced by pilots' awareness of the desires of passengers and airlines for on-time arrival.

In recent years many airlines have established explicit requirements that approaches be stabilized by a given point in final descent (usually 1,000 feet above ground in instrument conditions). Stabilization is typically defined as having the aircraft in the final landing configuration and within fairly narrow tolerances for airspeed, descent rate, glideslope and lateral course deviations. To discourage the tendency of pilots to try to salvage unstable approaches, these airlines mandate executing a missed approach whenever these narrow tolerances are exceeded. However, subtle cognitive factors and organizational pressures can undermine adherence to this mandate (Helmreich and Merritt, 1998, Chapter 4).

At the time of flight 554, this company had not established specific airspeed, glideslope, and localizer deviations that would define the limits of a stabilized approach, beyond which a missed approach would be required. In its accident investigation report, the NTSB stated that:

Several ... MD-88 check airmen/flight instructors and the pilots of ... flight 554 stated
that [the company's] manuals did not contain a formal definition of a stabilized approach,
and that the only specific guidance concerning pilot actions during an unstabilized
approach was located in the windshear guidance section. A review of [company] flight and
pilot manuals supported their statements; although the word "stabilized" and the terms
"stabilized approach" and "unstabilized flightpath" appear several times, the manuals did
not define these terms, nor did they prescribe stabilized approach criteria (NTSB, 1997b,
p. 37).

Further, these manuals did not specify what action crews should take if an approach
became unstabilized. At the time of the accident, the company was in the process
of establishing formal criteria for stabilized approaches and later incorporated these
criteria into its procedures.

Flight 554 deviated substantially above the glideslope for several seconds. It
is possible that if the company had established and thoroughly trained stabilized
approach criteria, the captain might have executed a missed approach when he
deviated above glideslope and thereby averted the accident. However, although
stabilized approach criteria and training are highly desirable and do encourage pilots
to be more conservative in these situations, we suggest that they are only a partial
solution and that it is not certain whether they would have prevented this accident.
Stabilized approach criteria work best when applied at the defined altitude by which
the airplane must be stabilized, typically 1,000 feet above the ground for instrument
meteorological conditions. This gives the crew time to assess the situation and decide
whether they should go around.

The situation is much more challenging when the airplane is initially stabilized
but later deviates from the criteria close to the ground, when workload is high and
scant time is available for decision-making. Mandating a go-around when a specific
numerical tolerance is exceeded reduces the mental challenge to observing the
deviation and making a yes/no decision, but even so the captain's workload at this
point was so high that making the right decision would have been challenging. He was
flying the aircraft manually, searching for visual signs of the runway environment as
they emerged from the clouds, monitoring the instruments, trying to determine if the
airplane ahead was still on the runway, and probably considering whether to continue
the approach or go around. Contributing to his workload was the somewhat unusual
displacement of the localizer course (lateral guidance) from the runway centerline on
the ILS approach to runway 13 at LaGuardia. This required the captain to bank the
airplane right and then left to align with the runway centerline after entering visual
conditions, while simultaneously attempting to recapture the proper glidepath to the
runway. However, the first officer, as monitoring pilot, would have been in a better
position to monitor for deviations from stabilized approach criteria, had they been in
effect, and call them to the attention of the captain. Company guidance is typically
silent on how long a transient excursion beyond a given stabilized approach tolerance
can be accepted before a go-around is required – this is considered a matter of pilot
judgment that must take into consideration the specifics of the overall situation.
Although crews may have time to assess and correct transient excursions at 1,000

feet, as the airplane approaches the runway this becomes increasingly risky. For stabilized approach criteria to be maximally effective it may be necessary to require immediate initiation of a go-around at some defined altitude even if it appears that an excursion is transient and could be corrected.

The captain acquired visual contact with the runway environment shortly after he began correcting for the initial glideslope deviation, which may have influenced him to think that the approach could be continued safely. Normally, visual contact with the runway environment would have assisted the captain with the task of controlling the flightpath of the airplane. However, in this case the final approach was conducted over a featureless river, in heavy rain and fog, first with only the approach lights and then with the runway edge lights, which were spaced irregularly, in sight. This operating environment made the captain's perspective subject to misleading visual illusions.[2] As the approach continued, these illusions would have caused the captain to think that the flightpath remained too high when in fact the airplane had begun to undershoot the planned touchdown point.

At 1638:22, possibly wanting to rejoin the glideslope more quickly, the captain disengaged the autothrottle and shortly thereafter he manually reduced power. Although the airplane responded to these inputs by stopping the upward deviation, it remained above the glideslope.

At 1638:26 the first officer stated: "Speed's good, sink's 700 [feet per minute]". This callout provided incorrect information to the captain; the actual sink rate at that moment, derived from post-accident analysis of FDR data, was 1,200 feet per minute. The first officer based his statement on the vertical speed indications on his flight instrument panel. According to the NTSB, the first officer's callout was consistent with the characteristics of the type of vertical speed indicator installed in this airplane. This older type of indicator derives vertical speed from barometric pressure changes through a slow leak in an internal diaphragm, and consequently its indications lag the actual vertical speed. In contrast, many transport airplanes are equipped with an instantaneous type of vertical speed indicator that uses inertial reference data and is not subject to lags. Thus, the first officer received incorrect information that he then provided to the captain, who may have been influenced to make larger pitch and power changes to regain the glideslope than he would have done had he known the true vertical speed.

As the airplane descended through 200 feet above the ground at 1638:29,[3] it remained above the desired glidepath to the runway but was sinking at an increasing rate. At this time the captain made his last nose-down pitch input, which he held for the next 2 seconds. At the end of that period, about 4 seconds before contacting the seawall, the airplane was descending through 125 feet above the ground at 1,500 feet per minute. Airspeed had decreased to approximately 5 knots slower than the target approach speed.[4] The first officer told the captain: "A little slow, a little bit slow". According to the first officer's recounting of these events to investigators, it was at about this time that he noticed the flight's descent path slide down from the runway toward a projected touchdown in the approach lights. He noticed this shift from the view out the windshield. At 1638:34 the first officer challenged:

"Nose up ... nose up". About this time, the captain was reacting to the sink rate and impending undershoot by applying nose-up pitch input and thrust. Because of the airplane's reduced airspeed, its momentum in descent, and the lags that are inherent in turbine engine power application, the descent rate did not begin to decrease until an additional 2 seconds had passed. The airplane crashed short of the runway just as the pitch and power inputs had begun to take effect.

We think that several factors may have contributed to the captain's failure to identify and correct the sink rate before it was too late. The captain had intentionally increased the sink rate to regain the normal descent path to the runway. As we have said, timing is critical when correcting from a high sink rate to a normal sink rate at low altitude; the captain was attempting an inherently difficult task, which was further complicated by the degraded and misleading visual information through the windshield. Both crewmembers were aware that the electronic glideslope signal was unusable below 200 feet; this special characteristic of the approach to runway 13 deprived the crew of potentially helpful glidepath information. The crew did not recall seeing the visual approach slope indicator (VASI), which would have provided the only valid out-the-windshield guidance to a safe glidepath down to the flare point. We do not know whether the heavy rain obscured the VASI lights or made them less salient, or whether the pilots did not cross-check them under heavy workload.

Further, the captain was using monovision contact lenses, which may have adversely affected his depth perception to some degree.[5] With one eye corrected for distance vision and one for near vision, the captain would have been using only one eye to judge descent rate and ground proximity. Binocular vision (stereopsis) is not the major determinant of human perception of depth beyond around 30 feet for most tasks – the brain has other mechanisms for calculating depth and rate of change of depth from the information received from a single eye. The NTSB report included as an appendix a NASA study showing that when highly experienced pilots had one eye covered their accuracy in landing on a predetermined spot was not altered (NTSB, 1997b, pp. 130–6). However, they chose to execute a steeper approach, apparently because they were not comfortable with the vision restriction and chose to be more conservative. Also, they reported experiencing higher workload with one eye covered.

The US Air Force does not allow pilots to use monovision contact lenses because of concern that the blurred input to the brain from the eye corrected for near vision might interfere with processing of information from the eye corrected for far vision (NTSB, 1997b, p. 144). This is a prudent precaution; however, we are not aware of published scientific studies revealing to what extent this interference might affect pilots' judgment of glideslope and sink rate or how this interference might interact with the effects of vision illusions resulting from reduced visual information in heavy rain.

The NTSB concluded that the captain's use of monovision contact lenses increased his dependence of monovision cues for depth information, making him more vulnerable to the illusions caused by reduced visibility and irregular spacing of runway lights, and causing him to misjudge his flightpath and descent rate. While this conclusion is plausible, we suggest that factors other than the captain's use of monovision contact lenses very probably affected the crew's performance, perhaps more substantially than the use of the lenses. Just as the above-glideslope deviation developed quickly, the final events in this sequence also occurred very rapidly. FDR data indicate that only about 5 seconds elapsed from the time that the high sink rate began to the start of the captain's (unsuccessful) recovery attempt. During some of this time, the high sink rate was inaccurately displayed on flight instruments because of lags in the vertical speed indicator. The descent from well above the glideslope to impact short of the runway occurred within a span of 7 seconds. The captain's attempted recovery from the high sink rate began about midway through that period.

This rapid deterioration in flight dynamics is consistent with the captain mistiming a difficult attempt to rejoin the glideslope from above. The workload induced by the deteriorating flight dynamics and the degraded visual scene would have been quite high, making it difficult for the captain to assess whether the situation was under control or required a go-around. It is appropriate to execute a go-around once a pilot becomes aware that the outcome of the approach is uncertain. However, perceiving and evaluating risk factors, and selecting an appropriate response, are themselves mental processes subject to degradation under high workload (Staal, 2004, pp. 84–5). Thus, ironically, pilots' ability to evaluate a rapidly evolving problem and change their plan of action is undercut by the moment-to-moment demands of responding to the problem.

The first officer's callouts suggest that he was monitoring the flightpath and providing the captain relevant information about the above-glideslope deviation, airspeed deterioration, and below-glideslope deviation. We think that the wording of the first officer's callouts could have been phrased to characterize the threat more clearly and forcefully; however, he had to rely on personal techniques because the airline did not specify callouts for flightpath deviations. In fact, the NTSB concluded that the first officer's verbal input surpassed what was required by company guidance at that time. The company's flight operations manual instructed the pilot not flying to monitor the flight instruments "though the flare" and "call out significant deviations to minimize the effects of possible visual illusions for the pilot flying" (NTSB, 1997b, p. 35). The manual also specified that the pilot not flying should monitor airspeed and sink rate through touchdown. However, in its description of "pilot not flying duties" when approaching decision altitude on the type of instrument procedure that flight 554 was executing, the manual also stated: "Adjust scan to include outside references and verbalize those observed" (NTSB, 1997b, p. 35). Recognizing the competing responsibilities in these procedures for the monitoring pilot to attend to cues both inside and outside the airplane, we find it understandable that a crewmember would not be able to perform all of these tasks to the degree necessary for identifying rapidly developing changes and trends.

Like most companies, this airline did not assist monitoring pilots by specifying instrument scan techniques to best allocate their attention among the assigned tasks. The first officer involved in this accident recalled that during the last seconds of the approach he was primarily scanning the flight instruments and glancing through the windshield for outside references. It was during this period that the lagging vertical speed indicator caused the first officer to report an incorrect descent rate ("sinking 700"). We note, however, that 2–3 seconds after this statement, the vertical speed indicator would have accurately displayed the high sink rate. If the first officer had immediately noticed the high sink rate when it was displayed on his indicator and called it out instantly, the captain might have been alerted to begin flightpath correction 3 seconds or so earlier than he did. However, most or all of these 3 seconds would have been consumed by the first officer finding words to articulate his observation and the captain hearing and interpreting the callout and initiating a response. Thus it is conceivable, though far from certain, that if the first officer had monitored the flight instruments continuously, rather than occasionally glancing outside, and had immediately and forcefully challenged the captain, the outcome might have been different. We think that better guidance on monitoring procedures would clearly benefit the airline industry (Sumwalt et al., 2002). However, it is unrealistic to expect perfect monitoring to make up for the demands imposed by unstabilized approaches.

Concluding discussion

In this accident, an approach that was destabilized in response to a potential need to go around led to a snowball effect of rapidly changing events and pilot control inputs during the last seconds of the flight. Workload and time compression during this period impeded the crew's ability to thoughtfully analyze their situation and respond effectively.

The last few hundred feet of an approach by definition allow only a narrow margin of tolerance. Unstabilized approaches increase workload and time pressure, and they further reduce the margin for error to the point that even highly experienced crews cannot be expected to make safe landings with the high degree of reliability required for airline operations. This has been borne out by the long history of air carrier accidents in which aircraft undershot or overshot the landing runway following an unstabilized approach. Recognizing the threat, most air carriers have now developed procedures and trained crews to avoid unstabilized approaches, and when they occur, to respond by executing a missed approach.

We suggest that when the captain allowed the airplane to deviate above the glideslope, given the weather conditions and the proximity of the ground at that point, no crew, no matter how skillful or experienced, could have continued to a safe landing with the level of reliability required for flights carrying passengers. This company's lack of specific procedural "bottom-line" standards requiring a missed approach may have made the accident of flight 554 more likely. In recent years, many air carriers (including this one) have provided explicit definitions of unstabilized approaches and policies for executing missed approaches. Given the powerful human bias to attempt to salvage a landing, we argue that reliable compliance with these guidelines will require educating pilots about the extremely narrow margin for error with unstabilized approaches, especially in conditions of bad weather and high workload, using accidents such as this one as illustrations. Plan continuation bias and the difficulty of quickly and correctly assessing whether attempts to salvage an approach will work should be emphasized, and the issue of whether and under what circumstances momentarily deviations from stabilized approach criteria can be tolerated should be discussed explicitly. In addition to establishing stabilized approach criteria, air carriers should emphasize to pilots that going around from unstabilized approaches is mandatory, not optional, should establish no-fault go-around policies, and should emphasize – especially to first officers – that the monitoring pilot must forcefully challenge an unstabilized approach. These procedural steps may help pilots to more reliably counter the human cognitive tendency to persist with the current plan of action despite cues suggesting the plan should be changed. Explicit guidance and emphatic training are necessary to counter inherent economic and organizational pressures to salvage an approach that is not working out, for whatever reason.

In this accident the first officer, performing the role of the monitoring pilot, provided callouts and challenges of flightpath deviations that exceeded the company's requirements. Yet the first officer did not challenge the flightpath deviations effectively enough to prevent the accident. The NTSB report suggests that it is desirable for air carriers to specify instrument scan policies and callouts by the monitoring pilot. This accident illustrates both the importance and the time-critical nature of monitoring. While it is natural for the pilot not flying to glance up periodically to monitor the visual approach, turning attention away from flight instruments even for a couple of seconds is dangerous and can be disastrous in the final moments of an approach. At least one airline has recently begun a program to increase emphasis on monitoring (Sumwalt et al., 2002). We suggest that company guidance on monitoring procedures should be detailed rather than generic, and that simulation training should provide practice and feedback in performing those procedures.

Further, based on the fact that the monitoring pilot in this accident was misled at a critical time by false information from the inherent lags of the non-instantaneous type of vertical speed indicator, the NTSB recommended that air carriers:

... make their pilots aware (through specific training, placards, or other means) of the type of vertical speed information (instantaneous/non-instantaneous) provided by the vertical speed indicators installed in their airplanes, and to make them aware of the ramifications that type of information could have on their perception of their flight situation (NTSB, 1997b, p. 71).

We think that this is important information for flight crews, and we further note that air carriers might devote special attention in this area to pilots transitioning from aircraft equipped with the instantaneous type of indicator to aircraft equipped with the non-instantaneous type of indicator. These pilots may have developed greater reliance on accurate vertical speed indications than is warranted by the equipment they would be using.

In its analysis of the critical last 10 seconds of this flight, the NTSB discussed the multiple sources of visual illusion and then noted:

> Although the airport and weather conditions that existed at the time of the accident combined with the irregular (and shortened) spacing of the runway lights presented a potential challenge for any pilot landing on runway 13, other airplanes used the ILS DME approach to runway 13 around the time of the accident and landed without incident (NTSB, 1997b, p. 59).

The NTSB then questioned "why the captain of Delta flight 554 was unable to land safely," and it answered with a conclusion that the captain's use of monovision contact lenses:

> ... resulted in his (unrecognized) degraded depth perception, and thus increased his dependence on monocular cues (instead of normal three-dimensional vision) to perceive distance. However, because of the degraded conditions encountered by flight 554, the captain was not presented with adequate monocular cues to enable him to accurately perceive the airplane's altitude and distance from the runway during the visual portion of the approach and landing. This resulted in the captain's failure (during the last 10 seconds of the approach) to either properly adjust the airplane's glidepath or to determine that the approach was unstable and execute a missed approach (NTSB, 1997b, p. 59).

The use of monovision contact lenses may well have contributed to the accident by further impairing the captain's processing of visual information that was already substantially impoverished and conducive to illusions; however, existing scientific knowledge is not sufficient to determine with certainty how much the contact lenses contributed to this accident. We suggest that at least three additional, related issues should be considered:

1) Other flights landing that day did not necessarily share the workload and risk factors that flight 554 encountered from the destabilized approach and the crew's attempt to salvage the approach at low altitude.
2) There have been many air carrier accidents prior to this one in which an airplane undershot the runway with a high sink rate that developed, and remained uncorrected, in poor-visibility conditions. These have given rise to studies of the phenomenon and universal cautions for pilots to avoid "ducking under" when they sight the approach lights in low visibility. Monovision lenses were not at issue in any of those accidents. Therefore, the other workload, risk, and perceptual factors that made this approach difficult were capable of resulting in an accident without the additional factor of the contact lenses.
3) When experienced flight crews execute challenging approaches in low-visibility conditions, performance varies appreciably as a function of the specific conditions, workload, crew interaction, and random factors. Variability in performance occurs both across pilots and within individual pilots. Repeated approaches under the conditions faced by the crew of flight 554 might yield safe landings hundreds of times and an accident once, depending on subtle

variations in conditions and interactions of factors that can be described only probabilistically.

Therefore, it is unrealistic to assume that because a given crew can manage a challenging approach most of the time they will always be successful in similar conditions and it is unrealistic to attribute the crash of one flight while others land safely to a single differential factor, such as the captain's use of monovision contact lenses. The prohibition against using monovision contact lenses while flying is highly appropriate, given their potential to degrade some aspects of visual performance. However, given the multiple risk factors in the operating environment of flight 554 and the history of similar accidents, we are far from certain that this accident would have been averted if the captain had not been wearing monovision lenses. Therefore, although banning the use of monovision contact lenses by pilots was a positive outcome of this accident and should eliminated a risk factor, it is crucial for the airline industry to continue and expand efforts to address the threats posed by unstabilized approaches and last-moment changes in flightpath, especially in bad weather.

Notes

1   The autopilot was disconnected at this time, so the captain was manually controlling the airplane's pitch attitude and flightpath. However, with the autothrottle system still connected, engine thrust was automatically being adjusted to maintain the selected airspeed. Therefore, engine thrust would increase as the captain raised the nose to reduce the descent, and it would decrease as he pitched the nose down to steepen the descent.

2   The accident report (NTSB, 1997b, pp. 51–3) discussed visual illusions that might have affected this flight by giving the pilots the impression that the airplane was higher/farther from the runway than it actually was: featureless terrain illusion (the river's surface), atmospheric illusions (rain on the windshield distorting and fog foreshortening the view ahead), and ground lighting illusion (overflying an unlit water surface). Also, on p. 17, the report stated that the runway edge lights on runway 13 were irregularly and more closely spaced than usual, which might have made the pilots perceive their aircraft to be higher above the runway and on a steeper glidepath than it actually was.

3   At about this time, with the airplane below 200 feet, the glideslope signal became unusable (as specified on the approach chart). Therefore from this time onward we cannot compare FDR data for the airplane's flightpath with those for the glideslope path (that is, we cannot evaluate glideslope deviation). In a subsequent section we will discuss the glidepath references that were available to the pilots during the visual descent below 200 feet, when they could no longer make use of the glideslope indication.

4   The NTSB concluded that windshear did not adversely affect the airplane's flightpath, despite a greater than 40-knot reduction in headwind component in the last 1,000 feet of the descent. The NTSB also quoted a Delta flight operations manual statement that heavy rain can have the same adverse aerodynamic effects as windshear. The manual recommended adding a 20-knot increment to reference speed in these conditions. See NTSB, 1997b, p. 39. The accident crew applied an 8-knot additive based on the reported wind, obtaining a target speed of 131 knots, and during the seconds prior to landing the airspeed deteriorated to less than the original reference speed of 123 knots.

5   Monovision contact lenses provide correct focus for far targets to one eye and correct focus
    for near targets to the other eye. This allows presbyopic individuals to discern both far and
    near objects without using bifocal or reading spectacles. The FAA prohibits pilots from
    using monovision lenses while flying, in part because switching between disparate inputs
    from the two eyes may impair visual processing. However, the captain and his optometrist
    stated they were unaware of this prohibition, and the captain's aviation medical examiner
    was not aware that the captain was using monovision lenses.

Chapter 19

American 1420 – Pressing the Approach

Introduction

On June 1, 1999 at 2350 central daylight time, American Airlines flight 1420, a McDonnell-Douglas MD-80, crashed into an approach light structure off the departure end of runway 4R at Little Rock, Arkansas. After landing fast and long on the runway in thunderstorm conditions, the airplane drifted to the right and then skidded back and forth as the captain fought to maintain directional control and stop the airplane with brakes and thrust reversers. The airplane then departed the left side of the runway and continued past the end of the pavement at high speed. The airplane collided with the approach lights, caught fire, and was destroyed. The captain and 10 passengers were killed; the first officer, the four flight attendants, and 105 passengers received serious or minor injuries, while 24 other passengers were uninjured.

The captain and first officer had started their workday during mid-morning at Chicago (O'Hare), Illinois, flying to Salt Lake City, Utah, then to Dallas/Fort Worth (DFW), Texas. Arrival traffic at DFW became congested by evening; the crew's flight from Salt Lake City inbound to DFW was delayed in a holding pattern, and it arrived late, at 2010 central daylight time. Flight 1420 from DFW to Little Rock was scheduled to depart at 2028 and arrive at 2141, but the airplane for that service was delayed, and the pilots became concerned. At about 2200, the first officer telephoned a company flight dispatcher to suggest that the airline substitute another airplane or cancel the flight. The airline substituted another MD-80, and the flight pushed back from the gate at 2240, 2 hours 15 minutes behind schedule.

The captain of flight 1420 was one of the airline's chief pilots at O'Hare. Serving as a manager for the 6 months preceding the accident had limited his recent flying time, but he had continued to fly regularly. He was quite experienced in the MD-80, qualified as a captain on the type since 1991 and as a check airman since 1998. He had accumulated 5,518 hours as a pilot-in-command in the MD-80. The first officer was new to this airline, but he was an experienced pilot. He had been flying at the airline for four months and had accumulated 182 hours as an MD-80 second-in-command; previously, he had flown extensively in various corporate jet aircraft types.

In its investigation of this accident, the NTSB found that the crew of flight 1420 conducted the approach and landing while a severe thunderstorm with strong crosswinds, heavy rain, and low visibility was affecting the airport. The crew did not arm the airplane's ground spoilers that normally extend automatically after landing to dissipate excess lift and improve braking performance. Also, in their attempt to stop the airplane, the crew applied reverse thrust to the degree that it disrupted airflow over the airplane's rudder and further degraded directional control. The NTSB determined that the probable causes of the accident were "the flight crew's failure to discontinue the approach when severe thunderstorms and their associated hazards to flight operations had moved into the airport area and the crew's failure to ensure that the spoilers had extended after touchdown". Contributing to the causes of the accident were:

> ... the flight crew's (1) impaired performance resulting from fatigue and the situational stress associated with the intent to land under the circumstances, (2) continuation of the approach to a landing when the company's maximum crosswind component was exceeded, and (3) use of reverse thrust greater than 1.3 engine pressure ratio after landing (NTSB, 2001j, p. xii).

Significant events

1. The crew attempted to reach Little Rock before the thunderstorms that were active in the area

Before the flight, the crew received and reviewed a printed weather briefing package prepared by the company that forecast a risk of thunderstorms in the Little Rock terminal area. The weather package also relayed a National Weather Service warning that an area of severe thunderstorms had formed in the vicinity of Little Rock. At 2254, while flight 1420 was en route, the crew received a message from the company dispatcher assigned to the flight that was conveyed by datalink to the printer in the cockpit. The dispatcher informed the crew:

> Right now on radar there is a large slot to Little Rock. Thunderstorms are on the left and right, and Little Rock is in the clear. Sort of like a bowling alley approach. Thunderstorms are moving east-northeastward toward Little Rock and they may be a factor for our arrival. I suggest expediting our arrival in order to beat the thunderstorms to Little Rock if possible (NTSB, 2001j, p. 32).

This printed weather report clearly indicated to the crew that thunderstorms would be a factor in the arrival at Little Rock. The dispatcher's predictions about the movement of the storms relative to the destination at arrival time now provided the crew with an up-to-date, accurate and clear perspective of the situation that they would encounter.

Flight dispatchers are responsible for monitoring the operation of several company flights at any given time. Dispatchers interact with flight crews to provide relevant information and to participate with the captain in cooperative, safety-oriented decision-making; for example, both the captain and the dispatcher must agree that it is safe to release a flight from its origin airport. Regulations do not prohibit dispatchers from also making recommendations promoting the efficiency of flight operations. Thus it is not surprising that the dispatcher assigned to flight

1420 concluded his message about the weather with a suggestion to expedite the approach. However, this suggestion conceivably biased the crew towards continuing their approach into the thunderstorm area.

We do not know whether the pilots considered alternative courses of action, but had the dispatcher provided the crew with additional information about alternatives for diversion (such as the weather at alternate airports, en route delays, and fuel planning data) or conducted a discussion about diversion, he might have prompted the pilots to at least consider other, more conservative, options. Arguably, a dispatcher on the ground may be in a better position to maintain an objective perspective that fosters consideration of more conservative options than a pilot who is immersed in the immediate flight situation, both because the dispatcher has a broader perspective on weather, fuel, and diversion alternatives, and because the dispatcher is more removed from the workload and stressors of the flight. However, a dispatcher's perspective may be affected by the large volume of flights handled during the course of a career. With few exceptions, all of these flights are conducted successfully to their destination in a large range of difficult weather conditions. Consequently, operation in such conditions may come to be perceived as routine and manageable, and the level of threat may be underestimated. All individuals are subject to "availability bias", which leads them to underestimate threat if their experiences of similar situations have all had positive outcomes (Tversky and Kahneman, 1974). This bias may have helped the dispatcher of flight 1420 to feel it appropriate to suggest that the crew expedite their approach; however, we suggest that this message may have added to the pressure that flight crews typically exert on themselves to land at their destination on time.

Arriving in the vicinity of Little Rock, the flight crew discussed the need to expedite the approach. At 2324:47, according to CVR data, the captain stated: "We got to get over there quick". The first officer stated: "I don't like that ... that's lightning", and the captain replied: "Sure is". The crew were probably observing the evolving weather, using both the onboard weather radar display and the out-the-window view as they continued toward Little Rock, noting that both the airport and the city were visible and the weather areas were to the northwest of the airport. The first officer later testified that the weather appeared to be 15 miles from the airport and that he and the captain believed there was "some time" (NTSB, 2001j, p. 3) to make the approach.

The crew's decision to continue the approach, hoping to arrive at the airport before the thunderstorm, was not unreasonable based on the information they had received at this time. Bias in favor of completing the flight at the planned destination is understandable, given the importance of reliable service in the airline industry. However, as is apparent in the discussion that follows, the crew of flight 1420 continued to adhere to this plan with remarkable tenacity in the face of contrary indications that they received later in the flight.

We suggest that the sequence of events from this point in the flight – still early in the approach – all the way through to the landing are best analyzed as a continuing process of assessment, reaction to events, and reassessment that is routine for airline pilots operating in proximity to a thunderstorm. During thunderstorm seasons airlines regularly operate in the general vicinity of storms, weaving around the cells of weather, sometimes holding for improved conditions, occasionally diverting, but usually landing at the planned destination. To assess the threat of continuing an approach in the vicinity of thunderstorms, crews must assemble a mental picture of a complex, dynamically changing situation from diverse indicators: onboard weather radar, controller reports, reports from preceding aircraft, and out-the-window observations (if not in instrument conditions). Crews are not provided with explicit guidelines on how to assemble a picture from these diverse indications that often provide ambiguous cues about overall storm development and movement; instead, they are expected to use experience and judgment to make decisions that directly affect the safety of the flight.

Flying into bad weather presents both tactical and strategic challenges. Tactical challenges involve identifying thunderstorm cells, deciding which way to deviate around them, and configuring the airplane for turbulence. While dealing with these tactical challenges crews must concurrently address strategic issues such as whether to continue to the planned destination and, if not, what alternatives to consider. Because these situations are dynamic, crews must repeatedly seek out and evaluate relevant information and assess its implications. Ideally, decisions made to continue in proximity to a thunderstorm should be provisional, and crews should continuously reassess conditions as an approach continues and revisit both tactical and strategic plans. We therefore analyze the further events of flight 1420 in terms of tactical and strategic decision-making and discuss the crew's continued assessments and reactions to the changing weather conditions at the airport.

2. The crew did not infer from the information they received about surface winds that the thunderstorms had already arrived at the airport

The flight was handed off to the Little Rock approach control facility and accepted radar vectors for an instrument landing system approach to runway 22L. Up to this time, according to the CVR, the crew had been observing the thunderstorm area that was ahead of the flight on radar and through the windshield. They discussed the situation and agreed that the thunderstorms were an adequate distance from the Little Rock airport for the flight to continue inbound to the destination. At 2334:11 the air traffic controller transmitted the following information: "… We have a thunderstorm just northwest of the airport moving, uh, through the area now, wind is two eight zero (direction from which the wind is blowing, in degrees) at two eight gusts four four (average and gust speed in knots)."

According to the CVR, the crew reacted to this information by discussing the limitations that the air carrier had established for landing on a wet runway in crosswind conditions,[1] which is a tactical consideration. However, in addition to the tactical significance of the controller's wind report (that is, whether the winds exceeded the company's crosswind limits for landing as the pilots were discussing), we suggest that this information also had strategic significance that was not discussed by the crew. The large increase in surface wind values suggested that the outflow of down-rushing air from the thunderstorm had reached the airport. The boundaries of thunderstorms are not precisely delineated; a thunderstorm's wind-generated effects on flight operations (including combinations of downdrafts, windshear, and turbulence) may extend beyond the heavy rain in the storm cell revealed by radar. Further, if an airport experiences these effects when it is downwind of the center of the storm, conditions are likely to worsen before they improve; the wind gusts in that case are the leading edge of the storm. This storm cell was located to the southwest of the airport, as the crew of flight 1420 could see on radar, and it was moving northeast, which the crew was aware of from their preflight weather information and the dispatcher's datalink message. The strategic implications of the wind report received by flight 1420 were that the storm already had arrived at the airport and that conditions would likely deteriorate even more.

Ideally, the updated weather report from the controller would have triggered the crew to conclude that their attempt to reach the airport before the thunderstorm had failed and to reconsider their plan of continuing the approach.[2] However, based on the crew's recorded conversations, they apparently continued to judge that the thunderstorm remained a safe distance away from the airport. Perhaps they were relying on the onboard weather radar data that evidently showed the heavy precipitation to have not reached the airport yet, and perhaps they were reassured by being able to maintain visual contact with the field throughout this period.

Relying on some indicators (radar returns and visual contact with the airport) to the exclusion of other information (surface winds) may seem to reflect inadequate knowledge of thunderstorms; however, other interpretations may be relevant. Research has revealed that experts in many domains often do not formally analyze the situations confronting them in a deliberate, analytical, systematic manner but rather compare the current situation with others, previously experienced (described as "recognition-primed decision-making" by Klein, 1997). The process of automatically retrieving and recognizing prototypical situations is typically advantageous because it enables experts to decide on a plan of action more efficiently and accurately than novices, who must analyze situations in a tedious step-by-step process. This efficiency can be especially advantageous in time-critical situations; however, we suspect that recognition-primed decision-making is less effective when information trickles in from diverse sources, especially when these sources are not entirely consistent with each other. Research indicates that experts are vulnerable to not fully processing information and to failing to completely assess situations when under time pressure, stress, high workload, or the effects of fatigue (Staal, 2004, pp. 84–5). This vulnerability may be exacerbated in a dynamic environment of diverse and changing information cues.

The crew of flight 1420, who were experiencing all these challenges, may have compared the radar data and the view out the windshield with their recollections of previous experiences of operating successfully in close proximity to a thunderstorm, and in doing so perhaps missed the implications of the wind report: that the thunderstorm had now arrived at the airport and that conditions would probably deteriorate even more. If their previous experiences were typical of air carrier pilots, they almost certainly would have had far more experience flying approaches to completion in similar conditions than aborting approaches. The crew's repeated references to the storm's proximity suggest that they correctly believed the situation to be a close judgment call. Repeated exposure to similar situations in which flights were continued to landing without adverse outcome makes all pilots vulnerable to building up a mental model that underrepresents the level of threat in these situations (another example of availability bias). The crew's discussion of the legality of landing in the existing wind conditions (both here and later in the approach) without discussing whether to break off the approach suggests they were more focused on tactical issues than on strategic issues. Perhaps crews are prompted to think about legality habitually because the issue arises for every approach involving appreciable crosswind or tailwind or limited visibility. Also, it is probably much easier for pilots to discuss legality because these issues involve directly comparing numerical values for currently reported winds with numerical values for prescribed limits. In contrast, decisions on strategic issues require subjective evaluation of a complex set of factors for which only general guidelines are available. Further, the piecemeal fashion in which weather information trickled in to the crew may have made it more difficult to hold in mind all sources of information and to integrate that information for strategic analysis.

During this period of the flight, and to some extent in later periods, the crew seemed more reactive than proactive. For example, to be more proactive, the captain could have assigned the role of flying pilot to the first officer when weather complications appeared, which would have allowed the captain to focus on the strategic aspects of continuously reassessing their situation and planning an appropriate course of action. A more proactive approach might have allowed the crew to recognize that the thunderstorm was too close to the airport to continue and might have prompted them to delay the approach or to divert to another airport.

Under high workload and stress, individuals attempt to simplify their tasks and reduce mental demands (Wickens and Hollands, 2000, pp. 488–9; Staal, 2004, p. 76). We suspect that one way pilots may unwittingly simplify task demands in these challenging situations is to shift from a proactive stance to a more reactive stance, responding to each event as it occurs, rather than managing the overall situation strategically. Conceivably, fatigue may also induce a shift to reactive responding. Research reveals that fatigue affects human performance adversely, especially in terms of flexibility in thinking, updating strategies in the face of new information, insight, and the general need to plan for future actions (Durmer and Dinges, 2005; see also NTSB, 2000c). The accident pilots had been awake for more than 16 hours at the time of the approach, were awake at a time they would normally have been asleep or winding down for sleep, and were undoubtedly tired. We will discuss the effects of fatigue in more detail later in this chapter.

3. The crew changed to the approach to runway 4R

At 2339:32 the air traffic controller transmitted: "…The wind's kinda kicked around a little bit right now it's, uh, 330 [degrees] at 11 [knots]". The first officer replied: "Okay, well, that's a little bit better than it was". The captain noticed that the northwesterly wind reported by the controller represented a tailwind component for the planned landing on runway 22L. At 2339:45 the controller added: "And, uh, right now I have a, uh, windshear alert. The center field wind is 340 at 10. North boundary wind is 330 at 25. Northwest boundary wind is 010 at 15". The captain suggested that the flight change its approach to runway 4R, and the first officer made this request to the air traffic controller who approved it.

In this exchange the flight crew was given new reports suggesting that the winds had decreased below crosswind limits and also that the flight should land in the opposite direction from the original plan. The crew received, assimilated, and reacted appropriately to both of these aspects of the new information. However, they had no apparent reaction to the fact that the new information also included a windshear alert. Once again the crew had considered the tactical implications of the wind report – favoring runway 4R – but not necessarily its strategic implications. We note, though, that pilots may downplay the significance of a windshear alert when it is accompanied by reports of decreased windspeeds, as in this case. The moderate windspeeds and changes in wind direction transmitted by the three sensors mentioned in the windshear alert could have implied (to any pilot) that the weather phenomena associated with the windshear were not severe. Further, crews frequently receive windshear alerts from ATC when approaching airports in the vicinity of thunderstorms and continue the approach without incident. By itself the existing low-level windshear alerting system (LLWAS) (especially the older model, with which many pilots formed their expectations about windshear reports generated by the system) is not reliably diagnostic of windshear, frequently providing false alarms. In general, it is well established that systems with high false alarm rates are frequently disregarded (this is described as the "cry-wolf effect" by Bliss and Dunn, 2000). As mentioned earlier, it may be especially difficult for pilots to infer the strategic significance of information when it includes apparently conflicting elements; in this case, windspeed reduction and windshear advisory.

In summary, the weather information received by the crew at this time of the flight may have seemed encouraging with regard to continuing the approach. Also, the crew began taking some precautionary actions in response to each identified risk factor: in this case, they correctly identified a tailwind component in the new wind reports and acted quickly to change runways. These actions may have given them confidence that they were compensating for the risks of the operation with proactive responses.

4. The crew continued the approach despite progressively deteriorating conditions

With the change to runway 4R, the approach controller vectored the flight in a series of turns away from the airport to reposition it onto the new final approach course. Consequently for approximately seven minutes the airplane's weather radar antenna was pointed away from the airport and the thunderstorm area that lay to the northwest of the field, so the crew could not observe the movement and development of the thunderstorms during that period. Also, during this same time that the airplane was maneuvering southeast of Little Rock and while it was established northwest-bound to intercept the final approach course, the captain could not see the airport and the weather immediately around the airport through the windshield and side windows, given his seating position on the left-hand side of the cockpit. The first officer had a better view of the area from his side of the airplane. The conversation recorded on the CVR during this period includes several references to the captain's inability to see the airport. The first officer reported the airport in sight and encouraged the captain to continue the approach. This conversation is consistent with the views that each pilot was able to obtain from his respective side of the aircraft.

At 2342:27, the controller informed the flight crew: "American 1420, it appears we have, uh, second part of this storm moving through. The wind's now, uh, 340 [degrees] at 16 gusts 34 [knots]". The flight crew acknowledged the controller. The first officer asked the captain: "You wanna accept a short approach? Want to keep it in tight?" The captain replied: "Yeah, if you see the runway 'cause I don't quite see it." The first officer continued: "Yeah, it's right here, see it?" The captain grunted and said: "You just point me in the right direction and I'll start slowing down here". The first officer then added, most likely referring to the weather area: "[expletive], it's going right over the field".

These conversations indicate that the crew had started recognizing that the weather was affecting flying conditions at the airport at this time. Their reaction was to further expedite the approach rather than to take a more conservative action. Also, in continuing with the approach, they did not appear to respond to the reported wind gusts that were greater than the crosswind limitations for a wet runway. During this period, the first officer seemed to have been encouraging the captain to continue the approach and to expedite the operation. Based on hindsight, the first officer's strong prompts might be considered to be undue influences on the captain, discouraging him from responding conservatively; however, considering the first officer's better view of the airport from his seat position it was natural, and even necessary, for him to verbally lead the captain toward the airport if the expedited approach were to be continued. On the other hand, it is important to note that the first officer's last comment, which is the one that most seems to express concern that the situation is really worse than previously thought, might better be viewed as an attempt to dissuade the captain from continuing with the approach. In this scenario, the first officer's wording may have been too subtle for the already busy captain to pick up on. Fischer and Orasanu (2000) reported that first officers typically use hints instead of direct suggestions to captains and that these hints are usually unsuccessful in changing the captain's actions. To obtain the greatest reliability, air carriers must train first officers to communicate directly and forcefully when perceiving a threat and must train captains not only to accept this directness but also to be alert for more subtle communication.

At 2344:19 the captain said: "… See we're losing it [the airport]. I don't think that we can maintain visual [contact]". The first officer transmitted to the controller that "There's a cloud between us and the airport", and the controller once again began to vector the flight onto the ILS approach course. At 2345:15, in a discussion of his decision to abandon the visual approach, the captain said to the first officer: "I hate droning around visual at night in weather with no idea where I am". The first officer's reply suggested the difficulty of the decision to accept vectors onto the instrument approach course: that in abandoning the visual approach for the ILS, the flight would experience a closer encounter with the weather area: "Yeah, but the longer we go out here the … See how we're going right into this …" The captain concurred.

The pilots were clearly aware at this point that their operation was caught between two risk factors: night visual maneuvering in poor weather if they continued directly toward the airport, and proximity to thunderstorms ahead of the flight if they accepted the southwesterly vector heading for the ILS approach. That the pilots apparently did not consider climbing away from the airport to avoid conflict with the thunderstorm (to wait for better weather at Little Rock or proceed to an alternate airport, either of which would have been a viable alternative) shows how strong their commitment was to the original plan of landing at the planned destination without delay. Pilots speak of this kind of behavior as "get-there-itis", a form of plan continuation bias, discussed in previous chapters.

The first officer next requested that the controller turn flight 1420 onto the ILS approach course as close to the airport as possible, which would expedite the approach and keep the flight away from the weather areas that were encroaching on the ILS final segment. As the flight began a right turn to the north to join the final approach course, the captain was once again able to assess weather conditions on final and at the airport, using weather radar and visual cues. At 2346:52 he said: "Aw, we're going right into this". Simultaneously the controller informed the crew, "American 1420, right now we have, uh, heavy rain on the airport … visibility is less than a mile, runway 4 right RVR [visibility reading] 3,000 [feet]".

At the crew's request the controller verified the RVR value and added: "The wind 350 [degrees] at 30 gusts 45 [knots]". The first officer read back: "030 at 45, American 1420". The first officer's mistaken readback of the wind direction as northeasterly (030 versus 350 degrees) would have suggested that the winds were now aligned with runway 4R and would not have signified an out-of-limits crosswind component, although it would have signified a worsening of the thunderstorm weather at the airport. His next statement to the captain suggests that the first officer actually understood the wind to have been northeasterly (as opposed to merely reading the wind direction back incorrectly): "[unintelligible] 0 forecast right down the runway." We cannot ascertain the captain's understanding of the wind direction and crosswind component at this time, without knowing whether he attended to the controller's transmission, the first officer's readback, or neither of these messages.

It is also noteworthy that the controller failed to correct the first officer's incorrect readback of the wind information he had just provided. Pilot-controller communications are most effective when three steps are followed: the controller transmits pertinent information in a prescribed format, the pilot reads back the critical elements of the transmission, and the controller verifies the readback is correct (Cardosi, Falzarano, and Han, 1999). This defense against communication errors was undermined when the controller working flight 1420 did not notice or take the time to correct the first officer. However, research on communications errors in air traffic control indicates that controllers' "hearback" of pilots' transmitted readbacks is often not performed reliably in daily operations (Monan, 1991; Cardosi et al., 1999). We note that on the day of the accident, the controller had worked the 0600 to 1400 shift, and he had only slept 4 hours before returning to the Little Rock control tower for the 2300 to 0700 shift. Research has shown fatigue to often cause individuals to accept performance of decreased quality from others as well as from themselves (Caldwell and Caldwell, 2003, p. 19) and this may help explain why the controller failed to notice, or noticed but failed to react to, the first officer's incorrect readback.

The crew's conversation next turned to the legality of landing in the existing conditions. At 2347:22 the captain said: "3,000 RVR, we can't land on that". The first officer consulted a flight publication and reported that the required minimum visibility was 2,400 RVR, to which the captain replied: "Okay, fine". The first officer reinforced: "Yeah, we're doing fine". The captain stated: "All right". The crew did not discuss and apparently did not overtly consider the implication of the onset of heavy rain combined with gusty winds: a worsening thunderstorm condition on the field.

The NTSB accident investigation report cited a study performed by scientists at the MIT Lincoln Laboratories revealing that it is not uncommon for airline crews to continue approaches in conditions similar to those faced by flight 1420. As part of an evaluation of the performance of new weather radar equipment, the MIT scientists correlated recorded weather radar returns and the radar tracks of flight operations inbound to the DFW airport during periods of heavy thunderstorm activity (Rhoda and Pawlak, 1999). Coincidentally, they made an important discovery about the behavior of airline flight crews: most of the crews confronting thunderstorms while on approach to their destination penetrated the storm cells during the approach. Flight crews were more likely to penetrate when flying after dark, within 10–15 miles of the airport, and when operating more than 15 minutes late (factors that might contribute to get-there-itis). This pattern of behavior was consistent across air carriers. These findings suggest that there is a norm in the air carrier industry to operate in close proximity to thunderstorms when approaching to land and that penetration of thunderstorm cells is common. These results also suggest that pilots often respond to the pressures of being late, near the end of their workday and near the airport (when they have almost attained the goal of completing the flight, and when their flexibility to deviate around weather is limited) by taking risks when confronting weather conditions. We conclude from this study that many airline crews in the situation of the crew of flight 1420 might also have penetrated the weather area.

Airliners that penetrate storm cells usually do not crash – none of the flights observed in the MIT study injured passengers or damaged aircraft severely. After penetrating storms and landing uneventfully several times, pilots may build up an inaccurate mental model of the risks involved. In evaluating situations people are heavily influenced by their personal experience (not necessarily consciously), but the small sample size of personal experience can give a distorted perception of the level of risk. The crew of flight 1420, like many other airline pilots, may have penetrated storm cells before without adverse outcome. Conversely, other pilots may have encountered severe turbulence when penetrating a cell and come away with a much higher perception of risk and consequently become much more conservative in flying in the vicinity of thunderstorms. Because individuals are vulnerable to cognitive biases distorting perception of risks, it is incumbent on the airline industry and on each company to develop explicit policy and training based on systematic analysis of risk in specific situations, such as that faced by the crew of flight 1420.

The MIT study findings also reveal shortcomings in the information available to pilots about thunderstorm location and severity. Assuming that their onboard weather radar was properly operated,[3] the crews observed to continue their flights through heavy precipitation areas conducted these operations despite radar displays of heavy precipitation. Clearly the information provided by existing onboard weather radar is not sufficiently specific or accurate to allow pilots to distinguish hazardous-looking but benign weather from truly hazardous weather. Thus pilots must supplement their weather radar information with information from additional sources, such as low-level windshear reports, ride reports from preceding flights, and ground-based terminal Doppler weather radar. Unfortunately, this additional information is not always available or complete. Also, ground-based sources typically provide alerts at conservative levels, which can lead pilots to discount or downplay the significance of this information. In the face of incomplete and ambiguous information and vague company guidance, pilots may tend toward either excessive conservatism or risk-taking, depending in part on the outcome of their previous experiences with thunderstorm encounters. We suggest that providing pilots with definitive information about weather hazards would allow them to avoid both excessive conservatism and excessive risk-taking. They could conduct flight operations in all weather conditions that are safe to fly in and deviate around the relatively limited number of unsafe conditions. However, in order to obtain these safety and operational advantages, the pilot community would have to be convinced that this weather information is highly reliable, accurate, and unbiased.

5. The crew did not perform the last five items of the Before Landing checklist, one of which was arming the spoilers, and they continued the approach despite reports of wind conditions exceeding carrier-specific crosswind limitations

At 2347:44 the captain ordered: "Landing gear down", the sixth of ten items on the Before Landing checklist (the first five had been performed in an earlier part of the approach, as required by company procedures). This was followed by the sound of the landing gear in transit. (The flying pilot, in this case the captain, calls for actions such as lowering the landing gear, and the monitoring pilot executes this commanded action.) At 2347:49 the captain added: "And lights [unintelligible] please". (He was probably asking the first officer to turn on the landing lights; this was not a checklist item.) For the next four seconds the only sounds recorded in the cockpit were from the captain trimming the stabilizer. At 2347:53, the controller transmitted a new windshear alert, which included information about a 45-knot gust at the center of the airport.

The ten items on the Before Landing checklist are not performed together, rather they are executed over time during the approach. The airplane was equipped with mechanical checklists, and company procedures called for the monitoring pilot (the "pilot-not-flying" in the company's terminology) to switch the light off on each item on the checklist as it was performed.[4] The airline's DC-9 operating manual stated:

> After each item has been accomplished, the pilot-not-flying will call out that item on the checklist, call out the appropriate response and then move the corresponding switch on the Mechanical Checklist [installed on the center control pedestal between the two pilots]. Any item that cannot be verified by the pilot-not-flying as accomplished will require a challenge and response. ALTIMETERS and FLT INSTR & BUGS will be challenged by the pilot-not-flying and responded to by both pilots. When all items have been accomplished, the pilot-not-flying will advise: "Before Landing checklist complete" (NTSB, 2001j, p.71).

The crew of flight 1420 deviated from company procedures after extending the landing gear by failing to perform the remainder of the items on the checklist. The omitted steps included arming the spoilers for automatic extension after touchdown and checking that they were armed. Conceivably, the captain's request for the landing lights momentarily diverted the first officer's attention at a time he would normally have continued with the habitual activity of performing the checklist. The windshear alert received in the cockpit shortly after the landing gear extension may have further distracted the first officer. During the 2½ minutes between lowering the landing gear and touchdown on the runway the crew received additional weather advisories, intercepted the localizer for the final approach, and struggled in the turbulence to keep the airplane aligned with the localizer and to find the runway when they broke out of the clouds. Pilots, like all other individuals, are vulnerable to forgetting to perform habitual tasks when interrupted, distracted, overloaded, or preoccupied, and when the cues that normally prompt execution of the task do not appear (Dismukes et al., 1998; Dismukes and Nowinski, forthcoming). Although we do not know why the first officer did not resume the Before Landing checklist, all of these factors were present and may have contributed to this oversight. Also, because the first officer was new to the company, he may not have yet established performing the company's procedures as strong habit, which could have increased his vulnerability to distraction.

We note that the company's procedures did not require the flying pilot to explicitly call for resumption of the Before Landing checklist when the landing gear was lowered. Rather, the monitoring pilot was supposed to continue without prompting with the final five items of the checklist. Research on checklist performance (Degani and Wiener, 1993) suggests that the call to initiate a checklist is an important cue and organizing element on the flight deck because it serves to involve both crewmembers in ensuring that a checklist is at least started. In this case, the captain could have linked his call for the landing gear with a call for completion of the checklist. If this call had been required by the company and routinely performed by the captain, both pilots might have been less likely to forget to complete the checklist in the workload and stress of the final approach of flight 1420.

The airline's manual indicated that, as part of the Before Landing checklist, the monitoring pilot was responsible for announcing that the spoiler lever had been armed. However, the manual did not indicate which pilot was responsible for physically arming the spoiler lever (NTSB, 2001j, p.72). NTSB investigators interviewed several of the company's pilots, instructors, and check airmen after the accident. They found that pilots had been instructed during their simulator training that the monitoring pilot was to arm the spoilers. However, line pilots told investigators that in practice the captain usually armed the spoilers regardless of whether acting as flying pilot or monitoring pilot, because the MD-80's spoiler handle is located on the captain's side of the center control stand.

Interference between procedures as trained and checked and as actually performed on the line is always a potential source of confusion and error. In this case the captain, as a check airman who had not recently performed much regular line flying, may have been relying on the first officer to arm the spoilers for landing as specified in company procedures, but the first officer may have become accustomed to the line norm of the captains arming the spoilers. Thus the captain's and the first officer's habit patterns may have been disjointed, and each pilot may have unconsciously depended on the other to arm the spoilers. Although they had flown two flights together earlier in the day, under the high workload, stress, and fatigue of this flight, each may have unwittingly reverted to his most strongly established pattern, and neither may have noticed that the other had not armed the spoilers.[5]

We note that at the time of the accident, company policy did not require both pilots to visually and verbally confirm the arming of the spoilers (confirmation was required for several other items on the Before Landing checklist). As discussed in previous chapters, the most reliable way to obtain participation in a checklist by the flying pilot is to require specific verbal responses from that pilot. After this accident the company changed its Before Landing checklist to require the flying pilot to specifically confirm spoiler arming. Although we cannot know whether this measure would have prevented the overloaded crew of flight 1420 from overlooking arming of the spoilers, it does provide additional protection.

We note that the crew of flight 1420 did not catch their failure to arm the spoilers or to complete the Before Landing checklist in spite of the airline's use of a mechanical checklist. The mechanical checklist is valuable for helping pilots avoid skipping checklist items or losing their place in the checklist because it requires a physical switch to be moved after execution of each item. If the switch is not moved, a light remains illuminated beside the omitted item, and pilots are likely to notice this light when scanning the instrument panel. However, no countermeasure to error is perfect. Effectiveness of the mechanical checklist might be improved by linking the call "Before Landing checklist complete", already required by the company, to a specific point in the approach that could serve as a reminder cue to prompt pilots' memory. We understand that the company now does this by requiring a checklist complete call in conjunction with the mandatory altitude call at 1,000 feet.

As previously mentioned, the air traffic controller transmitted new information at 2347:53, signifying further deterioration of weather conditions: "Windshear alert, centerfield wind 350 [degrees] at 32 gusts 45 [knots], north boundary wind 310 at 29, northeast boundary wind 320 at 32." The captain's reaction was to tell the first officer, "Add 20", a reference to maintaining extra airspeed during the final approach to compensate for gusts and windshear. The first officer confirmed the airspeed increment. This was another example of the crew reacting to new information about hazards by making a conservative tactical response, appropriate as far as it went, but failing to analyze and respond to the overall implications of the new information. Neither pilot referred to the crosswind component, which was now well in excess of company limitations for a wet or slippery runway (the company's crosswind limit for these conditions was 20 knots) (NTSB, 2001j, p. 79). We also note that, following standard procedure for a windshear advisory, the controller provided the windspeed, wind direction, and gust level at three airport locations. The controller's message contained seven numbers in addition to other information, which is at the upper limit of human working memory capacity, even when individuals have no other tasks to perform. Given that this crew was experiencing high workload, it is not surprising if they misunderstood or failed to process this information (Barshi and Healy, 2002). This may have caused the crew to miss the implication of some of the numbers transmitted at the beginning of the message. Further, several of the numbers were similar, increasing vulnerability to confusion.

At 2348:12 the air traffic controller added: "… The runway 4R RVR is now 1,600". This indicated that the controlling visibility measurement was now below landing minimums for the ILS approach. The crew's conversation after receiving the report once again focused on the legality of continuing the approach, and they pressed on. (It was legal for the crew to continue descending to the decision altitude because they had begun the final approach segment with adequate visibility reported at the airport.) They did not discuss the implications of the reduction in visibility – in fact, the core of the thunderstorm cell now lay over the landing runway – nor apparently did they consider that the RVR reading of 1,600 feet further reduced the crosswind limitation for landing, to 10 knots (NTSB, 2001j, p. 79). Thus, by two different measures, company procedures did not allow the flight to attempt to land at this point. Further, in a strategic sense, the crew was pushing beyond the limits of good judgment regarding thunderstorm operations. However, for the crew to make this strategic analysis they would have needed to retrieve from memory their understanding of thunderstorm characteristics and the fact that the runway would be wet and slippery. They would have had to add the wind information to the picture and compare the results to the airline's crosswind limitations, which they also would have had to recall from memory. This is in fact a straightforward, though attention-consuming mental task for experienced pilots, once they are triggered to perform the task.

The problem is that, under high workload conditions, fatigue, and stress, crews may fall into a reactive mode in which they respond only to the moment-to-moment demands of the situation and lose sight of strategic issues. This reactive mode has advantages – it reduces mental workload to manageable levels by allowing pilots to rely on highly learned procedural skills to automatically respond to task demands as they arise.[6] But the reactive mode also has major problems: overloaded pilots are less able to identify threats and errors and to reassess their situation. Pilots in this mode are less likely to recognize the combined implications of multiple situational factors – for example, to infer from the presence of both heavy rain and low visibility that the normal crosswind limitation must be replaced by much more stringent limitations found in the operating manual. Further, the piecemeal manner in which diverse information often arrives over time works against mental integration of the information, especially under high workload. Obviously, it is desirable for pilots to take a proactive stance in which they continuously update their mental representations and analyze situations strategically. Unfortunately this requires mental capacity often preempted by heavy workload. Ironically, task saturation may preoccupy pilots so heavily that they do not recognize that they are task-saturated.

The first officer made the required callout when descending through 1,000 feet above the ground. At that time he also noticed that the final flap configuration was not set, which was required to be done by 1,000 feet. At 2349:02 he asked the captain: "Want 40 flaps?" The captain replied: "Oh yeah, I thought I called it". The first officer then set and confirmed the flap extension for landing. We suggest that the captain's failure to complete configuring the airplane for landing by the required altitude is strong evidence that his performance was impaired by the high workload, his fatigued state, or both acting together. Further evidence is that he failed to make several required callouts during the approach: "Track-Track" when he noticed the initial movement of the localizer display; "Outer Marker" and the crossing altitude when the flight passed the outer marker; and later, "Landing" to inform the first officer of his plan at decision altitude. Also, we note that the first officer's call for final flaps was perhaps his last chance to notice that he had not accomplished the last five items of the checklist, including arming the spoilers. Under the existing situation and workload, the opportunity was missed.

After the accident the first officer recalled that the crew experienced a feeling of time compression during the final approach segment. He told investigators, "I remember that around the time of making the base-to-final turn, how fast and compressed everything seemed to happen". During this time, which was the period when the spoilers were not armed and the checklist was not completed, the cognitive demands of assimilating the worsening weather situation and the crew's unhappiness about conditions on the approach, as they expressed in comments recorded by the CVR ("We gotta get there quick … I hate droning around here visual at night in weather without having some clue where I am … Aw, we're going right into this …") were adding to the crew's workload and sense of pressure. The NTSB characterized the combined effects of the workload of conducting a time-shortened approach and the distractions of the worsening weather as "situational stress", continuing:

> Research has demonstrated that decision-making can be degraded when individuals are under stress because they selectively focus on only a subset of cues in the environment. As a result, any situation assessment may be incomplete, and the resulting decision, even when made by an expert, may be degraded. Stress can also impede an individual's ability to evaluate an alternative course of action, resulting in a tendency to proceed with an original plan even though it may no longer be optimal (NTSB, 2001j, p. 141).

The NTSB also considered how the flight crew was affected by fatigue. The crew had been awake for more than 16 hours at the time of the approach, and they were flying at a time of day when they were accustomed to being asleep (in other words, it was later than their normal bedtime). As part of its investigation, the NTSB interviewed Dr David Dinges, a prominent researcher on fatigue and associated human performance issues. In this interview, Dr Dinges described the effects of fatigue on human performance:

1. Performance on cognitive tasks shows somewhat more variability, both between and within subjects.
2. There is a tendency for vigilance decrements to occur when a task requires monitoring or detecting signals. This is associated with general difficulty overall in sustaining attention ….
3. Short-term and working memory errors increase. It can become more difficult to remember what was done and what was not done.
4. Cognitive slowing occurs on self-paced tasks. If the person can control the pace of work they will slow down, and slow the pace of the work, to maintain accuracy and hold performance up as they get tired or fatigued. However, if the task is work-paced, thereby preventing the maintenance of accuracy at the expense of speed, errors can be increased.
5. There tends to be a loss of time perception, which may be associated with cognitive slowing, and people begin to fail to appreciate whether their actions are timely enough.
6. There is perseverance on ineffective solutions, a tendency to keep trying the same old solution even if it doesn't work. People have difficulty coming up with a new way to solve a problem when fatigued.

7. There is a willingness to take some risks … for example in the Cambridge Cockpit Study, as reported by Hockey and Bartlett, the more tired aviators became … the more likely they were to cut some corners ….

8. There is a tendency to not pick up on peripheral events or to pay less attention to peripheral events. Peripheral events are defined in context and are often dependent on what the person is doing, what they see as their priority task, what problems they are confronted with, at what rate, etc.

9. An individual's reaction time can slow.

10. The above factors can combine to produce a loss of situational awareness, which can involve a neglect of routine actions and a failure to plan adequately for future actions (NTSB, 2000c, p. 3).

Dr. Dinges further described the allocation of cognitive resources by a fatigued person as follows:

> … Motivated, committed, professional people allocate resources to what they see as important when they are tired and have to get a job done … by putting extra resources, extra compensatory effort, into that task or modality. As a result, the person may not perform as well on other concurrent activities. It is more difficult for a fatigued person to allocate cognitive resources to multiple channels; and they have to expend more available cognitive resources to what they see as the most critical task at a given moment (*ibid.*, p. 4).

Based on his review of the evidence about flight 1420, Dr. Dinges concluded:

> Total wake time [of more than 16 hours] may have contributed to vulnerability to error … This prolonged wakefulness, coupled with the fact that the accident occurred at night approximately 2–2½ hours past the captain's habitual bedtime, make it highly likely that the captain was fatigued at the time of the crash … Fatigue was apparently one of a number of things that might have been relevant to performance errors … The way things were being prioritized by the captain during the final minutes of the flight fit what is known about fatigued performance (*ibid.*, p. 6).

The NTSB concluded that the rest and duty patterns of the crew of flight 1420 were consistent with fatigue. We suggest that fatigue probably exacerbated the crew's vulnerability to errors intrinsic to human cognitive limitations and the demands of the situation that developed in the last minutes of the flight. The snowballing overload situation that developed would have challenged any flight crew, well-rested or not. During the 2 minutes or so from landing gear extension to touchdown the crew struggled to maintain the correct flightpath in turbulence, interpret and mentally integrate successive weather reports, assess whether company procedures permitted them to land in these conditions, visually locate the runway, and then realign themselves when they saw it. Through its effects on working memory, fatigue may have increased the crew's vulnerability to forgetting to arm the spoilers and to failing to complete the checklist. Fatigue may also have increased the overloaded crew's persistence in continuing the approach, rather than considering alternatives, and may have made it difficult for them to recognize the growing risk of their situation.

6. The crew performed an unstabilized approach to touchdown

At 2349:12 the captain stated: "This is … this is a can of worms". The airplane was experiencing turbulence and the captain did not yet have the runway in sight, although the first officer apparently did see the runway. At 2349:31 the captain stated: "I got it, I got it", most likely referring to visual contact with the runway environment. At 2349:46 the first officer reported: "500 feet [above runway elevation]".

The first officer recalled after the accident that the flight began to lose lateral alignment with the final approach course and runway at approximately 400 feet above runway elevation. At 2349:56, one of the pilots stated: "Aw [expletive], we're off course". The first officer then stated, at 2350:00: "We're way off". According to the first officer's post-accident recollections, he made this statement because the airplane was deviating off the localizer course to the right and the edge lights on the right-hand side of the runway were drifting to his left (suggesting that unless the captain corrected the airplane's path the flight would land in the grass to the right of the paved surface of the runway). Almost simultaneously the captain stated: "I can't see it". According to FDR data the airplane was approximately 15–20 feet above the ILS decision altitude (215–220 feet above runway elevation) when the captain made that statement, apparently having lost visual contact with the runway. Approximately 3 seconds later, when the captain stated: "Yeah, I got it", the airplane had descended 10–30 feet below the decision altitude and was seconds from touchdown. Then, just prior to landing, the ground proximity warning system activated with two "sink rate" warnings. According to the FDR the airplane was descending through 70 and 50 feet above the ground when these warnings of excessive descent rate activated.

These recorded comments of the flight crew and correlated FDR data show that in several respects (landing configuration, sink rate, and lateral alignment) the airplane was in an unstabilized approach from 1,000 feet above ground level to touchdown. NTSB investigators noted that the air carrier had established guidelines for the stabilized approach, but these were only recommended "techniques" rather than required standard operating procedures (NTSB, 2001j, pp. 74–5). As we have suggested in our discussions of several other accidents (see Chapters 5, 9 and 18), the absence of strict bottom-line definitions for the stabilized approach can invite crews to push the boundaries of a safe operation.

We note that the first officer attempted to alert the captain about the airplane's alignment with the runway centerline just prior to landing with his callout of: "We're way off". Further, the first officer told investigators after the accident that he had quietly urged the captain to execute a go-around at this time; however, no statement to this effect was recorded by the CVR. The airline's DC-9 operating manual stated, "On final, a callout will be made any time any crewmember observes LOC [localizer] displacement greater than ⅓ dot and/or G/S [glideslope] displacement greater than ½ dot. The other pilot will acknowledge this deviation" (NTSB, 2001j,

p. 75). Although the first officer clearly attempted to alert or challenge the captain, the first officer weakened his challenge by not using the airline's standard callout phrasing for the course deviations that would have more clearly conveyed to the captain he had exceeded the prescribed limits.[7]

Further, it is important that the airline had not established a specific, required response, such as to execute a go-around, when the prescribed limits for a stabilized approach were exceeded (The airline has since established explicit limits.) Investigators learned from interviews with the airline's flight managers that captains were expected to use their own discretion in determining the maximum deviation tolerances for the localizer and glideslope courses. Consequently, even if the first officer had used standard terminology to challenge the deviations, it is uncertain how the captain would have responded. We suggest that establishing strictly defined bottom lines for continuing or missing the approach would help pilots make appropriately conservative decisions under time pressure and high workload. This and other approach-to-landing accidents illustrate how crews can become so intent on completing an approach in challenging conditions that they fail to interpret course deviations as signs that the approach cannot be continued safely. Also, as we have noted, crews may have previously landed under apparently similar conditions without mishap and without recognizing that the safety margins were narrow, reinforcing the habit of pressing on without reanalyzing the situation.

7. After landing the crew did not recognize the lack of spoiler auto-deployment, did not extend the spoilers manually, used excessive reverse thrust, and delayed obtaining maximum braking

The airplane touched down on runway 4R to the right of the centerline and in a sliding motion further to the right. During the landing rollout the airplane veered left and right by as much as 16 degrees before departing the left side of the runway at high speed.

Investigators determined that the airplane would have stopped successfully on the runway if the spoilers had deployed. The spoilers did not auto-deploy on landing because the crew had not armed the system while on final approach. However, had they noticed that the spoilers had not auto-deployed, the crew could have deployed the spoilers manually after touchdown. At the time of the accident the airline's procedures established the captain as responsible for extending the spoilers manually if auto-deployment did not occur after landing. There was no required callout for spoiler deployment in the carrier's operating manual, but both pilots were advised to check for auto-deployment after touchdown (NTSB, 2001j, p. 75).

We suggest that crew monitoring of spoiler auto-deployment may be unreliable, even in less demanding situations, especially absent a specific procedural requirement, such as a callout, that draws the crew's attention inside the cockpit to the center console just after landing.[8] The spoiler system does not provide salient aural or visual cues to signal the crew if the spoilers do not deploy; non-deployment is indicated only by the spoiler handle on the center console remaining in the forward position.

Pilots might happen to notice if the spoiler handle does not move aft following touchdown; however, their attention is strongly directed outside at this time. Further, crews become accustomed to spoilers deploying automatically, which is normally very reliable, and the absence of a normal event is easily overlooked, especially under high workload, if not announced by a salient cue such as a warning horn or light (Wickens and Hollands, 2000, p. 217).

The difficulty that pilots generally have with noticing and correcting failure of spoilers to auto-deploy was evident from NTSB investigators' observations of the company's pilots in training: several spoiler non-deployments occurred during landing practice in the simulator, but none of these failures were called out by the pilots. During one landing the first officer manually deployed the spoilers, which was inconsistent with procedures requiring the captain to take this action; in the other landings neither pilot deployed the spoilers.[9] Further, following the flight 1420 accident there was another directional control incident with a company MD-80 that also involved spoiler non-deployment. During this event neither pilot noticed that the spoilers had not auto-deployed, and neither manually deployed them (NTSB, 2001j, p. 56).[10]

The skidding and veering of the aircraft to the left and right after flight 1420's landing would have been particularly distracting for any flight crew. The NTSB investigation report concluded that the workload of the directional control problem "may have prevented [the pilots] from detecting that the spoilers had not automatically deployed" (NTSB, 2001j, p. 134). Also, according to witness statements, the CVR transcript, and weather reports, the aircraft encountered rain and hail at touchdown. The loud noise of hail striking the windshields and fuselage and the accompanying reduction of visibility would have further drawn attention away from the inside of the cockpit and the spoiler handle. To improve the reliability of flight crew monitoring of spoiler deployment, the NTSB suggested adding a callout of spoiler deployment to standard operating procedures.

Following this accident and the subsequent incident, the airline added a required callout of spoiler deployment (the monitoring pilot was required to call "deployed" or "not deployed") to draw crews' attention to the system after landing. We suggest that this safeguard should help if rigorously practised, but it, too, can fail under the workload and distraction of a landing with directional control problems. We also note that several other aircraft designs incorporate a feature that deploys the spoilers automatically, regardless of arming, when the pilots select reverse thrust after landing. Such a system likely would have been effective in preventing or minimizing the severity of this accident. Given that spoiler deployment is essential for obtaining adequate braking and directional control, and spoiler arming and monitoring are both vulnerable when crews are under high workload or stress, a backup system for auto-deployment seems desirable.

According to information obtained from the FDR, during the landing roll the captain used reverse thrust exceeding 1.6 engine pressure ratio (EPR). This amount of reverse thrust disrupted the airflow over the rudder control surface and reduced the crew's ability to yaw the airplane with rudder pedal inputs, which investigators determined was a factor in the flight's directional control problems. This "rudder-blanking" phenomenon of reverse thrust was well known in the MD-80 operational community prior to the accident. Although 1.6 EPR was the normal reverse thrust value for landing on a dry runway, airline pilots had been instructed to use a different procedure for landing in slippery conditions, when directional control from the rudder surface and pedals might be critical. In these conditions, the carrier's operating manual instructed pilots to limit reverse thrust to 1.3 EPR on the "slippery portions of the runway" except in an "emergency situation" (NTSB, 2001j, p. 82).

But it is difficult for humans to remember in the heat of the moment that a highly practised procedure must be modified for an infrequent situation (described as "habit capture" by Reason, 1990, p. 68). Landings on slippery runways are done far less frequently than landings on dry runways, so pilots are vulnerable to reverting to the habit of using more than 1.3 EPR reverse thrust. Vulnerability to habit capture increases when pilots are under high workload (Betsch, Haberstroh, Molter, and Glöckner, 2003), as occurs when controlling the airplane on a slippery runway. One countermeasure would be for crews to take the time, prior to beginning final approach, to pre-brief the special procedures that will be needed for landing on a slippery runway. The time and attention required for this briefing[11] is another argument in favor of buying time (executing a missed approach if necessary) to avoid a rushed approach and landing.

Training in special procedures should help crews apply them more reliably when called for by circumstances. We do not know the nature of the training or subsequent online experience that the crew of flight 1420 had received, but the simulator training sessions observed by the NTSB after the accident suggest that the accident crew may have received inadequate training in reverse thrust operations on slippery runways. Investigators found that, at least during the observed simulator training sessions, pilots were not being taught the correct procedures. In the two sessions on slippery runway procedures that were observed, pilots practised landings using the normal reverse thrust target (1.6 EPR), and instructors did not mention the company's procedures to limit reverse thrust to 1.3 EPR. In another training session observed by the NTSB the instructor taught students that 1.6 EPR was acceptable unless a crosswind was present. Pilots performed most of their practice landings in slippery runway conditions using 1.6 EPR.

Further, although company materials were explicit about the rudder-blanking problem (correctly informing pilots that the rudder would lose all effectiveness at 1.6 EPR reverse thrust), we suggest that the procedure limiting reverse thrust to 1.3 EPR in slippery conditions was rendered imprecise by including the "except in an emergency" clause. This clause was also in the manufacturer's flight crew operating manual for the airplane (NTSB, 2001j, p. 83), and it had probably been included by procedural designers to avoid suggesting that pilots should limit reverse thrust even when in danger of sliding off the end of a slippery runway. However, failing to define the nature of the emergency that might make rudder-blanking a worthwhile risk was potentially confusing for pilots and did not reveal that a trade-off between deceleration and directional control would be involved in exceeding 1.3 EPR.

The airplane was equipped with an autobrake system that was designed to apply the brakes immediately after touchdown and wheel spin-up.[12] At its maximum setting the autobrake system could provide only slightly less braking pressure than that provided by a pilot's maximum manual pressure on the top sections of the rudder pedals; however, autobraking would be adequate for most dry and wet runway situations. Further, air carrier line operational and incident/accident experience suggests that in practice pilots rarely achieve maximum deceleration performance using manual braking, perhaps because habits of braking moderately and smoothly are so strong. Consequently autobraking may provide better deceleration performance than pilots can reliably produce with manual braking. Use of autobraking was optional in the airline's procedures, and the captain of flight 1420 elected to use manual braking for the landing at Little Rock.

FDR information revealed that 5 seconds elapsed after landing before pilot-applied braking began, and 11 seconds elapsed before the pilots achieved maximum wheel brake pressure. We suggest that the crew's delay in applying maximum braking probably occurred because they were busy controlling the airplane directionally in the seconds after touchdown. It is difficult to coordinate holding full pedal pressure for manual braking while modulating the rudder pedals for steering, especially during a landing in which the airplane is veering directionally, requiring large, fast-changing pedal steering inputs. Thus, although manual braking may in principle provide greater maximum brake pressure and deceleration rate, in practice autobraking may outperform manual braking during the most critical landing applications – on a slippery runway.

We note, however, that if the crew of flight 1420 had selected autobraking for this landing they would have been surprised to find that the autobraking system did not operate, because that system is designed to apply the brakes only after the spoilers have deployed. Thus, the flight would have encountered an adverse interaction between two automated systems (autospoiler and autobrake) in which the failure to arm one system results in the loss of both. Moreover, in this interaction the disabling of the autobrakes is not annunciated and would remain latent until the crew was immersed in the critical post-landing rollout situation. The crew would then have had to recognize the failure of autobraking from the lack of deceleration during rollout and apply brakes manually, and this could have resulted in an even greater delay in braking. Although there may be valid engineering reasons for linking the autospoiler and autobrake systems, making both systems dependent on the pilots' remembering to arm the spoilers (or to deploy them manually) is poor design from a human factors standpoint.

Concluding discussion

This accident would likely have been averted if the crew had recognized that the crosswinds exceeded maximum limits, recognized the danger of continuing an unstabilized approach, or recognized the thunderstorm's influence on landing conditions, and had discontinued the approach. The NTSB also concluded that the aircraft would not have run off the end of the runway if the crew had armed the spoilers, so the accident likely would not have occurred if the crew had corrected only that omission. However, these failures did not occur in isolation but rather resulted from the confluence of many factors – as is true of most airline accidents. Conducting the approach in the vicinity of thunderstorms placed heavy workload demands as the crew attempted to assess the weather, locate the airport visually, switch to an instrument approach to a different runway and maneuver the aircraft. It is likely that these workload demands, exacerbated by fatigue, contributed to the crew's inadequate processing and interpretation of the controller's weather reports, omission of arming the spoilers, and omission of the last items of the Before Landing checklist. Vulnerability to the challenges faced by flight 1420 may be more widespread than has been recognized; the accident investigation revealed that penetration of storm cells is common with approach operations in the vicinity of thunderstorms.

Deeper understanding of accidents such as this requires going beyond naming errors and contributing factors. We must look deeply at the inherent character of human cognition and how cognition is affected by the way line operations are typically conducted. Research has shown that once individuals embark on a planned course they are slow to re-evaluate their plan even in the face of growing evidence that conditions have changed. This propensity to plan continuation error grows worse as individuals near completion of their planned task, especially when they are tired. Reinforcing this inherent vulnerability in the case of the crew of flight 1420 was the industry norm of conducting approaches in the vicinity of thunderstorms. Thunderstorm weather information is complex and ambiguous, and few guidelines are available to crisply define when an approach should be terminated. Once committed to the challenging approach into Little Rock the crew of flight 1420 became task-saturated, increasing their vulnerability to error and undercutting their ability to reassess whether they should continue the approach.

We suspect that task saturation interacted with other cognitive vulnerabilities to prevent the crew from recognizing that continuing the approach was not a good idea. Weather information trickled in piecemeal, and high workload made it harder to integrate this information and recognize that conditions were deteriorating. Stress narrows the span of attention, causing individuals to focus on the most salient aspects of threat, which is probably good in some situations (such as being attacked by an assailant) but is problematic when individuals need to step back to integrate diverse information to assess the overall situation. Under high workload and time pressure, experts such as pilots may slip into a reactive mode in which they deal with the moment-to-moment demands of a situation as they arise, relying on automatic execution of highly practised responses. This reactive mode reduces the mental workload to manageable proportions and allows crews to handle the immediate task demands, but it also prevents crews from keeping track of the larger picture and from reassessing their situation.

Obviously it is desirable for pilots to take a strategic approach, especially in situations that are not routine, but maintaining a strategic approach is harder than may be apparent. Thinking strategically makes heavy demands on mental resources such as attention and working memory at a time when ongoing tasks are competing for those resources. Also non-routine situations, such as the approach into Little Rock, share many features with routine situations that are normally handled by executing standard procedures. Initially, it may not be possible to distinguish a non-routine situation from a routine one, and by the time the difference is manifest, crews may be too overloaded to recognize the implications of the divergence. Fatigue exacerbates the problem by sapping mental resources and by diminishing motivation to invest extra mental effort. Thus, ironically, it is most difficult for crews to take a strategic approach when they most need to do so.

A similar analysis can help us understand why crews in the situation of flight 1420 are vulnerable to forgetting to arm spoilers and forgetting to complete checklists. Procedures such as arming spoilers are normally extremely reliable because they are highly practised and become habitual. But the very cognitive features that make habits reliable under normal conditions make them vulnerable to error under certain conditions. Execution of habitual actions is initiated not by explicit thought but by perception of environmental cues strongly linked in memory to the action, or by executing a previous action so linked. But if the initiating event or cue does not occur or if the individual's attention is diverted from noticing the cue, the individual is vulnerable to omitting the procedural action without noticing the oversight. Checklist procedures are designed to provide backup protection against this vulnerability. However, initiation of a checklist and resumption of a suspended checklist are subject to the same vulnerability. The design of the accident airline's Before Landing checklist procedure at the time of flight 1420 was not as robust as it could have been, but the airline has since made several improvements. This accident illustrates both the importance of checking and monitoring procedures and the need to address hidden vulnerabilities of these procedures.

The NTSB determined from the crew's duty/rest period duration and timing that the crew was very likely fatigued. We suggest that the effects of fatigue upon the crew's performance in this accident are of particular concern because this crew was "normally" fatigued – their duty and rest schedules were not unusual for air carrier pilots and were within legally permitted limits. This suggests a systematic issue for the airline industry: it may not be uncommon for airline pilots to perform their flight duties while impaired by fatigue to some degree. However, this is not a simple problem to address. Fatigue is not an all-or-nothing state but a matter of degree. It is difficult for individuals to accurately assess the extent to which fatigue is affecting their performance, and it is difficult for investigators to determine the degree to which fatigue contributed to an accident. Not surprisingly, duty and rest cycle requirements are sometimes a contentious issue among labor, management, and regulators.

The aviation system relies substantially upon resources outside the cockpit to enhance and maintain the safety of operations, and assistance from outside individuals can be invaluable when crews face threatening situations, especially if a crew is tired and task-saturated. We suggest that airline dispatchers, removed from the immediate demands of flying the airplane and moment-to-moment tactical decision-making, can help crews keep the strategic picture in mind. Naturally, airline managers encourage dispatchers to consider efficiency and customer service, just as pilots are encouraged. However, we believe that airlines should explicitly encourage dispatchers to maintain their broader perspective on safety and to avoid being drawn into excessive focus on mission completion.

Even the most skilled and experienced of pilots are vulnerable to error in the conditions encountered by flight 1420. Airlines can safeguard against error by:

1. periodically reviewing and revising procedures to protect against hidden vulnerabilities;
2. establishing firm "bottom-line" limits, such as stabilized approach criteria, that mandate specific conservative responses, such as executing an immediate go-around; and
3. training crews to establish a strong habit of proactively assessing and continuously re-evaluating unfolding situations so they can take a strategic approach rather than just reacting to the sequence of situational demands at a tactical level.

To take a strategic approach crews must be able to keep their workload well within a comfortable range. Flight 1420 suggests that workload management training should be expanded and emphasized. In particular, crews should be taught to recognize the insidious effects of task saturation and to immediately respond by "buying time", for example by going into holding.[13] However, this training will be effective only if companies make apparent to pilots that crews who do buy time when necessary, at the cost of on-time performance, will not be penalized.

Finally, the airline industry should recognize that nothing can completely eliminate vulnerability to accidents if landing approaches are normally conducted in proximity to thunderstorms. Norms of operating under these conditions expose flights to the rare risk of entering conditions in which the aircraft cannot be controlled, as well as to the much more common risks engendered by decreased reliability of crews under the conditions experienced by the crew of flight 1420. The most effective way the airline industry could reduce the occasional accidents that occur on approaches in the vicinity of thunderstorms would be to adopt a more conservative policy, requiring that approaches be discontinued earlier than is currently the norm. However, the strong competitive pressures within the industry and strong public demand for on-time arrivals would make it very difficult for any one airline to adopt a more conservative policy on its own. Thus an industry-wide approach, considering all of the costs and benefits, and the trade-offs between schedule reliability, operating expenses, and safety, is required.

Notes

1   Airlines establish maximum allowable crosswind and tailwind components as a function of visibility and whether the runway is dry or wet.

2   Orasanu has reported that crews typically do not discuss risk explicitly, even though they may address risks implicitly through indirect discussion (Orasanu, Fischer, and Davison, 2002). The crew of flight 1420's discussion of the legality of landing in the existing wind conditions may have been an example of such an indirect discussion of risk. However, we base our conclusions about this crew's risk evaluation not on their verbalizations about the situation, but rather on their reaction to continue with the approach.

3   We do not know what the radar systems installed on the airplanes operating into DFW actually displayed; their radars should have shown heavy precipitation if operated properly, with active adjustment of the radar beam by the pilots using the antenna tilt control that is provided in the cockpit. One concern about the accident flight crew is the first officer's report that the crew set the antenna tilt to 15 degrees nose-up. If that was truly the setting, the crew's weather radar display may have understated the severity of the weather in the Little Rock area. Airline crews receive limited initial training on using weather radar effectively and are expected to develop their skills on the line. We do not know of any study of how well experienced airline pilots learn to operate weather radar to fully extract the information available.

4   Instead of the paper checklists used by most airlines, American Airlines uses a mechanical checklist. The pilot not flying reads each item on the checklist and moves a switch that causes the checklist to indicate that that item has been performed.

5   After the accident the airline amended its DC-9 manual to require the captain to arm the spoilers.

6   Tasks that are mentally demanding when being learned become automatic through extensive practice under what is called "consistent mapping" conditions. Think of the challenge of initially learning to drive a car. When task performance becomes automatic, it requires much less mental effort and conscious supervision. Considerable research has addressed the nature of automatic versus "controlled" (essentially, conscious) processing, but our comments about a reactive mode into which pilots may slip under high workload is speculative – empirical research on this topic could contribute significantly to aviation safety.

7   We note that the first officer was in his initial, probationary year of employment at the airline, and the captain was one of his supervisors. The extreme power distance between the two members of the crew may have inhibited the first officer's performance in challenging the captain's conduct of the flight.

8   Crew verification of spoiler auto-deployment was likely to have been an industry-wide problem at the time of this accident, although the NTSB investigation only developed factual material about the airline involved in the accident.

9   During the simulator training session in which spoiler non-deployment occurred the instructor made no comment to the students about their failure to accomplish manual deployment. Although it is difficult to conclude from a single observed training session, this suggests that the air carrier's quality control over its training program was deficient in this area at the time of the accident. This illustrates the importance of organizations evaluating themselves critically. Evaluation should include gathering data in areas such as student performance during training (emphasized by the FAA Advanced Qualification Program, or AQP) and then analyzing these data critically. It is in the critical analysis of

data that the airline industry has considerable room for improvement, even under the FAA AQP.

10 American flight 9503 (MD-83, Palm Springs, February 2000 – NTSB, 2000d).

11 The approach briefing by the flight 1420 crew occurred before the beginning of the 30-minute CVR loop, so we do not know to what extent the crew briefed the challenging conditions that lay before them. Briefing the special conditions of an approach, identifying options, and specifying bottom lines for discontinuing the approach is an important tool by which crews can prime themselves (especially with regard to potential exceptions, such as the 1.3 EPR limitation) and reduce vulnerability to fixating on continuing the approach.

12 Evidence indicated that the tires did not hydroplane and therefore wheel spin-up occurred immediately after touchdown.

13 Thanks to Doug Daniels of Delta Air Lines for showing one of the authors an example of an effective workload management training program.

Chapter 20

Flightcrew-Related Accident Data: Comparison of the 1978–1990 and 1991–2001 Periods

Our study is to some extent an update and extension of an NTSB study of accidents in which crew factors were found to be causal or contributing (NTSB, 1994a). Thus it is instructive to compare our findings with the major features of the NTSB study. The two studies used similar criteria for case selection: both included all of the accidents involving air carriers operating under 14 CFR Part 121 regulations that occurred in the US during their respective time periods (1978–1990 and 1991–2001), for which the NTSB conducted a major investigation and concluded that the flight crew caused or contributed to the cause of the accident.[1] Major investigations were defined as those to which the NTSB assigned a multi-disciplinary "go-team"[2] and then adopted a complete aviation accident report or summary report. In both studies, the selected cases were restricted to major accident investigations because the NTSB obtains a very comprehensive factual record for these accidents. It validates these facts through stringent evaluation by parties external to the investigation (including air carriers, pilot associations, aircraft manufacturers, and the FAA) and carefully analyzes implications of the factual data. Usually the NTSB publishes a formal report of these investigations, and often it holds a public hearing that may elicit further input.

Caution is required in comparing the frequency with which various factors appeared in the accidents in the two studies. Because the sample size (the number of accidents) was small, apparent trends may represent only random variation. Unless we explicitly identify a difference between the two studies as statistically significant, the reader should not assume the apparent trends are real. Also, when a large number of variables are compared between two groups, a few of those variables will by chance reach arbitrary criteria for statistical significance unless those criteria are set very high. Conversely, when numbers from the two studies appear to be similar, random variation may also be at play, hiding real trends too small to be detected with small sample sizes. Thus, with a few exceptions that will be discussed, we combine the data from the two studies and focus on the implications of the combined data.

Incidence of crew-caused accidents

The number of accidents per year decreased substantially between the two periods (Table 20.1). When we adjust for the large increase in the number of airline flights in the later period, we see a dramatic decrease in the accident rate, especially for accidents attributed to crew error (Table 20.2). This decrease is statistically significant ($p < 0.05$).

Table 20.1   Incidence of major, crew-caused air carrier accidents in the US

	1978–90	1991–2001	1978–2001
Number of accidents	37	19	56
Accidents per year	2.8	1.7	2.5

Sources: NTSB (1994a) and this study.

Accident rates are usually calculated on the basis of either the total number of hours flown by all aircraft or the total number of departures (essentially, the number of flights). Because accidents occur most often in either the takeoff or approach/landing phase of flight and because the average number of hours per flight may shift over time we prefer to calculate accident rate in terms of number of departures. Information on annual number of airline departures was not available from the NTSB until 1984; hence Table 20.2 compares accident rates between 1984–1990 and 1991–2001.

Table 20.2   Rate comparison of major US air carrier accidents: "Crew-caused" and all other

	Time period		
	1984–1990	1991–2001	1984–2001
Air carrier departures (100,000s)	504.7	1037.2	1541.9
"Crew-caused" major accidents (study cases)	20	19	39
Rate per 100,000 departures	.0396	.0183	.0253
Other major accidents	9	13	22
Rate per 100,000 departures	.0178	.0125	.0143

Source: NTSB, 2005.

The dramatic decrease in "crew-caused" accident rates is statistically significant ($p < 0.05$); however, the smaller decrease in other major accidents, involving a smaller sample size, was not statistically significant. Taken at face value, these data suggest that most of the reduction in major accidents in the airline industry from the 1980s through the present resulted from improvements in crew performance. This apparent improvement may have come about through the widespread adoption of crew resource management training throughout most of the industry, the evolution of threat and error management concepts, and growing use of highly automated flight decks and enhanced navigation and control displays. However, interpretation of these data is complicated by the possibility that NTSB criteria for attributing causal factors to crew performance may have shifted over the years through changes in interpretation and perhaps even policy. Understanding of the probabilistic nature of human error and of the diverse factors that influence the incidence of error is growing in the airline industry, partly through the efforts of the research community (for example, Perrow, 1999; Reason, 1990; Dekker, 2002).

In the 1990–2001 period the NTSB chose not to cite crew performance as causal or contributing in several accidents in which it was theoretically possible for the flight crew to have recovered from upset attitudes, for example: United flight 585 (NTSB, 2001k), Fine flight 101 (NTSB, 1998c), and USAir flight 427 (NTSB, 1999). Apparently the NTSB recognized that recovery in these accidents, while theoretically possible, was not highly probable because of limitations of existing training and because of the inherent variability of skilled performance in these demanding situations. However, the NTSB also did not cite crew error in some comparable cases in the 1978–1990 period (such as American flight 191 (NTSB, 1979), Pan American flight 759 (NTSB, 1983)), so we do not know whether a shift in criteria for citing crew error actually occurred.

Comparisons between operational contexts of the accidents in the 1978–1990 and 1991–2001 periods

Some of the most interesting findings of the 1994 NTSB study involved characteristics of the flights and crewmembers, which we refer to as the operational context of the accident.

Period of day

Table 20.3 compares the distribution of accidents into three 8-hour periods, chosen in the NTSB study.

Table 20.3   Period of day

	Per cent of "crew-caused" accidents		
	1978–1990	**1991–2001**	**1978–2001**
Local time of accident			
Morning–midday (0600–1359)	27	21	25
Afternoon–evening (1400–2159)	43	53	46
Overnight (2200–0559)	30	26	29

Distribution was similar in the two periods, within the limits of statistical uncertainty. The NTSB examined all scheduled flights for calendar year 1988 and found that the overnight time period was over-represented in the population of "crew-caused accidents" relative to this sample of normal flights (30 per cent of accidents versus 13 per cent of normal flights). We performed a similar evaluation of flights during 1996, near the midpoint of our study period, and found a similar over-representation of the overnight period among the accident flights compared to these normal flights. The greater vulnerability to accidents at night might result from several factors: it is more difficult to visually identify and avoid terrain and obstructions at night, aircraft control can be more difficult in nighttime visual conditions, and interpretation of instruments and displays is sometimes harder under artificial illumination. Performance-decreasing effects of crew fatigue are likely to highest in the overnight period because of de-synchronization of circadian sleep/wake cycles. The similar distribution of accidents in the two studies suggests that overnight flight continues to present increased risk. However, caution is required in interpreting these data because it is possible that the spectrum of types of operation differs among the three time periods (for example, cargo versus passenger).

Phase of operation

Table 20.4 shows the distribution of accidents in the two study periods over the six phases of flight. The distributions are quite similar, within the limits of statistical uncertainty, and closely resemble the distribution reported for accidents worldwide (Boeing, 2004). Even though the takeoff and approach/landing phases present the shortest periods of exposure to risk, these phases incurred the highest number of accidents. The Boeing data show the ratio of accidents to exposure duration was by far the highest during approach and landing. Concerned with the substantially higher risk during approach and landing, the industry has developed training aids and other tools to help reduce this risk (FSF, 2000). Among these tools are terrain awareness and warning systems (TAWS) with terrain displays and aural warnings and constant angle non-precision approaches (CANPA) that eliminate stepdown fixes and provide an instrument display of the safe descent path to the runway.

Table 20.4   Phase of operation

	Per cent of "crew-caused" accidents		
	1978–1990	**1991–2001**	**1978–2001**
Taxi	2.7	0.0	1.8
Takeoff	27.0	26.3	26.8
Maneuvering	2.7	5.3	3.6
Cruise	8.1	0.0	5.4
Descent	8.1	5.3	7.1
Approach/landing	51.3	63.1	55.4

Non-Crew Causal/Contributing Factors

In addition to crew factors the NTSB cited factors external to the crew as causal or contributing in many of these accidents (Table 20.5).

Table 20.5   Non-crew factors involved in accidents

	Per cent of accidents		
	1978–1990	**1991–2001**	**1978–2001**
Weather	37.8	26.3	33.9
Mechanical	32.4	15.8	26.8
Other persons	40.5	63.2	48.2
No other factors (flight crew only)	21.6	21.1	21.4

Note: Totals more than 100 per cent because of the citation of multiple factors in most accidents.

The NTSB cited at least one factor in addition to the flight crew in almost 80 per cent of the accidents in both time periods. This reflects the NTSB's long-standing record of recognizing that most accidents result from interaction of multiple types of factors.

Flight delay status

We followed the procedure that the NTSB used in its 1994 study to evaluate the delay status of the accident flights. While the US Department of Transportation uses gate arrival within 15 minutes of scheduled time as its criterion for on-time operation, that criterion clearly cannot be applied to accident flights. Consequently the NTSB in its study defined a late flight as one that departed more than 15 minutes behind schedule, or one that was delayed en route so as to be no longer able to arrive within 15 minutes of the scheduled time.

Information on flight delay status was available for 31 of the 37 accidents in the earlier period and 15 of the 19 accidents in the later period. The percentage of flights operating late, for which data were available, was similar in both periods (Table 20.6).

Table 20.6   Flight delay status

	Per cent of accidents		
	1978–1990	**1991–2001**	**1978–2001**
Flights operating late	55.0	53.3	54.4

Data for the delay status of a sample of non-accident flights cited by the NTSB indicated that no more than 28 per cent of flights departed late and no more than 35 per cent of flights arrived late during the period studied by the agency. Thus more accident flights were behind schedule than would be expected from the distribution of normal flights, however, the NTSB did not analyze whether the divergence between accident and normal flights was statistically significant. In the period of our study, statistics on on-time performance are available only for the period 1995–2001; these data indicate that 16 to 20 per cent of flights departed late and 19 to 24 per cent arrived late (BTS, 2004a).

Pressure to maintain scheduled arrival time might conceivably lead flight crews to make less conservative decisions and, in particular, might contribute to plan continuation errors such as failing to discontinue a planned approach when it becomes inappropriate/dangerous to do so. This pressure could be externally generated or self-imposed, conscious or unconscious. However, we note that several of the eight accidents in our study that were operating late did not manifest overt evidence of time pressure on crew decision-making. For example, the factors cited by the NTSB in the approach of American flight 1572 (Chapter 3) in poor weather – the way in which automation was used, the small margin of clearance for the non-precision approach, and so on – appear unrelated to time pressure. Similarly, the response of the crew of ValuJet flight 558 (Chapter 13) to an inadequate checklist and the response of the crew of American flight 1340 (Chapter 17) to an autopilot-induced pitch oscillation at low altitude were almost certainly not related to the late operation of these flights. Also, it is conceivable that NTSB investigators are more likely to note an accident flight's delay status if the flight were late than if it were not, a possible source of bias in the data. Thus, it is not clear from existing data to what extent operating late may influence crew performance.

Crew fatigue

In the 1994 study, the NTSB examined several measures of crew duty and rest for possible effects of fatigue on performance. A comparison of the crewmembers' time since awakening (TSA) with on-duty time and the accident's time of occurrence suggested that pilots in the accidents that occurred in the afternoon through overnight not only had been awake and on duty longer (as might be expected), but also had been awake for a longer period before beginning their flight duties. The NTSB expressed concern that "pilots working late shifts [might] be more subject to the effects of fatigue because they devote the latter part of their period of wakefulness to the work shift", (NTSB, 1994a, p. 30) while pilots working early shifts might be off duty and attending to personal activities during the end of their waking day. The NTSB study calculated median and upper/lower quartile values of time since awakening for the 17 captains and 15 first officers for whom data were available among the 37 crews involved in the accidents in its study period. The study found that the group of pilots who had been awake longer than the median value made more errors overall, and in particular more errors of omission, than the pilots who had been awake for less time. The pilots who had been awake longer also made significantly more procedural and tactical decision errors. We did not adopt the NTSB's methods for enumerating and classifying errors during the accidents, so we are unable to compare the number and type of errors in the two studies. However, the distribution of TSA was quite similar in the two groups of accidents (Table 20.7).

Table 20.7   Time since awakening (TSA)

		1978–1990	1991–2001
Captains			
	Accidents for which data available	17	11
	Upper quartile TSA (hours)	14.3	14.0
	Median TSA	12.0	10.4
	Lower quartile TSA	6.5	7.6
First officers			
	Accidents for which data available	15	12
	Upper quartile TSA (hours)	13.6	12.5
	Median TSA	11.0	10.0
	Lower quartile TSA	5.2	5.6

Note: Because these data are medians and we do not have NTSB data on distribution of the samples for the period 1978–1990, we cannot calculate medians for the period 1978–2001.

Although the data seem to suggest greater vulnerability to error at longer TSAs, these data are also consistent with the fact that most accidents occur during the approach/landing phases of flight (that is, at the planned end of at least the first flight in the duty period). Consequently, any fatigue effects of long TSA may be confounded with the inherent risk factors of approach and landing. Conversely, fatigue may contribute to some of the increased risk of accidents occurring during approach and landing.

In addition to TSA, crew performance may also be affected by the circadian period, over which alertness varies systematically, and by the extent to which the pilots have adapted their sleep/wake cycle to the period in which they are currently working (Caldwell and Caldwell, 2003). De-synchronization of the sleep/wake cycle by working swing shifts may have contributed to the relatively high accident rate of the overnight period previously discussed; unfortunately data are lacking with which this might be analyzed.

First officer experience

One of the striking findings of the NTSB study was that slightly more than half of
the first officers in those accidents had less than one year in that position/capacity at
the airline (Table 20.8). We found similar results for the first officers in our sample of
accidents; seven out of the 17 for whom the data were available had less than 1 year
of experience as first officers at their airlines. These seven pilots had a median of 118
hours of experience as first officers at their current airline. (A few of these pilots had
previous experience as first officers at other airlines or experience as flight engineers
at their current airline; however, these data are incomplete.)

Table 20.8   First officers with less than 1 year of experience in position

	1978–1990	1991–2001	1978–2001
Accidents for which data available	32	17	49
Number of first officers in initial year in position	17	7	24
Per cent of first officers in initial year in position	53	41	49

To what extent is it typical for pilots to have less than one year of experience as a first
officer at their current airline? The answer varies substantially among airlines as a
function of how rapidly the airline expands. To explore this question in its 1994 study
the NTSB sampled four airlines of various sizes and growth rates and found that the
first officers at two of the airlines had experience profiles similar to those involved
in the accidents from 1978 through 2000 (with a distribution weighted toward less
experience), whereas the first officers at the other two airlines had greater experience.
The NTSB concluded that although the distribution of first officer experience in the
accidents "may indicate that the first year of experience is critical for first officer
performance", this distribution also might have been an artifact of airline growth
rates and fleet utilization (NTSB, 1994a, pp. 35–6).

It is conceivable that low time as a first officer at an airline could increase risk
of accident appreciably. Although airline first officers are trained to high standards
and typically have considerable experience, during the first year first officers are
to some extent still honing their skills at flying the particular airplane, monitoring,
and detecting errors. During the first year first officers are typically on probation
(unless they have previously held flight engineer positions at the same airline), and
conceivably may be less willing to challenge the captain's decisions and actions.
For example, evaluation of weather and effectiveness of monitoring by the first
officer seem to have played a role in American flight 1340 (Chapter 17) (first officer
experience 182 hours) and USAir flight 405 (Chapter 12) (first officer experience
29 hours). However, our review of the circumstances of the other accidents in our

sample suggests that in most cases greater experience among the first officers would probably not have affected the outcome.

In summary, the data do not allow firm conclusions about whether limited experience among about half of the pilots in the two study periods contributed to the accidents. However it is very clear that inadequate monitoring and/or challenging was an important issue in most of these accidents, even those with highly experienced first officers (see, for example, Southwest flight 1455 (Chapter 5)). This is further discussed in a later section in this chapter.

Flying/monitoring pilot assignment

In most circumstances captains and first officers exchange assignments as the flying and monitoring pilot on alternate flight legs. Therefore it is reasonable to expect that the captain will be serving as the flying pilot and the first officer as the monitoring pilot on approximately 50 per cent of all flights. Yet when the NTSB examined crew assignments for the accident flights in the 1994 study, the agency found that the captain was the flying pilot for 81 per cent of the flights – much greater than expected.

Regardless of crew assignment, the captain retains final command authority in all situations. Consistent with overall command authority, we might expect captains to choose to fly a leg in which they anticipated unusually demanding conditions posed, for example, by bad weather or special airports. In its 1994 study, the NTSB attempted to control for this possibility by excluding several cases from its analysis of crew assignment in which the captain might have chosen to fly what otherwise would have been the first officer's leg. The NTSB study also examined the effect of excluding accidents in which the captain took over in the course of the flight, perhaps because of concern with approaching conditions. Even with both exclusions the captain was the flying pilot in over half of these accidents; however, the NTSB did not analyze whether this was statistically significant.

In our study we compared crew assignment data for the 37 accidents between 1978 and 1990 and the 19 accidents between 1991 and 2001, using three metrics: flying pilot at the beginning of the flight ("captain's leg to fly"), flying pilot at the time of the accident, and rapid turnovers of control from the first officer to the captain during the accident sequence (Table 20.9).

Table 20.9   Crew assignment

	Per cent of accidents		
	1978–1990	**1991–2001**	**1978–2001**
Captain's leg to fly	73	53	66
Captain flying at time of accident	81	79	80
Rapid takeovers	5 (2 accidents)	21 (4 accidents)	

The data on captain's leg to fly for the 1991–2001 period did not show nearly as much bias toward the captain that the data from the earlier period showed (53 per cent versus 73 per cent, respectively). Combining the data from the two periods, we find that it was the captain's leg to fly on 66 per cent of the accident flights; the difference in this percentage from the expected 50 per cent was not statistically significant. Regardless of whose turn it was to fly, in both periods the captain was flying at the time of the accident in most of the flights. This increase, from 73 to 81 per cent, and 53 to 79 per cent, respectively, for the two time periods, indicates that the captain took over the flying role at some point during the flight. Furthermore, in the combined period 1978–2001, the captain was flying at the time of the accident in 80 per cent of the flights, and this difference from the expected 50 per cent was highly significant statistically ($p = 0.0014$ for a two-sided Fisher's Exact test).

Of the six accidents involving transfer of control in the 1991–2001 period, four involved a rapid takeover by the captain in response to an unforeseen operational circumstance (and there were two similar occurrences in the earlier group). In the Continental flight 1943 accident (Chapter 9), the first officer was uncomfortable with the approach and pointedly turned over control to the captain after the captain would not let him execute a missed approach; in TWA flight 843 (Chapter 2), the first officer suddenly gave control to the captain after V1 while mistakenly stating that the airplane would not fly; in American flight 102 (Chapter 10) the first officer expressed desire to execute a missed approach on short final, but the captain overruled him and took over to continue the landing; and in Continental flight 795 (Chapter 11) the captain became concerned about the airspeed indications – not realizing these indications were false – and took control during the takeoff roll to execute a rejected takeoff maneuver.

In two accidents between 1991 and 2001 the captain took control in different circumstances and in a much less rapid fashion. The captain of ATI flight 805 (Chapter 14) took control after the first officer was unable to execute either of two attempts at an ILS approach, but then the captain became disoriented and lost control of the aircraft during the climb-out. At this point the first officer took back control of the airplane but was unable to recover before crashing. In the American flight 1340 (Chapter 17), the captain routinely assumed control as the airplane approached Category II ILS decision height in accordance with the airline's standard operating procedures for a low-visibility, captain-monitored approach, and the critical events of the accident all occurred within the few seconds after the captain took control.

The circumstances of the four accidents involving rapid, unplanned takeovers suggest that transfer of control to the captain is a critical situation that should not be undertaken lightly, especially when under extreme time pressure or when the takeover is performed in order to continue a landing attempt in difficult conditions. When a captain takes over as flying pilot in these situations, it is probably best for the captain to perform a missed approach. Further, as the events of ATI flight 805 suggest, first officers should be trained to make a rapid transition to the non-flying role in which they must effectively monitor and sometimes challenge the captain who has just assumed control.

Crew familiarity

 In the accidents studied by the NTSB, 44 per cent of the crews for whom data were available had never flown together prior to the accident flight, and 73 per cent had never flown together prior to the day of the accident – that is, they had completed one or more flights earlier that day but had not previously flown together before the day of the accident. Suspecting these percentages to be much higher than would have occurred by chance, the NTSB collected data on crew pairing from four airlines and calculated that the percentage of crews for whom a given flight would be their first flight together ranged from 2.8 to 10.5 among these four airlines, and further calculated that the percentage of crews for whom a given day would be the first day flown together ranged from 6.8 to 30.3.

 We examined crew familiarity in the accidents for which data were available in our sample, but found that the percentages of crews on their first leg together or their first day together was much lower than in the previous sample (Table 20.10). However, the sample size for both periods is small, and the differences between the two periods, while suggestive, fall short of statistical significance. Looking at the data combined for the period 1978–2001, we see that the percentages of accident crews on either their first flight together or their first day together are still considerably greater than one would expect from the comparison the NTSB made from data from the four airlines sampled. However, these data should be interpreted with caution   we do not have access to a broad or current sample of typical crew pairings across the industry.

 It would not be surprising if in fact being on the first flight or first day together contributed to some of these accidents. Although airline procedures and training go a long way to enable to newly formed cockpit crew to work together effectively as a team from the moment they meet, it is natural for team effectiveness to grow as the crew members gain experience with each other. A landmark study by Foushee, Lauber, Baetge, and Acomb (1986) revealed that crews who recently flew together made substantially fewer errors in a challenging simulation flight.

Table 20.10   Crew familiarity

	1978–1990	**1991–2001**	**1978–2001**
First flight together	7	2	9
Accidents for which data available	16	16	32
Per cent	44	13	28
First day together	11	5	16
Accidents for which data available	15	15	30
Per cent	73	33	53

Error type classifications

The NTSB identified 302 discrete crew errors among the 37 accidents in its study. These errors were classified into one of nine categories based on a classification scheme used by NASA (Ruffell Smith, 1979):

1. aircraft handling
2. communication
3. navigational
4. procedural
5. resource management
6. situational awareness
7. systems operation
8. tactical decision
9. monitoring/challenging.

Tactical decision and monitoring/challenging errors were especially prominent, occurring in 68 per cent and 84 per cent of the accidents respectively. Tactical decision errors were defined as "improper decision-making, failing to change course of action in response to a signal to do so; failing to heed warnings or alerts that suggest a change in course of action" (NTSB, 1994a, p. 47). Monitoring/challenging errors were defined as "failing to monitor and/or challenge faulty action or inaction ... by another crewmember".

Rather than enumerating and classifying types of error, our study focused on analyzing the interaction of environmental circumstances, task demands, and organizational factors with human cognitive characteristics. However, to facilitate comparison with the NTSB study, we analyzed the occurrence of tactical decision and monitoring/challenging errors, as defined by the NTSB, among the 19 accidents in our sample. We found the incidence of tactical decision errors in our sample to be about the same as in the NTSB study; the combined data show that tactical decision errors occurred in 70 per cent of accidents (Table 20.11).

Table 20.11   Incidence of tactical decision errors

Per cent of accidents		
1978–1990	**1991–2001**	**1978–2001**
68	74	70

In the 1978–1990 period the most common kind of tactical decision error found by the NTSB was failure by the flight crew to execute a go-around when an unstabilized approach situation required it. That kind of error occurred during 13 of the 37 accidents (35 per cent). Perseverance in unstabilized approaches and failure to execute a go-around occurred in a similar percentage of accidents that we studied

(Table 20.12), which suggests that this continues to be an important risk area in air carrier operations.

Table 20.12   Failure to go around from unstabilized approach

Per cent of accidents		
1978–1990	**1991–2001**	**1978–2001**
35 (13 accidents)	37 (7 accidents)	36 (20 accidents)

We found that the incidence of monitoring/challenging errors in our sample was somewhat less than in the NTSB sample but still quite high; in the combined 1978–2001 period 79 per cent of the accidents involved monitoring/challenging errors. Thus, increasing emphasis on and training in challenging and monitoring has considerable potential for improving safety (Sumwalt et al., 2002; 2003).

Table 20.13   Incidence of monitoring/challenging errors

Per cent of accidents		
1978–1990	**1991–2001**	**1978–2001**
84	68	79

Concluding discussion

Although the data presented in this chapter must be interpreted cautiously, comparison of the periods 1978–1990 and 1992–2001 reveals a large reduction in the percentage of accidents in which the NTSB identified crew performance issues as causal or contributing. This reduction may reflect advances in training and operating procedures, growing recognition by the NTSB of the complex etiology of human error, or both. Trend information for most other variables was not statistically reliable because of the small size of both samples. However, combining the data from the two periods gives a better sample and reinforces concern with several problematic areas initially identified by the 1994 NTSB study, especially: overnight operations, approach and landing, tactical decision-making, failure to go-around from unstabilized approaches, and monitoring.

Simply identifying and enumerating problems is not sufficient to understand why these problems occur and to develop countermeasures. However, combining this statistical information with analysis of cognitive vulnerability to error in the specific circumstances of accidents is a far more powerful approach. In the final chapter we draw together factors that cut across many of the accidents discussed in this book. This provides a foundation for our suggestions for ways in which the airline industry can reduce vulnerability to crew error and help crews manage diverse threats they may encounter.

Notes

1   Both studies added one case which did not fulfill all of these criteria but which were
     equivalent to the other accidents for the purposes of the study. The 1994 study included
     a September 1989 aircraft incident at Kansas City in which a Boeing 737 struck wires
     short of the runway threshold and then made a successful missed approach, landing safely
     (NTSB, 1990a). Although the event was not an accident according to the agency's damage
     and injury criteria, the NTSB performed a major investigation of this event and published
     a complete report on its investigation. Similarly, our study includes the May 1997 non-
     fatal accident of an Airbus A-300/600R at West Palm Beach, Florida (American flight
     903 (Chapter 15) – NTSB, 2000b). The NTSB performed a comprehensive "go-team"
     investigation of this accident and compiled a standard, major accident factual record
     validated through the party process. Although the agency did not publish a complete
     report on this event, the factual record was equivalent to those of the other cases.
2   These investigations are signified in the NTSB accident/incident database with
     identification codes that include the designators "MA" or "AA". Additionally, regionally
     managed accident investigations (designated "FA" in the database) were included in case
     selection for both studies if a multi-disciplinary team performed the investigation and the
     NTSB published a complete report on the accident.

Chapter 21

Converging Themes:
The Deep Structure of Accidents

We began this book by asking two questions:

1) Why do highly skilled professional pilots make errors with consequences potentially fatal to themselves as well as to their passengers?
2) How should we think of the role of these errors when we seek to prevent future accidents?

In seeking answers to these questions it is crucial to avoid hindsight bias (Fischhoff, 2003; Dekker, 2002, pp. 16–20). Knowing the disastrous outcome of a flight makes it easy to identify things the crew could have done differently to prevent the accident, but of course the crews in these 19 accidents could not foresee the outcome of their flights. In our analyses, we have tried to describe events as they unfolded around the pilots, and we have tried to identify the factors that might have influenced the pilots' responses, given the situation as they understood it at the moment.

Maintaining and enhancing aviation safety requires deep understanding of the inherent nature of skilled performance of experts – in this case, pilots. Although much remains to be learned, scientists now know a fair amount about the nature of skilled performance. Humans are able to perform tasks far beyond the capabilities of computers, but some degree of variability is inherent in human performance – skill and error spring from the same perceptual and cognitive processes (Reason, 1990, p. 1). Error has a random aspect, but the probability of error can be understood in terms of the interaction of four kinds of factors:

1) the characteristics and limitations of human cognitive and perceptual processes;
2) the demands of tasks being performed;
3) events in the environment in which tasks are performed;
4) social and organizational factors that influence how experts typically approach their tasks.

In the preceding chapters we analyzed in detail how these interactions might influence the performance of a representative sample of airline pilots placed in the situations of the accident pilots. Although we cannot say with any certainty what caused the errors of the accident pilots themselves, this approach makes their errors far less mysterious. And although errors cannot be completely eliminated, understanding these interactions can provide ways to reduce the frequency of errors and ways to prevent errors from leading to accidents.

The topic of this book required us to focus on aspects of accident crew performance that were problematic, but it is crucial to view these aspects in the larger context of the overall situation and the way the aviation system operates. The overwhelming majority of airline flights operate without incident, the flight crews managing a wide range of demands so effectively that the underlying challenges are not obvious to casual inspection. Further, every day of the week, an airborne flight crew deals with some unanticipated situation – equipment failure, passenger medical problem, severe weather, or some other anomaly – using their skills to prevent the situation from becoming an emergency. The theme of this book is that in the rare occasions when airline crews are not able to manage situations adequately, it is most often because of limitations of the overall aviation system rather than inherent deficiencies of the pilots.

Each of these 19 accidents we studied is unique, with limited overlap among surface features. This heterogeneity of the outward form of airline accidents is a challenge to those attempting to improve safety. Even if the airline industry developed countermeasures aimed at each of these 19 accidents, these countermeasures might have limited benefit because the next 19 accidents are likely to have different surface features. Thus it is crucial to seek common underlying factors that might be addressed broadly. In this final chapter we attempt to find commonalities among the deep structure of these accidents.

In almost all of these accidents (and many others) multiple factors interacted over time to produce the final outcome. For example, the accident of American flight 1572 (Chapter 3) involved very close terrain clearance margins on the non-precision approach – perhaps closer than many pilots are aware exist – a strong crosswind that led the flying pilot to use a more demanding than usual method to track the approach course, the workload demands of non-precision approaches, the airline's use of QFE altimeter procedures, barometric pressure falling unusually rapidly, the approach controller's failure to update barometric information, tower closure because of broken windows, crew errors in setting their altimeters, the flying pilot's use of the autopilot's altitude capture mode to level at MDA, and the monitoring pilot's use of non-standard phraseology for callouts. Elimination of any one of these factors might conceivably have prevented the accident. This largely random and complex confluence among situational factors, organizational factors, and crew errors is one of the reasons each accident is unique and difficult to anticipate.

In this book we frequently raise a question that has seldom been explicitly addressed in the literature on aviation safety: Under what circumstances is it reasonable to assume crew performance will be reliable? By "reliable" we mean that, in a large population of highly experienced airline pilots, virtually all will perform the given task correctly and effectively, and individual pilots will rarely make serious errors performing the task. Occasional errors are inevitable even among the best of pilots; however, these errors should be minor or should be readily detected and corrected. In several chapters we point out that, although airline pilots could be expected to perform a certain task reliably under benign conditions, it is unrealistic to expect reliability under less benign conditions involving some combination of high workload, time pressure, stress, inadequate or confusing information, perceptual and cognitive limitations, inadequate training, and competing organizational goals.

Reliability is a matter of degree; even under benign conditions expert pilots will occasionally make serious errors. Thus it is crucial to detect errors and to prevent them from escalating into accidents. To accomplish this, airlines have established monitoring and checklist procedures to help crews catch their own errors, and air traffic controllers provide additional monitoring. These safety measures are buttressed by cockpit equipment systems such as traffic collision and avoidance (TCAS), ground proximity warning (GPWS), and configuration warning systems. These procedures and systems have substantially increased reliability of the overall air transport system; however, in several chapters of this book we have seen that error-trapping procedures are themselves vulnerable to the limits of human reliability, and that warning systems sometimes fail at the worst possible moment to operate as intended. Thus the challenge is to find ways around the imperfect reliability of humans and machines, a subject we will return to at the end of this chapter.

Common themes

Aspects of crew performance that contribute to accidents are commonly labeled "errors" – for ease of discussion we have followed this nomenclature, though later in this chapter we explain why the label "pilot error" can be misleading and may abet simplistic conclusions. As exemplified by American flight 1572, the errors discussed in previous chapters are quite diverse, as were the situations to which the crews were responding. Rather than attempting to categorize these errors by some theoretical model, we sought themes that might reveal commonalities among the accidents. We found that almost all of the significant events of these accidents clustered around six such themes, defined in terms of both the actions and failures to act of the crews and the situations that confronted them:

1. Inadvertent slips and oversights while performing highly practised tasks under normal conditions

These slips and oversights occurred in routine situations that pilots would not consider challenging. Some examples are overlooking a checklist item (Continental flight 795 – Chapter 11), Continental flight 1943 – Chapter 9), remembering an altimeter setting incorrectly (American flight 1572 – Chapter 3), and slightly misjudging the landing flare (Federal Express flight 14 – Chapter 6). These examples closely resemble the errors pilots themselves not infrequently describe in their voluntary safety reports to the Aviation Safety Reporting System (ASRS) (Loukopoulos et al., 2003, 2006) and which cockpit observers have noted (for example, Diez, Boehm-Davis, and Holt,

2003; Helmreich et al., 2004) in routine flight operations. Scientists consider these occasional errors to be within the normal range of performance of skilled experts. Although the probability of making an error in any one instance of performing a skilled task is relatively low, crews perform so many procedural steps in the course of a flight that the overall probability of making some sort of error is fairly high. Line observation safety audits (LOSAs) reveal that on most routine flights crews make at least one error (Helmreich et al., 2004; FSF, 2005). It is extremely rare for these errors to line up with situational factors in a way that leads to an accident; nevertheless, errors do reduce the margin of safety, so it is important to reduce the frequency of errors. To do so, we must start by recognizing that it is unrealistic to assume that humans will perform any task with perfect reliability, no matter how important the task. Further, the occurrence of error is probabilistic, rather than deterministic, which means that is virtually impossible to know the causes of an error in a single instance. However, the factors influencing the frequency of occurrence of errors among a large sample can in principle be determined. Thus in each accident chapter we described what is known about how various factors contribute to vulnerability to the kinds of errors attributed to the accident crew.

2. Inadequate execution of highly practised normal procedures under challenging conditions

These accidents involved slips and omissions similar to those described in the preceding paragraph; however, the probability of error is much higher in these conditions because of challenging demands of the crews' tasks. For example, the probability of forgetting to arm the spoilers was higher than usual in the situation of American flight 1420 (Chapter 19) because the crew was attempting to assess the weather, locate the airport visually, switch to an instrument approach to a different runway and maneuver the aircraft –challenging conditions that induced high workload and possibly stress. High workload, stress, and the fatigue of a long day are all factors that impair basic attentive processes. Performance of complex tasks is especially affected, as illustrated by loss of control in an accident involving high workload, stress, fatigue, and misleading information in a challenging approach with little margin for error (American International flight 808 – Chapter 4).

Our analysis of the accidents that occurred in challenging conditions reveals that many aspects of crew performance are sometimes affected: manual control of the aircraft, monitoring the status of the aircraft, identifying hazards and errors, decision-making, and intervention by first officers and flight engineers. The higher probability of error in challenging situations, and the tendency for these situations to snowball, increases the risk of accidents occurring. Thus it is crucial that displays, controls, alerting and warning systems, training, and operating procedures be designed realistically to anticipate greater vulnerability to error and to propagation of error under challenging conditions.

3. Inadequate execution of non-normal procedures under challenging conditions

Three of these accidents challenged the crew to recover from an upset attitude: in one case, a spiral dive (Air Transport International flight 805 – Chapter 14), in another, a stall (American flight 903 – Chapter 15), and in the third, windshear (USAir flight 1016 – Chapter 1). Upset recovery in large swept-wing jets is inherently challenging, requiring immediate and precise execution of the appropriate recovery procedure. Airline pilots are trained in these maneuvers; however, the amount of training is limited, and the form of training varies among airlines. The only upset recovery training that an airline is required to provide is for the specific condition of windshear; following a series of windshear accidents the FAA mandated that airlines conduct recurrent simulator training for identifying and escaping from this situation, typically spaced between 6 and 18 months.

All pilots are initially trained to recover from stalls, however airline pilots are taught to recover from imminent stalls at the onset of the stickshaker warning and do not get an opportunity to practise recovery from a fully developed stall. Because one of the largest categories of airline accidents is failure to recovery from upset attitudes, many airlines now provide at least one session of simulator training in recovery from upsets, including nose-high, low airspeed conditions and spiral dives. The industry has, in recent years, taken up an active interest in this important issue affecting aviation safety, and has produced a training aid (FAA, 2004c) to provide guidance for air carriers. Also, for the past several years the FAA has been considering recommendations from the NTSB and other parties to make upset recovery training mandatory.

A recent study examined the performance of airline pilots in executing recoveries from spiral dives, windshear, and other upset situations (Gawron et al., 2003). Although the study had design limitations and must be interpreted with caution, it produced a troubling finding: most of the pilots in the experiment, regardless of whether they had received upset training, were unable to recover from most of the upset situations. One possible interpretation of this finding is that simulation training may fail to replicate the cognitive factors influencing upset recovery. Upset attitude situations in actual flight operations typically involve surprise, stress, high workload, ambiguous indications, and/or confusion, which greatly increase the difficulty of quickly and correctly identifying the nature of the upset and executing the correct recovery procedure. Another potentially relevant factor is that the flight performance models of existing flight training simulators are not accurate outside the normal range of flight maneuvers. Thus, upset training may fail to capture accurately how actual transport aircraft respond in upset situations. Another factor, finally, may be that the quality and depth of upset training varies among airlines. To address this concern, an industry consortium has developed training aid materials to standardize upset attitude training (FAA, 2004c).

We did not treat in this book several other airline accidents involving loss of control in which the NTSB did not cite the crews as causal or contributing (for example, the September 8, 1994 Boeing 737 accident near Aliquippa, Pennsylvania in which the rudder's hydraulic mechanism jammed and the rudder reversed (NTSB, 1999)) because the situations these crews encountered were so challenging that the NTSB judged that typical airline crews could not have been expected to recover reliably. However, the challenges to crew performance in these accidents had much in common with the three accidents involving loss of control that we analyzed: surprise, ambiguous cues, high stress, high workload, and the need to respond quickly with a maneuver not frequently practised. Experienced airline crews sometimes recover from these situations and sometimes do not; clearly these situations push the boundaries of human skill.

Not all non-normal situations involve high workload, stress, and the need to respond quickly, yet crews are still vulnerable to error in these situations when they must perform unpractised procedures if those procedures are not well written. Being unable to raise the landing gear did not impose extraordinary workload or stress on the crew of ValuJet flight 558 (Chapter 13); however, the procedure for "Unable to Raise Gear" was written in a way that was ambiguous and easy to misinterpret, which this crew did while preoccupied with preparing to land.

4. Inadequate response to rare situations

These situations included a false stickshaker activation just after rotation (Trans World flight 843 – Chapter 2), an oversensitive autopilot that drove the aircraft toward the ground near decision height (American flight 1340 – Chapter 17), anomalous indications from airspeed indicators that did not become apparent until the aircraft was past rotation speed (Continental flight 795 – Chapter 11), and an uncommanded autothrottle disconnect for which the annunciation was not salient (American flight 903 – Chapter 15). The first three of these situations required extremely rapid responses – the crews had at most a few seconds to recognize and analyze a situation few pilots have ever encountered and for which no pilots are trained, and to choose and execute the appropriate action. Surprise, confusion, and stress undoubtedly hamper performance in these conditions. No data exist on what percentage of highly skilled airline pilots would be able to execute the most appropriate action in these situations; however, we suggest that these situations severely challenge human capabilities and that it is unrealistic to expect reliable performance, even from the best of pilots.

5. Judgment in ambiguous situations that hindsight proves wrong

These situations included continued approach toward airports in the vicinity of thunderstorms (USAir flight 1016 – Chapter 1), which broke off the approach, and American flight 1420 (Chapter 19), which attempted to land (further discussed in the next section) and failure to positively ensure that wings were clear of ice before takeoff (USAir flight 405 – Chapter 12, and Ryan flight 590 – Chapter 7).

No algorithm exists for crews to calculate exactly how far they may continue an approach in the vicinity of thunderstorms before it should be abandoned. Company guidance is typically expressed in rather general terms. Thus the crew must make this decision by integrating fragmentary and incomplete information from various sources as they go along. Thunderstorm accidents are not common, which suggests that for the most part crew judgment works out acceptably, but not always, as USAir flight 1016, American flight 1420, and previous accidents reveal. One might think that these accidents occurred because the judgment of the crews that crashed differed from that of their peers; however, the only study that directly sheds light on this issue suggests a different interpretation. The Lincoln Lab radar study described in Chapters 1 and 19 revealed that many crews approaching airports in the vicinity of thunderstorm cells penetrated the cells during the approach without adverse outcome (Rhoda and Pawlak, 1999). Thus the difference in outcome between the accident flights and non-accident flights in similar conditions may be partly or even largely a matter of chance. If so, this type of accident will continue to occur occasionally until either systems can be developed to provide crews with more definitive information or the airline industry develops more conservative norms for holding or diverting in these situations. The latter solution could be applied immediately but would increase delays, costs, and customer dissatisfaction.

Pilots are mandated by the FAA and trained to ensure that wings are free of frost or ice before takeoff. That much is clear – what is less clear is how they are to know that wings are indeed free in some situations. Because the F-28 (USAir flight 405) and the DC-9-15 (Ryan flight 590) do not use leading edge devices, common among many airliners, they are especially susceptible to wing contamination in even minute amounts. The NTSB determined that at the time of these accidents the airline industry did not provide pilots with adequate procedures and criteria to ascertain whether wings were contaminated in common winter operating conditions. (Improvements have been made since the time of these accidents, but some ambiguities remain.) These two accidents also clearly illustrate the role of actual operating norms. USAir 405 deiced twice before attempting to take off. Two other aircraft deiced about the same time as USAir 405 and were in line behind it preparing to take off when it crashed. Ryan 590 did not deice, nor did any of the other aircraft preparing to depart the airport around the time of the accident.

6. Deviation from explicit guidance or standard operating procedures

Use of beta thrust in flight (Simmons flight 3641 – Chapter 16), landing from highly unstabilized approaches (Southwest flight 1455 – Chapter 5) and Continental flight 1943 – Chapter 9), and landing in wind/runway conditions beyond published limits (American flight 1420 – Chapter 19) are striking examples of this theme. Notably, each of these accidents occurred during the approach to landing phase of flight. In some cases a captain who deviates or allows deviation from explicit company guidance may do so willfully and in a manner atypical of his or her peers. But in other cases these deviations may not be especially uncommon, an example of actual operating norms diverging from the ideals expressed in company guidance (Snook, 2000, Chapter 6). It would have been extremely useful to NTSB investigators if information had been available about operating norms in the situations of the crews of these four accidents. Not all deviations are deliberate – crews may get so caught up in the high workload of trying to make a challenging approach work out that they lose track of whether they are operating within permitted limits. Plan continuation bias, discussed later in this chapter, was very probably at play in the four accidents involving deviation from explicit guidance and in many other accidents discussed in this book.

Cross-cutting factors

Human cognitive vulnerability, task demands, environmental events, and social, cultural, and organizational factors interacted in many ways in these accidents. Several specific patterns of interaction that appear repeatedly in our analysis may underlie many of the errors identified by the NTSB.

Concurrent task management and workload issues

These factors appeared explicitly or implicitly in the great majority of these accidents. In some cases workload and time constraints were quite high in the final stages of the accident sequence (see for example, American flight 1420 – Chapter 19) and Southwest flight 1455 – Chapter 5). Compounding the workload problem, crews may be required to integrate a high volume of diverse information to evaluate their situation. Under these constraints pilots may fail to note subtle cues and are less able to integrate and interpret information from multiple sources. They may also revert to a reactive mode; rather than strategically managing the situation, they may respond to each demand as it arises, without prioritization, because they lack sufficient free mental resources to take a strategic approach. Monitoring and cross-checking may also suffer.

In other cases adequate time was available to perform all required tasks; however, the inherent difficulty of reliably switching attention back and forth among concurrent tasks may have hampered performance (see, for example, American flight 1572 – Chapter 3). Even experienced pilots are vulnerable to becoming preoccupied with one task to the momentary neglect of other tasks and to forgetting to complete tasks when interrupted or distracted or forced to defer a task (Dismukes et al., 1998; Loukopoulos et al., 2003, 2006; also see discussion of prospective memory in Dismukes and Nowinski, forthcoming). More effective monitoring might have helped many of the 19 accident crews prevent or detect most of the errors made (Sumwalt et al., 2002); unfortunately, because monitoring is itself a task that must be performed concurrently with other tasks, it is also subject to the fragility of attention switching among tasks.

Situations requiring very rapid response

To our surprise, this factor occurred in nearly two-thirds of these accidents (see for example, American flight 1340 – Chapter 17). We were surprised because wise instructors often caution pilots against the dangers of rushing, which has contributed to many aviation incidents and accidents (McElhatton and Drew, 1993; Karwal, Verkaik, and Jansen, 2000). We suspect that the vast majority of challenging situations confronting airline pilots are indeed best met with deliberate, measured responses; however, the rare unfamiliar situations requiring rapid response are so vulnerable to error that they show up disproportionately in our sample of 19 accidents. Scientists distinguish between two forms of cognitive processing: "automatic," in which highly practised responses to a familiar task can be quickly executed with a minimum of deliberate effort; and "controlled," in which unfamiliar situations are managed through slow, effortful reasoning and deliberation (Shiffrin and Schneider, 1977; Schneider, Dumais, and Shiffrin, 1984; Norman and Shallice, 1986). In unfamiliar situations requiring very rapid response, no automatic response set is available, and the pilot does not have time to assess the situation adequately and to fashion the most appropriate response using controlled processing; thus error is likely.

Plan continuation bias

This was apparent in at least nine of these 19 accidents. (We have used the term "get-there-itis" but see also the discussion of "press-on-itis" in FSF, 1998, p. 36). This bias manifests itself as difficulty recognizing the need to revise a plan of action when conditions change, especially when the plan is habitual and the goal – landing, for example – is close to completion (Nagel, 1988; Orasanu et al., 2001). Only limited research has been conducted on plan continuation bias, but it appears to be intrinsic to human cognition (Muthard and Wickens, 2003), and it can be quite powerful. Several factors that may contribute to this bias in aviation operations are discussed in Chapters 4 and 5 (see also Wickens and Hollands, 2000, pp. 310–13).

Equipment failures or design flaws

This factor appeared in about two-thirds of these accidents. In some cases a design flaw or equipment failure precipitated the chain of events leading to the accident, such as the false stall warning in Trans World flight 843 (Chapter 2), and the oversensitive autopilot equipment in American flight 1340 (Chapter 17); and in other cases a flaw or failure undermined the efforts of the crew to manage their situation, such as the non-activation of the windshear warning system in USAir flight 1016 (Chapter 1), and the non-activation of the stall warning system in USAir flight 405 (Chapter 12), Ryan flight 590 (Chapter 7), and American flight 903 (Chapter 15). One of the major consequences of these equipment failures and design flaws was to present the crews with misleading cues or to fail to provide normally expected cues, discussed next.

Misleading or absent cues contributed to many crew errors

In addition to equipment failures and design flaws, misleading or absent cues resulted from inadequate crew communication, such as the premature callout of rotation speed in USAir flight 405 (Chapter 12), and the omission of standard callouts for the unstabilized approach of Southwest flight 1455 (Chapter 5). If the pilots who received erroneous cues, such as a false stall warning or a premature speed callout, had not been in situations severely constrained by time and workload, they probably would not have been misled but, as it was, the erroneous cues misdirected the pilots' initial responses.

   In other accidents, warning systems that pilots have been trained to recognize and rely on as diagnostic of the situation failed to alert the crews: stall warning systems failed to activate in American flight 903 (Chapter 15), USAir flight 405 (Chapter 12), and Ryan flight 590 (Chapter 7), and windshear alerting equipment failed to activate in USAir flight 1016 (Chapter 1). Although stalls and windshear can be recognized from other indications, aircraft designers include warning systems for these hazards because pilots may not react quickly enough to less salient indications, especially in the presence of surprise, confusion, high workload, and stress. Also, the association between equipment alerting and the condition to which alerted may conceivably become so strong during training that pilots are biased to preconsciously assess the absence of an alert as indicating that the aircraft is not stalling or not in windshear.

   The effects of misleading and absent cues are similar in some respects to the effects of ambiguous cues and incomplete information, illustrated by accident flights operating in the vicinity of severe weather (USAir flight 1016 and American flight 1420), discussed earlier in this chapter.

Inadequate knowledge or experience provided by training and/or guidance

This factor appeared in more than a third of these accidents. In some cases pilots were not provided adequate guidance about problems known by some segments of the industry to exist; for example, the greater vulnerability of wings without leading edge devices to even minute amounts of frost (Ryan flight 590, as described in Chapter 7, and USAir flight 405, described in Chapter 12). Inadequate training may have played a role in the three loss of control accidents discussed earlier in this chapter. Also, the crews of Tower flight 41 (Chapter 8) (inappropriate use of tiller on take-off roll) and ValuJet flight 558 (Chapter 13) (incorrect execution of a non-normal procedure) found themselves in challenging situations for which they had received training, but the experience they received from that training was of inadequate fidelity to the actual situation, inadequately detailed, or incomplete. It is not practical to provide specific training for every situation that might arise – for example, the false stall warning in TWA flight 843 (Chapter 2) –which raises the question of how best to provide generic training and procedures that will work in a broad range of situations, including those that are not likely to be anticipated.

Hidden weaknesses in defenses against error

These were revealed in many of these accidents. In recent years the airline industry has made considerable progress in developing procedures to prevent or catch errors and to manage threats to safety. Checklists, cross-checking procedures, monitoring, and stabilized approach criteria are examples of powerful safety tools, yet the preceding chapters reveal that all of these tools are themselves vulnerable to error.

For example, with extensive practice, procedures such as preparing the cockpit for flight become highly automatic, requiring minimal conscious effort. This automaticity, an inherent property of human learning and skill, is normally advantageous – if pilots had to deliberately search memory for what step to perform next and how to do it, flight operations would proceed at a tortoise pace, and it might not be possible to manage the concurrent tasks required to operate an aircraft at all. Yet automaticity has specific vulnerabilities; for example when a perceptual cue that normally triggers a procedural step is absent, pilots are vulnerable to omitting the step and not noticing the omission. Also, pilots, like all humans, are vulnerable to seeing what they expect to see from long experience; thus a pilot checking the status of an item thought to be already set may not notice that on one rare occasion it is not actually set. Perhaps this is why the captain of Continental flight 795 (Chapter 11) did not detect that the pitot-heat system was not turned on. Stabilized approach criteria and guidelines for go-arounds are undercut by the factors contributing to plan continuation bias. And errors have a way of snowballing that undercuts defenses – for instance, a pilot-induced oscillation on landing engenders such high workload that the pilot may be too slow to recognize that the only solution is to go around (see, for example, Federal Express flight 14, recounted in Chapter 6).

Although these accidents reveal that safety measures such as checklists, cross-checking, monitoring, and stabilized approach criteria are not perfect, they are of course crucial defenses against error. Without these defenses, the airline accident rate would undoubtedly be far higher. In the final section of this chapter we suggest countermeasures that can help shore up the weaknesses of existing defenses against error.

Other cross-cutting factors

Stress may have played a role in many of these accidents, but the extent is hard to assess. Stress is a normal biological response to threat; however, in complex situations requiring controlled cognitive processing, acute stress hampers skilled performance by narrowing attention and reducing working memory capacity (Driskell and Salas, 1996; Staal, 2004). The combination of stress and surprise with requirements to respond rapidly and to manage several tasks concurrently, as occurred in several of these accidents, can be lethal. The NTSB named fatigue as a causal factor in American International flight 808 (Chapter 4), and fatigue may well have been involved in other accidents. Unfortunately it is usually very difficult to know if accident crews were fatigued, and so we cannot even hazard a guess about the prevalence of fatigue effects in these 19 accidents. Finally, social, cultural, and organization factors are so pervasive that they inevitably play roles in every normal flight and in every accident. Rather than listing these factors as a separate category, we have tried to identify specific examples of their potential influence in each chapter.

The concept of causality in accidents

The NTSB is charged by Congressional mandate (*Independent Safety Board Act of 1974*) to find the "probable cause" of accidents, but the concept of causality is tricky, especially in accidents involving human error. Even in the case of an accident resulting from an identified materials failure, such as United flight 232 (NTSB, 1990b), the probable cause cited by investigators was complex, involving "the inadequate consideration given to human factors limitations in the inspection and quality control procedures" that allowed an engine fan disk with a pre-existing crack to remain in service.

It is natural for society to want to understand what caused an accident, and because crew actions and omissions are often proximal to the final events of an accident it is tempting to identify those actions and omissions as "the probable cause". However, almost all the accidents discussed in this book involved a complex interaction of inherent human performance characteristics with task demands, environmental events and conditions, and social and organizational factors. Scientists have pointed out that labeling in hindsight the imperfect performance of crews as causal under-represents the confluence of events leading to an accident and reduces motivation to make changes that might prevent future accidents (see, for example, Perrow, 1999, Reason, 1990; Dekker, 2002; Strauch, 2002).

Investigators readily acknowledge the multiple and interactive nature of causal factors in aircraft accidents. As exemplified by its work on United 232, the NTSB has increasingly sought to uncover factors underlying human error. In investigation reports, the agency often recognizes these as "contributing factors" if an unambiguous link can be identified between the factor and the accident. But when the connection is uncertain or probabilistic, as is often the case, the agency has traditionally discussed these factors only in the body of the accident investigation report, without drawing conclusions about them. Because of the difficulty of linking a specific crew action – such as not extending flaps – with certainty to a specific underlying factor – such as momentary distraction – these underlying factors have not often been listed by the NTSB as causal or contributing. The agency does recognize the importance of underlying factors in many of its recommendations for safety improvements; however, perhaps because the crew has the last chance to avert an accident in the making, crew errors are often listed prominently in the "probable cause" section of NTSB reports.

The *Standards and Recommended Practices* document of the International Civil Aviation Organization (ICAO, 2001) defines "cause" as "actions, omissions, events, conditions, or a combination thereof, which led to the accident or incident". Further, the "conclusions" section should "list the findings and causes established in the investigation ... The list of causes should include both the immediate and the deeper systemic causes". However, ICAO, unlike US law, does not require citation of a single probable cause in an accident. Several countries' accident investigation authorities do not name a probable cause of accidents. For example, the Australian Transportation Safety Board limits itself to identifying and analyzing the role of the contributing factors, and listing them sequentially as "findings"; the Transportation Safety Board of Canada lists "findings as to causal and contributing factors" (unranked) and as well as "findings as to risk"; and the UK Air Accidents Investigation Branch lists "findings" and also "causal factors", the latter without distinction as to primary or contributing.

We suggest that US lawmakers and investigators consider that highlighting pilot error in the "probable cause" statement may draw readers' attention away from the inevitability of human error and may under-represent the factors that produce error. Admittedly, the degree of influence of those factors often cannot be determined with certainty in a given accident. We further suggest that the concept of probable cause is weighted toward a deterministic perspective, whereas modern scientific perspectives describe human error as probabilistic in nature. The chance combination of errors with multiple situational factors leading to accidents is, as we have illustrated, clearly probabilistic.

One might assume that making errors in situations that experienced pilots normally manage without great difficulty is evidence that the accident pilots were deficient in some way and were not representative of airline pilots – what Dekker (2002) calls the "bad apple" theory. Perhaps they lacked knowledge, skill, or conscientiousness? We found no evidence for this contention and suggest that the burden of proof is on anyone who would make it. The background, experience, and training of the 19 accident crews seem to be quite typical of airline crews. The NTSB investigators uncovered no evidence of unusual shortcomings in these pilots' performance in training or previous flights that might have predicted these accidents (In investigations of other accidents the NTSB has occasionally found such evidence, but in most accident investigations the data available are not sufficient to meaningfully compare the history of performance of the accident crew with that of their peers.)

For the most part, crew performance during these accident flights, to the extent it can be determined from the NTSB reports, seems quite similar to that of the many crews we and others have observed in actual flight observations and in recurrent flight training simulations (Loukopoulos et al., 2003, 2006; Helmreich et al., 2004; Berman and Geven, 2005). Many of the errors cited in the NTSB reports are similar in kind and circumstances to the errors pilots often make on normal flights, as reflected in their voluntary submissions to the ASRS. Fortunately, in these ASRS-reported incidents, the errors and operational conditions did not line up in one of the rare ways that produce accidents.

Even the few accidents that involved deviation from explicit guidance or standard operating procedures should be interpreted cautiously; one should consider the actual norms for operating on the line – is the accident crew's deviation unique or do similar deviations occur occasionally or even frequently in similar conditions? Unfortunately, little data on actual operating norms is currently available. One should also consider the ways in which human information-processing characteristics constrain pilots' ability to assess adequately in the heat of the moment the possible consequences of deviations that may seem common and acceptable when the outcome is not known.

Airline accidents in developed countries have become extremely rare events because of advances in the design of equipment, operating procedures, and training. Although modern equipment is highly reliable, the sheer volume of operations – some 8,804,262 air carrier flights per year in the US alone (BTS, 2004b) – means that every day one or more flight crews experience some sort of equipment failure. Crews routinely deal with these equipment failures, with the vagaries of weather, and with various other non-normal situations such as passenger medical emergencies, drawing upon skill and experience to resolve the problem uneventfully. Crew performance is generally quite reliable; but with errors being inevitable over the course of millions of flights crews must cope with the consequences of errors – which they usually do successfully. When rare accidents do occur it is almost always because events, operating conditions, and errors happened to combine in a way to slip through the multiple defenses erected by the airline industry. When this happens it is inconsistent with the fundamental realities of human performance, and counterproductive to safety, to focus too narrowly on crew errors or to assign the primary causes of the accident simply to those errors. Rather, almost all accidents involve vulnerabilities in a complex sociotechnical operating system (Perrow, 1999; Reason, 1990), and causality lies in the probabilistic confluence of many factors, of which pilot error is only one.

Implications and countermeasures

It is highly unrealistic to expect crews – no matter how well trained, skilled, and conscientious – to never make errors. Nor can humans with their imperfections be automated out of the system, for only humans can deal with unexpected and novel situations and only humans can make value judgments among competing options with advantages and disadvantages. Thus to maintain and improve safety we must design all aspects of the system with the foreknowledge that human operators will commit errors. When equipment, procedures, and training are designed to reflect the characteristics and limitations of human cognitive and perceptual processes, it becomes possible to limit the frequency of errors, improve early detection of errors, and limit the propagation of errors into accidents. The object is to design the operational system to be resilient to the equipment failures, unexpected events, and human errors that inevitably occur.

Comparison of the accident rates between 1978–1990 and 1991–2000 (Chapter 20) reveals improvement in aviation safety, apparently derived at least in part by reduction in crew-related accident causes. In recent years the airline industry has paid increased attention to human factors issues, the original concepts of crew resource management (CRM) have been refined, and new concepts such as threat and error management (TEM) (Helmreich et al., 1999; Gunther, 2004a; Veillette, 2005) and risk management training (Barcheski, 2001) have emerged. But clearly a residue of tough problems remains, and new challenges arise from an operating environment of financial instability in the airline industry, security threats, evolving cockpit automation, and new air traffic control procedures and systems being introduced to accommodate growing density of air traffic.

Looking to the future, the issue of diminishing returns arises because many of the more straightforward ways to protect against human error have been identified and are in place. Further improvement in safety (or even maintaining current levels of safety) requires the entire airline industry to shift its perspective on accidents now attributed to crew error. To reduce pilots' vulnerability to error we must first abandon unrealistic expectations about human performance, especially the assumption that if expert pilots can normally perform a particular task well, we can expect them to never make errors in that task. When pilots make errors that lead to accidents or near-accidents, unless explicit evidence is obtained that the pilots involved differed substantially from peers in skill or conscientiousness, the event should be interpreted as an indication of system vulnerability rather than inadequacy of the pilots (The fact that pilots made errors and were involved in an accident does not in itself constitute evidence that these pilots differed from their peers.) Remedies should be sought by analyzing how characteristics of the system and of the operating environment at large interact with cognitive vulnerabilities inherent to humans – a topic requiring considerably more research and close collaboration between the research community and the airline industry.

We urgently need much better information on how the airspace system really operates and on the range of ways in which airline crews respond to the challenges posed. For example, how often and at what airports do controllers issue slam-dunk clearances and last-minute runway changes? How do crews respond to these challenges and how close do they come to the edge of the safety envelope? How close to storm cells do flights come during arrival and departure, and how much of the variation among flights is due to crew judgment and how much to chance? One way of generating this information is through flight operations quality assurance (FOQA) programs (FAA, 2004d; FSF, 2004) that collect data from the aircraft data bus on many parameters of the aircraft's configuration movement through space, and control inputs made by the crew.

Early research on FOQA focused on detection and analysis of "exceedances" (operation beyond prescribed flight parameter values). More recently, NASA's Aviation Performance Measuring System (APMS) project has been developing tools to analyze precursor conditions associated with those exceedances. For example, Chidester (2004) reported analysis of APMS data revealing that unstabilized approaches were often preceded by high-energy arrivals. More than 1 per cent of 16,000 flights conducted by three air carriers were in higher than desirable energy states (high speed, low drag, and/or high thrust settings) below 10,000 feet and failed to become stabilized by 1,000 feet, but continued to land, exceeding acceptable values for multiple parameters after touchdown. Although these preliminary data must be interpreted with caution, this research illustrates the potential of FOQA programs to uncover the factors that drive vulnerability to accidents.

Although the number of airlines developing FOQA programs is growing, because of concerns with confidentiality and liability the industry has not yet found ways to share the data. Lacking an industry-wide database it is not possible to generate a comprehensive picture of the threats within the airspace system; consequently, the ability of the research community to help analyze those threats will be limited unless ways can be found to make data available across the aviation system. Recently NASA has been developing an Information Sharing Initiative under the Aviation Safety and Security Program to address this problem.

Another program that can provide information on the challenges of flight operations and the norms of crew performance is the line operations safety audit (LOSA) (Tullo, 2002; ICAO, 2002a, 2002b; FSF, 2005). Under this program, trained observers sitting in the cockpit jumpseat on a substantial cross-section of normal flights can provide detailed information on the threats encountered, errors made, how those threats and errors are managed, and the extent to which operations conform with or deviate from the expectations established in company procedures. LOSA can be supplemented by the Aviation Safety Action Program (ASAP) (see FAA, 2002; Harper and Helmreich, 2003; Gunther, 2004b), which is modeled after the Aviation Safety Reporting System, but is airline-specific. Under ASAP, crews can submit reports about system safety vulnerabilities, many of which would otherwise remain unknown except to the direct participants; in exchange for this information the reporting crew receives immunity from regulatory sanctions. Airlines have found LOSA and ASAP invaluable for identifying areas within their individual operations that require more attention; however, to date only limited data have been published that would allow the industry to develop a comprehensive picture of the issues.

To fully exploit the information generated by FOQA, LOSA, and ASAP it is necessary to go beyond simply identifying problem areas and increasing training emphasis. For example, if an airline were to find that the actual norms for checklist use fall short of the ideals expressed in company manuals, it would be essential to analyze the discrepancy in terms of organizational factors, task demands, design of procedures, and the characteristics and limitations of human cognitive processes. This analysis would point to aspects of operating procedures and equipment design that could be revised to reduce risk substantially.

The norms that arise for group behavior represent a kind of equilibrium among competing influences. To shape those norms an airline must understand the competing influences and must understand that implicit incentives and disincentives can operate as powerfully as explicit incentives and disincentives. For example, if an airline discovered significant deviation from its published stabilized approach criteria, it would be essential to uncover the forces that discourage crews from aborting unstabilized approaches. Pilots undoubtedly internalize industry-wide concerns with on-time performance and fuel costs, they may consciously or unconsciously view having to go around as appearing unskillful, and they may fear recrimination. Further, they may not fully understand the logic of requiring stabilized approach criteria to be absolute bottom lines. We have heard pilots, even check pilots who are responsible for ensuring standardization at airlines, argue that being unstabilized is not a big problem as long as they can get the aircraft stabilized before touchdown. What these pilots may not realize is that the cognitive demands for getting the aircraft stabilized just before touchdown may undermine their ability to assess how well the situation is resolving. And having salvaged unstabilized approaches in the past may have created an inaccurate mental model of the margins of safety involved. For all these reasons, airlines are not likely to shift actual norms simply by publishing criteria for stabilized approaches. Establishing no-fault go-around policies is a step in the right direction, but still not sufficient. If stabilized approach criteria are to be taken as hard bottom lines rather than merely as guidelines, the logic must be fully explained to pilots, and training, checking, and incentives and disincentives must be consistently and emphatically employed to reinforce this policy.

The concept of bottom lines goes beyond stabilized approach criteria. In various situations crews may become so focused on making their plan of action work that they lose their ability to assess how close they are coming to the margins of safety. This excessive focus may be the product of both plan continuation bias and task saturation. Task saturation is insidious because once pilots become task-saturated they have no free cognitive resources to recognize that they are task-saturated and to evaluate the potential outcome of their situation. Pre-established hard bottom lines simplify decision-making in these situations and allow busy crews to recognize more easily that it is time to abandon a plan rather than continuing to struggle to make it work. However, task saturation can even prevent crews from recognizing that they have reached bottom-line limits, so even these valuable procedural safeguards are imperfect.

Pilots, airline managers, instructors, designers of equipment, and designers of operating procedures must be well educated about human cognitive characteristics and limitations and how those characteristics and limitations come into play in typical flight operations. With this knowledge pilots can anticipate cognitive vulnerabilities such as plan continuation bias and forgetting to perform task elements when interrupted or when juggling concurrent tasks. Forewarned, pilots can to some degree counter these vulnerabilities on their own. However, more formal changes are essential.

Procedures designers and operational managers can beef up existing procedures to reduce cognitive vulnerability substantially. For example, it is easy for briefings to become an automatic recitation because of the repetitiousness of airline operations. More broadly, this repetitiousness can lull pilots into a reactive mode in which they simply respond automatically to events rather than thinking ahead proactively and strategically. But briefings can be used as a tool with which crews look ahead and question whether the situation they are approaching is truly routine, to identify any unusual aspects or challenges, and to prepare options. This proactive stance helps maintain situational awareness and may reduce vulnerability to plan continuation bias.

Laboratory research has shown that prompting individuals to consider alternatives improves judgment by preventing them from prematurely settling on a mental model of the situation confronting them (Hirt et al., 2004, and references therein). This is an example of debiasing, which might also be used to counter the several cognitive biases discussed in this book (also, see Wickens and Hollands, 2000). Although more research is required to extend these findings to aviation settings, it would be worth exploring whether flight crews could be trained to use debiasing techniques – for example, by explicitly asking each other during briefings what ways their appraisal of the upcoming situation might prove wrong, and by periodically revisiting their initial appraisal. Debiasing techniques could be practised in line oriented flight training (LOFT) (that is, full mission training in realistic flight simulators) and would also be useful in analyzing performance during LOFT debriefings.

Checklists are of course a major defense against equipment failures and pilot errors. However, checklists themselves are vulnerable to cognitive limitations (Degani and Wiener, 1990, 1993; Barshi and Healy, 1993). With extensive practice, checklist responses become automatic and can detach from actual checking. Pilots may unwittingly look at items to be checked without seeing the actual status because of the long string of previous flights in which the items are in the expected position. Initiation and resumption of checklists are vulnerable to being forgotten when pilots are interrupted or forced to perform tasks out of the normal sequence. These vulnerabilities may be reduced in several ways:

1. Pilots can develop the habit of executing checklists in a slow, deliberately paced manner that allows controlled processing of information; also, it helps to touch or point to items being checked.
2. Checklist initiation can be anchored to salient events that always occur (for example, top of descent).
3. The flying pilot will monitor the monitoring pilot's execution of checklist items far more reliably if the flying pilot is required to make a verbal response.
4. Interruptions and tasks performed out of normal sequence should be treated as red flags, and salient cues can be created as reminders to complete tasks (such as placing a suspended checklist in the throttle quadrant).

The airline industry is starting to recognize the importance of monitoring as a defense against threats and errors (Sumwalt et al., 2003). However, monitoring is generally performed as a concurrent task and is itself vulnerable to the fragility of concurrent task performance, especially in periods of high workload or stress. Research is needed to develop ways to maintain reliable monitoring.

Airlines and aircraft manufacturers should systematically review existing normal and non-normal operating procedures, both in the context of daily operations, to assess the extent to which these procedures protect against or contribute to cognitive vulnerabilities. For example, initiation of checklists should be sited in the sequence of tasks in a way to minimize interruptions and to reduce the need to defer checklist items. Other normal procedures, such as parameter callouts by the monitoring pilot, should be evaluated for the information value they provide relative to the distraction they cause from the monitoring of other parameters. Non-normal procedures require especially thorough scrutiny for consistency with cognitive limitations (Burian, Barshi, and Dismukes, 2005). Because non-normal procedures are practised infrequently, they place heavier demands than normal procedures on limited cognitive resources; workload in non-normal situations is often high, and confusion and stress can further strain cognitive resources. Scrutiny should go beyond cockpit procedures to examine how the procedures of ATC, maintenance, and dispatch contribute to or protect against aircrew vulnerability to error.

Training can be improved in various ways. Accident case studies are sometimes used in ground school, which is a good way to get pilots' attention, but to be truly effective case studies should systematically analyze the interleaving of cognitive factors, task demands, situational factors, and social and organizational influences. Simulation training of emergencies too often consists merely of practising execution of the checklist procedure, and crews rarely experience the full range of demands and workload that may arise when managing an emergency all the way to completion of the flight (Burian et al., 2005).

Upset attitude training in flight simulation training would benefit from recurrent exposure, including the element of surprise, and using realistic events to initiate upsets, for example, with control system failures. Line oriented flight training (LOFT) is well established as a uniquely valuable tool for confronting crews with complex decision scenarios in a full-mission environment, yet not all airlines provide LOFT on a recurrent basis. Also, simulation training can be so demanding and so busy that pilots may not glean from the experience all they might learn from how their decisions played out and how they worked together as a team. Facilitated debriefing provides a powerful tool with which crews can review the situations they encountered in simulation training and analyze how effectively they managed those situations (Dismukes and Smith, 2000).

The design of cockpit displays and controls has advanced greatly in the last half century by systematic incorporation of human factors principles. Yet some shortcomings are still evident. False positive and false negative warning alerts can mislead crews in subtle but powerful ways. Equipment designers should thoroughly examine potential scenarios in which false warnings might come into play and how crew performance might be affected and should design warning logic accordingly. There is also growing evidence that existing methods of annunciation of automation mode changes are not well matched to human cognitive characteristics, which contributes to crews failing to notice changes in the mode in which the airplane is operating (Sarter and Woods, 1997; Mumaw et al., 2000).

Although modern airliners are highly automated, pilots remain in the cockpit in part because only human experts can exercise appropriate judgment in ambiguous situations involving complex issues; for example, when deciding whether to take off and when deciding whether to land if thunderstorms are in the vicinity of the airport. By definition, the outcome of ambiguous situations is uncertain, and human judgment cannot always be perfect in these situations. These kinds of ambiguous situations confront airlines with difficult cost–benefit trade-offs. An airline can reduce the risk of an accident by establishing (and enforcing) extremely conservative criteria but at the cost of expensive fuel, delays, and passenger dissatisfaction in an extraordinarily competitive market. In this environment airlines typically provide general guidance and expect crews to exercise good judgment, which may be the most rational approach to such ambiguous situations. But on the rare occasions these situations result in accidents, it seems inappropriate and counterproductive to safety to fault crew judgment, absent evidence that the accident crew's judgment and actions differed substantially from the actual norms of the airline and the industry. Rather these accidents should be viewed as system accidents resulting from the lack of adequate information provided crews, inherent difficulties of assessing ambiguous situations, and the less than extremely conservative guidance given to pilots by the industry.

The frequency of this type of system accident can be reduced by providing crews more complete information (for example, about weather), by developing better ways to display information in the cockpit, and by providing more explicit guidance for decision-making in ambiguous situations. This guidance however, must be realistic and consistent with what crews are actually expected to do. If formal guidance is conservative, then the industry must back it up by demonstrating to pilots that following the guidance takes precedence over production pressures such as on-time performance.

Final thoughts

Although this book focuses on the cognitive underpinnings of pilot error, the issues and principles discussed apply to the skilled performance of professionals in all domains in which safety is a concern. We hope that this book helps readers better understand the errors made by conscientious but imperfect experts on whom our lives depend – not just pilots but also air traffic controllers, mechanics, medical personnel, law enforcement officers, and many more. And finally, we hope that this book will make the frustrating little errors we all make in everyday tasks a little less mysterious.

Glossary

AAS:

  altitude alerting system: designed to alert the crew when the aircraft approaches and departs a pre-selected altitude. The altitude alerting system typically references altitudes set in the MCP (mode control panel) and consists of an aural warning (momentary "beep"), accompanied by an illuminated annunciation when the aircraft approaches within 900 feet and/or deviates by more than 300 feet from the selected altitude.

ADI:

  attitude director indicator (also attitude indicator or artificial horizon): instrument that depicts aircraft attitude (pitch and roll). ADIs commonly depict the sky in blue and the ground in brown, thus providing an intuitive reference to the horizon which lies between the two. Pitch is depicted by up/down movement of the depicted horizon against a fixed airplane symbol. Roll is depicted by the left/right rotation of the depicted horizon line against the same aircraft symbol and may also be judged by the movement of an index mark against fixed calibration lines along the circumference of the instrument. The ADI instrument may also incorporate flight director symbols (for example, vertical and horizontal command bars) that cue the pilot to adjust the airplane's pitch and roll attitudes.

AFS:

  automated flight system: controls both the navigation (autopilot) and the thrust management (autothrottles) of an aircraft together, or separately. At the heart of the AFS lies a flight management computer (FMC in Boeing terminology) which accepts inputs from the pilots, manages it using information stored in regularly updated databases (such as location and other facility information for airports, runways, and navigational aids; route structure; approach procedures) and with information it also receives from the aircraft instruments, and calculates performance parameters necessary for various modes of flight. The desired flight mode is selected and data input by the pilot using buttons on an MCP (mode control panel) and a CDU (control display unit). The selected mode at each moment in time is indicated on the flight mode annunciator, displayed on the pilots' instrument panels.
  Examples of automated flight modes are:

  - level change mode: pitch and thrust are coordinated so that the aircraft climbs or descends to a selected altitude while maintaining a selected airspeed;
  - heading select mode: roll is controlled so that the aircraft turns to and maintains a selected heading;

- lateral navigation mode (LNAV): roll is controlled so as to intercept and track a selected route stored in the FMC database;
- speed mode: controls thrust so that the aircraft maintains a selected airspeed;
- vertical speed mode: controls pitch and thrust to maintain a selected climb or descent rate;
- altitude hold function: controls pitch to maintain a level altitude and thrust to maintain a selected airspeed.

ailerons:

hinged, movable surfaces on the trailing edge of each wing used to provide control of the airplane about the roll axis. Ailerons are primarily controlled by moving the control wheel (yoke) to the left or the right – the ailerons move simultaneously in opposite directions. To roll ("bank") the aircraft to the left, the pilot moves the control wheel to the left, causing the left aileron to deflect upwards and the right aileron to deflect downwards. This causes the left wing to drop and the right wing to rise, and the aircraft to roll around its longitudinal axis. On turbojet aircraft roll control is augmented by spoiler surfaces. Use of the ailerons must be coordinated with the rudder.

altimetry:

method of calculating altitude (height). Three methods are used in aviation:

- QNH: in reference to MSL (mean sea level);
- QFE: in reference to the elevation of the airport surface (that is, the altimeter is set to indicate 0 while the aircraft is on the ground); and
- QNE: in reference to a standard pressure datum of 29.92 inches of mercury.

angle of attack:

angle at which the airstream meets the wing. The greater the angle of attack, the more lift generated on that wing – up to the critical angle of attack at which airflow begins to separate from the wing and the wing loses its lift (stalls).

annunciator panel:

centrally located panel of labeled fault indications corresponding to different aircraft systems. Generally, the indications are amber and are accompanied by an amber "Master Caution" light to direct pilots' attention to the annunciator panel.

anti-ice system:

designed to prevent ice from forming on aircraft surfaces (as compared with a deicing system which removes already-formed ice). Ice can form as a result of low temperatures combined with moisture in the air and is very dangerous because it affects the aircraft's performance. The anti-ice system typically uses hot, high-pressure bleed air from the engines to protect the leading edge surfaces and engine intake lips.

AOM:

aircraft operating manual.

AP:

autopilot: provides automatic aircraft pitch and roll inputs. The AP physically moves the aircraft flight control surfaces (ailerons, elevator), which may of course also be manipulated by the pilot flying the aircraft. *See also* AFS (automated flight system)

APLC:

airport performance laptop computer: a laptop computer used to compute aircraft performance parameters. Calculations are accomplished based on pre-loaded performance limitation data.

approach:

procedures and parameters that define the manner in which an aircraft will approach the destination airport and ultimately land. Pre-defined approaches are published for each airport – one runway at a large airport may be reached using several different kinds of approaches, depending on the weather conditions and the technology in use. Common types of approaches include:

- visual approach: conducted in visual reference to terrain;
- instrument approach: conducted using instrument references;
- precision/non-precision approach: with/without an electronic glideslope;
- ILS approach (see ILS: instrument landing system);
- coupled approach: flown by an autopilot that is coupled to the flight controls;
- missed approach: transition from descending on the approach to climbing to a pre-established missed approach altitude;
- final approach: the final portion of the approach that terminates with the landing;
- stabilized approach: a final approach descent that is stabilized with respect to a number of parameters, typically including airspeed, aircraft configuration (gear down and flaps set), establishment within on-course and on-glidepath tolerances, and engine thrust;
- unstabilized approach: violation of any of these criteria at a specific altitude above ground or distance from the runway.

APU:

auxiliary power unit: a small turbine engine that provides an additional source of electrical power and pneumatics.

ASAP:

Aviation Safety Action Program: a voluntary program in which pilots and other airline personnel report incidents to a joint company, labor union, and FAA panel that decides on corrective actions and provides the reporters, in turn, with limited immunity from FAA sanctions.

ASRS:

Aviation Safety Reporting System: incident reporting system run by NASA. It collects voluntarily submitted aviation safety incident reports from pilots, air traffic controllers, flight attendants, mechanics, ground personnel, and others involved in aviation operations. Analysis of the de-identified data helps identify deficiencies in the National Aviation System, and supports efforts taken towards their resolution and prevention. More than 600,000 reports have been submitted to date.

AT:

autothrottle: provides automatic thrust control to achieve airspeed commanded by the pilot through the MCP or the flight management computer. On Boeing aircraft, the AT physically moves the thrust levers, which may of course also be manipulated by the pilot flying the aircraft. *See also* AFS (automated flight system).

ATC:

air traffic control: facilities that manage air traffic by issuing route, altitude, and speed instructions to aircraft within specified sectors of air space:

- terminal radar control facility: provides approach control services to aircraft arriving, departing, or transiting airspace controlled by the facility. Typically separated into "Approach" and "Departure."
- airport traffic control tower ("Tower"): provides service to aircraft operating in the vicinity of an airport or on airport runway(s). Authorizes aircraft to land or take off or to transit an area of airspace within its jurisdiction. At larger airports, movement on airport taxiways is commonly controlled by a separate facility ("Ground"). At smaller airports, Tower may also provide approach control services.
- ARTCC: air route traffic control center : provides service to aircraft within controlled airspace and principally during the en route phase of flight. There are 20 ARTCCs in the continental US.

ATIS:

automatic terminal information service: recorded terminal (airport) area information (for example, current surface weather conditions, landing and departing runways, runway and taxiway conditions, communication frequencies) of importance to arriving and departing aircraft. Broadcast continuously over a frequency specific to each airport and, in many locations, also datalinked to equipped aircraft. Reports are updated every hour and identified by a sequential letter of the alphabet (referred to using the phonetic alphabet, for example, "Alpha" for the letter A, "Bravo" for the letter B, etc.). Upon initial contact with the air traffic controller, a crew reports the most recent ATIS information it has received (for example, "Carrier 123, we have information Delta."

autobrake:

provides braking after touchdown by automatically controlling brake pressure. It has a number of different settings of deceleration rates, including an RTO (rejected takeoff) setting. Many carriers require pilots to manually select the autobrake setting before takeoff and landing.

availability heuristic:
information that is used frequently is retrieved from long-term memory more readily than infrequently used information. This can bias individuals to overestimate the probability of events for which they can readily retrieve information.

bad apple theory:
the belief that the overall operation of a complex system would be optimal and reliable if the erratic behavior of some unreliable operators were somehow eliminated.

barometric pressure:
pressure caused by the weight of the air above a given point. At sea level it has a mean value of one atmosphere or 15 pounds per square inch (equivalent to 29.92 inches of mercury). Pressure values reduce with increasing altitude and vary with meteorological conditions.

base leg:
see pattern.

briefing:
verbal conference conducted between the pilots before the beginning of certain phase of workload that will be requiring coordination and therefore an agreed-upon plan; for example, before takeoff, or before starting an approach to the destination airport. A briefing is also conducted between flight crew (pilots) and cabin crew (flight attendants) prior to a sequence of flights. In their standard operating procedures, many carriers specify the important points that must be covered in a particular briefing.

bugs:
see speed bugs.

callout:
specific utterances made by the monitoring pilot that serve to aid and enhance the general situational awareness of the flying pilot. Callouts are specified by each air carrier's standard operating procedures, most often refer to instrument readings, and are specific to each flight phase (for example, during the takeoff roll the monitoring pilot will call out the aircraft speed as indicated by the airspeed indicator – "100 knots"… "V1"… "Rotate"). In some cases, callouts are indicated only if certain parameters have been exceeded and the ongoing action must be discontinued (for example, during the approach to landing, the monitoring pilot will call out the deviation from any of a number of parameters for a stabilized approach, as set forth in the flight operations manual).

CANPA:

constant angle non-precision approaches: instrument approaches that do not use a transmitted electronic glideslope signal but still incorporate a steady, constant angle of descent profile, most often with the airplane's onboard flight management system generating an electronic glidepath.

CDU:

control display unit: keyboard and monitor of the FMC (flight management computer). Two CDUs are typically installed on the control pedestal between the pilots, one on the left and the other on the right side so that they are most immediately accessible to the pilot on the respective seat. See also AFS (automated flight system).

challenge:

a verbal utterance made by the monitoring pilot to alert the flying pilot that a specific flight parameter limit has been exceeded or an undesired aircraft state is occurring. These challenges are specified in airline standard operating procedures as a required function of the monitoring pilot; thus they do not connote interpersonal friction or insubordination. Besides being meant to inform the other pilot, they are also intended to prompt the other pilot to respond. Challenges must continue until any adverse situation is corrected. *See also* checklist, for another context in which this term is used.

change blindness:

failure to notice changes in a visual scene. Because noticing such changes effectively depends on comparing two images (that is, the two versions of the visual scene), change blindness may be related to memory – a failure to store information about the first image, or a failure to compare the second (current) with the first (earlier) image.

check airman:

airline pilot who is qualified to evaluate the performance of other pilots.

checklist:

list of actions to be accomplished prior to a particular event (such as a takeoff) that, when executed in the specified order, help ensure that the aircraft and its crew are ready to safely undertake that event. Checklists typically refer to actions already accomplished by memory (that is, in the course of a procedure), thus adding a layer of protection against errors and omissions and verifying that critical procedural steps ("killer items") have been accomplished. Checklists referred to in this book are read from a printed, laminated card and are executed in a challenge-and-respond manner. When a checklist is called for by the flying pilot, the monitoring pilot locates and physically holds the checklist card, challenges (reads out loud) each line and verifies that the intended action has already been performed and the expected outcome has been achieved (for example, when the checklist calls for the engine ignition switches to be turned on, the pilot visually confirms that they are on by looking at the switches). The monitoring pilot must then utter a verbal response to confirm that the intended action has been accomplished using the exact verbiage prescribed. Some checklists involve one pilot challenging the item and the other pilot confirming and responding with the proper response. Once the specified actions have been challenged and responded to, the monitoring pilot announces the checklist "complete.

One other type of checklist referred to in this book is a mechanical checklist located on the center aisle panel between the pilots that allows them to move a switch to reflect completion of each item, thus keeping better track of their progress along the checklist.

check ride:

airline pilots are periodically given "proficiency checks" in which they are required to perform challenging normal and abnormal procedures in a high-fidelity flight simulator, and they are also given "line checks" in which a senior captain – a check airman – flies with the pilot being checked on a regular line flight to evaluate performance and adherence to company procedures.

confirmation bias:

a tendency to seek and use information that confirms a hypothesis or belief, and not notice or use information inconsistent with the hypothesis or belief.

control wheel/column (collectively referred to as "yoke"):

device used by the pilot to manipulate the aircraft's roll attitude by turning the wheel clockwise or counterclockwise, and its pitch attitude by pushing or pulling on the wheel to move the control column to which the wheel is mounted in a forward or aft direction. The aircraft referred to in this book provide each pilot with a control yoke. Pilots exerting force on the control column to move it aft, and pitch the airplane up, are applying "back pressure".

CRM:

crew resource management: a set of principles that pilots and others are taught to use to make effective use of all available resources – human, equipment, and information. Interaction and coordination among team members are emphasized. The concept of "team" includes but is not limited to flight deck crewmembers, cabin crew, air traffic controllers, dispatch, and maintenance. CRM principles are couched in various ways but in general address topics such as workload management, coordination and communication, leadership and support, situation awareness, and decision-making.

CVR:

cockpit voice recorder: a recording of sound in the cockpit, which captures pilots' utterances and ATC communications, as well as some non-verbal sounds. The sounds are captured by a cockpit area microphone located near the pilots, and also (in most cases) by the pilots' headset microphones. The data are stored in a crash-resistant case. Until recently most CVRs were continuous loop devices that taped over previous recordings after 30 minutes, a process which caused loss of crucial information in some accidents. The most modern CVRs use solid state memory and are capable of recording somewhat longer periods.

datalink:
direct communication method between ground stations and aircraft that displays written messages containing important flight information to the crew.

d/b/a:
doing business as (equivalent to UK t/a, trading as).

DA:
decision altitude (or decision height – DH): a specified altitude in a precision approach at which a missed approach must be initiated if required visual references have not been acquired. DA is referenced to altitude above mean sea level as measured by a barometric altimeter, while DH is referenced to altitude above the runway threshold elevation as measured by a radar altimeter. DAs (or DHs) are one of the many parameters specified in an approach procedure, with the purpose of ensuring safe clearance from obstacles during the approach or missed approach.

declarative knowledge:
knowledge to which individuals have conscious access and can report directly (verbally or otherwise).

deicing:
the process of removing ice that has already accumulated on aircraft surfaces. This can be achieved either on the ground or in the air. Ground deicing is accomplished by spraying a glycol-based liquid over the airframe. There are different types (I, II, and IV) of liquid depending on their effectiveness in preventing further ice formation (anti-ice protection). Deicing in the air is accomplished using air from the pneumatic system (to inflate, then deflate the surface, thus cracking the ice off) or engine-bleed air (to heat the surface and thus melt the ice).

depressurization:
see pressurization.

deterministic:
the future status of a deterministic system can be accurately predicted based on its history.

DH: decision height:
see DA.

dispatchers:
airline ground personnel who consent to the safety of initiating a flight (jointly with the captain), monitor the flight from takeoff to landing, and collect and transmit to the

crew weather and other important information that may affect the flight. The dispatch function is required for major airlines in the US.

DME:

distance measuring equipment: *see* VOR.

EGPWS:

enhanced ground proximity warning system. *See also* GPWS (ground proximity warning system).

EPR:

engine pressure ratio: the pressure ratio across different sections of a gas turbine engine, an indirect measure of thrust that pilots use to set power on some turbine-powered aircraft.

FAA:

Federal Aviation Administration (of the US). The government agency that regulates flight operations and safety aspects of commercial aviation in the US.

FD:

flight director(s): *see* ADI.

FDR:

flight data recorder: equipment that records parameters involving aircraft motion, engine status, and in some installations control inputs, control surface movements, and the status of various other aircraft systems. The data are shielded in a crash-resistant case. The number of parameters varies from 13 on older systems to hundreds on modern systems.

final approach:

see approach, pattern.

final report:

most major aviation accident investigations performed by the NTSB result in a detailed final report known as a "Bluecover" report (the name is derived from an earlier – but not current – color scheme) that follows the ICAO Appendix 13 format for an accident report, first summarizing relevant factual information about the accident, then analyzing the facts, and finally reporting the agency's findings, causal determinations, and recommendations for safety improvement. Such a report was available for 17 of the 19 accident cases that we review in this book. Sometimes the NTSB publishes the results of a major investigation in a less extensive, "summary" or "brief format" report. In most of these summary reports the discussion of the facts and analysis of the accident is much less extensive than in a Bluecover report. For the two major accident cases we analyze for which the NTSB did not produce a major accident report, we also reviewed publicly available background reports by NTSB investigators ("group chairman factual reports") in the areas of flight operations, human performance, and data recorders.

fix:

geographic location that airplanes can navigate to or from using radio or other electronic navigation technologies. Flight plans, routes, and approaches are composed of a series of fixes.

fire handles:

one for each engine, to be used for extinguishing fires. When pulled, they isolate the respective engine from its fuel, hydraulic, and electrical connections. When twisted they release extinguishant into the engine compartment. They are typically red and have warning lights installed directly on them for easy identification. When an engine is on fire, the corresponding fire handle will illuminate.

flaps:

structures used to modify the surface of the wing of an aircraft. When extended, they increase the wing's lift by increasing its curvature and its surface area, thereby allowing the aircraft to fly at relatively slow speeds without losing lift. This is particularly important both at takeoff and the final stages of an approach (before landing). Flap position settings in the Boeing 737 are 0, 1, 2, 5, 10, 15, 25, 30, and 40 degrees. The desired setting is selected by positioning the flap lever on the control stand and monitored on the flap position indicator on the first officer's instrument panel. Flap settings are calculated based on the performance characteristics of the aircraft, its weight, the prevailing weather conditions, and possible speed restrictions prior to every takeoff and landing. Flap positions 0–15 provide increased lift and are normally used for takeoff. Flaps 15–40 provide both increased lift and drag to permit slower approach speeds and greater maneuvering capability, and are normally used for landing.

flare (landing):

applying control column back pressure to increase the airplane's pitch attitude during the final seconds of the flight, when the airplane is just a few feet above the runway surface. This reduces the airplane's descent rate and results in a gentle landing.

FMS:

flight management system: *see* AFS.

FOM:

flight operations manual (also flight operating manual): multi-volume reference document specifying basic design characteristics, specifications, and performance constraints of the aircraft, as well as the carrier's standard operating procedures for operating the aircraft. These guidelines define the intended use of the aircraft so that it meets both safety and efficiency goals as set forth by the manufacturer and the carrier.

Each air carrier authors its own FOM based largely on the manufacturer's operations manual and according to specific guidelines set forth by the FAA.

FOQA:

flight operations quality assurance: voluntary air carrier safety program that involves the routine monitoring of many parameters of flight operations for events that exceed safe limits and the analysis of trends over time.

flying pilot:

the pilot who controls the aircraft in flight. This is different from the pilot in command who is responsible for the flight and is always the captain by virtue of positional authority. The flying pilot manipulates the control yoke, thrust levers, and MCP/FMC settings. *See also* monitoring pilot.

fuel shutoff levers:

levers that control the supply of fuel to an engine. They are opened in the act of starting an engine, and closed again to shut it down.

gate hold:

flight delay specified by air traffic control that holds a departing aircraft at its gate.

glidepath:

descent profile during the final phase of an aircraft's approach for landing at an airport's runway. When conducting an instrument approach (ILS), the electronic glideslope information transmitted from near the runway guides the pilot or the AFS along the required glidepath.

glideslope:

system of vertical guidance embodied in the ILS indicating the vertical deviation of the aircraft from its optimum path of descent.

go-around:

aborted landing of an aircraft. Pilots are always ready to execute a go-around, according to a specific procedure, if certain criteria for a stabilized approach have not been met in the final stages of an approach.

GPS:

global positioning system: constellation of satellites that provides extremely accurate position information to aircraft that are equipped with a GPS receiver.

GPWS:

ground proximity warning system: provides warnings and/or alerts to the flight crew when certain conditions that signify dangerous proximity of the aircraft to the ground are met (for example, excessive terrain closure, altitude loss after takeoff, descent below specific altitude). The various modes are associated with different lights and aural warnings (such as "pull up" and "sink rate").

ground shift mechanism:
provides input to various aircraft systems as to whether an aircraft is in the air or on the ground. Operates using an air/ground safety ("weight-on-wheels") sensor that is activated when the weight of the airplane compresses one or more of the gear struts. The ground shift mechanism is important in preventing inadvertent gear retraction on the ground and inadvertent extension of ground spoilers in flight, and in automatically activating ground spoiler extension upon landing.

ground spoilers:
hinged panels close to the trailing edge of the wing that spoil lift upon touchdown on the runway and thus help control landing distance and improve braking. They usually deploy automatically, after the pilots have armed the ground spoiler activation lever.

heading select mode:
see AFS.

hindsight bias:
natural human tendency to evaluate past actions and decisions in light of what is now known about that situation. This bias can lead accident investigators, for example, to oversimplify the situation faced by an accident crew and to assume that things that are blatantly obvious to all after-the-fact should have also been equally obvious to the accident crew at the time they arose.

holding:
air traffic control instruction to an airborne flight to maintain its position by circling within a defined airspace.

horizontal situation indicator:
flight instrument used to display aircraft position relative to a navigation aid such as GPS or VOR; or to intercept and fly to or from any of the 360 compass "radials" that emanate from the navigation aid.

ICAO:
International Civil Aviation Organization: International organization associated with the United Nations that establishes standard practices and recommended practices for aviation operations.

ILS:
instrument landing system: provides lateral and vertical guidance to an aircraft approaching a runway by using signals from two separate systems, a localizer and a glideslope transmitter, respectively. The signals are displayed in the cockpit on

a course deviation indicator and/or arc fed into the AFS for the autopilot to track automatically.

IMC:

  instrument meteorological conditions: weather conditions that require pilots to fly using instruments rather than outside visual references (VMC or visual meteorological conditions).

inattentional blindness:

  failure to notice a visible but unexpected stimulus because attention is focused on some other aspect of the viewed display. Unlike change blindness, it does not appear to be linked to short-term visual memory as it does not require comparing images stored in memory.

INS:

  inertial navigation system (or IRS: inertial reference system): provides the position, velocity, and attitude of the aircraft by measuring accelerations (and, through integration, displacements) from a fixed starting position and attitude that pilots enter at the beginning of each flight.

jumpseat:

  supplementary seats in a cockpit primarily for the use of instructors, check airmen, inspectors, and other persons visiting the cockpit. An aircraft will typically have up to two cockpit jumpseats.

landing gear warning horn:

  loud aural warning that sounds to alert the crew that landing appears imminent (low thrust, low altitude, flaps set for landing) but the landing gear is still retracted. Designed to prevent crews from landing with the gear still retracted.

LLWAS:

  low-level windshear alert system. *See also* weather: Ground-based windshear detection system that uses several sensors for wind speed and direction located in various positions around the airport to identify localized areas of changing winds. The data from these wind sensors are integrated to identify changes that are characteristic of wind shear and provide an alarm to the control tower that includes the specific information about differences in the winds that were sensed at two or more locations.

load factors:

  ratio between the load currently applied to the aircraft structure from lift that is being generated in excess of the airplane's weight, and the airplane's weight in unaccelerated flight. An airplane turning in a 60-degree bank is experiencing a load factor of 2.0; that is, twice its normal weight. High load factors increase the speed at which the airplane will stall and thus its minimum controllable airspeed.

localizer:
>   lateral guidance provided by an ILS indicating the horizontal deviation of the aircraft
>   from alignment along the centerline of the runway.

local rationality assumption:
>   principle that one should try to understand how past actions and decisions made sense
>   in the moment, given the "local" circumstances at that time. Avoiding the influence of
>   hindsight bias, a pilot's behavior can be understood as rational when assessed in light
>   of the incomplete knowledge, goals, frame of mind, and pressures that the pilot was
>   trying to balance and address at the time of the (erroneous) decision or action.

LOFT (line oriented flight training):
>   training provided to flight crews using a high-fidelity flight simulator that incorporates
>   realistic scenarios and challenges crews to manage abnormal situations in real time.

long landing:
>   landing beyond the touchdown zone of a runway (normally defined as the first 3,000
>   feet).

LOSA (line operations safety audit):
>   Voluntary air carrier safety program, endorsed by the FAA and ICAO, that involves
>   the collection of data on crew, organization, and system performance. The LOSA
>   methodology was developed in the late 1990s by the University of Texas Human
>   Factors Research project in conjunction with major US airlines. Using observations
>   from routine flights and structured interviews of crewmembers, it enables the systematic
>   assessment of operational threats and cockpit crew errors and their management.

marker beacon:
>   device transmitting signals from stations on the ground, close to the runway, that when
>   received by the aircraft activate an indicator in the cockpit and produce an audible
>   tone. When incorporated in an instrument approach, such beacons (outer marker,
>   middle marker, and inner marker, as installed) inform pilots that they are a specific
>   distance from the runway:
>
>   − outer marker: located around 5 miles from the runway threshold. Emits a two-
>   dash, 400 Hz tone and activates a blue indicator.
>   − middle marker: located closer to the runway so that in low-visibility conditions
>   it signals that visual contact with the runway is imminent. Emits an alternate dot-
>   dash, 1300 Hz tone and activates a yellow indicator.
>   − inner marker: located around the runway threshold area. For certain approaches
>   that are used during very low-visibility conditions, the inner marker signifies the
>   imminence of arrival at the runway threshold. Emits a dot (6 per second), 3000 Hz
>   tone and activates a white indicator.

master caution:

> amber indication that illuminates whenever a caution indication on the annunciator panel is activated, thus directing pilots' attention to it.

MCP:

> mode control panel: pilots' primary interface to the AFS. Located centrally, just below the glare shield, it allows either pilot to manipulate key flight parameters (such as altitude, rate of climb, heading) for the autopilot and autothrottles to follow, or to turn over lateral and/or vertical navigation to the paths programmed in the FMC.

MDA:

> minimum descent altitude: the lowest altitude to which descent is authorized on a non-precision instrument approach, as specified on the published approach procedure, until pilots obtain visual contact with the runway environment and are able to continue the descent visually. It is expressed in feet above mean sea level.

MEL:

> minimum equipment list: FAA-approved document that authorizes dispatch of a flight with specified equipment inoperative, including the required maintenance actions and any operational conditions that are required to ensure safety.

microburst:

> *see* weather.

monovision contact lenses:

> provide the correct focus for distant targets to one eye and the correct focus for near targets to the other eye. This allows presbyopic individuals to discern both far and near objects without using bifocal or reading spectacles.

monitoring pilot:

> sometimes also referred to as non-flying pilot. Responsible for monitoring the flying plot actions, aircraft dynamics, radio communications, and aircraft systems. In most cases the monitoring pilot is responsible for performing checklists, either alone or in cooperation with the flying pilot. *See also* flying pilot.

MSL:

> mean sea level.

N1:

> The rotation speed of a jet engine's fan section, expressed as a percentage of maximum. Pilots use N1 on many aircraft types as a reference for setting thrust.

NAV:

> navigation radios: NAV receivers allow the aircraft to receive signals transmitted from stations on the ground (VOR and ILS frequencies) and to display the aircraft position

in relation to those stations. Stations are either automatically tuned by the AFS or manually tuned ("dialed") by the pilots in flight.

norms:

practices that are not written and required but are common practice. Norms may deviate from formal procedures when the latter do not allow human operators to perform their jobs efficiently and/or safely, or are not enforced. Routine deviation from formal procedures may occur repeatedly without mishap and come to be perceived (often incorrectly) by operators to involve little risk and in time become common practice.

nosewheel steering system:

for taxiing on the ground, airline pilots typically steer using a hydraulic nosewheel steering system. On most aircraft, the pilot can make steering inputs using both the rudder pedals for maintaining runway alignment and gentle turns, as well as a nosewheel steering tiller, or hand wheel, for the greater nosewheel deflections needed for turning more tightly.

NTSB:

National Transportation Safety Board (of the US): US government agency responsible for investigating and determining the probable cause of civil aviation accidents.

OPC:

onboard performance computer: one carrier's version of the airport performance laptop computer (APLC).

overhead panel:

collection of gauges, switches, and indicators located over the pilots' heads and extending from above eye-level to almost behind their heads.

overspeed (propeller):

condition in which the propellers and turbine engines are rotating faster than allowed, which can result in propeller and/or engine failure, drag increase, and loss of control.

pattern:

aircraft typically approach and land at airports using at least portions of a standard traffic pattern that is defined in relation to the landing runway. The final approach leg of the pattern is that portion in which the aircraft is aligned with the runway and ends with touchdown. The base leg of the pattern immediately precedes the final leg and is flown perpendicular to the runway, requiring a 90-degree left or right turn to establish the aircraft on final approach. The downwind leg of the pattern precedes base leg and is flown parallel to, and in the opposite direction of, final approach. Crosswind and upwind legs may also be flown and complete a rectangular pattern around the runway.

PFD:
> primary flight display: an aircraft instrument combining various pieces of information that were in the past displayed on separate instruments (such as airspeed, altitude, vertical speed, turn and bank information, radio navigation information).

PIO:
> pilot-induced oscillation: condition in which a pilot makes flight control inputs (usually involving pitch) slightly out of phase from those actually required to correct for a flight path deviation, such that the deviations worsen in an oscillation of increasing magnitude.

plan continuation bias:
> failure to revise a plan of action when the situation diverges from the premises on which the plan was originally built. For example, pilots may fail to recognize that changes in weather conditions along the intended flight path make the original plan inappropriate.

power distance:
> degree to which the less powerful members of a group expect and accept differences in the levels of power among group members.

pressurization:
> because atmospheric pressure decreases with altitude, aircraft must be pressurized so as to maintain inhabitable levels of pressure. This is typically accomplished using high-pressure bleed air from the engines and a pressurization controller which controls its outflow. Proper depressurization of an aircraft must be achieved by the time an aircraft lands on the ground so as to avoid structural stress on the airframe and discomfort to its occupants.

probabilistic:
> situations in which the outcome cannot be uniquely determined from the initial conditions. Random variations among contributing factors allow a range of possible outcomes that can only be described statistically.

QFE, QNE, and QNH:
> *see* altimetry.

QRH:
> quick reference handbook: an indexed handbook commonly provided by air carriers for pilots to use for performing checklists for emergency and abnormal situations; the QRH also may include performance data and other information that pilots need to be able to obtain readily while in flight.

radar altimeter:
> device which measures altitude directly above the ground when an aircraft flies low over the terrain. It is primarily used during the approach and landing phases, especially when in low-visibility conditions.

recognition-primed decision-making:
> a theoretical construct within the field of naturalistic decision-making (decisions made by experts within their domain of expertise). This construct, supported by empirical evidence, asserts that experts usually do not formally analyze the characteristics of situations and assess options sequentially. Rather, experts recognize the essential characteristics of situations from previous encounters stored in memory and quickly generate a response option that "satisfices" rather than optimizes. The response option is often evaluated through mental simulation.

rejected takeoff:
> transitioning from taking off to stopping the aircraft on the runway, because of engine failure or other condition that poses a risk for continuing the takeoff.

representativeness bias:
> the mental process by which we diagnose a situation by evaluating the extent to which the available cues match those stored in long-term memory and believed, through experience, to represent a particular hypothesis. If a match is made, then the situation is determined to fit the hypothesis.

rotation:
> the act of increasing the aircraft's pitch attitude (raising the aircraft's nose) during takeoff to allow the wings to begin to develop lift.

RPM:
> revolutions per minute: engine rotational speed, commonly expressed as a percentage of maximum allowable RPM.

rudder pedals:
> pairs of foot pedals in front of each of the pilots' seats that control the position of the hinged movable surface attached to the rear of the vertical stabilizer, and thus aircraft yaw. The rudder is used in coordination with the spoilers and ailerons when effecting turns for comfort and efficiency.

runway:
> – RVR: runway visual range: measurements of visibility (in the US, expressed in feet) pertaining to a specific runway or a portion of the runway.
> – numbering system: runway numbers indicate the magnetic direction in which they point, rounded to the nearest ten degrees and divided by ten. For example, runway 7 points 70 degrees or in a northeasterly direction. Each runway can be used in either direction, and hence has two numbers. Runway 10 becomes Runway 28 when used in the opposite direction.

RVR:
> *see* runway.

sink rate:
> rate of descent: also a warning mode of the GPWS alerting pilots to excessive descent rate at low altitude.

slam-dunk:
> an approach situation in which air traffic control requires the aircraft to remain at a relatively high altitude until close to the destination airport, thus requiring a very steep gradient path once finally allowed to descend. This challenges the crew to get the aircraft stabilized on the proper target airspeed, descent rate, and glidepath before landing.

source memory:
> memory for the context in which a piece of information was originally learned.

speed bugs:
> rather than rely on memory for a number of different critical speed settings (for example, V1), small plastic tabs around the indicator can be placed to mark the desired settings. Once the airspeed indicator needle points to the tab, the pilot can immediately recognize that the particular speed has been attained. On aircraft with electronic flight instrumentation, the speed bugs may be part of the video display rather than mechanical devices.

speeds:
> monitoring the aircraft speed either on the ground or in the air is particularly critical during certain phases of flight, such as takeoff, the final stages of the approach, and landing:

- V1: takeoff decision speed: speed below which a pilot can reject the takeoff and still be able to stop the aircraft on the runway remaining. At and beyond this speed, the aircraft can successfully climb to clear all obstacles despite an engine failure and crews are trained to continue the takeoff.
- Vr: takeoff rotation speed: speed at which the flying pilot applies control column back pressure to rotate the aircraft.
- V2: minimum takeoff safety speed: speed that will allow an aircraft that experiences an engine failure to remain fully controllable and maintain an FAA-required climb gradient.
- Vref:
  landing reference speed: speed to be flown on final approach with the aircraft established in the final landing gear and flap configuration; adjusted with additives for steady wind and gust conditions.
- Vmo: maximum (certified) operating airspeed.
- maneuvering speed: maximum speed at which the pitch control (control column) can be rapidly manipulated without overloading the structure of the aircraft.

spoilers:
> hydraulic-powered, movable surfaces on the upper surfaces of the wings that assist in roll control.

stabilizer:
> the horizontal stabilizer is a fixed horizontal surface on the tail of the airplane that contributes to pitch stability. The vertical stabilizer is a fixed vertical fin that contributes to yaw (directional) stability.

stall:
> condition in which an excessive angle of attack causes loss of lift due to disruption of airflow over the wing. Stall recovery usually involves reducing the angle of attack to "break" the stall, and adding power to begin a climb.

stall warning system:
> warning designed to alert the crew that the aircraft is about to enter a stall situation. Typically consists of motors that vibrate each of the two control columns (stickshaker), thereby delivering both a vibrotactile and an aural signal to the pilots. The warning system is energized in flight at all times, but is automatically deactivated on the ground.

STAR:
> standard terminal arrival route: a series of pre-defined navigational fixes designed to transition an aircraft from the en route environment to an instrument approach that is aligned with the runway.

stickshaker:
> *see* stall warning system.

takeoff warning system:
> system that monitors parameters essential for a safe takeoff (such as flap position and pitch trim) and provides an aural warning, such as a loud, intermittent horn, to alert pilots when the aircraft is not properly configured for takeoff.

TAWS:
> terrain avoidance warning system, *see* GPWS.

TCAS:
> traffic collision and avoidance: system capable of identifying the distance, direction, and altitude of nearby aircraft (that are suitably equipped), calculating whether these aircraft pose a collision threat, and providing advisories about the best action to take in order to avoid a collision.

thrust reversers:
mechanism by which engine thrust is directed forward to help bring the aircraft to a stop.

trim:
control capability provided to pilots for balancing the aircraft's pitch, roll, or yaw. Trim may be accomplished by repositioning the center positions of the rudder and ailerons, and by repositioning the entire horizontal stabilizer; in other applications trim surfaces are hinged sections of the ailerons, rudder, and elevator. Pilots trim the aircraft using electric trim switches or manual controls to relieve the pressure necessary on the control wheel and rudders while keeping the aircraft in the desired attitude. Setting the trim tabs to positions calculated prior to takeoff based on load and performance data redefines the corresponding flight control surface to a neutral position relative for the takeoff climb. In transport aircraft designs, autopilots also have the capability to trim one or more control surfaces.

TSA:
time since awakening.

VASI:
visual approach slope indicator: system of lights that provide visual descent guidance information to pilots during the approach. When viewing the lights from above a specific angle, the pilot sees white lights, and below that angle, red lights. When the aircraft is tracking the visual glidepath correctly, the pilot should see a combination of red and white lights.

vectors:
heading and speed instructions given by an air traffic controller to the crew of an aircraft. Most commonly an aircraft will receive vectors on approach to the destination airport, designed to intercept the published final approach course. Controllers also may provide delay vectors (in lieu of holding), turning an aircraft away from the most direct course in order to achieve the desired spacing between aircraft.

vertical speed mode:
see AFS.

VOR:
VHF omni-directional radio: navigation system that broadcasts a VHF radio signal. Each station emits signals that encode angle, thus allowing the aircraft's instruments to determine the radial (that is, the direction from the VOR station) along which the aircraft is flying. A VOR station is often collocated with DME (distance measuring equipment), allowing aircraft to also determine distance from the VOR station.

weather:

- buildups: clouds with vertical development that may become rain showers or thunderstorms.
- convective activity: thunderstorm.
- microburst: a small-circumference area of rapidly downrushing wind (as occurring in the case of US1016 described in Chapter 1).
- windshear: windspeed or wind direction changes caused by a variety of meteorological phenomena (such as thunderstorms, microbursts, mountain waves). Windshear can affect aircraft performance and, depending on the intensity and duration of exposure, have dangerous effects on aircraft airspeed or altitude. An aircraft is particularly vulnerable to the effects of windshear when close to the ground (that is, when departing or arriving).
- windshear alert: warning provided by the LLWAS (low-level windshear alert system) that is installed at many air carrier airports. Also, Doppler radar equipment installed at some airports and onboard windshear detection equipment provide windshear alerts.

windshear:
see weather.

wing contamination check:
action required of flight crews before attempting to take off in certain winter weather conditions. It involves a direct examination of the critical aircraft surfaces within five minutes of takeoff by a crewmember (or qualified personnel outside the aircraft) to ascertain that snow or ice is not adhering to the aircraft's surfaces.

working memory:
a system in which memory items are temporarily retained in a state of high availability to facilitate performance of tasks at hand. Items not in current use revert to long-term memory, from which access is generally slower and more effortful.

Bibliography

Adams, J.M., Tenney, Y.J., and Pew, R.W. (1995). "Situation awareness and the cognitive management of complex systems", *Human Factors*, **37** (1), 85–104.

Air Transport Association [ATA] (1998). Human Factors Committee, Automation Subcommittee, *Potential Knowledge, Policy, or Training Gaps Regarding Operation of FMS-generation Aircraft*. Second Report.

Arkes, H.R., and Blumer, C. (1985). "The psychology of sunk cost", *Organizational Behavior and Human Performance*, **35**, 129–40.

Austen, E.L., and Enns, J.T. (2003). "Change detection in an attended face depends on the expectation of the observer", *Journal of Vision*, **3** (1), 64–74. Retrieved October 29, 2006 from http://journalofvision.org/3/1/7/.

Baddeley, A.D. (1972). "Selective attention and performance in dangerous environments", *British Journal of Psychology*, **63** (4), 537–546.

Barcheski, R. (2001). "Incorporating risk assessment training into airline curricula." In *Proceedings of the 11th International Symposium on Aviation Psychology*. Columbus OH: Ohio State University Press.

Barshi, I., and Healy, A.F. (1993). "Checklist procedures and the cost of automaticity", *Memory & Cognition*, **21** (4), 496–505.

Barshi, I., and Healy, A.F. (2002). "The effects of mental representation on performance in a navigation task", *Memory & Cognition*, **30**, 1189–1203.

Beilock, S.L., Carr, T.H., MacMahon, C., and Starkes, J.L. (2002). "When paying attention becomes counterproductive: Impact of divided versus skill-focused attention on novice and experienced performance of sensorimotor skills", *Journal of Experimental Psychology: Applied*, **8** (1), 6–16.

Beringer, D., and Harris, H.C. (1999). "Automation in general aviation: Two studies of pilot responses to autopilot malfunctions", *International Journal of Aviation Psychology*, **9**, 155–74.

Berman, B., and Geven, R. (2005). Personal communication.

Besco, R.O. (1994). "To intervene or not to intervene? The copilot"s Catch 22." In *Proceedings of the 25th International Seminar of the International Society of Air Safety Investigators*, **27** (5), pp. 94–101. Retrieved October 25, 2005 from http://s92270093.onlinehome.us/CRM-Devel/resources/paper/PACE.PDF.

Betsch, T., Haberstroh, S., Molter, B., and Glöckner, A. (2003). "Oops, I did it again –relapse errors in routinized decision making", *Organizational Behavior and Human Decision Processes*, **93** (1), 62–74.

Bliss, J.P. and Dunn, M.C. (2000). "Behavioural implications of alarm mistrust as a function of task workload", *Ergonomics*, **43** (9), 1283–1300.

Bliss, J.P., Freeland, M.J., and Millard, J. (1999). "Alarm related incidents in aviation: A survey of the Aviation Safety Reporting System database." In *Proceedings of the HFES 43rd Annual Meeting* (pp. 6–10). Santa Monica CA: HFES.

Boeing (2004). *Statistical Summary of Commercial Jet Airplane Accidents: Worldwide operations 1959–2003.* Retrieved November 22, 2004, from http://www.boeing.com/news/techissues/.

Brandimonte, M., Einstein, G.O., and McDaniel, M.A. (eds) (1996). *Prospective Memory Theory and Applications.* Mahwah NJ: Lawrence Erlbaum Associates.

Broadbent, D.E. (1958). *Perception and Communications.* London: Pergamon Press.

Brown, G.N., and Holt, M.J. (2001). *The Turbine Pilot's Flight Manual*, 2nd edn. Ames IA: Iowa State Press. (Originally published 1995).

Brown, S.C., and Craik, F.I.M. (2000). "Encoding and retrieval of information." In E. Tulving and F.I.M. Craik (eds), *The Oxford Handbook of Memory* (pp. 93 107). New York: Oxford University Press.

Bureau of Transportation Statistics [BTS] (2004a). *Table 1: Summary of Airline On-Time Performance Year-to-date through December 2004.* Retrieved January 12, 2006 from http://www.bts.gov/programs/airline_information/airline_ontime_tables/2004_12/.

Bureau of Transportation Statistics [BTS] (2004b). *National Transportation Statistics 2004.* Retrieved February 24, 2005 from http://www.bts.gov/publications/national_transportation_statistics/2004/html/table_01_34.html.

Burian, B.K., and Barshi, I. (2003). "Emergency and abnormal situations: A review of ASRS reports." In R. Jensen (ed.), *Proceedings of the 12th International Symposium on Aviation Psychology.* Dayton OH: Wright State University Press.

Burian, B.K., Barshi, I., and Dismukes, R.K. (2005). *The Challenges of Aviation Emergency and Abnormal Situations.* NASA Technical Memorandum 213462. Moffett Field CA: NASA Ames Research Center. Retrieved January 27, 2006 from http://human-factors.arc.nasa.gov/eas/download/BurianTM_final.pdf.

Caldwell, J.A., and Caldwell, J.L. (2003). *Fatigue in Aviation: A guide to staying awake at the stick.* Aldershot: Ashgate.

Cardosi, K., Falzarano, P., and Han, S. (1999). *Pilot-Controller Communication Errors: An analysis of Aviation Safety Reporting System (ASRS) Reports.* DOT/FAA/AR-98/17.

Cellier, J-M., and Eyrolle, H. (1992). "Interference between switched tasks", *Ergonomics*, **35** (1), 25–36.

Chidester, T.R. (2004). "Progress on advanced tools for flight data analysis: Strategy for national FOQA data aggregation." *Shared Vision of Flight Safety Conference.* San Diego CA.

Code of Federal Regulations (14CFR91). *Title 14: Aeronautics and Space, Volume 2, Chapter I, Part 91: General Operating and Flight Rules, Subpart C: Equipment, Instrument, and Certificate Requirements, Section 91.209.* Retrieved February 20, 2006, from the US Government Printing Office via GPO Access: http://www.gpoaccess.gov/cfr/index.html.

Code of Federal Regulations (14CFR121). *Title 14: Aeronautics and Space, Volume 2, Chapter I, Part 121: Operating Requirements: Domestic, Flag, and Supplemental.* Retrieved February 20, 2006, from the US Government Printing Office via GPO Access: http://www.gpoaccess.gov/cfr/index.html.

Cook, R.I., Woods, D.D., and Miller, C. (1998). *A Tale of Two Stories: Contrasting views of patient safety*. Technical report, National Health Care Safety Council of the National Patient Safety Foundation at the American Medical Association, Chicago IL, USA, 1998. Report from a Workshop on Assembling the Scientific Basis for Progress on Patient Safety. Retrieved February 3, 2006 from http://www.npsf.org/exec/front.html.

Curry, R.E. (1985). *The Introduction of New Cockpit Technology: A Human Factors Study*. NASA TM-86659.

Degani, A. (2003). *Taming HAL: Designing Interfaces beyond 2001*. New York: Palgrave Macmillan.

Degani, A., and Wiener, E.L. (1990). *Human Factors of Flight-Deck Checklists: The Normal Checklist*. NASA Report No. 177549. Moffett Field CA: NASA Ames Research Center.

Degani, A., and Weiner, E. (1993). "Cockpit checklists: Concepts, design, and use", *Human Factors*, **35** (2), pp. 345–59.

Dekker, S. (2002). *The Field Guide to Human Error Investigations*. Aldershot: Ashgate.

Diez, M., Boehm-Davis, D.A., and Holt, R.W. (2003). "Checklist performance on the commercial flight-deck." In R. Jensen (ed.), *Proceedings of the 12th International Symposium on Aviation Psychology* (pp. 323–328). Dayton OH: Wright State University Press.

Dismukes, K., Young, G., and Sumwalt, R. (1998). "Cockpit interruptions and distractions: Effective management requires a careful balancing act", *ASRS Directline*, **10**, 4–9. Retrieved January 4, 2005, from http://asrs.arc.nasa.gov/directline_nf.htm.

Dismukes, R.K. and Nowinski, J.L. (forthcoming). "Prospective memory, concurrent task management, and pilot error." In A. Kramer, D. Wiegmann, and A. Kirlik (eds), *Attention: From theory to practice*. New York: Oxford University Press. Retrieved January 27, 2006 from http://human-factors.arc.nasa.gov/flightcognition/download/promem_concurrenttask.pdf.

Dismukes, R.K., and Smith, G.M. (eds) (2000). *Facilitation and Debriefing in Aviation Training and Operations* (in the series Ashgate Studies in Aviation Psychology and Human Factors). Aldershot: Ashgate.

Driskell, J.E., and Salas, E. (eds) (1996). *Stress and Human Performance*. Hillsdale NJ: Erlbaum.

Durmer, J.S., and Dinges, D.F. (2005). "Neurocognitive consequences of sleep deprivation", *Seminars in Neurology*, **25**, 117–129.

Edwards, M.B., and Gronlund, S.D. (1998). "Task interruption and its effects on memory", *Memory*, **6** (6), 665–87.

Einhorn, H.J., and Hogarth, R.M. (1978). "Confidence in judgment: Persistence of the illusion of validity", *Psychological Review*, **85**, 395–416.

Enders, J.H., Dodd, R., Tarrel, R., Khatwa, R., Roelen, A.L., and Karwal, A.K. (1999). "Airport safety: A study of accidents and available approach-and-landing aids", *Flight Safety Digest*, **17**, 11–12, and **18**, 1–2, 213–248. Retrieved October

15, 2005 from http://flightsafety.aero/members/serveme.cfm/?path=/fsd/fsd_nov-feb99.pdf.

Eysenck, M.W. (ed.) (1994). *The Blackwell Dictionary of Cognitive Psychology*. Malden MA: Blackwell.

Federal Aviation Administration [FAA] (1994). *FAA/Industry Takeoff Safety Training Aid*. National Technical Information Service PB93780013. Washington DC.

Federal Aviation Administration [FAA] (2002). *Aviation Safety Action Program (ASAP)*. Advisory Circular 120-66B. Retrieved February 24, 2005 from http://www.airweb.faa.gov/Regulatory_and_Guidance_Library/rgAdvisoryCircular.nsf/1ab39b4ed563b08985256a35006d56af/61c319d7a04907a886256c7900648358/$FILE/AC120-66B.pdf.

Federal Aviation Administration [FAA] (2004a). *Air Traffic Control, Order 7110.65P* (Chapter 2, Section 7, Altimeter Settings). Retrieved February 1, 2006 from http://www.faa.gov/ATpubs/ATC/Chp2/atc0207.html#2-7-1.

Federal Aviation Administration [FAA] (2004b). *Aeronautical Information Manual* (Chapter 4: Air Traffic Control; Section 4: ATC Clearances and Aircraft Separation). Retrieved October 24, 2005 from http://www.faa.gov/atpubs/AIM/Chap4/aim0404.html.

Federal Aviation Administration [FAA] (2004c). *Airplane Upset Recovery Training Aid*. Revision 1, August 2004. Retrieved February 3, 2006 from http://www.faa.gov/other_visit/aviation_industry/airline_operators/training/index.cfm?print=go.

Federal Aviation Administration [FAA] (2004d). *Flight Operational Quality Assurance. Advisory Circular 120-82*. Retrieved February 24, 2005 from http://www.airweb.faa.gov/Regulatory_and_Guidance_Library/rgAdvisoryCircular.nsf/0/40c02fc39c1577b686256e8a005afb0a/$FILE/AC120-82.pdf.

Fischer, U., and Orasanu, J. (2000). "Error-challenging strategies: Their role in preventing and correcting errors." In *Proceedings of the International Ergonomics Association 14th Triennial Congress and Human Factors and Ergonomics Society 44th Annual Meeting*. Santa Monica CA: HFES.

Fischhoff, B. (1982). "Debiasing." In D. Kahnemann, P. Slovic, and A. Tversky (eds), *Judgment under Uncertainty; Heuristics and Biases* (pp. 422–44). New York: Cambridge University Press.

Fischhoff, B. (2003). "Hindsight # foresight: The effect of outcome knowledge on judgment under uncertainty", *Quality and Safety in Health Care*, **12**, 304–311. (Originally published 1975).

Flight Safety Foundation [FSF] (1998). *Flight Safety Digest*, Special FSF Report: Killers in Aviation: FSF Task Force Presents Facts about Approach-and-landing and Controlled-flight-into-terrain Accidents. November 1998–January 1999. Retrieved January 29, 2006 from http://www.flightsafety.org/members/serveme.cfm?path=fsd/fsd_nov-feb99.pdf.

Flight Safety Foundation [FSF] (2000). ALAR (Approach-and-landing Accident Reduction) Briefing Notes. *Flight Safety Digest, Special Issue*. August–November. Retrieved January 12, 2006 from http://www.flightsafety.org/members/serveme.cfm?path=fsd/fsd_aug-nov00.pdf.

Flight Safety Foundation [FSF] (2002). "International efforts raise awareness to prevent approach and landing accidents", *Flight Safety Digest*, **21** (12), 1–21. Retrieved October 15, 2005 from http://www.flightsafety.org/pubs/fsd_2002. html.

Flight Safety Foundation [FSF] (2003). "CFIT Checklist: Evaluate the risk and take action", *Accident Prevention*, **60** (11), 8–11. Retrieved October 15, 2005 from http://www.flightsafety.org/members/serveme.cfm/?path=/ap/ap_nov03.pdf.

Flight Safety Foundation [FSF] (2004). "Wealth of guidance and experience encourage wider adoption of FOQA", *Flight Safety Digest*, June–July. Retrieved February 24, 2005 from http://www.flightsafety.org/members/serveme.cfm?path=fsd/fsd_june-july04.pdf.

Flight Safety Foundation [FSF] (2005). "Line Operations Safety Audit (LOSA) provides data on threats and errors", *Flight Safety Digest*, February. Retrieved March 2, 2005 from http://www.flightsafety.org/pubs/fsd_2005.html.

Foushee, H.C., Lauber, J.K., Baetge, M.M., and Acomb, D.B. (1986). *Crew Performance as a Function of Exposure to High Density, Short-Haul Duty Cycles.* NASA Technical Memorandum 88322. Moffett Field CA: NASA Ames Research Center. Retrieved January 12, 2006 from http://humanfactors.arc.nasa.gov/zteam/PDF_pubs/Flight_Ops/Short_Haul_III/Flight_Ops_III.pdf.

Foushee, H.C., and Manos, K.L. (1981). "Information transfer within the cockpit: Problems in intracockpit communications." In C.E. Billings and E.S. Cheaney (eds), *Information Transfer Problems in the Aviation System.* NASA TP-1875. Moffett Field CA: NASA Ames Research Center.

Gann, E. (1961). *Fate is the Hunter.* New York: Simon & Schuster.

Gawron, V.J. (2002). *Airplane Upset Training Evaluation Report.* NASA/CR-2002-233405. May. Buffalo NY: Veridian Engineering.

Gawron, V.J., Berman, B.A., Dismukes, R.K, and Peer, J.H. (2003). "New airline pilots may not receive sufficient training to cope with airplane upsets", *Flight Safety Foundation's Flight Safety Digest*, July–August, 19–32.

Gillingham, K.K., and Previc, F.H. (1996). "Spatial orientation in flight." In R.L. deHart (ed.), *Fundamentals of Aerospace Medicine*, 2nd ed. (pp. 309–97). Baltimore MD: Williams & Wilkins.

Gunther, D. (2004a). "Threat and error management (TEM) workshop." Presentation at the *Second ICAO/IATA LOSA/TEM Conference* (November 3–4), Boeing Training Center, Seattle WA. Retrieved February 23, 2005 from http://www.icao.int/icao/en/anb/peltrg/conf/LOSA_Seattle_2004.pdf.

Gunther, D. (2004b). "Aviation Safety Action Program (ASAP): Applying the Threat and Error Management (TEM) Process to an ASAP Event." *ASPA/ICAO Regional Seminar, March 2004.* Retrieved January 21, 2005, from http://www.apythel.org/CRMyFFHH/MEX_Gunther_04.ppt.

Harper, M.L., and Helmreich, R. (2003). "Applying the Threat and Error Management model to an Aviation Safety Action Program." In R. Jensen (ed.), *Proceedings of the 12th International Symposium on Aviation Psychology* (April 14–17, 2003) (pp. 491–5). Dayton OH: Wright State University Press.

Helmreich, R., Klinect, J., and Merritt, A. (2004). "Line Operations Safety Audit: LOSA data from US airlines." Presentation at the *Second ICAO/IATA LOSA/ TEM Conference* (November 3–4, 2004), Boeing Training Center, Seattle WA. Retrieved February 23, 2005 from http://www.icao.int/icao/en/anb/peltrg/conf/ LOSA_Seattle_2004.pdf.

Helmreich, R.L., Klinect, J.R., and Wilhelm, J.A. (1999). "Models of threat, error, and CRM in flight operations." In *Proceedings of the 10th International Symposium on Aviation Psychology* (pp. 677–82). Columbus OH: Ohio State University Press. Retrieved January 4, 2005 from http://homepage.psy.utexas. edu/homepage/group/HelmreichLAB/Publications/pubfiles/Pub240.pdf.

Helmreich, R.L., and Merritt, A.C. (1998). *Culture at Work in Aviation and Medicine: National, organizational, and professional influences*. Aldershot: Ashgate.

Hess, R.A. (1997). "Feedback control models: Manual control and tracking." In G. Salvendy, *Handbook of Human Factors and Ergonomics*, 2nd edn (pp. 1249–94). New York: Wiley.

Hirt, E.R., Kardes, F.R., and Markman, K.D. (2004). "Activating a mental simulation mind-set through generation of alternatives: Implications for debiasing in related and unrelated domains", *Journal of Experimental Social Psychology*, **40**, 374– 83.

Hofstede, G. (1980). *Culture's Consequences: International differences in work-related values*. Beverly Hills CA: Sage.

Hopkin, V.S. (1980). "The measurement of the air traffic controller", *Human Factors*, **22**, 347–60.

Hopkins, G.E. (1982). *Flying the Line: The First Half-Century of the Airline Pilots' Association*. Washington DC: Airline Pilots Association, Int.

International Civil Aviation Organization [ICAO] (2001). *International Standards and Recommended Practices, Aircraft Accident and Incident Investigation: Annex 13 to the Convention on International Civil Aviation Edition*, 9th edn. Montreal, Canada: ICAO.

International Civil Aviation Organization [ICAO] (2002a). "The LOSA experience: Safety audits on the flight deck", *ICAO Journal*, **57** (4), 5–15.

International Civil Aviation Organization [ICAO] (2002b). *Line Operations Safety Audit*. ICAO Document 9803 (AN/761), 1st edn. Retrieved January 13, 2006 from http://www.icao.int/ANB/humanfactors/LUX2005/Info-Note-5-Doc9803alltext. en.pdf.

Jagacinski, R.J. (1977). "A qualitative look at feedback control theory as a style of describing behavior", *Human Factors*, **19**, 331–47.

Johnson, M.K., Hashtroudi, S., and Lindsay, D.S. (1993). "Source monitoring", *Psychological Bulletin*, **114**, 3–28.

Johnston, N. (2003). "The paradox of rules: Procedural drift in commercial aviation." In R. Jensen (ed.), *Proceedings of the 12th International Symposium on Aviation Psychology* (pp. 630–5). Dayton OH: Wright State University Press.

Kahneman, D., and Tversky, A. (1984). "Choices, values, and frames", *American Psychologist*, **39**, 341–50.

Kanki, B.G., and Palmer, M.T. (1993). "Communication and Crew Resource Management." In E.L. Wiener, B.G. Kanki, and R.L. Helmreich (eds), *Cockpit Resource Management* (pp. 99–136). San Diego CA: Academic Press.

Karwal, A.K., Verkaik, R., and Jansen, C. (2000). "Non-adherence to procedures – Why does it happen?" In *Proceedings of the Flight Safety Foundation, 12th Annual European Aviation Safety Seminar*, March 6–8, Amsterdam, Holland (pp. 139–56).

Keppel, G., and Underwood, B.J. (1962). "Proactive inhibition in short-term retention of single items", *Journal of Verbal Learning and Verbal Behavior*, 1, 153–61.

Klein, G. (1997). "The recognition-primed decision (RPD) model: Looking back, looking forward." In C.E. Zsambok and G. Klein (eds), *Naturalistic Decision Making* (pp. 285–92). Mahwah NJ: Erlbaum. (Originally published 1993).

Klein, G. (1998). *Sources of Power: How people make decisions.* Cambridge, MA: MIT Press.

Klinect, J.R., Murray, P., Merritt, A., and Helmreich, R. (2003). "Line Operations Safety Audit (LOSA): Definition and operating characteristics." *In Proceedings of the 12th International Symposium on Aviation Psychology* (pp. 663–668). Dayton OH: Ohio State University Press.

Klinect, J.R., Wilhelm, J.A., and Helmreich, R.L. (1999). "Threat and error management: data from Line Operations Safety Audits." In *Proceedings of the 10th International Symposium on Aviation Psychology* (pp. 683–8). Columbus OH: Ohio State University Press. Retrieved January 4, 2005 from http://homepage. psy.utexas.edu/homepage/group/HelmreichLAB/Publications/pubfiles/Pub241. pdf.

Koriat, A. (2000). "Control processes in remembering." In E. Tulving and F.I.M. Craik (eds), *The Oxford Handbook of Memory* (pp. 333–46). New York: Oxford University Press.

Latorella, K. (1999). *Investigating Interruptions: Implications for flightdeck performance.* NASA TM-1999-209707. Retrieved January 27, 2006 from http:// techreports.larc.nasa.gov/ltrs/PDF/1999/tm/NASA-99-tm209707.pdf.

Loft, S., Humphreys, M., and Neal, A. (2004). "The Influence of Memory for Prior Instances on Performance in a Conflict Detection Task", *Journal of Experimental Psychology: Applied*, 10 (3), 173–87.

Loftus, G.R., Dark, V.J., and Williams, D. (1979). "Short-term memory factors in ground controller/pilot communications", *Human Factors*, 21, 169–81.

Loukopoulos, L.D., Dismukes, R.K., and Barshi, I. (2003). "Concurrent task demands in the cockpit: Challenges and vulnerabilities in routine flight operations." In R. Jensen (ed.), *Proceedings of the 12th International Symposium on Aviation Psychology* (pp. 737–42). Dayton OH: Wright State University Press.

Loukopoulos, L.D., Dismukes, R.K., and Barshi, I. (forthcoming). *Beyond Workload: Managing concurrent task demands in everyday flight operations.* Manuscript in preparation.

McElhatton, J., and Drew, C. (1993). "Hurry Up Syndrome", *ASRS Directline*, 5, March. Retrieved February 28, 2005 from http://asrs.arc.nasa.gov/directline_ issues/dl5_hurry.htm.

Monan, B. (1991). "Readback, hearback", *ASRS Directline*, **1**, March. Retrieved September 10, 2005 from http://asrs.arc.nasa.gov/directline_issues/dl1_read.htm

Mumaw, R.J., Sarter, N., Wickens, C., Kimball, S., Nikolic, M., Marsh, R., Xu, W., and Xu, X. (2000). *Analysis of Pilots' Monitoring and Performance on Highly Automated Flight Decks*. Final project report: NASA Ames Contract NAS2-99074. Seattle WA: Boeing Commercial Aviation.

Muthard, E.K., and Wickens, C.D. (2003). "Factors that mediate flight plan monitoring and errors in plan revision: Planning under automated and high workload conditions", In R. Jensen (ed.), *Proceedings of the 12th International Symposium on Aviation Psychology*. Dayton OH: Ohio State University Press. Retrieved January 4, 2005, from http://www.aviation.uiuc.edu/UnitsHFD/conference/Dayton03/mutwic.pdf.

Mynatt, C.R., and Doherty, M.E. (1999). *Understanding Human Behavior*, 2nd edn. Boston MA: Allyn & Bacon.

Nagel, D.C. (1988). "Human error in aviation operations." In E. Wiener and D. Nagel (eds), *Human Factors in Aviation* (pp. 263–303). New York: Academic Press.

National Research Council [NRC] (1997). *Aviation Safety and Pilot Control: Understanding and preventing unfavorable pilot-vehicle interactions*. National Academy Press: Washington DC. Retrieved October 25, 2005 from http://www.nap.edu/openbook/0309056888/html/R1.html.

National Transportation Safety Board [NTSB] (1970). *Ozark Airlines Inc. McDonnell Douglas DC-9-15, N974Z, Sioux City, Iowa, December 27, 1968* (Report No. NTSB/AAR-70/20). Retrieved January 28, 2006 from http://amelia.db.erau.edu/reports/ntsb/aar/AAR70-20.pdf.

National Transportation Safety Board [NTSB] (1973). *Eastern Air Lines Inc. L1-1011, N310EA, Miami, Florida, December 29, 1972* (Report No. NTSB-AAR-73-14). Retrieved November 11, 2005 from http://amelia.db.erau.edu/reports/ntsb/aar/AAR73-14.pdf.

National Transportation Safety Board [NTSB] (1978). *Trans World Airlines Flight 505, McDonnell Douglas DC-9-10, N1065T, Newark, New Jersey, November 27, 1978* (Report No. NYC79IA013). Retrieved February 3, 2006 from http://ntsb.gov/ntsb/brief.asp?ev_id=38461&key=0.

National Transportation Safety Board [NTSB] (1979). *American Airlines, Inc. DC-10-10, N110AA, Chicago O'Hare International Airport, Chicago, Illinois, May 25, 1979.* (Report No. NTSB-AAR-79-17). Retrieved January 23, 2006 from http://amelia.db.erau.edu/reports/ntsb/aar/AAR79-17.pdf.

National Transportation Safety Board [NTSB] (1982). *Air Florida Inc. Boeing 737-222, N62AF, Collision with 14th Street Bridge, Washington DC, January 13, 1982* (Report No. PB82-910408, NTSB/AAR-82/08). Retrieved February 5, 2005 from http://amelia.db.erau.edu/reports/ntsb/aar/AAR82-08.pdf.

National Transportation Safety Board [NTSB] (1983). *Pan American World Airways Inc. Clipper 759, Boeing 727-235, N4737, New Orleans International Airport, Kenner, Louisiana, July 9, 1982* (Report No. PB83-910402, NTSB/AAR-83-02). Retrieved February 5, 2005 from http://amelia.db.erau.edu/reports/ntsb/aar/AAR83-02.pdf.

National Transportation Safety Board [NTSB] (1985). *Airborne Express Flight 125, McDonnell Douglas DC-9-15, Philadelphia, Pennsylvania, February 5, 1985* (Report No. DCA95AA013).

National Transportation Safety Board [NTSB] (1988). *Northwest Airlines Inc. McDonnell Douglas DC-9-82, N312RC, Detroit Metropolitan Wayne County Airport, Romulus, Michigan, August 16, 1987* (Report No. PB88-910406, NTSB/ AAR-88-05). Retrieved February 5, 2005 from http://amelia.db.erau.edu/reports/ ntsb/aar/AAR88-05.pdf.

National Transportation Safety Board [NTSB] (1988b). *Continental Airlines Flight 1713, McDonnell Douglas DC-9-14, Stapleton International Airport, Denver, Colorado, November 15, 1987* (Report No. NTSB/AAR-88/09). Retrieved January 28, 2006 from http://amelia.db.erau.edu/reports/ntsb/aar/AAR88-09.pdf.

National Transportation Safety Board [NTSB] (1989). *Delta Airlines Inc. Boeing 727-232, N473DA, Dallas-Fort Worth International Airport, Texas, August 31, 1988* (Report No. PB89-910406, NTSB/AAR-89-04). Retrieved February 5, 2005 from http://amelia.db.erau.edu/reports/ntsb/aar/AAR89-04.pdf.

National Transportation Safety Board [NTSB] (1990a). *US Air Flight 105, Boeing 737-200, N283AU, Kansas International Airport, Missouri, September 8, 1989* (Aircraft Incident Report No. PB90-910404, NTSB/AAR-90/04). Retrieved February 6, 2006 from http://amelia.db.erau.edu/reports/ntsb/aar/AAR90-04.pdf

National Transportation Safety Board [NTSB] (1990b). *United Airlines Flight 232, McDonnell Douglas DC-10-10, Sioux Gateway Airport, Sioux City, Iowa, July 19, 1989* (Report No. PB90-910406, NTSB/AAR-90/06). Retrieved February 24, 2005, from http://amelia.db.erau.edu/reports/ntsb/aar/AAR90-06.pdf.

National Transportation Safety Board [NTSB] (1991). *Ryan International Airlines DC-9-15, N565PC, Loss of Control on Takeoff, Cleveland-Hopkins International Airport, Cleveland, Ohio, February 17, 1991* (Report No. PB91-910410, NTSB/ AAR-91/09). Retrieved February 5, 2005 from http://amelia.db.erau.edu/reports/ ntsb/aar/AAR91-09.pdf.

National Transportation Safety Board [NTSB] (1992a). *USAir B737-400, N416US, Flushing, New York, September 20, 1989* (Report No. DCA89MA074). Retrieved February 12, 2006 from http://ntsb.gov/ntsb/brief.asp?ev_ id=20001213X29335&key=1.

National Transportation Safety Board [NTSB] (1992b). *Air Transport International Inc. Flight 805, Douglas DC-8-63, N794AL, Loss of Control and Crash, Swanton, Ohio, February 15, 1992* (Report No. NTSB/AAR-92/05).

National Transportation Safety Board [NTSB] (1993a). *Aborted Takeoff shortly after Liftoff, TWA Flight 843, Lockheed L1011, N11002, John F. Kennedy International Airport, Jamaica, New York, July 30, 1992* (Report No. PB93-910402, NTSB/ AAR-S3/02). Retrieved January 4, 2005 from http://amelia.db.erau.edu/reports/ ntsb/aar/AAR93-02.pdf.

National Transportation Safety Board [NTSB] (1993b). *Takeoff Stall in Icing Conditions, US Air Flight 405, Fokker F-28, N485US, LaGuardia Airport, Flushing, New York, March 22, 1992* (Report No. PB93-910402, NTSB/AAR-

93-02). Retrieved February 5, 2004 from http://amelia.db.erau.edu/reports/ntsb/aar/AAR93-02.pdf.

National Transportation Safety Board [NTSB] (1994a). *A Review of Flightcrew-involved Major Accidents of US Air Carriers, 1978 through 1990* (Report No. PB94-917001, NTSB/SS-94/01). Retrieved January 4, 2005 from http://amelia.db.erau.edu/cdl/ntsbss.htm.

National Transportation Safety Board [NTSB] (1994b). *Uncontrolled Collision with Terrain, American International Airways Flight 808, Douglas DC-8-61, N814CK, US Naval Air Station Guantanamo Bay, Cuba, August 18, 1993* (Report No. PB94-910406, NTSB/AAR-94/04). Retrieved January 27, 2006 from http://amelia.db.erau.edu/reports/ntsb/aar/AAR94-04.pdf.

National Transportation Safety Board [NTSB] (1994c). *Continental Airlines Flight 5148, Boeing 727-227, N16762, Chicago, Illinois, November 15, 1993* (Report No. CHI94FA039). Retrieved February 3, 2006 from http://ntsb.gov/ntsb/brief2.asp?ev_id=20001211X13714&ntsbno=CHI94FA039&akey=1.

National Transportation Safety Board [NTSB] (1994d). *Runway Departure following Landing, American Airlines Flight 102, McDonnell-Douglas DC-10-30, N139AA, Dallas-Fort Worth International Airport, April 14, 1993*. Washington DC. Retrieved January 27, 2006 from http://amelia.db.erau.edu/reports/ntsb/aar/AAR94-01.pdf.

National Transportation Safety Board [NTSB] (1994e). *Overspeed and Loss of Power on Both Engines during Descent and Power-off Emergency Landing, Simmons Airlines Inc. d/b/a American Eagle Flight 3641, N349SB, False River Airpark, New Roads, Louisiana, February 1, 1994* (Report No. NTSB/AAR-94/06, PB94-910408). Retrieved January 27, 2006 from http://www.airdisaster.com/reports/ntsb/AAR94-06.pdf.

National Transportation Safety Board [NTSB] (1995a). *Flight into Terrain during Missed Approach, USAir Flight 1016, DC-9-31, N954VJ, Charlotte/Douglas International Airport, Charlotte, North Carolina, July 2, 1994* (Report No. PB95-910403, NTSB/AAR, DCA94MA065). Retrieved January 4, 2005, from http://amelia.db.erau.edu/reports/ntsb/aar/AAR95-03.pdf.

National Transportation Safety Board [NTSB] (1995b). *Runway Overrun following Rejected Takeoff, Continental Airlines Flight 795, McDonnell-Douglas MD-82, N18835, LaGuardia Airport, Flushing, New York, March 2, 1994* (Report No. NTSB/AAR-95/01).

National Transportation Safety Board [NTSB] (1995c). *American Airlines 1340, Boeing 727-223, N845AA, Chicago, Illinois, February 9, 1998*. Attachment 12 to Operational Factors/Human Performance Group Chairman's Factual Report, Docket DCA98MA023.

National Transportation Safety Board [NTSB] (1996a). *Collision with Trees on Final Approach, American Airlines Flight 1572, McDonnell Douglas MD-83, N566AA, East Granby, Connecticut, November 12, 1995* (Report No. NTSB/AAR-96/05, PB96-910405). Retrieved January 27, 2006 from http://amelia.db.erau.edu/reports/ntsb/aar/AAR96-05.pdf.

National Transportation Safety Board [NTSB] (1996b). *In-flight Icing Encounter and Loss of Control, Simmons Airlines, d/b/a American Eagle Flight 4184, Avions de Transport Regional (ATR) Model 72-212, N401AM, Roselawn, Indiana, October 31, 1994. Volume 1: Safety Board Report* (Report No. AAR-96/01, adopted on 7/9/1996; Revision 9/13/02.) Retrieved October 23, 2005 from http://www.ntsb.gov/publictn/1996/AAR9601.pdf.

National Transportation Safety Board [NTSB] (1996c). *Runway Departure during Attempted Takeoff, Tower Air Flight 41, Boeing 747-136, N605FF, John F. Kennedy International Airport, New York, December 20, 1995* (Report No. NTSB/AAR-96/04).

National Transportation Safety Board [NTSB] (1996d). *ValuJet Airlines Flight 558, Douglas DC-9-32, N922VV, Ground Spoiler Activation in Flight/Hard Landing, Nashville, Tennessee, January 7, 1996* (Report No. PB96-910407, NTSB/AAR-96/07). Retrieved January 27, 2006 from http://www.ntsb.gov/publictn/1996/AAR9607.pdf.

National Transportation Safety Board [NTSB] (1997a). *Continental Airlines Flight 1943, Douglas DC-9, N10556, Wheels-up Landing, Houston, Texas, February 19, 1996* (Report No. NTSB/AAR-97/01, PB97-910401). Retrieved January 27, 2006 from http://amelia.db.erau.edu/reports/ntsb/aar/AAR97-01.pdf.

National Transportation Safety Board [NTSB] (1997b). *Descent below Visual Glidepath and Collision with Terrain, Delta Air Lines Flight 554, McDonnell Douglas MD-88, N914DL, LaGuardia Airport, New York, October 19, 1996* (Report No. PB97-910403, NTSB/AAR-97/03, NYC97MA005). Retrieved November 11, 2005 from http://amelia.db.erau.edu/reports/ntsb/aar/AAR97-03.pdf.

National Transportation Safety Board [NTSB] (1998a). *In-flight Icing Encounter and Uncontrolled Collision with Terrain, Comair Flight 3272, Embraer EMB-120RT, N265CA, Monroe, Michigan, January 9, 1997* (Report No. AAR-98/04). Retrieved October 23, 2005 from http://amelia.db.erau.edu/reports/ntsb/aar/AAR98-04.pdf.

National Transportation Safety Board [NTSB] (1998b). *In-flight Fire/Emergency Landing, Federal Express Flight 1406, Douglas DC-10-10, N68055, Newburgh, New York, September 5, 1996* (Report No. NTSB/AAR-98/03, PB98-910403, DCA96MA079). Retrieved January 27, 2006 from http://www.ntsb.gov/publictn/1998/AAR9803.pdf.

National Transportation Safety Board [NTSB] (1998c). *Uncontrolled Impact with Terrain, Fine Airlines Flight 101, Douglas DC-8-61, N27UA, Miami, Florida, August 7, 1997* (Report No. AAR-98-02). Retrieved January 28, 2006 from http://amelia.db.erau.edu/reports/ntsb/aar/AAR98-02.pdf.

National Transportation Safety Board [NTSB] (1998d). *Safety Recommendation* (A-98-3 through -5). Retrieved November 10, 2005 from http://www.ntsb.gov/Recs/letters/1998/A98_3_5.pdf.

National Transportation Safety Board [NTSB] (1998e). *American Airlines 903, Airbus Industrie/A300B4-605R, N90070, West Palm Beach, Florida, May 12, 1997.* NTSB Operations Group Chairman's Factual Report, Attachment 13, American Airlines Flight Manual, Part 1. Docket DCA97MA049.

National Transportation Safety Board [NTSB] (1998f). *American Airlines 903, Airbus Industrie/A300B4-605R, N90070, West Palm Beach, Florida, May 12, 1997*. NTSB Operations Group Chairman's Factual Report, Attachment 3. Docket DCA97MA049.

National Transportation Safety Board [NTSB] (1998g). *American Airlines 903, Airbus Industrie/A300B4-605R, N90070, West Palm Beach, Florida, May 12, 1997*. NTSB Operations Group Chairman's Factual Report, Attachment 19. Docket DCA97MA049.

National Transportation Safety Board [NTSB] (1998h). *American Airlines 903, Airbus Industrie/A300B4-605R, N90070, West Palm Beach, Florida, May 12, 1997*. NTSB Group Chairman's Aircraft Performance Study. Docket DCA97MA049.

National Transportation Safety Board [NTSB] (1999). *Uncontrolled Descent and Collision With Terrain, USAir Flight 427, Boeing 737-300, N513AU, Near Aliquippa, Pennsylvania, September 8, 1994* (Report No. AAR-99-01). Retrieved January 28, 2006 from http://amelia.db.erau.edu/reports/ntsb/aar/AAR99-01.pdf

National Transportation Safety Board [NTSB] (2000a). *Crash During Landing, Federal Express Inc. McDonnell Douglas MD-11, N611FE, Newark International Airport, Newark, New Jersey, July 31, 1997* (Report No. NTSB/AAR-00/02, DCA97MA055, PB2000-910402). Retrieved January 27, 2006 from http://www.ntsb.gov/publictn/2000/AAR0002.pdf.

National Transportation Safety Board [NTSB] (2000b). *American Airlines 903, Airbus Industrie/A300B4-605R, N90070, West Palm Beach, Florida, May 12, 1997* (Brief of Accident DCA97MA049). Retrieved January 27, 2006 from http://www.ntsb.gov/ntsb/brief.asp?ev_id=20001208X07893&key=1.

National Transportation Safety Board [NTSB] (2000c). *Human Performance Group Chairman's Factual Report, Addendum 1* to Report No. DCA99MA060, August 30, 2000. Retrieved November 11, 2005 from http://cf.alpa.org/internet/projects/ftdt/backgr/dinges.htm.

National Transportation Safety Board [NTSB] (2000d). *American Airlines Flight 9503, MD-83, N597AA, Palm Springs, California, February 16, 2000*. Incident No. DCA00IA027.

National Transportation Safety Board [NTSB]. (2001a). *Southwest Airlines Flight 1455, Boeing 737-300, N668SW, Burbank, California, March 5, 2000*. Recorded Radar Study, Specialist's Report of Investigation. NTSB Public Docket for Accident No. DCA00MA030, Docket. No.16752.

National Transportation Safety Board [NTSB] (2001b). *Southwest Airlines Flight 1455, Boeing 737-300, N668SW, Burbank, California, March 5, 2000*. Southwest Airlines Flight Operations Manual, Sections 6.44 and 6.52 (Normal Operations, Visual Approach), quoted in NTSB Operations Group Chairman's Factual Report, pp. 18–19. NTSB Public Docket for Accident No. DCA00MA030, Docket. No. 16752.

National Transportation Safety Board [NTSB] (2001c). *Southwest Airlines Flight 1455, Boeing 737-300, N668SW, Burbank, California, March 5, 2000*. Southwest Airlines Flight Reference Manual, Section 3.6.11 (Normal Operations, Approach—

Deviation Callouts for All Approaches), quoted in NTSB Operations Group Chairman's Factual Report, April 16, 2001, Attachment 21: Deviation Callouts for all Approaches. NTSB Public Docket for Accident No. DCA00MA030, Docket. No. 16752.

National Transportation Safety Board [NTSB] (2001d). *Southwest Airlines Flight 1455, Boeing 737-300, N668SW, Burbank, California, March 5, 2000.* Southwest Airlines Flight Reference Manual, Section 3.6.46 (Normal Operations, Approach—Go Around and Missed Approach), quoted in NTSB Operations Group Chairman's Factual Report, Attachment 24: Go Around and Missed Approach Procedure/Profile. NTSB Public Docket for Accident No. DCA00MA030, Docket. No. 16752.

National Transportation Safety Board [NTSB] (2001e). *Southwest Airlines Flight 1455, Boeing 737-300, N668SW, Burbank, California, March 5, 2000.* NTSB Operations Group Chairman's Factual Report, Attachment 1: Interview Summaries, p. 23. NTSB Public Docket for Accident No. DCA00MA030, Docket. No. 16752.

National Transportation Safety Board [NTSB] (2001f). *Southwest Airlines Flight 1455, Boeing 737-300, N668SW, Burbank, California, March 5, 2000.* Southwest Airlines Flight Operations Manual, Section 3.6.44 (Normal Operations—Approach, Visual Approach), quoted in NTSB Operations Group Chairman's Factual Report, Attachment 16: Visual Approach Procedure and Crew Coordination Callouts. NTSB Public Docket for Accident No. DCA00MA030, Docket. No. 16752.

National Transportation Safety Board [NTSB] (2001g). *Southwest Airlines Flight 1455, Boeing 737-300, N668SW, Burbank, California, March 5, 2000.* NTSB Operations Group Chairman's Factual Report, Attachment 1: Interview Summaries, p. 7. NTSB Public Docket for Accident No. DCA00MA030, Docket. No. 16752.

National Transportation Safety Board [NTSB] (2001h). *Southwest Airlines Flight 1455, Boeing 737-300, N668SW, Burbank, California, March 5, 2000.* Southwest Airlines Flight Reference Manual, Section 3.7.5 (Normal Operations, Landing and Postflight, Normal Landing Dry Runway), quoted in NTSB Operations Group Chairman's Factual Report, April 16, 2001, Attachment 20: Normal Landing Dry Runway. NTSB Public Docket for Accident No. DCA00MA030, Docket. No. 16752.

National Transportation Safety Board [NTSB] (2001i). *American Airlines 1340, Boeing 727-223, N845AA, Chicago, Illinois, February 9, 1998* (Aircraft Accident Brief No. NTSB/AAB-01/01). Retrieved January 27, 2006 from http://www.ntsb. gov/publictn/2001/AAB0101.pdf.

National Transportation Safety Board [NTSB] (2001j). *Runway Overrun during Landing, American Airlines Flight 1420, McDonnell Douglas MD-82, N215AA, Little Rock, Arkansas, June 1, 1999* (Report No. NTSB/AAR-01/02, DCA99MA060). Washington DC. Retrieved January 27, 2006 from http://amelia. db.erau.edu/reports/ntsb/aar/AAR01-02.pdf.

National Transportation Safety Board [NTSB] (2001k). *Uncontrolled Descent and Collision with Terrain, United Airlines Flight 585, Boeing 737-200, N999UA, 4*

Miles South of Colorado Springs Municipal Airport, Colorado Springs, Colorado,
March 3, 1991 (Report No. AAR-01-01). Retrieved January 28, 2006 from http://
amelia.db.erau.edu/reports/ntsb/aar/AAR01-01.pdf.

National Transportation Safety Board [NTSB] (2002). *Southwest Airlines Flight*
1455, Boeing 737-300, N668SW, Burbank, California, March 5, 2000 (Aircraft
Accident Brief No. DCA00MA030). Retrieved October 24, 2005 from http://
www.ntsb.gov/publictn/2002/AAB0204.pdf.

National Transportation Safety Board [NTSB] (2003). *Loss of Pitch Control on*
Takeoff, Emery Worldwide Airlines Inc. McDonnell Douglas DC-8-71F, N8079U,
Rancho Cordova, California, February 16, 2000 (Report No. AAR-03-02).
Retrieved January 28, 2006 from http://amelia.db.erau.edu/reports/ntsb/aar/
AAR03-02.pdf.

National Transportation Safety Board [NTSB] (2004). *In-flight Separation of Vertical*
Stabilizer, American Airlines Flight 587, Airbus Industrie A300-605R, N14053,
Belle Harbor, New York, November 12, 2001 (Report No. NTSB/AAR-04/04
PB2004-910404). Retrieved November 11, 2005 from http://amelia.db.erau.edu/
reports/ntsb/aar/AAR04-04.pdf.

National Transportation Safety Board [NTSB] (2005). *Table 5. Accidents, Fatalities,*
and Rates, 1986 through 2005, for US Air Carriers Operating Under 14 CFR
121, Scheduled and Nonscheduled Service (Airlines). Retrieved Janaury 12, 2006
from http://www.ntsb.gov/aviation/Table5.htm.

Norman, D.A., and Shallice, T. (1986). "Attention to action: willed and automatic
control of behavior." In R.J. Davidson, G.E. Schwartz, and D. Shapiro (eds)
(1986), *Consciousness and Self-regulation*, Vol. 4 (pp. 1–18), New York: Plenum
Press. (Originally published 1980).

Orasanu, J., Fischer, U., and Davison, J. (2002). "Managing and communicating
risk on the flight deck." Paper presented at the *Gottlieb Daimler and Karl Benz*
Foundation Colloquium on Interaction in High Risk Environments, Berlin, May
15, 2002.

Orasanu, J., Martin, L., and Davison, J. (2001). "Cognitive and contextual factors
in aviation accidents: Decision errors." In E. Salas and G. Klein (eds), *Linking*
Expertise and Naturalistic Decision Making (pp. 209–225). Mahwah NJ:
Lawrence Erlbaum Associates.

Parasuraman, R., Molloy, R., and Singh, I.L. (1993). "Performance consequences of
automation-induced complacency", *International Journal of Aviation Psychology*,
3 (1), 1–23.

Perrow, C. (1999). *Normal Accidents: Living with high-risk technologies*. Princeton
NJ: Princeton University Press. (Originally published 1984).

Raby, M., and Wickens, C.D. (1994). "Strategic workload management and decision
biases in aviation", *The International Journal of Aviation Psychology*, **4** (3), 211–240.

Reason, J. (1990). *Human Error*. New York: Cambridge University Press.

Reason, J. (1992). "Cognitive underspecification: Its variety and consequences." In
B.J. Baars (ed.), *Experimental Slips and Human Error: Exploring the architecture*
of volition (pp. 71–91). New York: Plenum Press.

Reason, J. (1997). *Managing the Risks of Organizational Accidents*. Aldershot: Ashgate.

Rhoda, D.A. and Pawlak, M.L. (1999). *An Assessment of Thunderstorm Penetrations and Deviations by Commercial Aircraft in the Terminal Area*. Massachusetts Institute of Technology, Lincoln Laboratory, Project Report NASA/A-2.

Rosekind, M.R., Gander, P.H., Connell, L.J., and Co, E.L. (2001). *Crew Factors in Flight Operations X: Alertness Management in Flight Operations Education Module*. NASA Technical Memorandum 2001-211385. Moffett Field CA: NASA Ames Research Center. Retrieved October 23, 2005 from http://humanfactors.arc. nasa.gov/zteam/PDF_pubs/ETM-X200.pdf.

Ruffell Smith, H.P. (1979). *A Simulator Study of the Interaction of Pilot Workload with Errors*. NASA Technical Report No. TM-78482. Moffett Field CA: NASA Ames Research Center.

Ryan, C. (1959). *The Longest Day: The classic epic of D-Day*. New York: Touchstone.

Sarter, N.B., and Woods, D.D. (1997). "Team play with a powerful and independent agent: Operational experiences and automation surprises on the Airbus A-320", *Human Factors*, **39** (4), 553–69.

Schneider, W., Dumais, S.T., and Shiffrin, R.M. (1984). "Automatic and control processing and attention." In R. Parasuraman and D.R. Davies (eds), *Varieties of Attention* (pp. 1–27). Orlando FL: Academic Press.

Shiffrin, R.M. and Schneider, W. (1977). "Controlled and automatic human information processing: II. Perceptual learning, automatic attending, and a general theory", *Psychological Theory*, **84**, 127–90.

Simons, D.J., and Rensink, R.A. (2003). "Induced failures of visual awareness", *Journal of Vision*, **3** (1), i. Retrieved 23 January, 2006 from http://journalofvision. org/3/1/i/.

Sivak, M., and Flannagan, M.J. (2003). "Flying and driving after the September 11 attacks", *American Scientist Online*, **91** (1). Retrieved November 22, 2004 from http://www.americanscientist.org/Issues/Macroscope/macroscope03-01.html.

Snook, S.A. (2000). *Friendly Fire: The accidental shootdown of US Black Hawks over Northern Iraq*. Princeton NJ: Princeton University Press.

Southwest Pilots' Association [SWAPA] (2002). *Southwest Airline Pilots' Association Submission to NTSB: Southwest Airlines Flight 1455, Burbank, California, March 5, 2000*. Party Submission—Southwest Airlines Pilots Association Submission, Docket DCA00MA030.

Staal, M. (2004). *Stress, Cognition, and Human Performance: A Literature Review and Conceptual Framework*. NASA TM 2004-212824. Retrieved January 4, 2005, from http://humanfactors.arc.nasa.gov/flightcognition/publications.html.

Stanton, N.A., Booth, R.T., and Stammers, R.B. (1992). "Alarms in human supervisory control: A human factors perspective", *International Journal of Computer Integrated Manufacturing*, **5** (2), 81–93.

Stokes, A., and Kite, K. (1994). *Flight Stress: Stress, fatigue, and performance in aviation*. Burlington VT: Ashgate.

Strauch, B. (2002). *Investigating Human Error: Incidents, accidents, and complex systems*. Aldershot: Ashgate.

Summala, H. (2000). "Brake reaction times and driver behavior analysis", *Transportation Human Factors*, **2** (3), 217–26.

Sumwalt, R.L. (1991). "Eliminating pilot-caused altitude deviations: A human factors approach." Paper presented at the *Sixth International Symposium on Aviation Psychology*, Columbus OH, 1991.

Sumwalt, R.L.III, Thomas, R.J., and Dismukes, R.K. (2002). "Enhancing flight-crew monitoring skills can increase flight safety." In *Proceedings of the 55th International Air Safety Seminar, Flight Safety Foundation* (pp. 175–206), Dublin, Ireland, November 4–7.

Sumwalt, R.L. III, Thomas, R.J., and Dismukes, R.K. (2003). "The new last line of defense against aviation accidents", *Aviation Week & Space Technology*, **159** (8), 66 (August 25).

Tullo, F. (2002). "LOSA shows promise to help increase air safety", *Aviation Week and Space Technology*, p. 70, January 21. Retrieved January 13, 2006 from http:// homepage.psy.utexas.edu/homepage/group/HelmreichLAB/Publications/Misc/ franktullo.html.

Tversky, A., and Kahneman, D. (1974). "Judgment under uncertainty: Heuristics and biases", *Science*, **185**, 1124–31.

Tversky, A., and Kahneman, D. (1981). "The framing of decisions and the psychology of choice", *Science*, **211**, 453–8.

US Department of Transportation [DOT], Federal Aviation Administration [FAA] (1980). *Instrument Flying Handbook*. Washington DC: US DOT/FAA.

Veillette, P. (2005). "Threat and Error Management", A*viation Week's Business and Commercial Aviation*, February 9, 2005.

Walters, J.M., and Sumwalt, R.L. III. (2000). *Aircraft Accident Analysis: Final reports*. New York: McGraw Hill.

Wickens, C.D. and Hollands, J.G. (eds) (2000). *Engineering Psychology and Human Performance*, 3rd edn. Upper Saddle River NJ: Prentice-Hall.

Wickens, C.D, Goh, J., Helleberg, J., Horrey, W.J., and Talleur, D. (2003). "Attentional models of multi-task pilot performance using advanced display technology", *Human Factors*, **45**, 360–80.

Wiener, E.L. (1989). *The Human Factors of Advanced Technology (Glass Cockpit) Transport Aircraft*. NASA CR-177528.

Wiener, E.L., and Curry, R.E. (1980). "Flight-deck automation: Promises and problems", *Erqonomics*, **23**, 995–1011.

Woods, D. and Cook, R. (1999). "Perspectives on human error: Hindsight biases and local rationality." In R.S. Durso et al. (eds), *Handbook of Applied Cognition* (pp. 141–71). New York: Wiley.

Zsambok, C.E., and Klein, G. (eds) (1997). *Naturalistic Decision Making*. Mahwah NJ: Erlbaum.

Index